High-Bounty Men in the Army of the Potomac

INTERPRETING THE CIVIL WAR
Texts and Contexts

EDITOR

Angela M. Zombek
University of North Carolina, Wilmington

Aaron Astor
Maryville College

Brian Craig Miller
Mission College

Joseph M. Beilein Jr.
Pennsylvania State University

Jennifer M. Murray
Oklahoma State University

Douglas R. Egerton
Le Moyne College

Jonathan W. White
Christopher Newport University

J. Matthew Gallman
University of Florida

Timothy Williams
University of Oregon

Hilary N. Green
University of Alabama

The **Interpreting the Civil War** series focuses on America's long Civil War era, from the rise of antebellum sectional tensions through Reconstruction.

These studies, which include both critical monographs and edited compilations, bring new social, political, economic, or cultural perspectives to our understanding of sectional tensions, the war years, Reconstruction, and memory. Studies reflect a broad, national perspective; the vantage point of local history; or the direct experiences of individuals through annotated primary source collections.

High-Bounty Men in the Army of the Potomac

Reclaiming Their Honor

Edwin P. Rutan II

The Kent State University Press

Kent, Ohio

© 2024 by The Kent State University Press, Kent, Ohio 44242
All rights reserved

ISBN 978-1-60635-486-5
Published in the United States of America

Cataloging information for this title is available at the Library of Congress.

28 27 26 25 24   5 4 3 2 1

To Lynne
You've made my life richer for fifty-six years

Contents

List of Maps, Tables, and Illustrations   ix

Acknowledgments   xi

Introduction   1

1   Demonization of the Late-War Replacements   13

2   Raising the Union Army   33

3   To Volunteer . . . or Not   48

4   The Quality of Late-War Replacements   64

5   Desertion   78

6   Late-War Union Soldiers in Battle   97

7   The Overland Campaign: May 4 to June 12, 1864   107

8   The Petersburg Campaign during 1864: June 15 to December 11   125

9   Second Reams's Station: August 25, 1864   140

10   Fort Stedman: March 25, 1865   152

11   The Five Forks Offensive: March 29 to April 1, 1865   177

Conclusion   203

Notes   212

Bibliography   282

Index   294

Maps, Tables, and Illustrations

Maps

Battle of Reams's Station   150
Battle of Fort Stedman, Confederate Breakthrough   153
Battle of Fort Stedman, Hartranft's Initial Positions   155
Battle of Fort Stedman, Union Counterattack   160
Lewis Farm to Five Forks   179
Battle of White Oak Road, Morning, March 31, 1865   182
Battle of Five Forks, April 1, 1865   186

Tables

2.1   Major Union Calls   35
2.2   Aggregate Present for the Union Army and the Army of the Potomac   36
3.1   One-Year and Three-Year Enlistment Terms for the July 1864 Call   58
3.2   Ratio of Military Compensation to Civilian Wages (Summer 1862), Abbreviated   60
3.3   Farmers, Farm Laborers, and Laborers in the Workforce by State   61
3.4   Ratio of Military Compensation to Civilian Wages (Spring 1864), Abbreviated   62
4.1   Oswego County Occupations (Percent), Abbreviated   71
4.2   Oswego County Average Ages and Birthplaces   72
4.3   Onondaga County Occupations (Percent), Abbreviated   73
4.4   Onondaga County Average Ages and Birthplaces   73
4.5   147th New York Occupations   75

4.6   149th New York Occupations   75

4.7   Eighty-First New York Replacements   75

4.8   Eighty-First New York Occupations (Percent), Abbreviated   76

4.9   Eighty-First New York Birthplaces   77

5.1   Pennsylvania and New Jersey Desertion: Later-Enlisting Volunteers   80

5.2   Pennsylvania and New Jersey Desertion: Comparison of Volunteers   81

5.3   Men Failing to Report after Being Drafted (Percent)   83

5.4   New Jersey Desertion: Late-War Replacements   85

5.5   Pennsylvania Desertion: Late-War Replacements   85

5.6   White Volunteers, Substitutes, and Draftees Raised by 1864 Calls   86

5.7   Desertion Rates: Late-War New Regiments   88

5.8   Desertion Rates: Late-War Pennsylvania Regiments   89

5.9   Desertion: Pennsylvania One-Year and Three-Year Volunteers and Substitutes   91

5.10 Recruitment Categories and Desertion: Pennsylvania and New Jersey   94

6.1   Battle Deaths: Pennsylvania Soldiers in the Army of the Potomac   98

6.2   Battle Casualties: Late-War New Regiments Not in Fox's Three Hundred   100

7.1   Old Pennsylvania Regiments with a Majority of Late-War Replacements   109

7.2   Army of the Potomac Force Levels (Present for Duty)   111

8.1   Support for President Lincoln in the 1864 Election   138

10.1 Hartranft's Division: Ages, Farmers, and Laborers   175

11.1 198th Pennsylvania Occupations (Percent)   197

Illustrations

40th New Jersey Recruiting Poster   18

Secretary of War Edwin Stanton   22

Provost Marshal General James B. Fry   22

War Dead at Antietam, Mathew Brady   54

Regimental Effectiveness Diagram   106

General Winfield Scott Hancock   141

Captain Nelson Penfield (125th New York Volunteers)   148

General John Hartranft   167

General Joshua Chamberlain   180

General Warren's Raid   191

Sixth Union League Regiment (198th Pennsylvania) Recruiting Poster   194

Colonel Horatio Sickel   195

Acknowledgments

I contacted Earl J. Hess about the idea for this book in November 2015. He strongly encouraged me to pursue the project and periodically passed along helpful suggestions and materials over the succeeding years. His constructive criticism of the first draft of the entire manuscript was invaluable. I am extremely grateful for his support.

As with my first book, one of the most rewarding aspects of this project was working closely with my longtime friend and fellow Civil War buff, Brian Dawe. We spent many an afternoon on the phone working through the particular challenge of the week. There is hardly a part of the book that Brian didn't help improve. Of particular importance, Brian created the latewarunionsoldiers.org website. He also put together the HIBO Database of soldiers, which was a critical tool for analyzing desertion, and mechanized the wage data and bounty data I collected to form the Economic Database and the Union Bounties (Eastern States) Database. I can't thank Brian enough.

Hal Jespersen does a superb job with maps, so naturally Brian Dawe and I wanted him to do them for this book. The care with which he prepared the maps and responded to our comments cemented our respect for his work.

Andrew Pace was such a great help on my first book that I asked him to do even more on this one, notwithstanding the fact that he had entered the doctoral program at the University of Colorado in the meantime. Andrew's questions and comments were always right on point as I wrote—and rewrote—the beginning chapters of the book.

The professional insight of Ken Miller, brigadier general, USAF (retired) and Ben Koerselman, colonel, USA (retired), fellow book club members in Park City,

Utah, helped with the development of chapter 6, "Late-War Union Soldiers in Battle" and chapter 10, "Fort Stedman: March 25, 1865."

Reed Spaulding from Park City did important legwork to help Brian Dawe put together the HIBO database.

I am extremely grateful to the staff of the Kent State University Press, the series editor, and the peer reviewer. Their carefully directed comments significantly improved my focus from the manuscript that I initially submitted to the present book, demonstrating that good editors are an author's best friends.

Introduction

The preservation of the Union and the end of slavery as the result of the Civil War are so fundamental to America's history that it is natural to want to portray the Union soldiers who paid the price of victory as noble men. A victory so significant has to have heroes. In our democracy, we cannot limit the heroes to statesmen such as Abraham Lincoln and generals such as Ulysses S. Grant. We need to make the common soldier a hero as well. A hero acts out of a sense of duty, not financial gain. We do not celebrate men motivated by financial gain as heroes.

Historians have long viewed the men in the Union army recruited later in the war, after the draft had been adopted and higher bounties offered, as unpatriotic and poor soldiers compared to the men who had enlisted in 1861 and 1862.[1] Historians have disparagingly referred to the men recruited for the Union army later in the war as "high-bounty" men.[2] Historians have characterized them as mercenaries, and on occasion with even more derogatory terms such as "offscourings of the world." Bruce Catton has written that: "in the great majority of cases these men were worse than useless." In contrast, "the historiography of the war has almost universally presented the volunteers of 1861, and to a great extent those of 1862, as the purest of patriots," as William Marvel recently noted.[3] James McPherson, author of the widely read *Battle Cry of Freedom,* recognized that 750,000 men joined the Union army later in the war but still concluded that "they did little to help win the war. This task fell mainly on the pre-bounty veterans of 1861 and 1862." He also commented that many of the recruits "deserted before they ever got into action and others allowed themselves to be captured at the first contact with the enemy."[4]

New regiments formed with "high-bounty" men have been disparagingly referred to as "high-number" regiments. My own work on a regimental history of the 179th New York Volunteers—a "high-number" regiment recruited in the spring and summer of 1864 when higher bounties and a conditional draft were in effect—led me to question the traditional view that high-bounty men were motivated solely by money and necessarily made poor soldiers as overbroad and too simplistic. For example, in the 179th New York's first battle on June 17, 1864, at Petersburg, the Confederates initially repulsed them, but they regrouped to carry the entrenched Confederate positions. Nearly 40 percent of the men engaged were killed or wounded, while only 5 percent were missing in action. That did not seem to me like men who were just motivated by money, looking for a quick exit from the war.[5]

Men may have had good reasons outweighing patriotism for not enlisting in 1861 or 1862. Differences in individual circumstances made for complex decisions on whether to volunteer or not.[6] For example, some men who did not volunteer in 1861 or 1862 had families to support. As J. Matthew Gallman noted in *Defining Duty in the Civil War: Personal Choice, Popular Culture, and the Union Home Front,* Northern society of the day did not view a decision to remain at home because of family responsibilities as unpatriotic.[7] Almost half of the men of the 179th New York Volunteers were married compared to only about 30 percent for the Union army as a whole. Family responsibilities may have prevented them from volunteering before the draft was in place. Similarly, about a fifth of the men who enlisted in the 179th New York in early 1864 were only eighteen or nineteen years old—too young to have enlisted in 1861 or 1862 without parental consent.[8] A presumption that the men who volunteered in 1864 were motivated solely by money and made poor soldiers seemed questionable to me.

There was also the nagging question that if the high-bounty men were really as bad as historians say, how did the North win the war? By the end of 1863, there simply weren't enough of the veterans of 1861 and 1862 left in the Army of the Potomac to carry the load by themselves and defeat the Army of Northern Virginia. It was only by bringing new men to the field in 1863, 1864 and 1865 that the Union army ultimately succeeded in the Petersburg Campaign.

Finally, even though the future of the nation was at stake, more than half of the men of military age in the North never served at all notwithstanding the high bounties and the draft. That group includes the nearly 90,000 men who bought an exemption from the draft by paying the $300 commutation fee, the nearly 120,000 men who procured substitutes to serve in their stead, the 160,000 men who failed to report after they were drafted, and the large number of men who fled their local communities to avoid enrollment in the draft system to begin with.[9] At least a large majority of the high-bounty volunteers actually served.

A reappraisal—based on data—is in order.

The goal of this project is to provide a balanced assessment of the motivation and performance of the high-bounty men and the high-number regiments compared to the men who volunteered in 1861 and 1862 and the "old" regiments they comprised. To provide a neutral starting point, I use the phrases *later-enlisting volunteers* (following Kenneth Noe's example) and *late-war new regiments* going forward rather than the loaded terms *high-bounty* men and *high-number* regiments. I define the *later-enlisting volunteers* as the men who enlisted in the Union army after the October 1863 call through the end of the war—excluding substitutes. I treat substitutes separately, even though they also received the much-criticized high bounties, because they did not enlist in their individual capacity and were a narrower class of men (generally foreign-born or younger than twenty-one). I also discuss draftees separately because they did not volunteer. I use the term *late-war replacements* to refer to volunteers, substitutes, and draftees as a group. I define *late-war new regiments* as new infantry regiments organized during the same time period. The term *late-war Union soldiers* refers to the *late-war replacements* and the *late-war new regiments* taken together. I define *old* regiments as infantry regiments organized in 1861 or 1862.[10] To make the project more manageable, I have limited the discussion to the Army of the Potomac and the states that provided the bulk of its troops—Connecticut, Delaware, Maine, Massachusetts, New Hampshire, New Jersey, New York, Pennsylvania, Rhode Island, and Vermont (hereafter referred to collectively as the "Eastern States").[11]

The reappraisal has three major components. First, the bounty system and the question of economic motivation are reexamined in chapters 1 through 3. Historians, senior Union commanders, and veterans from 1861 and 1862 have unjustifiably demonized both the later-enlisting volunteers and the bounty system based on the mercenary accusation. Second, the claims of rampant desertion among the late-war replacements and that they were of lesser quality than the volunteers of 1861 and 1862 are reviewed on objective grounds in chapters 4 and 5 by using data on desertion rates and factors such as occupation and place of birth. Third, to address the criticism that the late-war replacements made poor soldiers, their performance on the battlefield is assessed in chapters 6 through 11.

Demonization of the Late-War Replacements and the Bounty System

Both Union veterans from 1861 and 1862 and historians have long demonized the late-war replacements and the late-war new regiments, going back to the Civil War itself. The early-enlisting volunteers and senior army officers began the campaign during the war and continued it in their memoirs. Professionally trained historians continued the demonization at the beginning of the twentieth century, and their successors have continued it up to the present. As noted, not only have they labeled the later-enlisting volunteers and substitutes as mercenaries, they have also derided them with phrases such as *the offscourings of the world.* They have advanced these characterizations as broad generalizations without the broad-based facts necessary to support them. They generally have subjected the later-enlisting volunteers and substitutes to trial by anecdote and have presumed them to be guilty. For example, historians have recounted the case of the "Albany bounty jumper," who admitted to deserting and reenlisting for the bounty thirty-two times, without addressing whether that case was typical. When there are conflicting facts as to the performance of the late-war replacements in the field, historians rarely give the late-war replacements the benefit of the doubt.

Historians have largely relied on contemporary statements by the volunteers from 1861 and 1862 without taking appropriate account of their bias toward the late-war replacements. Not only was the traditional enmity of battle-hardened veterans toward raw replacements in play, but there was also the ill feeling caused by the higher bounties. The liberalization of the pension system for Union veterans in 1890, which many commentators argued disproportionately benefited the late-war replacements by removing the requirement that the disability be service-related, kept the criticism alive. Sound history requires proper consideration of that bias before repeating such serious accusations without appropriate qualification.

Senior officers in the Union army also had a bias against the later-enlisting volunteers and the late-war new regiments because neither fit in with their view of how recruiting should be done. Senior officers strongly preferred a stand-alone draft and regularly complained about the delay and cost of raising troops through bounties and the conditional draft. (By stand-alone draft, I mean a draft conducted without the options of "commutation" or "substitution"; with only the limited exemptions provided in the Enrollment Act of 1863; and with only nominal bounties offered to volunteers. By *conditional draft,* I mean a draft that was held only if the quotas were not completely filled by recruiting volunteers and substitutes.)[12]

Senior officers also generally opposed the creation of new regiments, preferring to send newly raised troops to the old regiments in the field that had been weakened by casualties from battle and disease. They also believed that training would be more effective in the old regiments than in new ones. By blaming the late-war replacements for Union defeats in battles such as Second Reams's Station and Poplar Spring Church, the generals diverted attention from their own mistakes.

Rehabilitation of the reputation of the late-war replacements cannot be achieved without rehabilitation, at least to a degree, of the reputation of the bounty system. A fair analysis of the bounty system must begin with 1862, when state and local bounties were offered with increasing frequency, not 1864 when bounties reached their high point. Regardless of whether patriotism was the driving motivation for volunteering in 1861, it was not as powerful as a motivating force by the middle of 1862. State and local governments increasingly offered bounties, a practice going back to the nation's beginnings, to induce men to volunteer. Newspapers regularly promoted the economic benefits of volunteering. For the Eastern States, it is not accurate to refer to the 1862 volunteers as "pre-bounty." With the conditional draft coming from the August 1862 call, the groundwork was laid for the carrot-and-stick approach that the Union would rely on for the rest of the war.[13]

The bounties combined with the conditional draft represented a delicate balance between the public's opposition to the compulsion of a stand-alone draft and the army's calls for large numbers of troops. The need to compete with the booming civilian economy resulted in higher bounties. State and local governments used the higher bounties to mitigate the impact of the draft on their more stable citizens, as well as the local economy, by drawing forth volunteers best situated to leave their homes and jobs for war. To be sure, the bounty system was extremely costly and very inefficient—both in terms of the disappointing percentage yield of troops for the field and the delay in getting them to the front. However, it worked (to borrow a phrase from Eugene Murdock and James McPherson).[14] The criticism that the bounty system created a "mercenary problem" (in the words of Fred Albert Shannon) is misplaced.[15] The real problem, as the *Brooklyn Daily Eagle* and other contemporary commentators noted, was that people in the North were "largely in favor of war, while being individually in favor of getting somebody else to do the fighting."[16] The bounty system was a financial solution—albeit one testing the bounds of pragmatism—to the very real challenge of raising a large number of troops at a time when Northern society was simply unwilling to accept a stand-alone draft. Northern society was, however, willing to bear the financial cost of the bounty system because it maintained the veneer of voluntary action by citizen-soldiers and mitigated the impact of the draft on a community's more stable and established residents, as well as the local economy.[17]

Historians advanced the proposition that the men who volunteered in 1861 and 1862 were motivated by patriotism rather than financial gain long ago without broad-based supporting data and have adhered to it ever since. William Marvel recently brought broad-based data to the issue for the first time in *Lincoln's Mercenaries*. Marvel pursued a wealth-based analysis using data from the 1860 census. He concluded that: "the earliest [Union] units were composed overwhelmingly of men from families claiming less than median wealth" and that "economic incentives exerted greater stimulus on Union enlistments than has been acknowledged." While Marvel rightly does not claim that the data prove that individual men in fact enlisted primarily for economic reasons, the data do at least raise a serious question about the primacy of patriotism as a motivation for enlistment in 1861 and 1862.[18]

Another data-based approach to the motivation issue is the "income-based" model that I pursue here, comparing the military compensation package—federal, state, and local bounties being the largest component—that was available in the summer of 1862 with civilian wages for specific occupations in the Eastern States. I estimate—subject to the timing of local bounties—that the military compensation package offered in the Eastern States in the summer of 1862 could have been viewed as "economically compelling" for a quarter and perhaps as many as half of the men in the civilian workforce. By "economically compelling," I mean that a soldier's military compensation over the course of a year—widely, though inaccurately, asserted as the likely duration of the war—would have been double his civilian wages.[19] (This estimate likely would not hold for the Western States.)[20]

To be clear, like Marvel, I am not trying to prove that money was the dominant motivation for volunteering in 1862. What I am trying to show is that the money could have been significant enough in 1862 that money cannot be dismissed as a motivation for enlisting in 1862, and that patriotism accordingly cannot simply be presumed to have been the dominant motivation in 1862. Patriotism should not be asserted as the dominant motivation for enlisting in 1862 without more proof than has been offered in the past.

Quality of the Late-War Replacements and Their Desertion Rates

The assertion that the quality of the men in the Army of the Potomac declined over time with the entry of the late-war replacements has been a recurring theme. However, the critics of the late-war replacements have not explained how they measured "quality." For example, Eugene Murdock simply concluded that "bounties went progressively upward while the quality of the men obtained went progressively downward" without explicitly explaining how he measured quality.[21] For historians, the lack of quality generally seems to be based on the subjective consideration of a presumed lack of patriotism of the late-war replacements and/or their asserted high desertion rates after enlistment. For many Civil War–era civilians, quality was measured by socioeconomic standing. There has been no effort by historians to compare the late-war replacements with volunteers from 1861 and 1862 based on objective criteria at the time of enlistment related to how a recruit likely would perform as a soldier.

Health is certainly an important criterion for evaluating potential recruits. Civil War–era army regulations required that recruits be "effective, able-bodied, sober, free from disease."[22] Because of lax physical examinations, the New York Agency of the Sanitary Commission estimated that "at least 25 per cent. of the volunteer army raised [in 1861 was] not only utterly useless, but a positive incumbrance and embarrassment, filling our hospital with invalids."[23] Patriotism did not compensate for physical disability. Physical examination procedures were subsequently tightened—though certainly not to perfection—with the result that the late-war replacements as a group were in better health than the volunteers from 1861 and 1862 had been when they entered the service.

Army regulations also required that recruits be "of good character and habits, with a competent knowledge of the English language."[24] Civilians also spoke of the need to recruit "good" men for the army. While there is no objective, quantifiable measure of good character, a man's occupation said something about what his community would presume his character to be. A yeoman farmer would command respect that a boatman could not. Whether a man was born in the United States or abroad could be indicative of his loyalty to the Union and/or his ability to speak English. A comparison of late-war replacements with the volunteers from 1861 and 1862 on these two factors could prove instructive on the issue of quality.

In order to make such a comparison over time, I selected two New York counties that had recruited new regiments over the course of the war—Oswego County and Onondaga County. Based on the objective criteria of occupation and place of birth (as well as age), the late-war 184th New York, which was raised in Oswego County in September 1864 and the late-war 185th New York, which was raised in Onondaga County at the same time, were comparable to the eight regiments raised in those two counties in 1861 and 1862 (and in fact better than some). While this sample is far too small to claim that it represents typical experience even in New York State, much less the Eastern States, it does at least raise a question about the universality of the alleged decline in quality with the influx of the late-war replacements.

Historians and the military have also criticized the late-war replacements for their alleged propensity to desert without actually quantifying the desertion rates. The data necessary to calculate the desertion rates have long been available, but that does not mean that the data exist in an easily accessible format for analysis.

Not only is the data on individual soldiers located in many disparate sources, but the data must be brought together to be electronically sortable. To facilitate more detailed analysis of desertion, the sortable HIBO Database has been created for this project. The HIBO Database, which includes more than a quarter million men, is comprised primarily of soldiers from the late-war new regiments in the Army of the Potomac, and soldiers from old regiments from Pennsylvania and New Jersey in the Army of the Potomac at the beginning of the Overland Campaign (with data going back to 1861).[25]

The desertion rates for the late-war new regiments (which generally did not have substitutes or draftees in their ranks) were not materially different from the desertion rates for the original complements of the old Pennsylvania regiments from 1861 and 1862. One difference is that desertion from the late-war new regiments tended to occur before the arrival of the regiment in the field, while desertion from the old Pennsylvania tended to occur from the field.

However, the late-war replacements in the old Pennsylvania regiments generally did desert at a higher rate than the original complement of the old Pennsylvania regiments. The desertion rate for the later-enlisting volunteers from Pennsylvania was around 20 percent compared to about 10 percent for the Pennsylvania volunteers from 1861 and 1862. The difference in New Jersey was even greater—about 30 percent of the later-enlisting volunteers deserted compared to about 12 percent for the volunteers from 1861 and 1862. Not surprisingly, the desertion rates for substitutes and draftees were significantly higher than for the later-enlisting volunteers in both Pennsylvania and New Jersey.

While the late-war replacements did desert more frequently than the volunteers from 1861 and 1862, two additional factors should be considered. First, a certain amount of desertion was inevitable no matter how laudatory the objective of the war, as Provost Marshal General Fry recognized. The larger the number of troops to be raised and the longer the duration of the war, the more severe the problem of desertion became. Had the Union resorted to a stand-alone draft rather than bounties and the conditional draft, desertion probably would have been even greater. One hundred thousand or more men left their local communities to avoid the initial enrollment. And that was when the bounties were available. Moreover, once the draft was initiated, on average, 20 percent of the men called in each of the drafts failed to report.[26]

More importantly, the Union took a variety of measures to successfully manage the desertion problem (as well as the impact of casualties from battle and disease) so that desertion did not adversely impact the operations of the Army of the Potomac. For example, the Provost Marshal General's Bureau was created in 1862, largely to address desertion. Partially disabled soldiers were organized into the Veteran Reserve Corps to perform noncombat duties, freeing up healthy soldiers for the front. Heavy artillery regiments garrisoning coastal forts were repurposed as infantry and sent to the field. African American men were also recruited. As a result, desertion by late-war replacements did not deprive Grant of the numbers of troops in the field necessary to implement as planned his strategy for defeating Lee.

Performance in the Field

As vigorously as the mercenary accusation has been made, it is important to remember that debating whether soldiers were patriots or mercenaries is beside the point in the midst of a war. The ultimate question is not whether men were in the army for good or for questionable reasons but rather how well they fought. While the mercenary epithet is a serious one, comments such as Bruce Catton's conclusion that the vast majority of later-enlisting volunteers were "worse than useless" are more damning in the end. To address the criticism that the later-enlisting volunteers made poor soldiers, it is not enough to show that they came from backgrounds similar to those of the volunteers from 1861 and 1862 or that the later-enlisting volunteers deserted less frequently than often implied. It is necessary to assess their performance on the battlefield.

Historians and men in the Union military have accused the late-war replacements of avoiding battle and leaving the danger of combat to the veterans from 1861 and 1862. However, the Pennsylvania data suggest that the battle deaths suffered by the later-enlisting volunteers from Pennsylvania were in line with the battle deaths suffered by the Pennsylvania veterans from 1861 and 1862 considering the later-enlisting volunteers' shorter time in the field. Further inquiry is necessary, but the claim that the later-enlisting volunteers shirked combat is subject to dispute. (The Pennsylvania data do suggest that the Pennsylvania substitutes and draftees did not engage in combat to the same extent as the later-enlisting volunteers.).[27] Moreover, it is necessary to go beyond casualty numbers for a proper assessment of the performance of the late-war replacements in the field. Even William J. Fox, author of the famous list of "Three Hundred Fighting Regiments," recognized that "large casualty lists are not necessarily indicative of the fighting qualities of a regiment."[28]

The alleged poor performance of the late-war replacements at Second Reams's Station has become the exemplar for the argument that they made poor soldiers. Accordingly, I have investigated in some detail the performance of both the late-war replacements and the veterans from 1861 and 1862 at Second Reams's Station.

I conclude that criticism along the lines of Richard Sommers's conclusion in *Richmond Redeemed* that the late-war replacements "wrecked" the Second Corps at Second Reams's Station is not justified, as discussed in chapter 9.[29] In fact, the Second Corps was defeated at Second Reams's Station primarily because after the Overland Campaign, the enlisted men—veterans from 1861 and 1862 as well the replacements from early 1864—were simply "fought out" in the words of Gen. John Gibbon and the officer corps to lead them had been decimated. The performance of the late-war replacements at Second Reams's Station was not materially different from the performance of the veterans from 1861 and 1862. Mistakes by key officers, including General Hancock, were a further factor.

Demonstrating that late-war replacements did not wreck the Second Corps is just the starting point in addressing the alleged poor performance of the late-war replacements. At the other end of the spectrum, there are battles where late-war replacements were critical to Union victory. Notably, the six late-war new regiments comprising Hartranft's Division of the Ninth Corps played a key role in staunching Lee's breakthrough at Fort Stedman in March 1865, as discussed in chapter 10. Fort Stedman was their first battle, but they were widely praised as having performed like veterans. Similarly, in the Fifth Corps, the late-war 185th New York and the 198th Pennsylvania in Chamberlain's Brigade of Griffin's Division were crucial to the Union victory in the Five Forks Campaign and literally saved the day at White Oak Road as discussed in chapter 11.

As the performance of these eight late-war new regiments demonstrates, late-war new regiments were capable of fighting quite effectively, even in their initial engagements. A natural question is how were they able to do so? Military historians have used the theory of "combat effectiveness" to guide the answers to questions like this. John A. Lynn provided the leading model of combat effectiveness, which he defined as "the quality of performance in combat" in *The Bayonets of the Republic* (1984), which assessed the performance of the Army of Revolutionary France from 1791 to 1794.[30] Other historians have followed his model in their assessments of the performance of other armies in the nineteenth and twentieth centuries. Two "systems" comprise Lynn's model—the motivational system, which examines "the motive force that drives [an army]," and the military system, which makes up the mechanisms of operation, including such factors as tactics, training, and weapons. Civil War historians have focused on motivation rather than the military system and have not dealt with combat effectiveness in a comprehensive manner.

Drawing on the work of Lynn and others, as well as the "readiness" concept used by the US Department of Defense to assess both large and small units, I have developed a streamlined model for assessing the performance of a smaller unit like a regiment. The first step is to determine whether the unit accomplished its assigned mission, including identification of elements of success (or failure) such as rapid (or slow) deployment, and extenuating circumstances such as weather or an unexpectedly large enemy force. The second step is assessment of the following essential capabilities to explain that performance: (1) motivation (morale and unit cohesion); (2) leadership; (3) training and discipline; (4) experience in the field; (5) actual versus authorized strength; (6) supply (food, arms, and equipment); and (7) demographics. This model is used to assess in detail the performance of the six late-war new regiments in Hartranft's Division and the performance of the late-war 185th New York and 198th Pennsylvania in Chamberlain's Brigade. This analysis demonstrates these eight late-war new regiments were indeed ready for battle and accomplished their missions. I do not contend that the stellar performance of these eight regiments was typical of the late-war new regiments in the Army of the Potomac as a group. However, solid performance—well above "poor"—was in fact typical of late-war new regiments in the Army of the Potomac during the Overland and Petersburg campaigns as discussed in chapters 7 and 8.

Late-war replacements did not just take the field in late-war new regiments. They also joined old regiments whose numbers had been severely depleted by battle and disease. The performance of these late-war replacements needs to be evaluated as well. In order to take a first cut at that analysis, I used the HIBO Database to identify old Pennsylvania infantry regiments in the Army of the Potomac, which were comprised of roughly a majority of late-war replacements on the eve of the Overland Campaign. The eighteen old Pennsylvania regiments so identified generally performed well in battle in both the Overland and the Petersburg campaigns based on the after-action reports of senior military officers and/or the evaluations of leading historians. While these eighteen old Pennsylvania regiments represent only a small part of the Army of the Potomac, their solid performance—combined with the solid performance of the thirty-plus late-war new regiments from nine different states—casts significant doubt on the assertion that the late-war replacements made poor soldiers compared to the veterans from 1861 and 1862.

Placing the performance in the field of the late-war Union soldiers in proper perspective lays the groundwork for a fair assessment of their contribution to the Union victory. The contribution of the veterans of 1861 and 1862 to the Union's victory was necessary—indeed indispensable—but it was not sufficient. The Confederacy still had armies in the field at the end of 1863 and 1864 despite the sacrifices of the men who enlisted in 1861 and 1862. Given the strength of the Confederate fortifications at Petersburg, the Army of the Potomac was not going to win the war in the East by frontal assault. Success depended on Grant's ability to stretch the Confederate lines to the breaking point by doggedly maneuvering further and further to the left. That strategy required putting more Union soldiers in the field. The late-war replacements, whether joining old regiments or arriving in late-war new regiments, provided the needed numbers of effective troops. There were not enough veterans from 1861 and 1862 left in the ranks in the spring of 1865 to have completed the final push without the infusion of the late-war replacements. As New Jersey's *Paterson Daily Press* wrote in September 1864,

> The country has already made prodigious and unprecedented exertions in the raising of armies; and if the fame and credit of what it has already accomplished were sufficient to rout Lee and Hood, we would strongly advise everybody to take his ease, and go on making money. But Jefferson Davis knows perfectly well how much we have done, and what great sacrifices we have made and yet the knowledge of it does not cause him to give way an inch. It is, in short, in what we will do and not in what we have once done, that our thunder lies.[31]

The late-war Union soldiers were a critical part of that "thunder."

CHAPTER 1

Demonization of the Late-War Replacements

Considering the heavy losses from both combat and disease suffered by the Army of the Potomac in 1862 and 1863, one would expect that the military would have heartily welcomed the late-war replacements in 1864 and 1865. It was not that simple. In the ranks, the seasoned veterans held the traditional enmity toward replacements who had not yet undergone the hardships of war. Many veterans were also jealous over the higher bounties that the later-enlisting volunteers and substitutes had received. For senior military leaders, the late-war replacements and the late-war new regiments did not conform to their views on how recruiting should be done. Accordingly, the military generally took a negative view of the late-war Union soldiers.

Historians have generally followed the military's negative view for more than one hundred years. As a result, historians have generally divided Union soldiers into two classes—the "patriots" of 1861 and 1862 who made "good" soldiers and the "high-bounty mercenaries" of 1863, 1864, and 1865 who made "poor" soldiers.[1] *Mercenary* is a strongly pejorative word whether used as a noun or an adjective—"motivated solely by a desire for money." A mercenary is the antithesis of a patriot fighting for a cause he believes in. A "patriot" is "somebody who proudly supports or defends his or her country and its way of life."

In his final report on the war, PMG James Fry harshly criticized the bounty system, especially the role played by local governments. Fry concluded that as the result of the price competition among localities, "the business of recruiting assumed a mercenary character." He also argued that "in time of war" the country "need[s] the service of better men than those who enter the Army simply for mercenary motives." While Fry was not the first to refer to bounty men as mercenaries, his position as provost marshal general gave official approval for others to follow the implication that the later-enlisting volunteers and substitutes joined the army solely for the money. It is easy to discern Fry's motivation for disparaging the late-war replacements. The military strongly preferred a stand-alone draft. Fry wanted to be sure that the Union army's reliance on the "carrot and stick"—bounties to induce volunteering backed up by the threat of a conditional draft—did not bog down recruiting during the next war as it had during the Civil War in his view.[2]

In *Battle Cry of Freedom,* published in 1988, winner of the Pulitzer Prize and probably the most widely read general history of the Civil War over the past thirty years, James McPherson followed Fry's criticism of the competition among local governments, referring to it as "a mercenary bidding contest for warm bodies to fill district quotas."[3] He was following a consistent line of historians preceding him. James Ford Rhodes, winner of the second Pulitzer Prize awarded for history, wrote in 1902 that the recruits of 1864 "were in great part mercenaries" but provided only a cursory reference to the amount of bounties. Ella Lonn, one of the earliest professionally trained historians to write on the Civil War, identified high bounties as one of the causes of Union desertion in her 1928 study, which remains the definitive treatment of desertion during the Civil War. In words similar to those of Rhodes, she concluded that "Reinforcements were constantly being sent to the armies, but they were for the most part mercenaries, immoral and cowardly."[4] Writing at the same time as Lonn, Fred Albert Shannon devoted an entire chapter to "The Mercenary Factor" in his study of the organization of the Union army.[5]

Eugene Murdock substituted "love of money" for "mercenary" in *Patriotism Limited* (1967). He followed earlier historians in drawing the line between the men who had enlisted in 1861 and 1862 and the men who enlisted thereafter: "The 'love-of-country' boys of 1861–62 had now given way to those who had to be bribed with bounties before they would enlist. These 'love-of-money' volunteers brought the Civil War bounty system to full bloom."[6] Murdock followed *Patriotism Limited* with his 1971 study of the Enrollment Act—*One Million Men: The Civil War Draft in the North 1862–1865*. Writing at the time of the hostility to the Vietnam-era draft, Murdock made clear where he stood: "For a democratic state, in a moment of national emergency, a universal, impartial draft of all citizens is the only way to raise an army."[7]

As Shannon noted, the practice of paying a bounty to volunteers—as opposed to drafting men—did have historical precedent going back to the beginnings of the nation. And, as Shannon recognized, the vast majority of Union soldiers were to some degree "bounty" men because bounties in smaller amounts had been paid since the beginning of the war. McPherson explained that away by stating that the "modest" bounties offered by the federal, state, and local governments in 1862 were "intended as a compensation for the economic sacrifice made by a volunteer and his family." He referred to the family support payments provided in 1861 as "implicit bounties," but also characterized them as "patriotic subsidies."[8] While that rationale has some validity, the facts do not entirely support it. The word *bounty* itself bespeaks a reward, not compensation to hold harmless. The bounty was an extra on top of regular monthly military pay. Moreover, state or local governments usually had a separate family support program as McPherson acknowledged.[9]

If a very small financial gain for the enlisting volunteer crosses the line between an acceptable "patriotic subsidy"/"modest" bounty and a "mercenary"/"high-bounty" payment, the line was crossed for farmhands and other low-paid men in 1862.[10] In July 1862, military compensation doubled civilian compensation in the Eastern States for occupations comprising as much as half of the workforce.[11] McPherson's characterization of the 1862 volunteers as "pre-bounty" should be revisited. See chapter 3.

Not only did critics question the patriotism of the late-war replacements, but they also often demeaned their very worth as human beings. Veterans in the field often criticized the late-war replacements in the strongest personal terms. As a result, historians have had ample contemporary source material to support their characterizations of the late-war replacements as "human refuse," "immoral and cowardly," "offscourings of the world," etc.[12]

At the time of the Civil War Centennial, Bruce Catton was the most widely read Civil War historian. His history of the Army of the Potomac was a landmark, and the third volume—*A Stillness at Appomattox*—won the Pulitzer Prize. At the beginning of *A Stillness at Appomattox,* Catton described the change in the composition of the Army of the Potomac that had occurred by the end of 1864: "Most of [the new recruits] were men who had joined up only because they got a great deal of money . . . , and in the great majority of cases these men were worse than useless."[13] He followed that statement with six pages of anecdotes detailing the evils of high-bounty men, bounty jumpers, conscripts, substitutes, and substitute brokers. He concluded that "There undoubtedly is exaggeration in some of these accounts. . . . Yet if there is exaggeration in the complaints there is not very much exaggeration."[14] While Catton acknowledged that some of the high-bounty men made good soldiers, in the end he left the strong impression that the great majority did not.[15] Bell Wiley also acknowledged in *The Life of Billy Yank* that there were some good late-war replacements, but in the end, he also left a negative impression, in part by lumping the later-enlisting volunteers together with substitutes and bounty jumpers.[16] The same is true of Eugene Murdock as well.[17]

As voluminous as the contemporaneous accounts by soldiers relied upon by historians are, a cautious dose of skepticism should accompany them. Probably since time immemorial, veterans have criticized replacements arriving in the field. During the Civil War, the payment of bounties introduced a new complication in the relationship between veteran and replacement. Moreover, if the veteran from 1861 or 1862 owned land, he was also paying for the higher local bounties himself through increased property taxes. And with the July 1864 call for troops, men could enlist for only one year rather than three and still get a high bounty. At the end of the war, the possibility that one-year men from the high-bounty summer of 1864 might be discharged before some of the three-year men was also a sore point for the veterans.[18] No matter how bravely a later-enlisting volunteer or substitute performed in the field, the monetary distinction would always be there.

In one of the more recent books addressing the late-war replacements, Steven J. Ramold noted that "Established volunteers, proud of their nationalistic impulse, scorned the later soldiers for their perceived lack of nationalism. Considering themselves true patriots, veteran soldiers looked down at those who needed a financial incentive to join."[19] The tension could arise even before the bounty men reached the field. When the commissioners of Blair County, Pennsylvania, adopted a fifty-dollar bounty in August 1862 for three-year recruits, two company commanders from the Seventy-Sixth Pennsylvania Volunteers, a three-year regiment organized in October 1861 that would go on to become one of Fox's Three Hundred, wrote an open letter to the citizens asking if their men would receive the bounty or just the new recruits, and "if not why?" They noted that when they had enlisted, "no other inducement was held out than that our country needed our services," and that they had responded "with true and patriotic hearts." They lamented that "*patriotism* is a *fine* thing, but *finer* is the 'almighty dollar,' is some peoples estimation, . . . judging from the response to the late calls" (emphasis in original).[20] Similarly, an 1862 volunteer in the 148th New York Volunteers led with the "high bounties" in the list of grievances he sent to his hometown newspaper in September 1864: "Quite a difference exists between the bounty given three years volunteers in 1862 and what is paid now for volunteers for one year. Then it averaged $90 for *three years* now $1200 for *one year*. . . . Is this justice? Is it good faith?"[21]

With the end of the war in sight, one veteran in an old regiment did not even see a need for replacements. On March 2, 1865, James Harper of the 139th Pennsylvania, a three-year regiment organized in August 1862, wrote that "We dont [*sic*] want any new men. The strength of our regiment increases slowly [from returning convalescent veterans] . . . and we prefer to serve what remains of our term by ourselves." However, Harper probably did not base his aversion to late-war replacements on personal experience. There were no draftees or substitutes in the 139th Pennsylvania and of the roughly fifty later-enlisting volunteers who joined the 139th Pennsylvania, only a couple deserted, while 10 percent of the men overall in the 139th Pennsylvania deserted.[22]

The late-war replacements could also be outsiders in a cultural sense. While Union regiments generally were not recruited in a single county or town, companies often were. Men often served with people they had known before the war. The late-war replacements coming into an old regiment were not necessarily from the same community as the veterans and not even necessarily from the same state. For example, over five hundred new recruits joined the Ninth New Hampshire, a three-year regiment organized in 1862, at the end of 1863 to compensate for heavy casualties. What had been a solidly rural regiment made up of New Hampshire men in 1862 now had a significant percentage of urban men from other states. Only about a third of the new men resided in New Hampshire. Over 40 percent came from New York City and other parts of New York State and an additional 8 percent each from Pennsylvania (primarily Philadelphia) and Massachusetts (primarily Boston).[23]

The bias of veterans toward the late-war replacements must be weighed when quoting veterans. Far too often, historians have conclusively described the character of the late-war replacements by using veterans' characterizations without appropriate caution. The bad reputation of the high-bounty soldiers and the high-number regiments as a group has on occasion deprived them of balanced, objective analysis of their performance. An example is the performance of the late-war Fortieth New Jersey in the final assault at Petersburg.

In the Sixth Corps' attack on April 2, 1865, Penrose's New Jersey Brigade led with the Fortieth New Jersey. Noting that the Fortieth New Jersey was "notorious" for desertion, A. Wilson Greene suggests that "The tough-minded Penrose may have selected this shaky regiment for front line duty both to deter its members from skulking during the attack and to absorb its share of the expected casualties, thus sparing the veteran regiments some measure of danger." Greene then recounted that "The 40th New Jersey, true to its reputation, broke no fewer than three times, although according to one witness, 'a portion did admirably.'"[24]

A more favorable view of the Fortieth New Jersey's performance is equally, if not more, credible. A portion of the Fortieth New Jersey did indeed perform admirably. Maj. Augustus Fay of the Fortieth New Jersey led the intermingled regiments of Penrose's Brigade into hand-to-hand combat in the Confederate lines.[25] General Wheaton recommended Fay and eight other officers of the Fortieth New

Jersey for brevet promotions for their service in the last campaign. Moreover, Wheaton cited nine enlisted men from the Fortieth New Jersey for "conspicuous bravery and good conduct"—more than the Fourth New Jersey (five), the Tenth New Jersey (seven), and the Fifteenth New Jersey (four), although the latter did have fewer men in the field.[26] Pvt. Frank Fesq of the Fortieth New Jersey received the Congressional Medal of Honor for capturing a Confederate battle flag.[27]

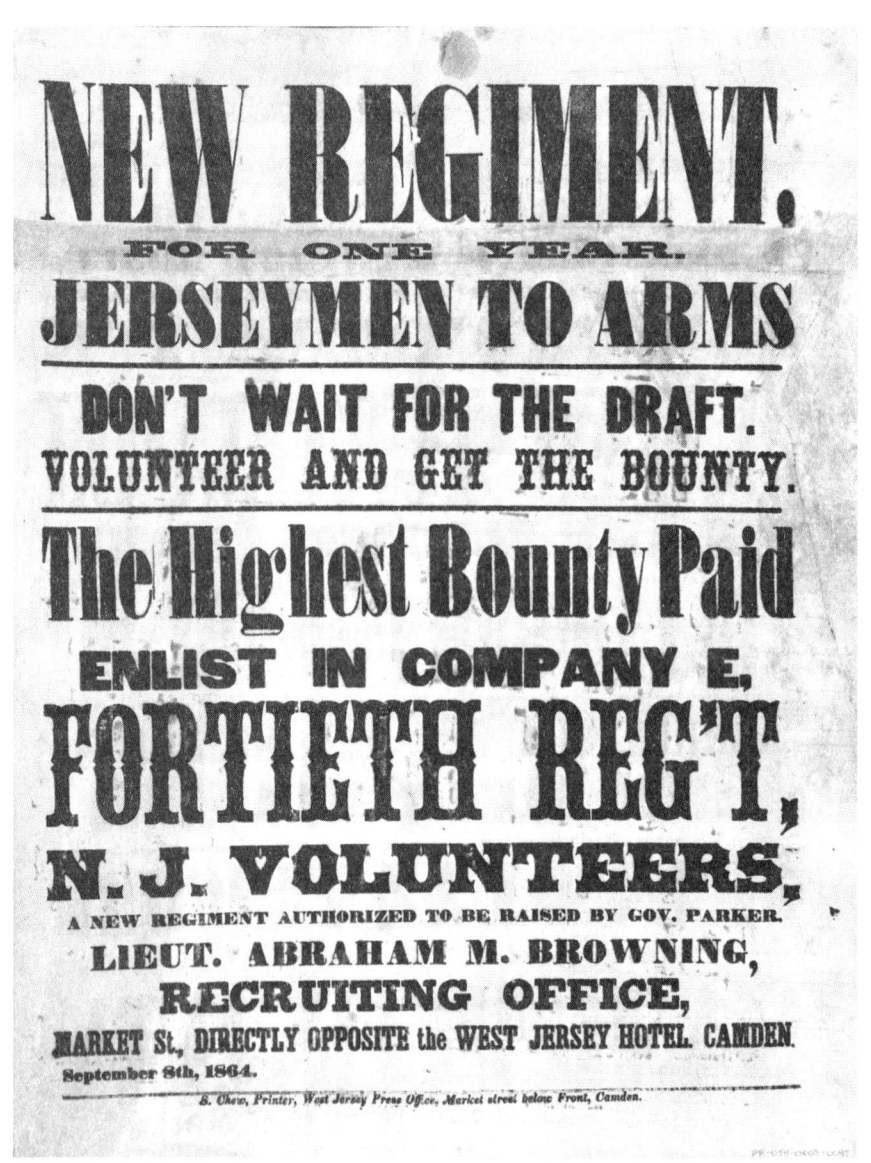

"New Regiment, for One Year, Jerseymen to Arms, Don't Wait for the Draft" (Reproduced by permission from the New-York Historical Society)

Penrose may have believed that the Fortieth New Jersey was his best choice to lead the assault. The Fortieth New Jersey was his only regiment commanded by a full colonel—Stephen Gilkyson, who had served for three years in the Sixth New Jersey and risen from captain to lieutenant colonel before being mustered out in September 1864 to organize the Fortieth New Jersey. A lieutenant colonel commanded the Fourth New Jersey and majors commanded the Tenth and the Fifteenth New Jersey.[28] The Fortieth New Jersey at five hundred strong may have been the largest of Penrose's regiments. The Tenth New Jersey was down to eighty men present for duty after the Battle of Winchester. Many replacements did join the Tenth New Jersey at the end of January 1865, but they were substitutes, and Penrose may have viewed them as less reliable and greener than the volunteers in the Fortieth New Jersey. Similarly, two hundred draftees and substitutes joined the Fifteenth New Jersey in late March. Large numbers of substitutes had also replenished the Fourth New Jersey from December 1864 through March 1865.[29]

Moreover, the Fortieth New Jersey did not necessarily break without cause (assuming that it did in fact break three times). The Confederate positions were quite strong, as described by Wheaton: "The work accomplished by the division on this day was the most difficult I had ever seen troops called upon to per-form. Massing and advancing in the dark, they successfully assaulted strongly intrenched [*sic*] and elaborately obstructed lines with a determination and gal-lantry that could never be excelled."[30] Penrose reported that the Confederate pickets had not been cleared, and as a result "the first and second lines became one," receiving "severe" fire from the pickets. Nonetheless, "the entire command pushed on, and in a few moments parts of each regiment had possession of the enemy's lines."[31] Penrose did not criticize the Fortieth New Jersey in his after-action report and praised the overall performance of his troops: "Though the command was in some confusion in the assault, yet in the afternoon's advance the men and the officers behaved to my satisfaction, especially as two-thirds of them were new men, and had not been in the army three months."[32]

Historians have all too often subjected the late-war replacements to trial by anecdote. Anecdotal evidence is, of course, an important part of historical analy-sis. It can provide the human dimension to an otherwise colorless set of facts on dates, places, movements, and conclusions about who won the battle. But if the anecdotal experience is not typical, it risks distorting the historical picture. Anecdotes presenting a sensational story are certainly enticing, but the question remains whether they represent typical experience.

Bounty jumpers certainly met the sensational test, going all the way back to the Civil War. The press regularly reported on successful escapes by bounty jumpers—as well as their punishment when caught. The serial bounty jumper made a particularly enticing story. The annual reports by state adjutant generals and the federal provost marshal general also discussed the problem of bounty jumping.[33] Several of these incidents developed enough notoriety for historians to include them in their writings. The Enrollment Branch of the Provost Marshal General's Bureau highlighted a serial bounty jumper in its end-of-the war report: "desperate characters presented themselves who would enlist and 'jump' bounties as often as opportunities presented. A man now in the Albany Penitentiary undergoing an imprisonment of four years confessed to having 'jumped the bounty' thirty-two times." James Rhodes, Fred Albert Shannon, and Shelby Foote included the Albany Bounty Jumper in their books. More recently, Geoffrey Ward included the Albany Bounty Jumper in his companion volume to Ken Burns's widely viewed documentary series on the Civil War.[34] Was the Albany Bounty Jumper typical of the late-war replacements (or even bounty jumpers as a group)? Serial bounty jumping certainly occurred, but it is unclear how frequently it occurred. McPherson was wisely cautious in stating that "some men" had become bounty jumpers and that "several" of them got away with the practice several times, but he may have underestimated the extent of the problem.[35] In an era without photo identification cards, fingerprints, and social security numbers, a successful bounty jumper could easily jump again in another location without being recognized.[36]

A large number of deserters from a contingent of late-war replacements sent to an old regiment in the field also met the sensational news test. In 1864, the *American Annual Cyclopedia* reported that "out of a detachment of 625 recruits sent to re-enforce a New Hampshire regiment . . . 137 deserted on the passage, 82 to the enemy's picket line, and 86 to the rear, leaving but 370 men, or less than 60 percent available for duty."[37] Rhodes, Lonn, and Foote included this New Hampshire anecdote in their books.[38]

One should also remember that bounty jumping did not begin in 1864 with the higher bounties. People complained about the practice of bounty jumping as early as September 1861, even though the bounties were substantially smaller.[39] To be sure, the typical volunteer in 1861 and 1862 was not a bounty jumper, but the typical later-enlisting volunteer in 1864 and 1865 was not a bounty jumper either.

Historians have often lumped together for discussion substitutes, conscripts, bounty jumpers, and later-enlisting volunteers who actually served without adequate attention to the differences among them. For example, substitutes in general deserted much more frequently than later-enlisting volunteers, as discussed in chapter 5. Historians have given attention to substitutes far out of proportion to their numbers. As a result, the later-enlisting volunteers who intended to— and did—serve suffer from guilt by association with substitutes and draftees.

Shelby Foote commented in *Red River to Appomattox* that the veterans from 1861 whose terms were expiring in 1864 "would have to be replaced, and mainly this would be done by the conscripts and substitutes who now were arriving as a result of Lincoln's February [1864] Call." Foote quoted a veteran that "Such another depraved, vice-hardened and desperate set of human beings never before disgraced an army."[40] In fact, later-enlisting volunteers comprised nearly 90 percent of the men raised under the February and March 1864 calls—only 48,000 of the 374,000 troops raised were conscripts or substitutes. For the February through December 1864 calls overall, later-enlisting volunteers comprised nearly 80 percent of the men raised.[41]

The men in the ranks were not the only ones who criticized the late-war replacements. Senior military leaders had their own reasons for doing so. The military and civilian leaders differed on two key recruiting policy issues that impacted their views of the late-war replacements and the late-war new regiments: conscription versus volunteering and using replacements for refilling old regiments in the field versus populating newly created regiments. The military preferred conscription to volunteering because the draft could raise large numbers of troops more quickly. The civilian leaders preferred volunteering because of the political cost of drafting. The military preferred using replacements to refill old regiments in the field because the veterans in the old regiments could quickly and effectively train the new recruits. State and local civilian leaders preferred creating new regiments because of the patronage opportunities—three field-grade officers and thirty company-level officers per regiment. The late-war replacements and the late-war new regiments did not fit into the military's view. The replacements were volunteers and substitutes who the military thought delayed the replacement process. And the regiments were, by definition, new. As a result, criticism from military leaders is not surprising.

Senior military officers much preferred a stand-alone draft to the combination of bounties and a conditional draft that the Lincoln Administration and the states pursued to entice volunteers. Time was the simple reason. The senior commanders needed troops in the field immediately and believed that a stand-alone draft would meet that need far more quickly than the prolonged process necessary to recruit volunteers with a subsequent—and usually delayed—draft to meet any shortfall. Senior military officials considered cost as well. At the end of 1864, Fry advised Stanton that the average federal cost of raising a man through the volunteer process was $244.69, while it was but $55.84 (and arguably only $33.86) through the draft.[42] State and local bounties added to the federal cost.

As efforts to fill the July 1864 call for three hundred thousand troops with volunteers were proceeding, Grant complained to Secretary of State Seward on August

Left: Secretary of War Edwin Stanton (Library of Congress); *right:* Provost Marshal General James B. Fry (Library of Congress)

19, 1864, about "'bounty jumpers' or *substitute men,* who enlist for the money, desert, and enlist again. Of this class of recruits [that is, substitutes] we do not get one, for every eight bounties paid to do good service."[43] Three weeks later, Grant sent a two-sentence complaint to Secretary of War Stanton: "I hope it is not the intention to postpone the draft to allow time to fill up with recruiting. The men we have been getting in that way nearly all desert, and out of five reported North as having enlisted we do not get more than one."[44] Stanton replied the next day that he had no plan to delay the draft and added a contrary view of the recruits then being obtained: "It is represented that the first recruits were a hard lot, but that recently the volunteers are equal to any that have taken the field during the war."[45]

Grant's statement that "nearly all [volunteers and substitutes] desert" is clearly an exaggeration. Grant did not explain how he derived his one in five and one in eight fractions. Timing probably accounts for some of the loss. Recruiters could not deliver the men to the field the day after they enlisted. However, desertion was undoubtedly a factor.[46] Grant's estimates are discussed further in chapter 5 on desertion.

The final, official statement by the military on conscription versus volunteering came in Fry's postwar report in 1866. Fry adamantly concluded that in a future military emergency, conscription was by far the preferable course of action over recruiting with bounties. Cost was the key factor, but Fry also pointed to the need for recruiting "better men than those who enter the Army *simply for mercenary motives.*"[47] Fry's conclusion favoring the draft became basic federal policy for the next hundred years, but his assertion that the bounty system produced "soldiers of an inferior class" is not supported by the facts as illustrated in chapter 4 on the quality of recruits. His assumption that the later-enlisting volunteers enlisted "simply for mercenary motives" also has never been proven.

The question whether new recruits would be assigned to existing regiments in the field or to new regiments to be created arose each time that Lincoln issued a new call for troops. Assigning them to old regiments could bring the old regiments back to full strength after heavy losses from combat and disease. Creating a new regiment would give a governor the opportunity to appoint some thirty officers. The patronage opportunity was significant. The monthly pay (including allowances) for Union infantry officers was $194 a month for a colonel, $170 for a lieutenant colonel, $151 for a major, $118.50 for a captain, $108 for a first lieutenant and $103 for a second lieutenant (although officers did have to pay for their food and other expenses). These positions were lucrative. For example, George Carpenter probably doubled his wages as a carpenter when he joined the 179th New York as a first lieutenant in the spring of 1864.[48]

Senior military officers all but unanimously preferred the old regiments throughout the war, believing they could more quickly and effectively train new soldiers. General Sherman probably was the most emphatic, writing in his memoirs that the policy of raising new regiments while old regiments "dwindle away into mere skeleton organizations" was the "greatest mistake made in our civil war."[49] In July 1862, McClellan wrote Lincoln that "I am very anxious to have my old regiments filled up rather than have new ones formed."[50] At the same time, he told Governor Morgan of New York: "The greatest benefit that can be conferred upon [the army] would be to fill to the maximum the old regiments . . . I would prefer 50,000 recruits for my old regiments to 100,000 men organized into new regiments, and I cannot too earnestly urge the imperative necessity of following this system."[51]

Notwithstanding the logic of filling the old regiments, the practice varied from year to year. The military's view lost out in 1862. Despite McClellan's strong personal appeal to Governor Morgan, New York sent sixty new three-year infantry regiments to the army during the last five months of 1862.[52] (That represented nearly two thousand patronage opportunities.) However, the military's preference for filling old regiments prevailed in 1863. New York created only one new infantry regiment in 1863—the 178th New York. Similarly, Pennsylvania raised nineteen new three-year regiments during the last five months of 1862, but none in 1863. Massachusetts raised eight new three-year regiments in August and September 1862. The only two new regiments that Massachusetts raised in 1863 were both African American troops. New regiments did regain favor in 1864, with Pennsylvania creating twenty-six, New York six, and Massachusetts six.[53]

In June 1863, Grant, while commanding the Army of the Tennessee, told Lincoln that he preferred using the men from the contemplated draft to fill old regiments. In Grant's view, a new recruit added to an old regiment "would become an old soldier, from the very contact, before he was aware of it." An old regiment had trained and experienced officers and men. An old regiment also had an existing logistical infrastructure that would have to be created for a new regiment. "Taken in an economic point of view, one drafted man in an old regiment is worth three in a new one."[54] Sherman held similar views,[55] as did Meade and Thomas.[56] Meade estimated that the regiments in the field needed 84,000 men to bring them back to full strength.[57]

It is hard to dispute that experienced officers will generally train new troops more effectively than inexperienced officers. But new regiments did not necessarily have to be officered by inexperienced men trading on political connections. As the war progressed, officers who had enlisted in 1861 but did not reenlist when their original regiment was mustered out formed an increasingly large pool of available veteran officers. For example, in New York, the thirty-plus two-year regiments that mustered out in the spring of 1863 proved to be an important source of experienced officers for the New York late-war new regiments being raised in 1864. The Union army's senior leadership did not overlook this source of experienced officers. When the Adjutant General's Office announced the veteran volunteers program, they included a provision that "New organizations will be officered only by persons who have been in service and have shown themselves properly qualified for command."[58] For example, in February 1864, Stanton authorized William Gregg, who had served as major in the two-year Twenty-Third New York, to raise an infantry regiment that became the 179th New York Volunteers. Gregg selected Franklin B. Doty, who had been a company commander in the Twenty-Third New York as his second in command. Several other officers from the Twenty-Third New York served in the 179th New York. Other men recruiting companies for the 179th New York had served as officers in the Twenty-First, Thirty-First, Thirty-Seventh, Thirty-Eighth, 126th, 141st, and 154th New York. Local newspapers highlighted this veteran experience in their reporting on the recruiting for these new regiments.[59]

Col. Thomas Livermore, who had volunteered in 1861 and commanded the late-war Eighteenth New Hampshire at the end of the war, recognized the importance for recruiting of his predecessor's standing in the community. He also commended him for resisting political influence: "Colonel Bell, although himself not a trained soldier, displayed rare judgment of men, great ability in organizing, and—what was of greatest importance to the future of the regiment—the strongest resistance to the clamors of politicians who sought commissions for their friends on political grounds."[60]

The military hierarchy also believed that new recruits would learn better and more quickly from the experienced noncommissioned officers and enlisted men in the old regiments. That makes sense, but the question arises whether that theory worked in practice when the veterans in the old regiments criticized the late-war replacements so severely. As with officers, there was a ready supply of veteran noncommissioned officers and enlisted men from 1861 who had left the service but could be induced to return for new regiments. The Adjutant General's Office also recognized that possibility. In the first six companies of the 179th New York, 10 percent or more of the enlisted men had previously served. Twenty percent of the enlisted men in the Eighteenth New Hampshire had previously served. Livermore noted that with the presence of these veterans, "the inexperienced recruits had all the advantages of instruction by experienced officers and association with practiced soldiers that they would have had in some of the old regiments then in the field in which there were not over two hundred veterans present for duty."[61] The experience of the veteran officers and noncommissioned officers who led the six late-war new regiments in Hartranft's Division was critical to these regiments' ability to perform like veterans at the Battle of Fort Stedman in March 1865, as discussed in chapter 10.

The military's preference for old regiments also assumed that the old regiment would have sufficient officers and enlisted men in the field to train the new recruits. However, the Overland Campaign and the beginning of the Petersburg Campaign took a heavy toll on the officers and noncommissioned officers, with captains often commanding regiments. A short-staffed regiment would have been hard pressed to conduct the necessary training for new recruits. The fact that the old regiments often received new recruits in large numbers over short periods of time, inundating the veterans, aggravated the problem. For example, over the course of the war, the number of replacements doubled the number of veterans in the original complement in the Seventh New Jersey.[62] Factoring in casualties in the original complement means the actual ratio in the field was significantly higher. Thus, a single veteran would have been responsible for training six or seven replacements—a challenging task. The theory that the old regiments would better train new recruits also assumed that the new recruits would learn soldiering by serving alongside the veterans. But new recruits did not always join the existing companies of the old regiments. New recruits often formed new companies and the benefit of shoulder-to-shoulder contact with veterans was lost.[63]

Finally, new regiments had advantages over old regiments for recruiting. The thirty-some officer commissions not only gave a governor patronage opportunities, they also induced prominent men in the community to recruit a company or a regiment. Fry recognized that the call of July 1862 was met in large part with new regiments in part due to "a more or less well-founded belief that, without the stimulus of commissions in new regiments, individual efforts, heretofore so successful in raising men, would not be made by influential parties in different localities." Maine's *Ellsworth American* noted in August 1862 that "The enlistments for new companies and the new regiments have been stimulated by the active and energetic exertions of those expecting commissions. This fact alone accounts for the rapidity with which companies are formed and why the several towns have furnished their quotas of men." Two years later, the Newark, New Jersey, *Sentinel of Freedom* noted that the authorization of a new one-year regiment "will no doubt stimulate volunteering."[64]

New regiments may also have attracted men who might not have been willing to serve in an old regiment. Henry Bull, a twenty-year-old farmer from Steuben County, New York, who enlisted in the 189th New York in August 1864, wrote his father that "We are all thankful for to be put into a new regiment."[65] New York's *Hornellsville Tribune* wrote in February 1864 that "The advantages of a new regiment to a raw recruit are manifold, and must be so well understood by men generally, that to mention them would be a work of supererogation."[66] Livermore, who had the experience of commanding a late-war new regiment, provided a more explicit explanation. He noted that a recruit in a new regiment "enlisted under a captain or lieutenant from his neighborhood. He had comrades[,] friends and old schoolmates . . . Each one started on a level with the rest of the regiment, and had an equal chance for promotion."[67] Livermore's case for new regiments was somewhat exaggerated, but considerations like this apparently led the governor of New Hampshire to conclude in the autumn of 1864 that "recruiting citizens of the state for new regiments presented small difficulty, while recruiting for old ones was impossible."[68]

Because the late-war replacements did not fit into the military's preferred method of recruiting, the military could disclaim responsibility for their performance. As a result, Union generals on occasion scapegoated the late-war replacements to explain away their failure in battle. Rather than acknowledging that the Union army was often throwing late-war replacements into battle with little or no training, generals could attribute failure to the alleged lesser caliber of men receiving high bounties to volunteer. After the Union defeats at Second

Reams's Station on August 25, 1864, and Poplar Spring Church on September 30, 1864, some of the Union generals involved blamed the late-war replacements—at least in part—for the defeats, rather than acknowledging the impact of their own mistakes and factors beyond the responsibility of the late-war replacements.

Gen. Winfield Scott Hancock, the commander of the Second Corps at Second Reams's Station, singled out three regiments for criticism: "Just at the time when a few minutes' resistance would have secured the repulse of the enemy, who were thrown into considerable disorder by the severity of the fire they were subjected to and the obstacles to their advance, a part of the line (composed of [the three regiments]) gave way in confusion."[69] Hancock then noted that the three regiments "are largely made up of recruits and substitutes. The first named regiment in particular is entirely new, companies being formed in New York and sent down here, some officers being unable to speak English. The material compares very unfavorably with the veterans absent."[70] Hancock's criticism of the late-war replacements became the military's standard view. Andrew A. Humphreys, who commanded the Second Corps after Hancock and had previously served as the chief of staff for the Army of the Potomac, noted in his 1883 history *The Virginia Campaign of 1864 and 1865* that "the extent of the injurious effect of the large number of raw recruits recently received had not been anticipated."[71] Livermore, who commanded a late-war regiment but who had also enlisted in 1861, followed the Hancock/Humphreys interpretation in his 1904 regimental history of the Eighteenth New Hampshire. "One of the saddest incidents of the Civil War was the subjection of the Second Army Corps, of glorious reputation, to dishonor at Reams' Station, by the infirmity of the recruits with which its ranks were encumbered."[72]

Two widely respected historians have agreed with the military view. Richard Sommers went so far in *Richmond Redeemed: The Siege at Petersburg* to state that "such men . . . wrecked the vaunted II Corps at Second Reams's Station. They might do the same to the V and IX Corps, too, for they infected both outfits."[73] However, Sommers did also state that heavy losses in the Overland Campaign "had shredded the very fabric of the [Second] corps" and point to the "high muster-out rate" of veterans and "the lack of proper training" for the replacements.[74] More generally, Earl J. Hess also wrote about the impact of the late-war replacements on the Second Corps: "[The poor quality of recruits] was a major reason that the 2d Corps, which had repulsed Pickett's Charge at Gettysburg and had fought so ferociously at Mule Shoe Salient, was only a shadow of its former self by the time it refused to attack the Confederate works at Petersburg."[75] Given the sterling reputation of Hancock and the Second Corps, looking elsewhere to lay the blame for the disaster at Second Reams's Station is understandable, but historians have blamed the late-war replacements for forces beyond their control as chapter 9 discusses.

Poplar Spring Church provides another example. On September 30, 1864, Potter's Division of the Ninth Corps was racing toward the Boydton Plank Road when a Confederate attack caught them by surprise. The Confederates routed Potter's Division and took over a thousand prisoners as Potter's Division retreated in chaos. Potter reported that "The majority of the troops behaved well, but the recruits (mostly substitutes, and many unable to speak English) behaved badly."[76] Gen. John Parke, the commander of the Ninth Corps, made the same point as Potter, explaining that the "new material requires time for drilling and disciplining," but also pointing out that "in the conscript and the substitute we do not find the same *elan* that displayed itself so gloriously in the patriotic volunteer" and that "we have to contend against the demoralizing influence of the bounty jumper, whose sole ambition is to shirk and desert."[77]

The order that Potter proceed toward the Boydton Plank Road "as rapidly as practicable, without reference to anyone else" caused the rout of his division, not the late-war replacements or the late-war new regiments on the field. While the Ninth Corps had moved in concert with the Fifth Corps earlier in the day, the Fifth Corps did not advance further, leaving Potter's right flank totally exposed as he moved toward the Boydton Plank Road.[78] The opportunity to gain the Boydton Plank Road may well have justified the risk of advancing "without reference to anyone else," but that risk underlay Potter's defeat, not the late-war replacements.

As opposed to Potter's Division, the Confederates did not rout Willcox's Division of the Ninth Corps at Poplar Spring Church. Gen. John Hartranft, who commanded the Second Brigade of Willcox's Division at the time, expressed his "entire satisfaction with the conduct of the regiments in the command and their commanding officers." Hartranft concluded that "They behaved nobly . . . especially, when the brigade was almost surrounded by the enemy, . . . All the regiments displayed a steadiness under trying circumstances, which speaks well of their discipline."[79] Two of the seven regiments in Hartranft's Brigade were late-war new regiments—the Twenty-Fourth New York Cavalry and the Sixtieth Ohio, which were organized in January 1864 and March 1864 respectively.[80] Another two were old regiments with late-war replacements constituting half their numbers—the Forty-Sixth New York and the Fiftieth Pennsylvania.[81]

After the war, the policy dispute in Congress about the appropriate pension benefits for Union veterans engulfed the late-war replacements. The Pension Act, adopted in 1862, protected disabled soldiers whose disability was service-related. Opponents of the repeal of the requirement that the disability be service-related saw the proposal as disproportionately benefiting the late-war replacements because they had endured the hardships of war for a much shorter time than the early war veterans. (This issue may have been more acute in the Western States, which had raised large numbers of "One Hundred Days" regiments during the war.)[82]

In 1881, the Grand Army of the Republic actively entered the pension debate for the first time. The *National Tribune,* the veterans' editorial voice, advocated using the pension system to recognize the veterans' service in preserving the Union.[83] In a July 1887 editorial, the *New York Evening Post* criticized the Grand Army of the Republic "as no longer a benevolent institution working for unselfish ends; it has become a machine for the procuring of pensions and offices." The *Post* noted that the GAR's then current membership of 350,000 included only about a quarter of the surviving veterans. "This one-fourth includes almost all the self-seekers, the men who were only tempted into the army by high bounties, and the men who are also trying to trade upon their services in the war."[84] Similarly, South Dakota's *Bismarck Weekly Tribune* wrote that the pension bill that President Cleveland had vetoed "would have doubled the pension list in a short time [and] have been chiefly a benefit to the high bounty men of the last year of the war."[85]

In 1890, Congress repealed the requirement that the disability be service-related. The change may have led Col. Thomas W. Hyde to skewer the late-war replacements in the Sixty-First Pennsylvania in his memoirs. The Sixty-First Pennsylvania was one of the regiments in his brigade during the final assault at Petersburg on April 2, 1865. He commended the two hundred veterans in the ranks, who captured two Confederate battle flags and condemned the three hundred "drafted men, substitutes and the like" who "disappeared" during the battle. "The 200, in my opinion, should all have large pensions, and the 300 should all have been shot or hung."[86] The 1890 amendment may have colored Hyde's recollection. Hyde ended his discussion with the comment, "It would be interesting to know how many of the latter lot [that is, the three hundred new men] in after days turned up pensioned by a grateful government, and still we wonder that the pension roll is not a roll of honor." A. Wilson Greene relied heavily on Hyde for his criticism of the Sixty-First Pennsylvania in *The Final Battles of the Petersburg Campaign.*[87]

Bounty men comprised the bulk of the men criticized by Hyde. If in fact the bounty men performed poorly on the field on April 2, they may have suffered from a lack of training and their officers' inexperience rather than cowardice. The bounty men were in companies (H, I, and K), which had joined the Sixty-First Pennsylvania only the month before the April 2 attack. The vast majority of the men in companies H and I had joined the army only in mid-February. Most of the men in Company K had been in the army for only three weeks or less when they went into battle on April 2.[88] Moreover, the new recruits were placed in separate companies, which prevented them from learning firsthand from the veterans. That violated Sherman's observation that "recruits distributed *among* older companies catch up, from close and intimate contact, a knowledge of drill, the care and use of arms, and all the instruction which otherwise it would take months to import" (emphasis added).[89] The officers in these three companies also had limited or no experience in the field.[90]

Rather than having "disappeared" out of "cowardice," these three companies may simply have gotten lost in the dark considering their lack of training and their officers' lack of experience. Hyde himself did not criticize these men in his 1865 after-action report. However, he did note that "some confusion occurred on account of the intense darkness." He recalled in 1894 that "A heavy mist made the moonless night more dark and gloomy . . . [A] very large proportion taking part in [the attack] got mixed up in the darkness and went the wrong way." General Getty himself reported in 1865 that "considerable confusion was caused by the character of the ground and the darkness of the night."[91]

As for the substitutes and draftees, they had been assigned throughout the various companies of the Sixty-First Pennsylvania from July 1863 through the fall of 1864, and their performance in battle had not been previously criticized.[92]

The division between the patriots of 1861 and 1862 and the mercenaries of 1863, 1864, and 1865 readily flows into the question of "who won the war?" The Grand Review of the Army of the Potomac and the Army of the Tennessee in Washington, DC, on May 24 and 25, 1865, was the high point in the public celebration of the Union victory. All the soldiers shared the ample glory that day. New regiments from 1864 marched side by side with the old regiments from 1861 and 1862. Late-war replacements in the old regiments marched alongside the remaining veterans from 1861 and 1862. To be sure, the *New York Times*'s veteran correspondent covering the parade recalled the heroic service of various old regiments—the "most glorious record" of the First Minnesota and Nineteenth Massachusetts—and the old veterans. But he also noted the contributions of the late-war new regiments, recalling General Hartranft, "who saved Fort Stedman, and beat back the enemy with a division of new troops never before under fire"—and late-war replacements—the "good and sturdy men" who had taken the place of the veterans in Ayres's Division of the Fifth Corps.[93]

Shortly after the war, the author of the history of a late-war new regiment, the Thirty-Seventh Wisconsin—one of Fox's Three Hundred, wrote that there was ample glory to go around for all "veterans" regardless of the date of their enlistment. "Though called into the field at a late hour, the services of the Regiment have been arduous and severe in the extreme, and, participating, as it has done, in the last closing scenes of the rebellion, it has shared in the honor and glory of winding up the secession movement."[94] But not all veterans agreed. Ill feeling among veterans toward the late-war replacements continued in some quarters after the war independent of the pension issue. Membership in the Grand Army of the Republic—the forerunner of the American Legion and the Veterans of Foreign Wars—was open to any man who had served in the Union forces at any time from April 12, 1861, to April 9, 1865, as long as he had been honorably discharged. In contrast, the smaller Union of Union Veterans limited membership to men who had enlisted before July 1, 1863—"before the large bounties were offered."[95] In an 1884 Memorial Day address delivered in Canandaigua, New York, veteran Theodore C. Bacon distinguished between those soldiers who volunteered early in the war and those who came later, referring to the former as "noble men—patriotic men, unselfish men—breasting the storm of bullets, with higher motives than the bounty . . . impelling them." Bacon claimed that the connection of material gains rather than patriotism to military service had "demoralized our armies, lost our battles, depraved the public sentiment, and burdened nations, states, counties and towns with prodigious accumulations of indebtedness."[96]

Historians have also questioned the contribution of the late-war replacements. As noted in the introduction, James McPherson concluded that the late-war replacements "did little to help win the war. This task fell mainly on the prebounty veterans of 1861 and 1862."[97] Other historians have also downplayed the contributions of the late-war replacements in their assessments of the fighting quality of the Union army and the Army of the Potomac over time. Bell Wiley concluded that "The fighting quality of the army as a whole seems to have reached its zenith in the early months of 1863 and to have declined thereafter until the end of the war."[98] That is implicit praise for the volunteers of 1861 and 1862 and implicit criticism for the late-war replacements. Earl J. Hess was more explicit in his assessment of the late-war replacements compared to the veterans from 1861 and 1862 in *The Union Soldier in Battle,* written in 1997: "By 1864, . . . the quality of these new soldiers was lower than it had ever been. . . . The Northern war effort was carried by the core of highly motivated men who had enlisted in 1861 and 1862, not by those questionable patriots who were brought into the army from 1863 through 1865."[99] Similarly, Hampton Newsome wrote in 2013 that the loss of veterans who did not reenlist and "the arrival of replacement troops of an indifferent quality had dramatically altered the [Army of the Potomac] . . . [T]he reliability of troops eroded noticeably. In engagements throughout the summer, Union forces reeled back under pressure they might have withstood earlier in the year."[100] There is no question that the combat effectiveness of the Army of the Potomac had deteriorated by the end of the Overland Campaign, but there is a legitimate question whether that was due to the heavy casualties of the campaign as opposed to the late-war replacements. As Hess acknowledges, the Army of the Potomac had an "enormous" need for replacements.

A quantitative assessment that looks only at the numbers of late-war replacements and their time in the field undervalues their contribution to the Union victory. A qualitative assessment recognizes that they helped the Army of the Potomac to rebuild both before and after the Overland Campaign. Without the infusion of new troops at these key times, the Army of the Potomac would not have been able to defeat the Army of Northern Virginia.

CHAPTER 2

Raising the Union Army

Lincoln stated his "general idea of this war" in a January 1862 letter to General Buell, with a copy to General Halleck. He began by noting that "we have the *greater* numbers, and the enemy has the *greater* facility of concentrating forces upon points of collision." He then concluded "that we must fail, unless we can find some way of making *our* advantage an over-match for *his;* and that this can only be done by menacing him with superior forces at *different* points, at the *same* time" (emphasis in original).[1]

Lincoln's strategic assessment was spot on. The North had a four-to-one advantage over the South in the number of white males between the ages of eighteen and forty-five.[2] However, the federal army was all but nonexistent in 1861. In the Northern states, the militia organizations were antiquated if they existed at all.[3] The North's manpower advantage would be decisive only if transferred from the census schedules to an army in the field, which would then have to deploy effectively. The North ultimately succeeded in doing so, but success required a fine-tuned and constantly changing balance of measures carefully tasked to respond to a variety of often conflicting political, economic, social, and battlefield realities. Federal, state, and local bounties played a critical role in that balance.

Grant proudly recalled in his *Memoirs* how well the civilian economy in the North had continued to function during the war: "The country, the towns and the cities presented about the same appearance they do in time of peace. The furnace was in blast, the shops were filled with workmen, the fields were cultivated, not only to supply the population of the North . . . but to ship abroad to pay a part of the expense of the war." In contrast, "the whole South was a military camp."[4]

The civilian economy in the North was so vibrant during the war by deliberate, if unstated, choice. The North decided that it would not sacrifice the civilian economy to preserve the Union (and later, to end slavery). Rather than raising an overwhelming force at the outset of the war or even as the war progressed, the North raised troops in multiple calls for moderate numbers of troops, generally two hundred or three hundred thousand at a time (Table 2.1). When Sherman proposed a call of six hundred thousand men in June 1863, he commented that "It may be that the industrial interests of the country will not authorize such a call, but how much greater the economy to make an army and fight out this war at once."[5] The use of multiple calls also reflected uncertainty as to the force levels necessary to win the war.

From today's perspective, a draft would answer the challenge of raising large numbers of troops, but not in 1861. Alexis de Tocqueville wrote in 1835 that "In America, conscription is unknown; men are enlisted for payment. Compulsory recruitment is so alien to the ideas and so foreign to the customs of the people of the United States that I doubt whether they would ever dare to introduce it into their law." While his assessment in 1835 has failed the test of time, it was still accurate as of the eve of the Civil War.[6] However, Tocqueville did note that the United States "has not had to sustain a single serious war" since the Revolution and concluded that "To assess what sacrifices democracies are capable of imposing upon themselves, we must await the time when" the United States "is forced to place in the hands of its government half of its income, as England has done, or has to throw a twentieth of its population on the battlefield, as France has done."[7] The North faced such a challenge during the Civil War, although Northerners did not recognize it when the war began. Up to that time, Americans had relied upon the tradition going back to Lexington and Concord of citizen-soldiers—men who voluntarily came to the defense of their country in times of military crisis.[8]

At the beginning of the Civil War, the federal government had hardly any troops for restoring the Union—just sixteen thousand—and they were widely dispersed throughout the country.[9] On April 15, 1861, President Lincoln issued a proclamation "call[ing] forth the militia of the several States of the Union, to the aggregate number of 75,000" to serve for three months (the maximum period allowed by the Militia Act, which was his source of authority).[10] However, three months was also consistent with the widespread—but totally unrealistic—expectation that it would not take very long to put down the Rebellion.[11] This was the first of nearly a dozen even larger calls over the course of the war (Table 2.1).

The states furnished over ninety thousand troops in response to this call.[12] These troops defended Washington and fought in the first Battle of Bull Run (July 21, 1861), but their term of enlistment expired before the Union army effec-

Table 2.1: Major Union Calls

Date	Number	Term	Adjusted Number	Raised
April 15, 1861	75,000	3 months	73,391	91,816
May 3, 1861[a]	540,000	6 mos. to 3 yrs.	611,827	700,680
July 2, 1862	300,000	3 years	334,835	421,465
August 4, 1862	300,000	9 months	334,835	87,588
July 7, 1863[b]	292,441	3 years		
October 17, 1863	300,000	3 years		
February 1, 1864[c]	200,000	3 years	467,434	317,092
March 14, 1864	200,000	3 years	186,981	259,515
July 18, 1864[d]	500,000	1, 2, or 3 years	357,152	386,461
December 19, 1864	300,000	1, 2, or 3 years	284,215	212,212

Source: Compiled from OR III:5, 1264–68; War Department, *Statement of Number of Men Called for by the President of the United States,* January 1892, RG94, entry 287, Miscellaneous Files, Envelope 132, No. 4. There are some internal differences among the numbers for July 1863 through July 1864. See OR III:5, 635–39.

[a] Includes the acts of July 22, and July 25,1861. Congress authorized acceptance of up to one million volunteers. OR III:5, 606–7. A formal call was not issued.

[b] The initial draft under the Enrollment Act, which was adopted in March 1863, began on July 7, 1863, and continued for several months. The number of names drawn was 292,441.

[c] The February call was for 500,000 but included the 300,000 from the October 1863 draft call. The adjusted number and the number raised includes the July draft and the October and February calls.

[d] The total includes 223,044 men raised for one year, 153,049 for three years , and 8,340 for two years.

tively organized them. Several weeks later, Lincoln issued a call on May 3, 1861, for forty thousand volunteers to serve for three years unless sooner discharged.[13] He had no legal authority to issue this call, under the Militia Act or otherwise, but hoped that Congress would ratify his action when it convened in July. By June 30, 1861, the Union army had 129,894 men present.[14] (See Table 2.2.)

The recruiting results over the next six months were even more impressive. Congress not only ratified the call in July as Lincoln had hoped but also authorized him to enlist up to one million volunteers for terms varying from six months to three years as he saw fit.[15] Lincoln did not issue a formal call for troops because Congress authorized him to "accept the services of volunteers" and thousands were stepping forward. At the end of 1861, the Union army had 477,193 men present. The Army of the Potomac had 208,604 men—its largest force.[16]

Widespread patriotic fervor among sufficient numbers of men was the primary driver of the North's success, but other factors also played an important role. Even after the defeat at Bull Run, Northerners generally believed that the war would be a short one. Northerners also did not understand the horrors of war. And the economy was relatively weak. In that context, the inducement of a large bounty or the spur of a draft to enlist were unnecessary. However, each of

Table 2.2: Aggregate Present for the Union Army and the Army of the Potomac

	Union Army	Army of the Potomac
June 30, 1861	129,894	
December 31, 1861	477,193	208,604
June 30, 1862	501,663	113,895
December 31, 1862	664,163	185,386
June 30, 1863	636,189	117,930
December 31, 1863	600,787	94,151
June 30, 1864	683,058	112,478
December 31, 1864	605,360	105,091
April 30, 1865	733,752	83,753

Sources: OR III:1, 301; OR III:1, 775; OR III:2, 185; OR III:2, 957; OR III:3, 460; OR III:3,
   1198; OR III:4, 1, 465; OR III:4, 2, 1034; OR III:4, 2, 1283.
Note: Due to transfers in and out of units, the composition of the Army of the Potomac
   changed throughout the war.

the factors that favored recruitment so much in 1861 changed over time to the Union's detriment.

The flood of enlistments in 1861 carried the Union into 1862. While the number raised seemed huge at the time, it represented only slightly more than 10 percent of the four million white males of military age potentially available to the North.[17] Shortly after Edwin Stanton became secretary of war in January 1862, he concluded that the Union had ample troops on hand and he actually shut down the federal recruiting apparatus in April—a mistake that quickly became obvious.[18]

After the failure of McClellan's Peninsula Campaign, the Army of the Potomac desperately needed reinforcements. As of June 30, 1862, the Army of the Potomac had 113,895 men "present"—down from 208,604 at the end of 1861.[19] Lincoln, with the help of Seward, orchestrated a new call for troops by soliciting a letter from most of the Union governors requesting him to "at once call upon the several States for such number of men as may be required to fill up all military organizations now in the field" as well as additional troops. Lincoln followed on July 1, 1862, with his call for three hundred thousand troops to serve for three years.[20] A month later, he issued a draft call for three hundred thousand militia men to serve nine months. The draft also applied to any shortfall under the July call.

The *Oxford Democrat* in Paris, Maine, noted that "The new quota of men . . . will make almost a million of men that already have gone into the service: and yet we have four times that number at home, able-bodied and fit for service," while the Confederate States "have pressed every man into the service that is capable of bearing arms." The *Troy Weekly Times* of New York commented that "if, with this superiority, we fail, then as a nation we deserve to die."[21]

The federal bounty remained at $100.[22] The initial response to the July 1862 call was slow. The "impulse of patriotism and love of adventure" referred to by the *New York Times* in 1861 were waning. As Fry recalled after the war, "The desire to enter the service, prompted by the first ebullition of military ardor had subsided." The *New York Evening Post* recalled the success in raising troops in 1861 "under great popular excitement, when the tented field presented to the imagination of the volunteer a picture of pleasing excitement, of adventurous life and dazzling honor." However, "now war has lost its charms, and the wooden leg replaces the laurel crown in the imagination of the soldier. . . . Can it be expected that the rush to arms will be as rapid as then?"[23] The economy was also recovering well in the summer of 1862. The *Columbia Spy* of Pennsylvania wrote in mid-July that "We now find affairs changed.—with the withdrawal of so many hands, and with the immense demand for supplies for our armies, has come work for every mechanic and laborer. [T]here is no lack of employment for willing hands."[24]

Historians often acknowledge the slow initial response to the July 1862 call but are less direct in acknowledging the role of bounties and the possibility of a draft in subsequently stimulating enlistments.[25] However, contemporary observers recognized the need for state and local governments to increase their bounties. The *Albany Atlas & Argus* succinctly stated the challenge—"To get recruits we must either offer large bounties or resort to drafting." The New London, Connecticut, *Weekly Chronicle* opined at the end of August that "It must be plainly evident by this time to every thinking person in the place that enlistments for the nine months' regiments cannot be raised without the inducement of a heavy bounty." Local governments offering bounties became the norm in the summer of 1862, not the exception. Eighty to 90 percent of the towns in Maine, Massachusetts, and Rhode Island offered bounties, as did nearly two-thirds of the cities and towns in New York (including New York City and Brooklyn, which accounted for a quarter of the population).[26]

The "carrot" of bounties and the "stick" of a conditional draft definitely succeeded the first time they were employed together. The July 2, 1862, call far exceeded its goal in the end, raising over four hundred thousand three-years men. (The August 4, 1862, call for nine-months men fell short of its goal with only 88,000 men raised.)[27] As of December 31, 1862, the Union army had 664,163 men "present"—an increase of over 150,000 men since June (and nearly 190,000 since December 31, 1861). The Army of the Potomac had 185,386 men present—an increase of over 70,000 since June, notwithstanding heavy casualties at Antietam and Fredericksburg and losses from disease.[28]

However, fewer men were volunteering by early 1863. As Fry recalled: "A general apathy prevailed throughout the country on the subject of volunteering."[29]

Overcoming historical tradition and public opposition, Congress finally adopted compulsory military service in the Enrollment Act in March 1863, as the Confederacy had done the year before.[30] Enrollment began in May, with the actual draft occurring on different dates in different localities, beginning in July and finishing late in the year. The riot in New York City is well known, but protection of the draft process also required troops in other areas, including certain districts in Pennsylvania. Even where there was no threat of violence, the public disliked the draft.[31]

Disruption of the local socioeconomic order was the real threat of the federal government's mandated draft, although towns also did not want to appear unpatriotic by failing to provide needed troops and individual liberty was a strong philosophical concern. New York Governor Seymour viewed the draft as a power play by the federal government.[32] Local communities used the bounty as their primary weapon against the potential disruption from the draft. Bounties could protect the most stable members of the community if they wished to remain at home by inducing others to serve.

Shortly after Lincoln announced the militia draft in August 1862, newspapers began expressing their communities' desire to avoid a draft. Initially, communities said they wanted to avoid the shame of not meeting their quota. On August 16, 1862, the *Poughkeepsie Eagle* proclaimed: "Heaven forbid that such a disgrace should fall on this great and wealthy county." At the end of August, Massachusetts's *Berkshire County Eagle* admonished its readers: "Let us see to it that no draft is needed in Massachusetts."[33] Beyond the issue of disgrace, considerations of economic class were in play. The *Brooklyn Daily Eagle* commented in mid-August that "It is desirable if possible to get that class to enlist that can best be spared, and if a draft is resorted to this is the very class who will escape." Similarly, the *Ontario Repository and Messenger* noted that "the great majority of the floating population have already gone" with the result that the current call "will necessarily fall upon our businessmen."[34]

Stanton concluded in January 1864 that it was "certain" that "a large portion of the people in every State prefer the method of contributing their proportion of the military force by bounty to volunteers, rather than a draft."[35] The *Hartford Courant* argued in August 1864 that "If labor is to be withdrawn from the community, it should be taken in a way to effect the least derangement of business. In this respect volunteering has an incomparable advantage over drafting. The point requires no argument." The *Poughkeepsie Daily Eagle* had earlier expressed concern that if the local quota were not met, "then follows the draft which will put upon the community more sorrow and suffering than the volunteer system by great odds."[36] The *Lewistown Gazette* of Pennsylvania encouraged the "business and monied men" of the community to contribute to the bounty fund to avoid the draft by pointing to the increased cost of labor: "Were a draft to take only the idle, the dissolute, and the nonproducing, the loss would be small, but every laboring man who is taken away hereafter—let his occupation be what it may—will cost every business man from $10 to $20 per head, and all other classes in proportion."[37]

Intense competition among most—but not all—of the towns in a state began with the July 1862 call and continued until the end of the war, causing a strong upward trend in local bounties.[38] The states also competed with each other.[39] The degree of the need of towns to compete to protect their local socioeconomic order varied significantly. While the federal government theoretically equalized local quotas based on population, the relative hardship of the men in the pool in responding to the draft was not the same in all communities. Not everyone could just pick up and leave for war. For example, a yeoman farmer would have to leave operation of the family farm to his wife and children. Communities (and states) with a high percentage of farmers in their draft pools were at a competitive disadvantage in recruiting soldiers and needed to reach beyond their town (and state) boundaries to meet their quota. The financial resources for funding their competitive effort also varied significantly.

The approaches of state and local governments to bounties and to the intensifying competition also varied significantly. Some states took the lead, sometimes to the extent of prohibiting local bounties, while other states deferred to their local governments or actively encouraged them to offer local bounties. And some states changed their approach.

Pennsylvania did not offer a state bounty during the war. Governor Curtin set the pattern in the summer of 1862 when he declined to summon a special session of the legislature to consider a state bounty after the July 1862 call. Instead, he exhorted local communities to offer bounties, which they did, although not in as large amounts as the communities in New England did. However, by the time of the December 1864 call, Curtin had changed his opinion about local bounties. In his January 1865 Message to the Legislature, he pointed to "the evils which have resulted from abuses of the system of local bounties which was begun, in an emergency by the voluntary and generous loyalty of our citizens . . . The result has been to the last degree oppressive to our citizens." Curtin's claim that "the people of Pennsylvania" had been "robbed" of the millions of dollars in local bounties paid during 1864 failed to impress the Legislature, which proceeded to increase the cap on local bounties from $300 to $400 and validated a number of local bounties of questionable legal authority.[40]

From the beginning of the war, Vermont offered additional pay of $7 per month as a bounty. In October 1862, the Legislature authorized municipalities to "grant and vote such sums of money as they may judge best" for bounties. A year later, the Vermont Legislature decided not to increase the state bounty for recruiting under the October 1863 call, preferring that towns should offer the necessary bounties. The cities and towns of Vermont responded to the October 1863 call by offering bounties ranging from $200 to $500—a substantial increase over 1862. By the time of the July 1864 call, Vermont faced a tight supply of men. (Farmers comprised nearly 40 percent of the workforce.)[41] One Vermont town unanimously adopted a resolution that it "cannot spare any more men from among her citizens to go to the war" and hired a recruiting agent to fill the town's quota elsewhere. The *Burlington Weekly Sentinel* reported that "all through Republican Vermont, the towns are offering enormous bounties and loading themselves down with unheard of taxes, in order to save their citizens from going to war." The Vermont adjutant general reported that "Town meetings were held throughout the State, and the selectmen of the several towns authorized to pay the most liberal bounties for recruits."[42]

At the end of 1863, New Hampshire paid a state bounty of $100, but Governor Gilmore urged the cities and towns to offer "reasonable bounties" as well to meet their quotas. As in Vermont, the supply of volunteers was drying up. (Farmers made up not quite a third of the workforce.)[43] The *New Hampshire Patriot and State Gazette* lamented in February 1864 that "The whole field has been completely gleaned to answer the last call." For the July 1864 call, the Legislature authorized the cities and towns to offer up to $100/$200/$300 for one/two/three years of service. (If they exceeded those amounts, the state bounty was cut off.) However, these amounts were not large enough. "F. F." from Concord wrote at the end of July that "The new military bill is found to be a clumsy and useless piece of legislation. It provides that the town bounty shall not exceed $300, while it is impossible to secure a single volunteer for less than five hundred. . . . The law must be evaded or recruiting will stop." Indeed, Governor Gilmore complained that "the towns pay no attention to the law limiting the amount of bounty."[44] The Legislature did later authorize towns and cities to pay their own residents any amount of bounty "deemed expedient." Several towns availed themselves of that authority to offer their residents a $1,000 bounty for one year's service.[45]

Other Eastern States also attempted to limit the bounties offered by their local governments. They often combined a prohibition on local bounties with a significant increase in the state bounty. However, these efforts to limit local bounties generally failed.

Connecticut had offered a small amount of additional monthly pay since the beginning of the war. At the end of 1863, Connecticut also began offering a significant state bounty—$300 for a three-year term (which was changed to $100/$200/$300 for one/two/three years for the July 1864 call). The Legislature prohibited town appropriations for bounties, but the prohibition did not apply to private subscriptions, even if turned over to the town. As a result, Connecticut towns were able to offer "large sums" as bounties.[46]

After announcement of the October 1863 call, the Massachusetts Legislature significantly increased the state bounty from $50 to $325 for a three-year enlistment. (The Legislature gave the volunteer the option of receiving $50 in advance and $20 per month over the three years instead of receiving the $325 in advance.)[47] The Massachusetts Legislature authorized towns to tax to fund bounties in March 1864, but only up to $125. When the July 1864 call came, the market demanded more. Noting that towns had only the powers granted to them by the Legislature, the *Lowell Daily Citizen and News* recognized the towns' dilemma: "How a city can go beyond the limit of [$125] for each volunteer, except by some dodge, is not apparent." A Massachusetts court enjoined a creative dodge by some Massachusetts towns of offering the bounty in gold—worth twice the currency then in circulation. More significantly, the $125 ceiling did not apply to bounties funded by private subscription. Towns relied on private citizens, who in some cases provided for a doubling of the local bounty.[48]

In December 1863, the governor of Maine prohibited local bounties greater than $200 paid to nonresidents. The *Lewiston Evening Journal* matter of factly observed that "Despite the order there will of course be evasion—as people generally understand that there is [sic] more ways than one of 'skinning a cat.'" The Maine adjutant general acknowledged in January 1864 that local governments were paying bounties as high as $500. When the state bounty was increased to $300 on February 20, 1864, the Legislature also in effect prohibited local government (or private) bounties altogether by providing that such amounts would be deducted from the $300 state bounty, and that municipalities would have no right of reimbursement from the state for amounts in excess of $300.[49] However, local governments did not comply and the state did not enforce the law. An Augusta correspondent reported that "The violation of the law was general, almost universal." Recognizing the widespread illegality, the *Portland Daily Press* observed that "Who doubts that a Union Legislature will legalize any such act done in good faith to furnish men for our armies in the field?" And the Legislature did so in 1865.[50]

New York went back and forth on local bounties. In February 1863, the Legislature ratified local bounties paid for the July 1862 call but revoked local authority two months later (except for procuring substitutes for drafted men). In February 1864, the Legislature again restored local authority. Local bounties did reach $1,000 and more in some parts of New York State. As for a state bounty, Governor Morgan had taken the initiative to offer a $50 state bounty at the beginning of the July 1862 call, but his Democratic successor, Horatio Seymour, did not increase the state bounty beyond $75 ($150 for old regiments), and the Legislature did not renew funding for enlistments after April 1, 1864. (Thus, the North's two largest states did not offer a state bounty during the July 1864 call.) However, the Legislature reversed course yet again for the December 1864 call. Following the recommendation of county supervisors at their state convention, the Legislature authorized a state bounty of $300/$400/$600 for one-/two-/three-year service and prohibited local bounties. The Legislature did allow up to $100 in "hand money" for procuring recruits, which often went to the volunteer himself.[51]

New Jersey provided only a monthly benefit of up to $6 rather than a fixed sum on muster-in as a bounty. In theory, the Legislature controlled local bounties because local governments could not levy taxes without legislative authorization and the Legislature did not grant blanket authorization. However, the Legislature routinely approved local government requests for bounty authorization, often months after the fact.[52]

Rhode Island was the only one of the Eastern States that succeeded in curbing local bounties. While Rhode Island paid the highest bounties in 1862, the cost led Governor Sprague and the Legislature to restructure the Rhode Island bounty. Sprague called a special session in August 1862 and the Legislature repealed the authority of towns to offer bounties and increased the state bounty from $15 to $300 for three years' service for the remainder of the July 1862 call and $150 for the nine months call in August. The net result was actually to reduce the state/local bounty component for a three-year volunteer from $315 ($15 state/$300 local) in the summer of 1862 to $300 ($300 state/zero local) in the spring of 1864. The increase in the federal bounty from $100 in 1862 to $300 in 1863/1864 did result in an overall increase in military compensation, although part of the increase was negated by the increase in civilian compensation from 1862 to 1864. The impact was even more dramatic for the July 1864 call. For the one-year term of enlistment, the state and local bounty in Rhode Island was only $100 ($100 state/zero local).[53]

The strong resistance by local governments to their state's attempts to limit the amount of the bounties that they offered demonstrates just how important the bounty was to them. The towns in the Eastern States were determined to manage the impact of the draft on their local economy and social order and the local bounty was their most effective means of doing so.

Local governments in the Eastern States in fact generally succeeded in limiting the impact of the draft on their community. For the September 1864 draft following the July 1864 call, only minimal numbers of men were drafted in Connecticut (twenty-one), Delaware (eighty-two), New York (forty-seven), New Hampshire (three), and Vermont (ten), with small numbers in Massachusetts, New Jersey, and Rhode Island as well. Nearly 2,400 men were drafted in Pennsylvania, but they still represented only 5 percent of Pennsylvania's quota. The 815 men drafted in Maine represented only 7 percent of Maine's quota. Even smaller numbers were drafted under the March 1864 call, although commutation was still available then.[54]

Returning to the Enrollment Act itself, the results from the first draft during the summer and early fall of 1863 were disappointing. Moreover, losses from combat and disease continued. By the fall of 1863, the Union army faced a serious manpower shortage. On October 19, 1863, Lincoln called for three hundred thousand volunteers to serve for three years. A draft to commence on January 1, 1864, would cover any shortfalls.[55]

The Lincoln Administration increased the federal bounty paid to new recruits enlisting in old organizations for three years to $300, with $60 paid upon muster-in and the remainder in six-month installments. Fry noted the need "to compare favorably with the price of ordinary labor."[56] The need to compete with the civilian labor market had become a continuing challenge. From 1862 to 1864, the average annual wage for many of the major occupations increased significantly. For example, in New York State, the average wage increased 34 percent for laborers (12 percent of the workforce); 50 percent for farm laborers (9 percent of the workforce); and 43 percent for carpenters (3 percent of the workforce).[57]

At the same time that the Union army was trying to raise more recruits, it also had to address the challenge of retaining its veteran troops. In 1861, government officials considered a three-year term of enlistment sufficient because they assumed that the war would be over fairly quickly. However, as the war dragged on longer than anticipated, the troubling prospect arose that the veterans from 1861 would return home before they had defeated the Confederacy. In the summer of 1863, a study by the Provost Marshal General's Bureau revealed that the terms of enlistment of nearly half of the volunteer regiments of infantry then in service would expire by the end of 1864–455 of 956 regiments.[58] Loss of these men would be catastrophic for the Union forces in the field. The War Department accordingly created the concept of the "veteran volunteer" in an attempt to retain these soldiers whose terms of enlistment would be expiring and to bring back soldiers whose enlistments had already expired.[59]

In return for a new three-year (or the war) commitment, the federal government offered soldiers in the field a bounty of $400 paid in seven installments with an advance payment of $25, one month's pay in advance ($13 for a private), a thirty-day furlough to be granted as soon as the exigencies of military service would permit, and special service chevrons "as a badge of honorable distinction."[60] Union authorities believed the $400 bounty was necessary to induce the veterans to reenlist. Men who had left the army after having served at least nine months—which would reach back to the men who had enlisted at the very beginning of the war—were also eligible. The returning soldiers would have the option of serving in an old regiment in the field or a new regiment to be "officered only by persons who have been in service and have shown themselves properly qualified for command."[61] Regiments—new or old—could use the "veteran volunteer" designation if at least half the men qualified as veterans.[62]

Implementation of the reenlistment program did not begin until the fall of 1863, when the campaign season had ended because the Union authorities thought that the soldiers might be more receptive then.[63] In the end, 136,300 of the eligible soldiers in the Union army as a whole reenlisted.[64] Stanton concluded that "the patriotic determination of these troops who had taken a prominent part in the war to continue it until brought to a satisfactory close was the foundation of the success which attended the enterprise." Similarly, Fry viewed it as "essential to the final success which attended our arms."[65] Historians agree.[66]

The reenlistment of these 136,000 veterans was important, but 400,000 late-war replacements were forwarded to the field between November 1863 and October 1864. New York raised more than sixty three-year regiments during the last half of 1861 and early 1862, roughly 60,000 men. While three-quarters of these New York regiments ultimately qualified for the veteran volunteer designation, the number of New York three-year men from 1861 and early 1862 who reenlisted was smaller than might at first appear due to the heavy casualties suffered since 1861. Only about 20,000 men reenlisted, split evenly between late 1863 and early 1864. In contrast, New York sent over 25,000 new volunteers and nearly 10,000 drafted men and substitutes to the Union army in 1863 and nearly 150,000 volunteers, substitutes, and drafted men in 1864.[67] Similarly, the impact in the Army of the Potomac was less significant than in the Union army as a whole. The eligible veterans represented only about a third of the Army of the Potomac's force at the time, and within that group only about half of the eligible soldiers reenlisted—27,000 men.[68]

In February 1864, Lincoln issued a call for another two hundred thousand men (in addition to the three hundred thousand men called for under the October 1863 draft). The *Yates County Chronicle* of New York wrote that "there can be no hope of raising the men by volunteering unless the bounties are kept up." New York's *Watkins Express* optimistically commented that "This will perhaps be the last call of the war for volunteers,"[69] but even two hundred thousand more troops was not enough. Only six weeks later, Lincoln called for another two hundred thousand troops on March 14, even though no significant combat operations had occurred in the meantime.[70] The *Hartford Daily Courant* had cut to the heart of the matter on March 5 in stating the strategic imperative for the North: "The country needs the men. . . . The rebellion long since culminated and is now rapidly on the wane. But it still has powerful armies led by able generals. Unless those armies are overpowered and broken in pieces by superior force, they will be able to protract the struggle indefinitely."[71]

The Union army significantly replenished its numbers in time for the Overland Campaign, but then suffered fifty-five thousand combat casualties by the end of the campaign in early June. The Union clearly needed additional troops again. Stanton wrote Lincoln on June 7 that "it is absolutely necessary that efficient means be taken with vigor and promptness to keep the Army up to its strength and supply deficiencies occasioned by the losses sustained by casualties in the field."[72] The public saw the need for more troops as well. The *Ontario County Times* of New York recognized at the time of the July call that "The rebels are still confronting our armies at different points with numbers sufficient to present formidable obstacles to a complete triumph of the Union cause, and the only way to . . . ensure the final overthrow of the rebellion is to reinforce our brave boys in the field."[73] The remaining veterans from 1861 and 1862 were not going to be able to win the war without the help of the late-war replacements.

With the Petersburg Campaign underway, Grant advised Lincoln on July 19, 1864, that he should "call for, say, 300,000 men to be put in the field in the shortest possible time. [T]his number of re-enforcements would save the annoyance of raids, and would enable us to drive the enemy from his present front, particularly from Richmond, without attacking fortifications." Grant further noted that "The enemy now have their last man in the field. Every depletion of their army is an irreparable loss."[74] Lincoln matter-of-factly responded that he had issued a call for five hundred thousand troops just the day before, "which [he] suppose[d] covers the case." A draft on September 5 would cover any deficiency.[75]

The Lincoln Administration made three important changes to the process for raising troops in the run-up to the July 1864 call. First, they reduced the term of service for draftees from three years to one to "lighten" the impact on the citizenry. Low citizen morale necessitated the move. (Citizen morale reached its nadir in August 1864).[76] Shortening the term of service overruled Fry's advice that the draft should continue to be for three years in order to maintain the full recruiting impact of the threat of the draft.[77]

Second, instead of the long-standing three-year term of enlistment, the Lincoln Administration gave volunteers the option of serving for one, two, or three years with a federal bounty of $100, $200, or $300, which was also seen as "lightening" the burden of military service. The Lincoln Administration apparently was quite serious about allowing new troops to enlist for only a year if they wished. Authorizations for new regiments sent to state governors generally specified the term of service as one, two, or three years "as the recruit may elect."[78]

The willingness to accept recruits under the July call for a one-year term suggests that Lincoln and Stanton were confident by then that the war would be over in a year. If they were wrong and the Union army had to continue fighting after the summer of 1865, the new one-year recruits from the July 1864 call would have returned home and the Union army would then have had available only the veterans from 1861 who had reenlisted in the winter of 1863 and early 1864 for three years and the three-year men from October 1863 through April 1864. The terms of the three-year men from 1862 would expire beginning in July 1865 and the Administration excluded them from the veteran reenlistment program at the end of July 1864.[79]

Third, Congress repealed the right of commutation at Lincoln's request. In Stanton's view, commutation was no longer necessary because the burden of military service under the draft was being lightened. Fry had proposed the repeal of commutation in early June when the early returns on the April draft showed that commutation was once again seriously eroding the number of men yielded by the draft. While commutation had its serious supporters—it was repealed on a party line vote, it was hard to argue with Fry's facts.[80] The military won on the repeal of commutation but lost on the first two changes.

The Petersburg Campaign brought heavy casualties during the summer and early fall of 1864. Nonetheless, the Army of the Potomac achieved enough tactical success to lay the groundwork for final victory. As the military campaign season ended in 1864, both sides understood that the war would be over in 1865. However, hard fighting still lay ahead, and the Union still needed more troops. As the *Brooklyn Daily Eagle* observed, "It is all very well to prove that the rebellion is on its last legs; what Mr. Lincoln needs is not logic, but men."[81] On December 19, 1864, Lincoln called for three hundred thousand more volunteers to serve one, two, or three years. A draft in February 1865 would cover any shortfalls in volunteers.[82]

During the critical year of 1864, the Union raised nearly eight hundred thousand white volunteers, substitutes, and drafted men. Volunteers comprised nearly 80 percent of this number, while substitutes and drafted men represented only 16 percent and 5 percent respectively.[83] At the end of 1864, the Army of the Potomac had over one hundred thousand men present and the Union Army overall over six hundred thousand. The North had been able to maintain both the Union army and the Army of the Potomac at roughly these levels since the end of 1862. See Table 2.2. Moreover, after four years of war, the Union still had over two million men enrolled in the draft system for potential call as of April 30, 1865.[84]

Returning to Lincoln's observation in January 1862 that the Union's strategic challenge was to make their population advantage an "over-match" for the

Confederacy's "greater facility of concentrating forces upon points of collision," the fact that the Union won the war suggests that the Union was able to do so. However, a more nuanced answer is called for.

In his *Memoirs,* Grant addressed the story line "of what a splendid fight the South had made and successfully continued for four years before yielding, with their twelve million of people against our twenty, and of the twelve four being colored slaves, non-combatants."[85] He pointed out that the people of the Confederacy had been almost totally committed to war, while the Union had been able to maintain a peace-time economy alongside the war effort. He also noted that "more than half the National army was engaged in guarding lines of supplies, or were on leave, sick in hospital or on detail which prevented their bearing arms." His conclusion? "There were no large engagements where the National numbers compensated for the advantage of position and intrenchment occupied by the enemy."[86] Grant was not a disinterested observer, but he implicitly made the valid point that the Union did not utilize its manpower advantage to the full extent theoretically possible. However, Grant's strategy during the Petersburg Campaign of extending Lee's lines to the breaking point did require large numbers of troops.[87] While the North did not come even close to putting the same percentage of military-age men in the field that the South did, the North did recruit enough men with bounties and the conditional draft to defeat the Confederate forces in the East.[88] Patriotism alone did not generate enough manpower for the North after 1861. Even in 1861, the economic motivation likely influenced men more than historians generally have acknowledged.

Paul Escott recently raised the question whether "Southern society put restrictions on the Confederacy's war effort and strategy that were not found in the North." He concluded that "It seems that Northern society did not hamstring the military strategists, for the North enjoyed some important advantages. Its population was so large that increasing demands for troops could be met and were met without widespread or lasting disruption."[89] However, societal opposition to conscription in the North *could* have proven to be a barrier to the military's strategic flexibility in using its manpower advantage but did not because the federal, state, and local governments pragmatically addressed the challenge. The reason that "fierce resistance" to the draft was rare and the army's increasing need for troops was met "without widespread or lasting disruption" is that the system of increasing bounties for voluntary enlistments, aided by commutation and substitution, successfully sidestepped Northern citizens' strong distaste for stand-alone conscription and its threatened impact on the local economy and social structure.

CHAPTER 3

To Volunteer . . . or Not

Historians have criticized the later-enlisting volunteers and substitutes as un-patriotic because they did not volunteer in 1861 or 1862. Historians have also criticized them as mercenaries because of the high bounties they received when they did enlist in 1863, 1864, and 1865. Both labels are overly simplistic. A man's individual circumstances bring multiple considerations into play that complicate his decision whether or not to go off to war. Historians have generally been too quick to judge the motivations of the late-war replacements.

When the war broke out, the North was as unprepared culturally for war as it was militarily. As the New York Sanitary Commission wrote to Lincoln in August 1862: "In the theory of our Government, every citizen is a soldier at the command of the President."[1] However, while the general notion of a "citizen-soldier" was well established in political theory, there was little cultural guidance for the individual man in deciding whether he himself should become a citizen-soldier or could remain at home. J. Matthew Gallman observed in *Defining Duty in the Civil War: Personal Choice, Popular Culture and the Union Home Front* that there was "no reason to know how to behave in the midst of a war of this magnitude. . . . The Civil War presented prowar northerners with no obviously recognized roadmap dictating how they should behave. . . . [M]ost northern civilians faced complicated choices, not unambiguous mandates."[2] Patriotism did not dictate that a man volunteer. As Gallman noted, "patriotic citizens might have good personal reasons to stay home."[3] "Patriotic citizenship merely required that men examine their own circumstances and consciences and contemplate volunteering in a forthright manner."[4] Lincoln himself acknowledged the complexity of the motivations involved in his "Opinion on the Draft" written in September 1863: "A variety of motives pressing, some in one direction and some in the other, would be presented to the mind of each man physically fit for a soldier . . . Among these motives would be patriotism, political bias, ambition, personal courage, love of adventure, want of employment, and convenience."[5]

Northern society recognized family obligations—honestly considered—as a proper reason for not volunteering.[6] As the *Rochester Daily Union and Advertiser* noted in July 1862, "There is plenty of patriotism, but it will not induce men to leave their families in want and go into the army."[7] Indeed, Congress explicitly recognized certain family responsibilities, such as the only son of aged or infirm parents dependent on him for support or a widower with children under the age of twelve, as exemptions in the Enrollment Act, which created the North's draft process in 1863.[8] Recognition of these exemptions when the draft was enacted in 1863 strongly suggests that they would have been recognized by society in 1861 as valid reasons for not serving without putting a man's patriotism in question.

As opposed to later periods in American history, the Enrollment Act did not recognize critical civilian occupations that warranted an exemption (other than certain government offices). However, Northern society did consider certain occupations to be more important than others. Fry lamented the plight of communities who had to fill their draft quotas with the men "which the country could least afford to spare—the actual producers—men fixed to the soil."[9] When hostilities broke out in 1861 and even as the war continued longer than expected, a farmer might well have thought that he could better serve his country as a farmer than as a soldier. As the *Poughkeepsie Eagle* wrote in August 1862, "It is quite as important too that the harvests should be secured in time." Men in other occupations also may have thought the Union needed them for critical civilian work.[10] Thus in 1861 and as the war progressed a man could decide to stay at home and not volunteer for a variety of socially acceptable reasons (or could volunteer for reasons other than patriotism).

The reflections of John Andrews, who was of military age in 1861 but did not volunteer until the late summer of 1864 when he joined as a second lieutenant, illustrate the variety of considerations a man could face in deciding whether to enlist. After a month in the field, Andrews recalled in his war journal the carefree days of college after the war broke out.

> During my whole college course . . . I felt as though I was not doing my duty. When the first blast of the war trumpet rang . . . , calling patriots to their country's rescue I felt that I ought to respond; but a dear mother lay at death's door . . . and I could not darken her last hours by expressing a wish to go. She died. I quietly pursued

> my studies till Fall and then another call for more men came and I spoke of going.
> . . . All my friends . . . told me I was foolish to think of going so long as my health
> remained as poor as it then was; father urged me not to go; my sisters were in tears
> every time I came into their presence; and I yielded. I would not, had I not felt
> that they were right—my health was too poor to endure a soldier's hardships and
> exposures.

> For three years I continued my studies, yet I could not but ask myself the question,
> at times, who will be to blame if our Union is destroyed? and the answer invariably
> came. Those young men who, like myself, remain at home while the great struggle
> is going on. During my last term I made up my mind that after my graduation I
> would even with my poor health give my services to the government till rebellion
> was crushed or my life ended.[11]

Andrews's thought process in 1861 and at later times up to mid-1864 addressed
what Gallman refers to as the "clear duty" to the nation "to take the decision seriously and draw conclusions that were not selfish."[12] Moreover, Andrews demonstrated a willingness to reconsider his initial decision not to volunteer.

The increased financial inducements that came into play with the July 1862
call for three hundred thousand men complicated a man's decision whether to
volunteer. The conditional draft in August and the adoption of the Enrollment
Act in March 1863 complicated matters further. And public understanding of the
gruesome reality of war greatly increased as the war continued.

Newspapers were quick to promote the economic benefits of volunteering as
state and local bounties increased for the July 1862 call. On July 18, 1862, the *Rochester Daily Democrat and American* provided a detailed economic assessment for
potential volunteers to show that they would make more money in the army than
in their civilian jobs: a private "receives . . . $13 per month, $100 bounty from the
General Government, and those from this State will now receive a special bounty
of $50 . . . This gives, besides rations clothing, &c., monthly wages of $25.75. *As a
pecuniary matter merely, can one man in ten do better than to enlist?*" At least five
other New York newspapers ran the same story.[13] The *Broome Republican* went
on to point out that "if, in addition to this, the towns, by private subscription or
otherwise, give $50 to the volunteer, as some have voted, the inducements are
still greater."[14]

In New Hampshire, the *Portsmouth Journal of Literature and Politics* refined
the financial analysis in even more detail, beginning with the statement that the
compensation of $833 for one year was "enormous" and then questioning: "How
many men in good business are making half of it?"[15] Similar economic analyses

appeared throughout the Eastern States.[16] The *Harrisburg Pennsylvania Daily Telegraph* spoke in qualitative terms: "The 'biggest thing,' not on ice, now-a-days, is the bounty extended to volunteers." While the bounties offered in 1862 were not as large as later in the war, they were still high enough for the 1861 veterans in the field to derisively call the recipients "bounty men."[17]

Local bounties increased over the next two years and newspapers continued to promote the economic benefits of volunteering over staying at home. In July 1864, the *Poughkeepsie Eagle* wrote: "Just look at it. The man who shoulders his musket gets first of all food and clothing, then the regular pay of $16 per month, then the Government bounty of $100, and finally the local bounty of $300. What other service holds out such strong temptations to the young man in a pecuniary point of view?"[18] Moreover, there was little, if any, social stigma in volunteering in response "to the lure of bounties" as long as the volunteer in fact intended to serve.[19]

The bounty payment clearly motivated Charles E. Hemphill, a twenty-one-year-old working as a farm laborer, to enlist in August 1864. Hemphill came from a poor family, with Hemphill and an older brother providing much of the support for their parents and six younger siblings.[20] Hemphill and a friend traveled over a hundred miles from Clearfield County, Pennsylvania, to Erie County and received a $500 bounty for enlisting for the quota of Wayne Township in Erie County. He sent the money to his mother with very explicit instructions on how it was to be disbursed: "you can pay John Patton $30 dollars & [?] Eycks [$13.75] for me & give Father $50 dollars to help make the first payment on the lot & the other [$400] you give to John Patton & tell him to do the best he can with it for me. . . . [I]f you wish to send Ada to school you may take one hundred & let her go where ever you want."[21]

But mercenary motivation and patriotic sentiment were not mutually exclusive in Hemphill's case. He wrote his mother in November 1864 that in the spring of 1865 "there will be a great slaughter of men and I am as liable to fall as any of them but if I do it will be in the defence of our 'Glorious old flag' which we are now fighting for."[22] Hemphill also took pride in being considered a good soldier in the late-war 211th Pennsylvania Volunteers. He was promoted to sergeant shortly after enlisting. He wrote his mother that: "our Col. and Lt. Col. both think a good deal of [James] Boal and I because I am right general guide for the regiment."[23] Hemphill was mortally wounded in the Battle of Fort Stedman.[24]

The late-war Thirty-Second Maine's Michael Kennedy, an eighteen-year-old who worked on the family farm, expected to receive a $300-plus bounty before leaving home. Two hundred dollars of Kennedy's bounty paid off the mortgage on the family farm and an unknown amount purchased livestock. After two months in the field, including the Battle of Spotsylvania, he wrote home that

"I am not sorry for enlisting yet if I got my discharge I should come home and enlist over again."[25] Abner Roberts, an eighteen-year-old farmer, served in the late-war 179th New York. Roberts may not have been enthusiastic about going to war, but he recognized his duty: "if I have got to go and fight I am willing to go." In addition to the federal and state bounties, Roberts received a town bounty between $300 and $550. The Confederates captured him in the 179th New York's first battle and he died at Andersonville. As Hemphill, Roberts, and perhaps Kennedy illustrate, late-war replacements were not ipso facto devoid of patriotic feeling. Indeed, the *Hartford Courant* reported in August 1864 that "Citizens are enlisting under the joint stimulus of patriotism and large bounties."[26]

High as the bounties were becoming, some commentators suggested that high bounties were fair compensation for the risks of war and the loss of opportunity to share in the benefits of the burgeoning civilian economy. New York Governor Seymour thought that the men leaving civilian life for the army "have a right to share in the prosperity of the community when so many are enriched by the operations of this war, and those who stay at home enjoy unusual wages. While the Government and people are financially prosperous, our armies ought to be filled by bounties, and not by coercion." The *New London Daily Chronicle* bluntly stated that "To bleed and die for one's country is not a duty so encircled about with patriotism that one ought to do it free gratis, when other men that should be equally as patriotically disposed, stay at home, clothing themselves in fine linen, and fare sumptuously every day." The *Portland Weekly Advertiser* opined that "*Equity* demands that the man whose work is the hardest, and at the same time dangerous [to] health, limb and even life, should have the largest pay."[27]

One should remember when considering the mercenary characterization that local communities affirmatively approved the bounties. Citizens debated the amount of bounties extensively at ad hoc war meetings and regular town meetings. Communities consciously decided on the higher local bounties, usually with majorities well above 50 percent. As the combined amount of federal, state, and local bounties increased, some people criticized the total as "high," but others in the Eastern States often referred to the bounties nonpejoratively as "liberal" to recognize that the amount was indeed generous but not necessarily without justification. A resident of Bristol, New Hampshire, which offered a local bounty of $200, stated in August 1862 that "This town acts on the very just principle that those who stay at home, should be willing to pay those who go, a liberal sum, to compensate them, in some small degree at least, for the suffering and hardships which they must necessarily endure." In Maine, the *Bridgton Reporter* commented in July 1862, after arguing the need for a "liberal" bounty to avoid a draft, that "those who volunteer will, as they should, be liberally paid for the sacrifice they make." Other newspapers expressed the same view.[28]

The North initially adopted conscription on August 4, 1862, when Lincoln ordered a "draft of 300,000 militia" for nine months' service. He further directed that the militia draft would also apply to any shortfall in the 300,000 volunteers called for in July.[29] George D. Fox from New Hampshire explained to his parents why he wanted to volunteer: "I am liable to be drafted and quite liable too as it will include about one man in four or five . . . If I enlist I shall receive $165.00 bounty when I am enlisted besides I can be in which Regiment I want to be. If I am drafted I shall receive no bounty & I shall be [?] of with some nasty lousy crew."[30]

While bounties were not as high as they later became and a draft was uncertain, the "carrot" and the "stick" of bounties and a conditional draft were definitely in play as communities responded to the July and August 1862 calls. A presumption that patriotism—not money and/or fear of the draft—was the sole motivation for the men who volunteered in the summer of 1862 is not justified by the evidence. Newspapers throughout the Eastern States featured bounties and/or the conditional draft in August 1862. Philadelphia's *Dollar Newspaper* concluded that "The bounty will operate with a great many, and the probability of being drafted on many more." New York's *Hornellsville Tribune* noted that the state bounty of $50, $25 of the federal bounty, and the first month's pay would be received upon joining a regiment, constituting "a most flattering inducement for volunteers." Not only that, but the *Tribune* advised: "Enlist at once and avoid your chance of being drafted." A recruiting advertisement in the *Pittsburgh Daily Post* trumpeted "Come up and Volunteer: If You Don't You'll Be Drafted!"[31] The Middletown, Connecticut, *Constitution* observed that "When the draft was not anticipated, some men opposed the bounty and discouraged enlistments. Not a word of it now. The expected draft has made them quiet and docile as lambs. They will pay any amount necessary to escape the draft." The *Delaware Gazette* of Delhi, New York, reported that "The papers from different parts of the country state that the recruiting has been much more lively since the order for drafting was issued."[32] In September 1864, the *Syracuse Daily Courier and Union* confirmed that the "carrot and stick" remained in full play: "The large bounties are attracting a numerous crowd of those who hunger after money, and who are frightened that the draft 'may gobble them up.'"[33]

Increased public understanding of the reality of war also impacted a man's decision whether to volunteer. There can be no doubt that the change in public understanding of the horror of war affected a man's willingness to volunteer, although neither the precise timing nor the precise degree of the change can be determined. In 1861, the general population had little if any understanding of the grim reality that war meant death and injury in brutal circumstances. The small number of casualties in the Mexican War had barely touched the general population and had occurred fifteen years before at that.[34] As James McPherson notes, "In 1861 many Americans had a romantic, glorious idea of war."[35] In 1861, people discussed the possibility of death in battle in heroic terms, if at all, as the death of Col. Ephraim Ellsworth, the Union's first war hero, exemplified. Ellsworth was shot after taking down a Confederate flag from the top of a hotel in Alexandria. The press lionized him.[36]

However, in 1862, the reality of massive casualties without individual glory in battles such as Shiloh, Antietam, and Fredericksburg began to hit home.[37] Photographs also provided a new visual reality for death on the battlefield.[38] The *New York Times* wrote of Matthew Brady's first exhibition after the Battle of Antietam:

War Dead at Antietam, Mathew Brady (National Archives)

"Mr. BRADY has done something to bring home to us the terrible reality and earnestness of war. If he has not brought bodies and laid them in our door-yards and along the streets, he has done something very like it."[39] For family men, the widely reported story of Sgt. Amos Humiston dying at Gettysburg with a photo of his three children in his hand added a personal element to the risk of enlisting.[40] Family men considering enlistment must have weighed the need to provide for the financial needs of their dependents in the event of their death.

A new dimension to the horror of war arose during the last half of 1864. Fry noted that Confederate mistreatment of Union prisoners of war "became generally known throughout the country." He observed that: "there was probably nothing in all the operations of the rebel armies or authorities which acted so unfavorably upon our recruitment as the inhumanity with which the insurgents treated the prisoners of war held by them."[41] In September 1864, the United States Sanitary Commission issued its two hundred page narrative of the hardships suffered by Union prisoners of war, which included several gruesome photos and numerous depositions.[42] Potential recruits knew that the risk of capture was not minimal.

Many years after the war, J. Howard Wert, who enlisted in 1864 in the late-war 209th Pennsylvania Volunteers, recalled that "in 1861, a wild wave of enthusiasm swept over the two belligerent sections, that rendered enlistment . . . an easy matter. War was then a dream, not a reality . . . Not so, in 1864. The stern and sober realities of hundreds of sanguinary fields . . . had permeated to the remotest corners of the land." Men thinking about volunteering in 1864 had to consider the risk of "death or a brief life blighted by disease and enervating wounds."[43] While it can be said that Wert was exaggerating at both ends, his account contains a good deal of truth.

Veterans from 1861 deciding whether to reenlist faced similar concerns. To encourage reenlistments, the War Department created the special program for "veteran volunteers" as previously discussed. An increase in the federal bounty to $400 and a thirty-day furlough were the key inducements. The furlough was critical in Meade's view. He believed that over half of the eligible men in the Army of the Potomac would reenlist "provided they can have at once a furlough of thirty days to spend at their homes." Fry was equally emphatic: "I am satisfied that the men will not re-enlist for three years longer without going home."[44] A Vermont veteran attested to the importance of the furlough: "Furloughs are the most precious privileges that the government allows their soldiers, and the prospect of going home has tempted a great many soldiers to re-enlist when nothing else would."[45] A soldier who reenlisted in order to receive a furlough to visit his family would not be considered a mercenary (although he was still acting out of selfish rather than patriotic motives).

While the furlough may have been necessary to induce veterans to reenlist, it is by no means clear that it was sufficient. A thirty-day furlough and a smaller bounty had failed in 1863 to retain the New York two-year men who had enlisted in 1861.[46] It is also noteworthy that the federal bounty was increased from $100 to $400 as part of the new offer for these veteran soldiers. The importance of the higher bounty is also demonstrated by the fact that when Congress voted to stop paying it effective January 5, 1864, Fry immediately expressed concern about the impact on reenlistments to Stanton. Stanton forwarded Fry's memo to Lincoln, who in turn requested Congress to extend the bounties. Stanton wrote that "a very large proportion of the forces now in service would have cheerfully re-enlisted for three years . . . and that such enlistments have been checked, and will, in great measure, be put to an end by the restriction imposed by the action of Congress." Congress extended the bounties.[47]

As important as the furlough was to the Vermont veteran quoted above, he was not indifferent to the bounty money. "It was a glad day for us when we turned our backs upon the old camp with our furloughs . . . and . . . a very respectable pile of greenbacks in our hands."[48] He did not have in mind just the federal bounty of $400. Because reenlisting veterans would be credited to their state quotas, they were also eligible for state and local bounties.[49] A company commander in the Sixth New Hampshire shopped around for some of his men. He wrote the selectmen of Surry, New Hampshire, which had not yet filled its quota: "There are some men in the Company who would like to re-enlist and be credited to the town that is paying the highest bounty. . . . [I]f you will please send documents so that these men will be sure of the bounty, I think I can procure some six men that would like to be credited to your town."[50] In Maine, Gov. Samuel Cony recounted to Stanton that the Fourteenth Maine "re-enlisted under the inducement of $300 offered by Maine." Rhode Island Governor Smith led with the $300 state bounty, giving the thirty-day furlough lower billing. Connecticut Governor Buckingham sent representatives to New Orleans to obtain reenlistments from the Ninth, Twelfth, and Thirteenth Connecticut by offering the $300 state bounty. He hoped for five hundred reenlistments but got fourteen hundred.[51] Thus, the high bounties prevailing in late 1863 and early 1864 became available to many men who had enlisted in 1861. Noting the "prejudice" that the early volunteers held against the late-war replacements because of the bounty, the *Philadelphia Inquirer* wrote in July 1864 that "There is no longer any ground for this. Both the volunteer and the re-enlisted men . . . have received heavy bounties, and no man is entitled to cast upon his comrade the slur of having sold himself as a soldier."[52]

Did these 136,000 veterans from 1861 lose their claim to patriotism if the high bounties and the furlough motivated them to reenlist? Or did they have two military careers—one motivated by patriotism, the other by self-interest? The experience of three years in the field certainly would have changed the parameters of their decision-making—some weighing against reenlistment, others in favor. In fact, over fifty thousand of the eligible veterans from 1861 chose not to reenlist.[53] Were they unpatriotic? They had put their lives at risk and endured the hardships of the field for three years, but they left the army before the Union defeated the Confederacy. McPherson wrote that they behaved like short-timers during the time remaining until their discharge. However, Joshua Chamberlain took a magnanimous view fifty years after the war: "It was a time when they were sorely needed; but we can scarcely blame those who thought duty did not call them to prolong their experiences."[54]

There was one significant category of veterans who had no opportunity to receive the higher bounties—the men who enlisted in the summer of 1862 for a term of three years. For example, from August through November 1862, New York raised sixty infantry regiments to serve for three years. These men were obligated to serve into the late summer and fall of 1865 and therefore were not eligible for the reenlistment program.[55] Thus while many of the three-year volunteers in 1862 had received higher bounties than had been available in 1861, they never had an opportunity to benefit from the even higher bounties prevailing from 1863 through the end of the war.

The Lincoln Administration introduced yet another variable for the individual man's decision whether to volunteer with the July 1864 call for five hundred thousand troops by offering a one-year term of service as an option, as discussed in the prior chapter. The *Pittsburgh Gazette* predicted that "As the draft can only be for one year, it is not probable that volunteering will be for any greater period, as, where there is a choice of periods of service, men naturally incline to choose the shortest."[56] However, if a man were interested in maximizing financial return and strongly believed that the war would be over within a year, enlisting for three years "or the war" with a significantly higher bounty could have been viewed as a good bet (the risk of battle and disease aside). Indeed, no less a person than New Hampshire Governor Gilmore said that "If I conceived it my duty, I would enlist in this war, not for one year, but for three years. I believe it would be a good operation, for I would get my three years bounty, with a tolerable certainty that this Rebellion would be finished within a year."[57]

In the event, maximizing financial gain lost out. Over half of the volunteers under the July 1864 call enlisted for only one year. However, the pattern varied significantly by state. Eighty percent of the Pennsylvania volunteers enlisted for only one year, while 95 percent of Connecticut volunteers enlisted for three years (see Table 3.1). The financial differences among the states were substantial. A

Table 3.1: One-Year and Three-Year Enlistment Terms for the July 1864 Call

	PA	ME	DE	NJ	NY	RI	VT	NH	MA	CT
One-Year	80	75	72	63	54	53	47	32	22	5
Three-Year	19	23	27	29	44	39	52	67	78	95

Source: Calculated from OR III: 4:2, 1266.

Note: Percentage totals do not equal 100 percent because the relatively small number of two- and four-year enlistments and commutations are not included.

three-year volunteer in Connecticut received an advance payment of $900 and a total cash payment over a year of $1,322. A one-year volunteer from Pennsylvania received an advance payment of only $433 and a total cash payment of $692.[58]

Economic data can provide some additional insight on the general impact of financial inducements on men's decisions whether to volunteer or reenlist. As noted, historians have traditionally contended that the men who volunteered in 1861 and 1862 were primarily motivated by patriotism rather than financial gain. However, using 1860 census data on median wealth, William Marvel recently concluded in *Lincoln's Mercenaries* "that the earliest [Union] units were composed overwhelmingly of men from families claiming less than median wealth," and that "economic incentives exerted greater stimulus on Union enlistments than has been acknowledged."[59] While that does not prove that individual men in fact enlisted primarily for economic reasons (and Marvel does not claim that it does), it does at least raise a serious question about the primacy of patriotism as the motivation for enlistment in 1861 and 1862.

Another way of testing the potential influence of bounties on volunteering is to compare the overall military compensation package—monthly pay; federal, state, and local government bounties (a significant part of which generally was paid in advance); and the imputed value of board—with civilian wages to determine whether it could be economically attractive to volunteer and, if so, to what extent. This is an income approach as opposed to Marvel's wealth approach.[60]

The methodology followed to develop the comparisons presented here is explained in detail on latewarunionsoldiers.org. However, one aspect of that methodology needs to be discussed here—assessing economic motivation. While not easy, it is much easier to calculate and compare the military and civilian compensation packages than it is to express the impact of that relationship on the decision whether or not to volunteer. When attempting to assess the motivation of an individual soldier, insight might come from his extant letters or diary—if they addressed the subject. Additional insight might come from circumstantial evidence such as the soldier's economic position. However, when trying to reach a conclusion about the motivating impact on soldiers in general, a general standard is necessary.

The newspapers cited earlier in this chapter broke down the components of military compensation and compared the total to civilian wages in general, but the newspapers did not directly address the critical question—how much better than civilian pay did the military compensation package have to be to motivate individual men to enlist primarily for economic reasons (notwithstanding the risks of war)?[61] A one-to-one ratio of military to civilian compensation presumably could attract men initially motivated to enlist by patriotism, but concerned that doing so would have an adverse financial impact on their families, because their family's financial needs could be covered. In that context, a one-to-one ratio (expressed as a 1.0 ratio) would cast the bounties as a "patriotic subsidy." However, the debate is not about those men. The debate is about whether there were men who enlisted just for financial gain.

Determining the ratio that would indicate that the military compensation package was so compelling that men would enlist just for financial gain, despite the hardship of separation from family and friends and the risk of death or injury from war, is no small challenge. Drawing on today's popular culture, which admittedly is not evidence-based social science, people view the prospect of "doubling your money" in a short period of time as an opportunity not to be passed up if you can possibly take advantage of it. Advertisements in Civil War–era newspapers demonstrate that Civil War–era men were familiar with the concept of doubling your money in a short time.[62] Based on that assumption, a ratio of 2.0 represents a military compensation package that *could* be "economically compelling," that is, large enough to motivate a man to enlist just for financial gain. (Whether a particular man considering a 2.0 ratio in fact enlisted just for financial gain is an independent question.) A ratio of 2.0 is an arbitrary benchmark. A potential volunteer might have had some interest in a ratio greater than 1.0 but less than 2.0, just not to the degree assumed to be "compelling."

To be clear, the objective is not to prove that money was the dominant motivation for volunteering in 1862. The objective is to show that the financial gain could have been large enough in 1862 that financial gain cannot be dismissed as a motivation for enlisting and that patriotism accordingly cannot simply be assumed to have been the dominant motivation in 1862.

Based on this approach, at least a quarter and as many as half of the men in the Eastern States as a group could have seen the military compensation package as economically compelling in the summer of 1862. (This estimate probably would not hold for the Western States.)[63] Differences in state and local bounties and differences in local wages cause significant differences among the Eastern States.

Table 3.2: Ratio of Military Compensation to Civilian Wages (Summer 1862), Abbreviated

Occupation	CT	DE	ME	MA	NH	NJ	NY	PA	RI	VT
Farmer										
Laborer	2.1	2.0	2.1	2.2	2.1	2.6	2.2	1.7	3.2	2.0
Farm laborer	3.0	3.0	3.0	2.5	3.0	3.8	2.9	2.6	3.8	2.9
Factory hand	2.1	2.0	2.1	2.2	2.1	2.6	2.2	1.7	3.2	2.0
Mariner	2.7		2.5	2.2		2.6	2.2	1.9	3.5	
Teamster	2.1	1.6	1.6	1.9	1.6	2.1	2.0	1.4	2.6	1.6
Blacksmith	1.4	1.3	1.3	1.2	1.5	1.6	1.1	0.9	2.0	1.3
Clerk	1.7	1.2	1.5	1.5	1.5	1.7	1.4	1.3	2.1	1.5
Carpenter	1.7	1.2	1.5	1.6	1.4	1.6	1.1	0.9	1.8	1.3
Molder-iron	1.6	1.2	1.2	1.4	1.5	1.5	1.3	1.1	1.9	1.2

Source: Economic Database, Wage Ratios (by state and year), latewarunionsoldiers.org. For more occupations, see
Economic Database.

Note: There is no income data available for farm owners or operators.

Volunteering could have been economically compelling for as many as 80 percent of the men in Rhode Island, but only 20 percent in Pennsylvania.[64] Not surprisingly, the ratios are highest and generally exceeded 2.0 for unskilled occupations such as laborers and factory hands.[65] The ratio generally was not economically compelling in the summer of 1862 for skilled workers (see Table 3.2).

Farmers who were the operators of their land, whether as the owners or renters, were by far the largest occupation category in the Eastern States in 1860 (see Table 3.3).[66] Considering the importance of this occupation, it is unfortunate that there is no reasonably available data on the income of farm operators as opposed to the wages of farm laborers. Moreover, not all farm operators were alike. A farmer might own his land free and clear, or more likely his land was mortgaged. Or a farmer might be a renter/tenant. He might be farming at the subsistence level or might have a large farm. Men often moved between owners or renters or between farmers and laborers "as their fortunes rose and fell." A farmer might have a large family providing a source of free labor—or not. And so on.[67]

Volunteering apparently was not economically attractive for New York farmers, using the 122nd New York, a three-year regiment from Onondaga County raised in August 1862 (and discussed in the next chapter) as the test.[68] Only about 1.5 percent of the men in the 122nd New York were classic yeoman farmers who owned their land. The yeoman farmers volunteering for the 122nd New York tended to be less wealthy than New York farmers as a group, although they were also younger, ranging in age from twenty-three to forty-three. For example, Charles Stevens (age thirty, married with no children), Niles Rogers (age twenty-nine, married with no children), and George Wilkenson (age forty-three, married with a teenaged

Table 3.3: Farmers, Farm Laborers, and Laborers in the Workforce by State (percent)

Occupation	CT	DE	ME	MA	NH	NJ	NY	PA	RI	VT
Farmer	19	20	31	10	30	14	19	20	11	39
Laborer	10	18	9	10	8	15	12	15	12	9
Farm laborer	7	11	8	4	9	9	9	8	6	14
Total	36	49	48	24	47	38	40	43	28	62

Source: Compiled from Kennedy, *Population of the United States in 1860,* passim.

daughter) had "Real Estate" and "Personal Estate" valued at $500/$100, $600/$50, and $500/$300 respectively.[69]

At the same time, the dearth of farmers who owned their land in the 122nd New York compared to the percentage of farmers in the New York population suggests that patriotism apparently also was not a sufficient motivation for them to volunteer. However, for a farm owner or operator, there were significant practical limitations on his ability to leave the farm behind and go off to war. His family might not be able to operate the farm (and pay the mortgage) without him. Leaving the farm behind simply may not have been a viable option for even the most patriotic farmer. Or a yeoman farmer may have felt that his patriotic obligations were met by continuing agricultural production for the civilian economy and/or sending one or more sons to war.

Instead, it was the military-age (or near military-age) sons of yeoman farmers who were the more likely candidates for enlistment than the yeoman farmer himself. The sons generally had little if any reported wealth of their own. For an eighteen-year-old son interested in marrying, fifteen or more years might be a long time to wait to inherit the family farm. They generally also had male, teen-aged siblings, so they potentially could be spared from the work of the family farm. For them, the advance payment of $127 and a total of $358 cash over one year could have been attractive.[70] Somewhat more than 10 percent of the men in the 122nd New York were sons of yeoman farmers.[71]

Military service probably was more attractive economically to farmers and their sons in New Hampshire, which offered a somewhat higher state and local bounty—$177, with a total cash payment of $408 over the course of a year, as well as Maine ($182/$413) and Connecticut ($177/$438). A "small farm" could be purchased for $250 in New Hampshire, while larger farms could be purchased from $600 to $800.[72]

Farm laborers were generally somewhat less than 10 percent of the workforce in the 1860 Census, with Vermont higher (14.0 percent) and Massachusetts lower (4.0 percent) (see Table 3.3). For farmhands, the federal, state, and local bounties, combined with a private's pay at $13 per month, presented an extremely lucrative offer in the late summer of 1862. In all the Eastern States the ratio of military to civilian compensation for the one-year test period was 2.0 or more (see Table 3.2). The bounties, which were paid in advance, by themselves were roughly the equivalent of a year's wages. Putting aside the separation from family and friends and the hardship and risks of going off to war—no small consideration—farm laborers throughout the Eastern States could have seen enlisting in the Union army as economically compelling in the late summer of 1862.[73]

Laborers generally represented around 10 percent of the workforce in the Eastern States, with Delaware (18.3 percent) and Pennsylvania (15.3 percent) having higher percentages.[74] The ratio for laborers was 2.0 or more in all the Eastern States except Pennsylvania (1.7 percent).

Federal, state, and local bounties increased substantially from the summer of 1862 to the spring of 1864. The vast majority of wage earners in the Eastern States in the spring of 1864 could have viewed volunteering for military service as economically compelling. The ratios were significantly higher than in the summer of 1862, reaching 4.6 for laborers and factory hands in Rhode Island (see Table 3.4). The same was true for the July 1864 and December 1864 calls, although for the one-year term of service the ratios fall somewhat below 2.0 for some of the higher paying civilian occupations.[75]

The ratios well in excess of 2.0 do raise the question of whether the bounties became too high. An economist would say "no" because that is what the forces

Table 3.4: Ratio of Military Compensation to Civilian Wages (Spring 1864), Abbreviated

Occupation	CT	DE	ME	MA	NH	NJ	NY	PA	RI	VT
Farmer										
Laborer	2.9	2.5	3.2	3.8	3.3	3.2	3.4	3.0	4.6	3.0
Farm laborer						4.8	2.4			
Factory hand	2.9	2.5	3.2	3.8	3.3	3.2	3.4	3.0	4.6	3.0
Teacher	3.4		5.1	2.5	5.6					
Boatman	2.9		3.2			3.2	3.4	3.0		
Weaver-wool	3.7			5.7					4.2	
Teamster	2.3	2.0	2.6	4.0	2.6	2.6	3.2	2.4	3.6	2.4
Blacksmith	1.9	1.6	2.0	2.4	2.6	1.8	2.1	1.5	2.9	1.9
Carpenter	2.2			3.0		2.4	1.6	1.6		
Molder-iron	2.4	1.5	1.9	2.6	2.5	2.2	2.4	1.8	2.7	1.8
Machinist	2.3			2.4	2.5	2.2	2.2	1.9		

Source: Economic Database, Wage Ratios (by state and year), latewarunionsoldiers.org. For more occupations, see Economic Database.

Note: Data not available for farm owners or farm laborers (other than New Jersey and New York).

of supply and demand yielded. Many contemporary observers certainly decried the bounties as too high, but, as noted, many others viewed liberal bounties as fair compensation for undertaking the risks and hardships of war, while men remaining at home prospered in the booming civilian economy. Communities generally accepted the higher bounties as the price of mitigating the draft on the local economy. The later-enlisting volunteers may or may not have had reasons for not enlisting in 1861 that their neighbors would have recognized as valid, but they did at least ultimately serve. Over 80,000 other men paid the $300 commutation fee to escape the draft. Nearly 120,000 other men paid the going rate to procure a substitute. These 200,000 men avoided military service altogether by financial means, which could be characterized as selfish if not strictly speaking mercenary. And another 160,000 men whose names were drawn in the draft avoided service by failing to appear.[76]

CHAPTER 4

The Quality of Late-War Replacements

Historians generally take the view that the men who joined the army in 1861 and 1862 made better soldiers than the men brought into the army by the draft and high bounties in 1863, 1864, and 1865 because they were more patriotic and not motivated by money. Some historians did not just question the patriotism of the late-war replacements. They have gone so far as to describe the recruits from the high-bounty period with phrases such as "human refuse." Even during the war, there were people who complained that the right sorts of men were not joining the Union army after 1861 and 1862.

Civil War–era sources provide guidance on what the qualities of a good soldier were. Army regulations provided that "Any free white male person above the age of eighteen, and under thirty-five years of age, being at least five feet three inches high; effective, able-bodied, sober, free from disease, of good character and habits, and with a competent knowledge of the English language, may be enlisted as a soldier." In his enlistment oath, the new soldier swore that he would "bear true allegiance to the United States of America," "serve them honestly and faithfully . . . ; observe and obey the orders of . . . officers appointed over me."[1] The Articles of War provided further guidance, not just with respect to conduct in battle (see Article 52, for example), but also for soldiers' general conduct. Article 24 prohibited "any reproachful or provoking speeches to another." Article 2 "earnestly recommended . . . diligently to attend divine services."[2]

"Good character and habits" were not just important to the military. Northern newspapers used a wide range of similar phrases to describe the men who would make good soldiers. Examples are: "excellent character, . . . can endure toil and fight to some purpose," "generally correct in their habits," "intelligent and vigorous," "purest principle and of the highest talents," "best developed and most capable," "bone and sinew of the country," "sense of duty," "brave and high-minded men," and "representing the best families in town."[3]

Complaints that recruits were not the right sort of men were not limited to the last half of the war. In July 1862, the *New York Times* opined that "The men who are coming forward are far superior, on the average, to those who have filled up the regiments that went from the State last winter [1861]. They . . . seem to be acting, not from impulse, or necessity, or in the belief that they will have an easy time of it, but from conscientious motives of patriotism."[4] The *Albany Evening Journal* commented that "The mass of volunteers have hitherto come from the laboring classes," while Canandaigua, New York's *Ontario Repository and Messenger* noted that "the great majority of the floating population have already gone." Similarly, a reporter for New York's *Otsego Republican* wrote in August 1862 after visiting the 121st New York at Camp Schuyler that "as we looked at the men, we could not but feel that they were the bone and sinew of Otsego and Herkimer, and far superior to the class of men who have heretofore enlisted."[5] All four newspapers disparaged the volunteers of 1861.

Patriotism as a motivation for enlistments was waning by the summer of 1862. "The vital difficulty . . . [of] obtain[ing] an adequate number of *good* soldiers," which Sherman noted in his memoirs, became even more challenging. Towns seeking to meet their quota of recruits faced the dilemma that there was no way to cast a net that would bring in only good men in sufficient numbers. Local communities raising bounties to attract more good men faced a practical problem, as the Manchester, New Hampshire, *Daily Mirror* explained: "The higher rate of wages you pay, the better class of men you can obtain; but where the work is open to all who apply, no high rate of wages will keep out the unskilled workman."[6] Nor does a draft distinguish among men of good, mediocre, and bad character. The army does not reject men on character grounds (other than criminal convictions). From the July 1862 call onward, not enough men of good character were willing to enlist based upon patriotic motivations alone. With laborers and farm laborers—many of them foreign-born—representing a fifth of the potential pool, there were bound to be recruits—Irish-born laborers, for example—whom some people considered not the right sort of men to preserve the Union. The problem continued. Two years later, the *Hartford Daily Courant* stated the hard reality of recruiting for the July 1864 call: "The *class* of men the army is most in need of will not come forward [for a $500 bounty order]. . . . It is worth an effort to obtain the right kind of men." Similarly, the Providence *Manufacturers' and Farmers' Journal* counseled: "Nor should the general effort be confined merely to the number of men recruited. We should not forget that the character of the men is of vital importance."[7]

The higher bounties for residents certainly reflected a desire to meet local quotas at a time when local men were in short supply, but at least in some communities the higher bounties also reflected a sensitivity to the need to fill the quota with local volunteers rather than substitutes and prospective bounty jumpers. New Hampshire's *Coos Republican* commented that local volunteers were "worth ten times their numbers of bounty jumpers or substitutes." The *Coos Republican* proudly reported in September 1864 that Lancaster had filled its quota with local residents—a "superior body of men"—by paying a "good" ($800) bounty, noting that "such men as these would not have gone but for one year, nor at a different bounty."[8] Other local communities also expressed their pride in their recruits during the high-bounty period, perhaps reflecting a belief that a cause as noble as preserving the Union had to be pursued with good men. In early 1864, Williston, Vermont, filled its quota with its own residents instead of recruits of "doubtful character, both moral and physical" provided from other areas by brokers. "The best specimens of intelligent and vigorous young men, citizens of Williston, now constitute its quota." In the fall of 1864, when the bounties in New York reached their highest levels, the *Elmira Daily Advertiser* reported that "Never before, perhaps, was a better class of human material being secured for our armies. The rural districts are sending forth their best developed and most capable young men." The editor of the *Alleghanian* accompanied the newly raised company in Ebensburg, Pennsylvania, to Harrisburg, reporting that he "can truly say that a better looking or a better-behaved set of men never came under his observation. . . . [T]hey comprise within their number men of the purest principle and of the highest talent, intelligent and good." In October 1864, Vermont's general superintendent of recruiting took pride in "the class of men which has been furnished" in response to the July 1864 call.[9] In March 1865, the governor of Maine reported to Fry that Maine was not only "getting volunteers rapidly" but also that "the men are of a good class."[10]

When Grant expressed concern in September 1864 about delaying the draft to allow volunteering to continue longer, Stanton responded that "it is represented that the first recruits were a hard lot, but that recently the volunteers are equal to any that have taken the field during the war."[11] Stanton said this at a time when bounties were reaching their highest levels. The *Pittsburgh Daily Commercial* saw greater support for the war in 1864 than in 1861. "High bounties may have had some influence in producing it, but generally it is to be attributed to a sense of duty, which all loyal and patriotic people must now feel. As has been said before, a better class of our population is now taking the field against the enemy."[12]

However, the reader should not accept any of these characterizations without question because they are all subjective conclusions reflecting unstated biases. Stanton, for example, had a strong political interest in supporting volunteering to minimize the political cost of the draft. The problem with much of the criticism directed to the alleged drop in quality of the men coming into the army after 1861 and 1862 is that it is based on undefined subjective considerations rather than objective analysis. Critics during the war often referred to the lower social class of the late-war replacements without specifically explaining just what it was about men from lower classes that made them poor soldiers. Historians, in turn, generally refer to a presumed lack of patriotism and/or greater propensity to desert as the explanation. (Desertion rates are discussed in the next chapter.) An analysis based on objective factors related to the capability of men to fight would be much more productive. From an objective perspective, health would be a key indicator of the quality of a recruit. Other objective criteria such as occupation and place of birth have some value as indicators of whether a recruit would make a good soldier.[13]

Health is the most direct indicator among these objective criteria. Army regulations required that recruits be: "effective, able-bodied, sober, [and] free from disease."[14] The army did not effectively enforce the requirements for the physical examination of recruits at the beginning of the war.[15] As patriotic as a man joining the Union army in 1861 may have been, he was not necessarily healthy enough for military service. The New York Agency of the Sanitary Commission wrote President Lincoln in July 1862 that "The careless and superficial medical inspection of recruits made at least 25 per cent. of the volunteer army raised last year [1861] not only utterly useless, but a positive incumbrance and embarrassment, filling our hospitals with invalids."[16] Fry later reported to Stanton that "A large part . . . (near 200,000) of the men accepted in the years 1861 and 1862 were soon found to be unfit for service, and were discharged."[17] Many, if not most, of these men must have known that they had a disabling condition—they knew their age, that they had a hernia, etc., but they volunteered anyway for their own reasons to the detriment of the army.[18]

Responsible military and medical officials understood the harm that had been caused and they conducted the physical examination of recruits more rigorously later in the war, though certainly not with perfection. Fry reported in 1866 that "such strict regard was paid to [recruits'] physical fitness, before accepting them, as to greatly reduce the enormous loss on account of discharges for physical disability, which had prevailed during the first two years of the war."[19] Thus, as a group the late-war replacements were healthier when they arrived in the field than the volunteers from 1861 and 1862. In that sense—clearly an important one— the late-war replacements made better soldiers than their predecessors.

Northern society probably considered occupation as the best demographic indicator of whether a man would be a good soldier. A man's occupation indicated his social standing in the community as well as his economic wherewithal. Outside the cities and larger towns, the yeoman farmers were the pillars of their communities. Their sons could be trusted to have been brought up with the same strength of character. In contrast, society had trusted men who did not own the land they farmed with the right to vote for only a generation or two. In the cities and towns, the good character of merchants and skilled tradesmen was presumed. The character of laborers was uncertain. Amos Judson of the Eighty-Third Pennsylvania concluded that "those who make the best and most reliable soldiers in the field were the best and most reliable men as citizens at home." Grant's reference in his *Memoirs* to European soldiers being "from a class of people who are not very intelligent" reflected the view that middle-class men made better soldiers. Overall, nearly half of Union soldiers had been farmers before the war, while somewhat more than 10 percent had been common laborers.[20] Declines over time in the percentages of men in middle-class occupations in regiments from the same area could be an indicator of a decrease in the number of good men in the recruiting pool.

Foreign birth could indicate that a man was less patriotic than his native-born counterpart or less likely to be committed to the Union. (The length of time that the foreign-born man had lived in the United States might temper that.) Foreign-born soldiers deserted more often than native-born soldiers.[21] Differences in place of birth could also present cultural differences affecting unit cohesion. For example, the Thirty-Seventh New York was primarily raised in New York City, but two of the companies came from Cattaraugus County in rural western New York State. One of the men from Cattaraugus County wrote home in 1861 that "our men are not very well satisfied with the regiment as most of them are Irish and some of the officers are rather rough." The Cattaraugus men tried to have their companies assigned to a different regiment.[22] Language differences could also create communication problems within a regiment. Battle required prompt and complete understanding of orders. Even day-to-day operations could be disrupted if soldiers could not understand or speak English.

Civil War–era commentators often dismissed the "floating population." Men who had strong ties to their community were less likely to desert. A community's increasing reliance over time on nonresidents to fill their local quotas could also be viewed as indicating decreasing quality in the pool of available men. Unfortunately, broad-based data on a soldier's actual residence at the time of enlistment are hard to find. Data on the town where a soldier enlisted and the town against whose quota he was credited are generally available. However, once the bounty system was in place, men frequently left their hometowns to enlist in another town and/or were credited to the quota of another town.[23]

Taking the organizational, technical, and logistical complexities of operating today's armies as a given, literacy is critical for an effective soldier. But literacy may also have been important for the Union soldier. In Grant's view, a literate man made a better soldier than an illiterate man. Compared to European armies, "Our armies were composed of men who were able to read, men who knew what they were fighting for."[24] At a more pedestrian level, the ability to read could be an important part of training. August V. Kautz wrote in *Customs of Service* that "heretofore the enlisted soldier has been dependent upon tradition for a knowledge of his specific duties." Kautz was "confident that every soldier who is desirous of learning his duties will feel grateful for this little volume, [which] places before them the means of studying for themselves what they so much desire to know."[25] How many Union soldiers read *Customs of Service* or similar manuals is unknown, but the opportunity was there. However, the literacy rates of men joining the Union army probably did not vary significantly over the course of the war. McPherson estimates that more than 90 percent of white Union soldiers were literate. With such a high rate of literacy, meaningful differences over time seem unlikely. Thus, literacy is not pursued further.[26]

Throughout history soldiers in the field have taken as a sign of impending victory an increasing reliance by the other side on old men and boys. But age is more an indicator of physical capability than character beyond the maturity of judgment that generally comes with age. The Union army as a whole (as opposed to the Confederate army) experienced no significant problem with the age of its troops as the war progressed. The standard age for enlistment was between eighteen and thirty-five. The average age at enlistment for the Union army overall was 25.8 years, somewhat below the midpoint between eighteen and thirty-five. The average age for individual years during the war was in the same range.[27]

Newspapers reported early in the war that there were married men who would have joined the army but for their economic inability to provide for their families in their absence. Higher bounties would have made it possible for married men to provide for their families. However, this project has not pursued marital status any further because of the lack of an answer to the threshold question: "During the Civil War, did single men make better soldiers than married men, all other things being equal?"[28]

Longitudinal Comparisons of Demographic Data

The fact that local communities continued recruiting throughout the war offers the opportunity to look for differences over time in objective criteria that are rough indicators of whether a man would be a good soldier or not, notably occupation and place of birth and, to a much lesser extent, age. While regiments were often comprised of companies from different parts of the state, this project has identified two sets of New York regiments primarily recruited in the same county over the course of the war—the Oswego County Regiments and the Onondaga County Regiments. This enables a comparison of the recruits raised in the same general area at different times.

Using occupation, place of birth, and age as indicators of whether a recruit would be a good soldier, the quality of the recruits for the regiments primarily raised in Oswego and Onondaga counties generally did not decline over the course of the war. In particular, the quality of the recruits for the late-war 184th New York and 185th New York was at least as good—and in some cases better—as for the regiments raised in 1861 and 1862. However, that was not the case for the 193rd New York, which was partially raised in Oswego County in the spring of 1865.

The Oswego County Regiments

Oswego County is located at the southeastern corner of Lake Ontario. Oswego was its largest city with a population of seventeen thousand. Lincoln carried Oswego County in 1860.[29]

The five regiments principally recruited in Oswego County were the Twenty-Fourth, Eighty-First, 110th, 147th, and 184th New York. Two companies of the 193rd New York were raised in Oswego County in early 1865.[30] The Oswego regiments were raised at different times when different conditions prevailed as to the draft and bounties.

Recruiting for the Twenty-Fourth New York—a two-year regiment—began in April 1861, the day after Lincoln's call for seventy-five thousand men.[31]

Recruiting for the Eighty-First New York, a three-year regiment, began in August 1861 and the regiment was organized in February 1862. Three companies from Rome were added in early 1862, but they are not included in the numbers analyzed here.[32]

Recruiting for the 110th New York, a three-year regiment, began at the end of July 1862 and was quickly completed. In addition to the $100 federal bounty, New York offered a bounty of $50, and Oswego County offered an additional $50. Half the towns offered no bounty, while the other half offered $25 to $50. The possibility of a draft was also pending.[33]

Recruiting for the 147th New York, a three-year regiment, began shortly after the 110th New York but progressed more slowly. The conditional draft was pending, but the 147th New York was ultimately filled without draftees.[34]

The 184th New York, a one-year regiment, was raised in the summer of 1864 and the men were mustered in August and September. The Oswego County bounty reached $400 and town bounties were as high as $600.[35]

Recruiting for the 193rd New York was authorized in January 1865. The 193rd New York did not reach the field until March 1865.[36]

There is little difference in terms of occupation, birthplace, and age between the late-war 184th New York recruited in the summer of 1864 and the four regiments recruited in 1861 and 1862. However, there was a noticeable decline in the occupational and birthplace profiles for the 193rd New York, which was recruited in the spring of 1865 as the war was ending. The 110th New York, organized in July 1862, presented the strongest occupational profile of the six Oswego regiments. However, the late-war 184th New York was not far behind the 110th New York and had a stronger occupational profile than the other regiments (see Table 4.1).

With respect to birthplace, more than 80 percent of the men in the late-war 184th New York were native-born, placing it close to the 110th New York and higher than the other Oswego regiments. However, only about 60 percent of the men in the 193rd New York were native-born. There was not a meaningful difference in age over time in the Oswego regiments.

Table 4.1: Oswego County Occupations (Percent), Abbreviated

	24th May 1861	81st Aug. 1861	110th July 1862	147th Sept. 1862	184th Sept. 1864	193rd Mar. 1865
Farmer	40.9	49.5	55.9	44.5	53.3	41.6
Laborer	11.7	7.8	4.8	9.5	9.5	22.4
Sailor	6.0	6.4	2.8	9.7	2.7	3.0
Boatman	4.3	5.9	2.5	2.9	3.8	5.4
Cooper	2.7	5.2	6.6	6.4	8.0	1.4
Carpenter	3.0	4.8	4.0	3.8	4.0	2.0
Shoemaker	2.3	2.0	1.3	1.2	0.5	2.0
Mechanic	4.9	3.4	5.3	1.6	2.8	2.1
Clerk	5.1	3.8	2.3	1.0	3.6	2.7
Teacher	1.3	0.3	0.6		0.2	0.4

Source: Compiled from Descriptive Books, Regimental Books for the individual regiments, NARA.
Note: For more occupations, see Table 4.1.A, Tables, latewarunionsoldiers.org.

Table 4.2: Oswego County Average Ages and Birthplaces

Birthplace	Oswego Co. 1860 Census	24th May 1861	81st Aug. 1861	110th July 1862	147th Sept. 1862	184th Sept. 1864	193rd Mar. 1865
New York State		70.3	70.9	81.4	65.5	79.0	54.9
Other US		8.0	4.7	5.0	4.9	4.0	7.0
Native-born	84	78.3	75.6	86.4	70.4	83.0	61.9
Foreign-born	16	21.7	24.4	13.6	29.6	17.0	38.1
Ireland		8.3	8.7	4.4	10.1	5.3	15.0
Canada		5.0	6.3	4.2	9.6	6.2	16.8
Germany		2.9	2.4	0.9	3.9	1.2	1.3
England		3.2	4.0	3.0	4.2	3.0	3.4
Other		2.3	3.0	1.1	1.8	1.3	1.6
Average age		23.5	25.3	26.1	27.0	25.9	25.5

Source: Compiled from Descriptive Books, Regimental Books for the individual regiments, NARA.
Note: Average age for the Union Army was 25.8 years.

The Onondaga County Regiments

Onondaga County is in the geographic center of New York State, just south of Oswego County. Syracuse was the largest city with a population of nearly thirty thousand. In 1860, Onondaga County went 61 percent for Lincoln, but dropped to 56 percent in 1864.[37]

The five regiments raised principally in Onondaga County were the Twelfth New York, the 101st New York, the 122nd New York, the 149th New York, and the 185th New York.[38]

The Twelfth New York, a two-year regiment, was organized in May 1861.[39]

The 101st New York, a three-year regiment, was formed in January 1862 by consolidating two regiments that had been slow in recruiting—the Second Onondaga and the First Union Brigade. It was discontinued in December 1862, when its men were transferred to the Thirty-Seventh New York.[40]

Recruiting for the 122nd New York, a three-year regiment, began at the end of July 1862 and was completed by the end of August. New York State had adopted a $50 bounty on July 17 and Onondaga County offered an additional $50 bounty. Half of the towns in the county offered no bounty, while $50 was the most common amount for the other towns.[41]

The 149th New York, a three-year regiment, started recruiting at the end of August 1862 and finished in a matter of weeks. Bounties remained the same.[42]

The 185th New York, a one-year regiment, completed recruiting within four weeks in August and September 1864. New York State did not offer a bounty for the July 1864 call. The county paid a total of $2.1 million in bounties, but the individual amount for specific calls is not available. Town bounties varied significantly, from zero (the most common) to $500.[43]

The late-war 185th New York presented one of the strongest occupational profiles of the Onondaga regiments.

With respect to the percentage of native-born men, the 185th New York exceeds the Twelfth New York and the 101st New York, which were raised in 1861 and early 1862, and falls between the 122nd New York and the 149th New York, which were raised in August and September 1862. That indicates that there was no drop-off in the quality of recruits in Onondaga County in the fall of 1864 as

Table 4.3: Onondaga County Occupations (Percent), Abbreviated

Occupation	12th May 1861	101st Oct. 1861	122nd Aug. 1862	149th Aug. 1862	185th Sept. 1864
Farmer	40.9	49.5	40.9	29.1	42.8
Laborer	11.7	7.8	14.1	22.7	8.3
Sailor	6.0	6.4	1.2	0.6	0.6
Boatman	4.3	5.9	2.6	4.0	0.8
Cooper	2.7	5.2	4.2	4.1	2.4
Carpenter	3.0	4.8	3.8	4.3	7.0
Shoemaker	2.3	2.0	2.9	1.2	2.1
Mechanic	4.9	3.4	2.4	1.9	2.8
Clerk	5.1	3.8	2.4	2.7	4.3
Teacher	1.3	0.3	0.5	0.5	0.9

Source: Compiled from Descriptive Books, Regimental Books for the individual regiments, NARA.
Note: For more occupations, see Table 4.3.A, Tables, latewarunionsoldiers.org.

Table 4.4: Onondaga County Average Ages and Birthplaces

Birthplace	Onondaga Co. 1860 Census	12th May 1861	101st Jan. 1862	122nd Aug. 1862	149th Aug. 1862	185th Sept. 1864
New York State		69.7	63.6	70.2	57.5	67.9
Other US		4.4	6.3	8.0	5.3	9.2
Native-born	77	74.0	70.0	78.2	62.8	77.1
Foreign-born	23	26.0	30.0	21.9	37.0	22.9
Ireland		12.6	12.4	8.5	12.5	6.0
Germany		4.6	8.5	2.9	15.7	9.1
England		4.4	3.6	6.3	4.8	3.9
Other		4.4	5.5	4.2	4.0	3.9
Average age		24.1	25.9	25.7	27.4	25.9

Source: Compiled from Descriptive Books for the individual regiments, RG 94, NARA. Data for the 12th and 101st New York compiled from New York Muster Roll Abstracts, Fold3.com.
Note: Average age for the Union Army was 25.8 years.

measured by place of birth. As with the Oswego County regiments, there was no significant difference in the average age of the recruits over time.

Refilling the Old Oswego and Onondaga County Regiments

Examining the personnel in the late-war new regiments from Oswego and Onondaga counties reveals only part of the recruiting picture. The old regiments in the field were also recruiting. Moreover, the army generally did not assign substitutes and draftees to the late-war new regiments in significant numbers. Recruiters seeking replacements for the old regiments from Oswego and Onondaga counties during the high-bounty period achieved mixed results. The occupations and birthplaces of the replacements in Oswego County's 147th New York and Onondaga County's 149th New York were similar to those of the men in the original complements of those regiments. However, the occupational and birthplace profiles for the late-war replacements for Oswego County's Eighty-First New York did decline.

During the several months following Gettysburg, the 147th New York received over five hundred replacements, most of them conscripts and substitutes. While conscripts and substitutes have been scorned by many of their fellow soldiers as well as historians, Charles Biddlecom, himself a draftee in the 147th who had served briefly in the Twenty-Eighth New York at the beginning of the war before receiving a medical discharge, did not see it that way: "There is in this regiment something like five hundred conscripts and substitutes and I do think them the best men for service I ever saw together."[44] The 1863 replacements were in fact quite similar to the original complement in terms of both nationality and occupation. The percentage of farmers was somewhat higher in the 1863 replacements (with the caveat that in both cases the soldier declared his occupation as "Farmer," while many in fact may have been "Farm Laborers"). In the other categories, changes in one occupation tended to be offset by changes in another. While the 1863 replacements were slightly less native-born than the original complement of the 147th New York, the difference is not substantial.[45] Thus, to the extent that quality is determined by nationality and occupation, the 147th New York's replacements were of similar quality compared to the original complement.[46]

The 149th New York is the only one of the Onondaga County regiments that received sufficient replacements to warrant further analysis.[47] The 149th New York received three hundred replacements in 1864, 90 percent of them in the first six months when bounties were lower than later in the year.[48] There was little difference in the distribution of occupations between the original complement and the 1864 replacements. The percentage of farmers was basically the same (with the usual caveat). The percentage of laborers did decrease by almost half, but

Table 4.5: 147th New York Occupations

Occupation	Original Complement	1863 Replacements
Farmer	44.5	46.1
Laborer	9.5	15.5
Sailor	9.7	3.1
Boatman	2.9	3.1
Cooper	6.4	1.6
Carpenter	3.8	3.1
Shoemaker	1.2	3.9
Mechanic	1.6	0.2
Clerk	1.0	1.3
Teacher	0.2	0.9

Source: Compiled from Descriptive Books, Regimental Books for the individual regiments, RG 94, NARA.

Table 4.6: 149th New York Occupations

Occupation	Original Complement	1863 Replacements
Farmer	29.1	30.3
Laborer	22.7	13.1
Sailor	0.6	3.7
Boatman	4.0	7.1
Cooper	4.1	0.7
Carpenter	4.3	3.7
Shoemake	1.2	2.4
Machinist	1.2	1.7
Clerk	2.7	5.7

Source: Compiled from New York Muster Roll Abstracts, Fold3.com.

Table 4.7: Eighty-First New York Replacements

Period	Number
Jan.-July 1862	100
Rest of 1862	149
1863	12
Jan.-Apr. 1864	75
Nov.-Dec. 1864	81
Jan.-Mar. 1865	70
Apr. 1865	233

Source: Compiled from unit roster, NYSMM.

increases in the percentages for other unskilled occupations largely offset that. There were decreases in some skilled occupations—notably coopers—but there were increases in others.

The 1864 replacements were slightly more foreign-born than the original complement, but the increase was only about five percentage points.[49] The average age of the 1864 replacements was actually younger compared to the original complement—25.8 compared to 27.4.[50]

The Eighty-First New York left Oswego County with about one thousand men. However, the Eighty-First New York lost heavily in battle as noted and became one of Fox's Three Hundred.[51] The Eighty-First New York received significant numbers of replacements throughout its service (Table 4.7).

The distribution of occupations for the second half of 1862 was very similar to the distribution for the original complement. However, there was a significant drop in quality for the 1864 cohorts. The percentage of farmers fell to 30 percent

Table 4.8: Eighty-First New York Occupations (Percent), Abbreviated

	Original Complement	July–Dec. 1862	Spring 1864	July–Dec. 1864
Farmer	49.5	50.7	30.0	9.8
Laborer	7.8	1.5	21.7	51.9
Seaman	6.4	7.4	10.0	1.9
Boatman	5.9	5.1	6.7	1.9
Cooper	5.2	0.7	3.3	
Carpenter	4.8	2.9		1.9
Clerk	3.8	4.4	1.7	
Mechanic	3.4	1.5	3.3	
Shoemaker	2.0	2.2	5.0	3.7

Source: Compiled from New York Muster Roll Abstracts, Fold3.com.
Note: The Original Complement dates from August 1861. For more occupations, see Table 4.8.A, Tables, latewarunionsoldiers.org.

for the spring 1864 cohort and just under 10 percent for the second half of the 1864 cohort. Laborers comprised half of the second half of 1864 cohort, the vast majority of whom were substitutes.

The birthplace distribution for the volunteers raised in the spring of 1864 was essentially the same as for the original complement. However, the replacements from the second half of 1864 were almost 90 percent foreign-born (see Table 4.9). Almost all these replacements were substitutes. While most of the replacements from the last half of 1862 and the spring of 1864 had enlisted in the same areas of Oswego County and the surrounding area, 40 percent of the replacements from the second half of 1864 enlisted in Buffalo or Rochester.[52] There was no significant difference in age between the original complement and the replacements.[53]

For the late-war new regiments from Onondaga and Oswego counties, there generally was no decline in quality as measured by occupation, place of birth, and age compared to the regiments raised in those counties in 1861 and 1862. Similarly, two of the old regiments from these two counties were able to find replacements of similar quality during the high-bounty period, but one was not. The 193rd New York, which was partially raised in Oswego County, does raise questions about recruiting in the spring of 1865.

These ten regiments from Onondaga and Oswego counties are not necessarily typical of the Union army as a whole—or even the regiments from New York State. The sample is too small to support broad conclusions.[54] However, the fact that there was generally no decline in quality—as measured by occupation and birthplace—over the course of the war in the recruits for these regiments in these

Table 4.9: Eighty-First New York Birthplaces

	1860 Census	Original Complement	July–Dec. 1862	Spring 1864	July–Dec. 1864
New York State		70.9	75.7	68.3	9.8
Other US		4.7	9.6	5.0	3.9
Total native	84	75.6	85.3	73.3	13.7
Total foreign	16	24.4	14.7	26.7	86.3
Ireland		8.7	8.8	10.0	33.3
Canada		6.3	1.5	8.3	37.3
Germany		2.4	0.7	1.7	2.0
England		4.0	3.7	6.7	11.7
Other foreign		3.0			2.0

Source: Compiled from New York Muster Roll Abstracts, Fold3.com. The Original Complement dates from August 1861.

two counties at least raises questions about the universality of the contention that the quality of Union recruits significantly declined after 1862.[55]

The Union army's recruiting challenge invokes the old saw that when it comes to quality, time, and price, you can have only two out of three. However, the Union military leaders did not just want all three, they also wanted quantity. At a time when the civilian economy was flourishing—and the populace wanted to keep it so—and prior calls had pulled roughly a million men into the army in 1861 and 1862, the Union army simply could not have all four. This was especially the case when many people believed that 20 percent and more of the eligible men (laborers, farm laborers, boatmen, foreign-born, etc.) did not come from the right class. A stand-alone draft could have given the Union time, quantity, and price, although with no assurance of quality. However, a stand-alone draft was politically unacceptable. The combination of bounties backed up by a conditional draft certainly failed on price and to an extent on time, but it delivered the necessary quantity of troops and—at least generally in Oswego and Onondaga counties—did so with essentially the same quality (as measured by occupation, birthplace, and age) as the veterans from 1861 and 1862.

CHAPTER 5

Desertion

Historians have criticized the bounty system for causing high desertion rates among the Union army's later-enlisting volunteers and substitutes, but they have made little effort to explore that criticism more deeply or to support it with data. Historians should consider a wide range of questions, with data informing the answers. For example, what was the actual desertion rate for the later-enlisting volunteers? What percentage of later-enlisting volunteers were "bounty jumpers" as opposed to ordinary deserters? How did the desertion rate for later-enlisting volunteers compare with the rate for the men who volunteered in 1861 and 1862? If there were differences, were they significant? And the ultimate question—what was the actual impact of higher bounties on desertion compared to other causes such as frustration with conditions in the field or homesickness? This chapter begins providing answers to these types of questions by looking at data for soldiers in Pennsylvania and New Jersey regiments in the Army of the Potomac at the beginning of the Overland Campaign (with data going back to 1861) or thereafter.[1]

Desertion Rates

Starting with the proper context is important. Desertion by late-war replacements was definitely a serious problem for the Union army in 1864 and 1865. However, desertion had been a serious problem since the beginning of the war. Indeed, before the war, desertion in the peacetime regular army was as high as a third per year.[2] Desertion quickly became frequent in 1861.[3] By the end of July

1862, "the absence of officers and privates from their duty under various pre-texts" had become such a "burden" that Stanton found it necessary to cancel all leaves of absence and furloughs.[4] He did so well before bounties had reached their highest levels. The War Department created the Provost Marshal General's Bureau in September 1862 primarily to address desertion. The first provost marshal general, Simeon Draper, reported that between 10 and 25 percent of the men raised in July and August 1862 had deserted. He noted that "nearly all of these men have received bounties; many of them have received bounties, deserted, re-enlisted, and deserted several times."[5]

When Gen. Joseph Hooker took command of the Army of the Potomac in January 1863, the situation with desertion "seemed almost hopeless."[6] Fry recalled that "desertion had greatly increased and had grown into a formidable and widespread evil." Several hundred soldiers a day were deserting and roughly a quarter of the Army of the Potomac was absent.[7] These were men who had volunteered in 1861 and 1862. Hooker ordered the arrest of deserters and tightened discipline. For a time, desertion in the Army of the Potomac dropped significantly.[8] However, based on the numbers officially reported, desertion started to increase again. The average number of Union soldiers deserting every month increased from 4,225 in 1863 to 7,561 in 1864, but fell somewhat to 6,449 in 1865.[9] That certainly looks like a substantial increase during the high-bounty period, but whether such an increase in fact actually occurred is not clear because of uncertainties about the officially reported data.[10] That makes it all the more important to try to quantify the various facets of desertion by the late-war replacements. It is also worth remembering Gary Gallagher's observation on Confederate desertion: "A careful look at patterns, numbers, and circumstances reveals that, as is almost always the case with history, the phenomenon was far more complex, and its impact less certain, than often assumed."[11]

Later-Enlisting Volunteers

Around 20 percent of later-enlisting volunteers in Pennsylvania regiments in the Army of the Potomac from the beginning of the Overland Campaign onward deserted. For New Jersey, the rate was about 30 percent. In both states, later-enlisting volunteers deserted at significantly higher rates in 1863 than in 1864 and 1865.[12] Improved security in transporting troops to the front after 1863 may be the explanation.

These desertion rates have two components: (1) desertion after enlisting but before reporting to the assigned regiment and being officially taken up on the books of the regiment (hereafter the Not Taken Up Factor), and (2) desertion after reporting to the regiment. For the first component, the Adjutant General 's

Table 5.1: Pennsylvania and New Jersey Desertion: Later-Enlisting Volunteers

Period	Pennsylvania			New Jersey		
	Number	Desertions	Percent	Number	Desertions	Percent
1863	2,209	438	19.8	760	264	34.7
1864	24,884	2,088	8.4	4,091	757	18.5
1865	2,470	144	5.8	2,711	532	19.6
1863–65	29,563	2,670	9.0	7,562	1,553	20.5

Source: HIBO Database.
Note: See introduction, note 25. Not Taken Up Factor (10 percent) not included. For a fuller discussion, see Methodology–5. Desertion–Not Taken Up Factor and No Further Record, latewarunionsoldiers.org.

Office estimated the loss between muster in and reporting to the assigned unit (which likely was primarily due to desertion) at 10 percent in October 1864.[13] For the second component, later-enlisting volunteers joining Pennsylvania regiments in the Army of the Potomac deserted at a rate averaging around 9 percent for 1863 to 1865.[14] In New Jersey, later-enlisting volunteers deserted after joining their regiments at an average rate around 20 percent from 1863 through 1865.[15]

Bounty Jumpers

Bounty jumpers comprised 15 to 20 percent of Pennsylvania's later-enlisting volunteers in the Army of the Potomac. Because 20 percent of Pennsylvania's later-enlisting volunteers in the Army of the Potomac deserted, the vast majority of these deserters can fairly be classified as bounty jumpers as opposed to standard deserters. However, that also means that four-fifths of Pennsylvania's later-enlisting volunteers in the Army of the Potomac were not bounty jumpers.

In *One Million Men,* Eugene C. Murdock posed basic questions about bounty jumpers but gave a frustrating answer: "What percentage of all bounty soldiers jumped? Did the jumpers comprise a significant portion of the troops raised? . . . Obviously, these questions cannot be answered statistically. No census of bounty jumpers was ever compiled, nor could one have been."[16] While Murdock was literally correct that the government did not undertake a census of bounty jumpers like the 1890 Census of Veterans, that does not mean that further statistical inquiry is impossible. By definition, bounty jumpers were deserters and there is a good deal of data on desertion during the high-bounty period.[17] Murdock had begun with the obvious point that not all soldiers who received a bounty deserted. But he overlooked the important point that not all bounty soldiers who deserted were necessarily bounty jumpers. Murdock defined a bounty jumper as a person "who would enlist for no other purpose than to pocket one or more large bounties" and then "stop at nothing to gain his freedom."[18] A bounty soldier who initially intended to serve but then left for home after six months in the field because of a family crisis or because he was tired of the war was certainly a deserter, but he was not a bounty jumper. The distinction is important because it affected the force level that a regimental commander of late-war replacements could rely on.

The guiding principle for a bounty jumper was to desert at the first opportunity after he received the bounty payment. As a result, as a group bounty soldiers who deserted shortly after enlisting probably can fairly be called bounty jumpers. The numbers of bounty soldiers who deserted after enlisting but before arriving in the field are large enough to demonstrate that there was often ample opportunity to desert quickly. Looking at the interval between a bounty soldier's enlistment and desertion dates can provide insight on whether he was likely a bounty jumper as opposed to a standard deserter. The later-enlisting volunteers who deserted after enlisting but before reporting to their assigned regiment—estimated at 10 percent for the Union army as a whole by the Adjutant General's Office in the fall of 1864—likely were bounty jumpers. In addition, later-enlisting volunteers who deserted within thirty days of reporting to the regiment also likely were bounty jumpers. For Pennsylvania, that would be roughly an additional 5 to 10 percent in addition to the Not Taken Up Factor for a total of roughly 15 to 20 percent of Pennsylvania's later-enlisting volunteers in the Army of the Potomac as bounty jumpers as opposed to standard deserters.[19]

Volunteers from 1861 and 1862 Compared to Later-Enlisting Volunteers

The men who volunteered in 1861 and 1862 to serve in Pennsylvania regiments in the Army of the Potomac deserted at rates around 10 percent. For New Jersey, the volunteers from 1861 and 1862 deserted at slightly higher rates than in Pennsylvania.

Table 5.2: Pennsylvania and New Jersey Desertion: Comparison of Volunteers

Period	Pennsylvania			New Jersey		
	Number	Desertions	Percent	Number	Desertions	Percent
1861	41,496	4,108	9.9	9,744	1,123	11.5
1862	23,761	2,937	12.4	4,765	663	13.9
1863–65	29,563	2,670	9.0	7,562	1,553	20.5
Not Taken Up			10.0			10.0
Total 1863–65			19.0			30.5

Source: HIBO Database.

Notes: See introduction, note 25. The Not Taken Up Factor is assumed to be zero for 1861 and 1862, which may be too low. For a fuller discussion, see Methodology–5. Desertion–Not Taken Up Factor and No Further Record, latewarunionsoldiers.org.

Later-enlisting volunteers deserted at higher rates than the volunteers from 1861 and 1862 in both Pennsylvania and New Jersey—about 10 percentage points higher for Pennsylvania and not quite 20 percentage points higher for New Jersey.[20] However, that higher desertion percentage for later-enlisting volunteers might be offset in part by the possibility that the volunteers from 1861 and 1862 may have been absent without leave more frequently than the later-enlisting volunteers. Unfortunately, the data necessary to compare absent-without-leave rates would be quite difficult to compile.

Significance of the Higher Desertion Rates by the Later-Enlisting Volunteers

The higher desertion rate for later-enlisting volunteers compared to the volunteers from 1861 and 1862 was large enough that it had to be addressed, but it did not materially impact the Union war effort because the impact was successfully managed. The magnitude of the challenge was also reduced by the fact that the Confederacy did not have the manpower reserves to offset the heavy losses it suffered in the Overland Campaign (and from desertion by its own soldiers).

The significance of the increase in desertion cannot be determined simply based on the size of the number. Whether the difference was significant depends on the impact of increased desertion on the Union war effort. The Union did not ignore the increase in desertion. The Lincoln Administration created the Provost Marshal General's Bureau in 1862, as noted. The Deserters' Branch estimated that the 77,181 deserters who were arrested since the branch had been created in the spring of 1863 represented "nearly two-thirds" of the total during that period (although the deserters who were returned to the field did not necessarily perform well as soldiers).[21] The Provost Marshal General's Bureau did not come close to eradicating desertion, but it prevented desertion from materially impairing operations. Lincoln did call for more troops five times from October 1863 through December 1864, but the large numbers of troops needed to replace the heavy casualties from the Overland Campaign and the beginning of the Petersburg Campaign, as well as disease, required the calls, not losses from desertion.[22] Even at that, the very round numbers of the Union's troop calls—300,000, 200,000, 500,000, and 300,000—suggest that Lincoln, Stanton, and later Grant could well have factored in losses from bounty jumpers and draftees who failed to report.

Rare is the commanding general who would not like more troops, but Grant did not report that he did not have enough troops to accomplish his objectives and would have to change strategy and/or postpone offensive operations.[23] Grant's Petersburg strategy of stretching Lee's forces to the breaking point required large numbers of additional troops, but the Union army found the necessary numbers. To maximize the number of troops for offensive operations, the Union army found ways to use its troops more efficiently. It reorganized partially disabled soldiers into the Veteran Reserve Corps to perform noncombat duties such as escorting recruits, freeing up troops for the front. The Union army repurposed heavy artillery units garrisoning harbor forts as infantry for the field. The Lincoln Administration authorized "hundred days" infantry regiments to free up troops performing railroad duty and other rear echelon functions. And the Union army also recruited African American men. Fry was perhaps the best witness for the case that the problem of desertion was successfully managed. As severe a critic of the bounty system as he was, he nonetheless concluded that the combination of bounties and the conditional draft "met the wants of the service."[24]

Another way of looking at the issue of increased desertion is to recognize it as unavoidable.[25] No one claims that high bounties were the ideal way to raise a large number of troops. The challenge is identifying an alternative that would have worked better under the circumstances. A stand-alone draft is the obvious candidate, but it was not politically viable in Congress or with the general public. However, even assuming that the congressmen of the day would go against public opinion and enact stand-alone conscription with the cooperation of state and local officials (and fees for substitutes were prohibited), desertion could well have been even worse. Many men left their homes to avoid enrollment even when large bounties were available to them. Without the bounties, the flight to avoid enrollment likely would have continued as additional boys became old enough to be subject to the draft. The number of men who failed to report after their names were drawn can be quantified—20 percent on average and nearly

Table 5.3: Men Failing to Report after Being Drafted (Percent)

State	July 1863	March 1864	July 1864	December 1864
Connecticut	8.1	a	15.4	a
Delaware	11.2	18.7	16.4	25.8
Maine	10.7	a	21.5	10.3
Massachusetts	9.0	24.1	a	a
New Hampshire	4.1	8.4	0.2	0.3
New Jersey	a	18.9	18.4	19.9
New York	16.5	22.7	33.6	29.3
Pennsylvania	13.6	26.8	28.6	10.3
Rhode Island	5.8	a	a-	a
Vermont	4.7	13.5	13.6	16.7
Eastern States	13.0	23.4	26.3	19.0
All states	13.5	24.0	28.5	20.5

Source: Calculated from OR III:5, 730–39.
Note: a = No names drawn or data not reported.

30 percent in July 1864 when civilian morale was at its lowest (see Table 5.3). Without bounties, that number could well have been even higher. If substitution were retained but bounties prohibited, market forces would have driven up the substitute fee to levels that likely would have encouraged bounty jumping. Holding the principal personally responsible for the desertion of his substitute could have had a real impact, but such a proposal was unrealistic.

Another possibility to consider is the fact that the later-enlisting volunteers were in better health than the volunteers from 1861 may have offset the impact of the greater desertion rate for later-enlisting volunteers. Whether a soldier in the field is lost to poor health or to desertion, the impact on the army is the same regardless of his patriotism (or lack thereof). The army has still lost a man either way. As discussed in the preceding chapter, Fry estimated that at least one hundred thousand of the recruits from 1861, 1862, and 1863 "were unfit for service when received." Improved physical examination of recruits meant that fewer later-enlisting volunteers were found to be unfit after reaching their units. This project has not quantified the difference between the volunteers from 1861 and 1862 and the later-enlisting volunteers, but it could be significant.

The Union had to raise large numbers of troops—far in excess of what patriotism alone could generate—and increased desertion was going to be an unavoidable result. The best that the Union army could do was effectively manage the impact of desertion on its way to raising the large number of troops necessary for victory in the field. It succeeded in doing so with the bounties and the conditional draft, efficient management of available troops and the efforts of the Provost Marshal General's Bureau, including more effective security and discipline.

Differences among Later-Enlisting Volunteers, Substitutes, and Conscripts

Later-enlisting volunteers, substitutes, and draftees deserted at very different rates in both Pennsylvania and New Jersey. The later-enlisting volunteers deserted the least frequently. Substitutes deserted at a rate twice that of later-enlisting volunteers.[26] Draftees deserted only slightly more often than later-enlisting volunteers in Pennsylvania but deserted less frequently than later-enlisting volunteers in New Jersey (see Tables 5.4 and 5.5).

Historians have often lumped volunteers, substitutes, and draftees together when discussing allegedly high desertion levels, despite the differences in their desertion rates. However, the numbers of draftees and substitutes were significantly smaller than the number of volunteers. For the four calls in 1864, nearly 80 percent of the men raised were later-enlisting volunteers.

The relatively high desertion rates for substitutes should not be surprising. A man could serve as a substitute only if he were not eligible for the draft. That

Table 5.4: New Jersey Desertion: Late-War Replacements

Period	Category	Percent of Database	Total	Desertions	Rate (Percent)
1864–65	Volunteers	59.3	6,802	1,289	19.0
	Draftees	4.0	456	21	4.6
	Substitutes	36.7	4,213	1,575	37.4
1863	Volunteers	100	760	264	34.7
1864	Volunteers	59.5	4,091	757	18.5
	Draftees	3.0	208	14	6.7
	Substitutes	37.5	2,577	1,087	42.2
	Combined	100	6,876	1,858	27.0
1865	Volunteers	59.0	2,711	532	19.6
	Draftees	5.4	248	7	2.8
	Substitutes	35.6	1,636	488	29.8
	Combined	100	4,595	1,027	22.4

Source: HIBO Database.
Notes: See introduction, note 25. Substitute data do not include unassigned men.

Table 5.5: Pennsylvania Desertion: Late-War Replacements

Period	Category	Percent	Number	Desertions	Rate (Percent)
1863–65	Volunteers	68.7	29,563	2,670	9.0
	Draftees	17.9	7,689	911	11.8
	Substitutes	13.4	5,763	1,204	20.9
	Combined	100	43,015	4,785	11.1
1863	Volunteers	31.2	2,209	438	19.8
	Draftees	60.2	4,259	786	18.5
	Substitutes	8.5	602	108	17.9
	Combined	100	7,070	1,332	18.8
1864	Volunteers	84.4	24,884	2,088	8.4
	Draftees	6.1	1,810	68	3.8
	Substitutes	9.5	2,793	679	24.3
	Combined	100	29,487	2,835	9.6
1865	Volunteers	38.2	2,470	144	5.8
	Draftees	25.1	1,620	57	3.5
	Substitutes	36.7	2,368	417	17.6
	Combined	100	6,458	618	9.6

Source: HIBO Database.
Note: See introduction, note 25.

Table 5.6: White Volunteers, Substitutes, and Draftees Raised by 1864 Calls

Call	Substitutes	White Volunteers	Drafted	Totals
February and March	34,913	325,366	13,296	373,575[a]
	9.3%	87.1%	3.6%	
July	58,086	146,392	26,205	230,683
	25.2%	63.5%	11.4%	
December	25,011	130,620	12,566	168,197
	14.9%	77.7%	7.5%	
Totals	118,010	602,378	52,067	772,455
	15.3%	78.0%	6.7%	

Source: Compiled from OR III:5, 635–37, 639.
Notes: Reenlisting veterans and African American recruits are not included.
   [a] Includes October 1863 draft call.

meant he was either under the age of twenty-one or foreign-born (or a veteran of at least two years' service). Being foreign-born or under the age of twenty-one did not preclude a man from volunteering once the draft was in place. Thus, if a man chose to become a substitute rather than volunteer, it is fair to say that he was usually motivated by financial considerations (although there undoubtedly were cases of men who came forward as a substitute for selfless reasons, such as serving in lieu of a relative or friend with family obligations). The combination of economic motivation and the fact that foreign-born men were more likely to desert than native-born men supports the relatively high desertion rate. Substitutes would also seem to have been more likely to desert en route.[27]

The likelihood that substitutes would desert in large numbers after receiving their bounty money was recognized early on. The adjutant general, Lorenzo Thomas, complained to Stanton in November 1862 that the substitute system "has become a real evil. . . . After receiving their money they desert, and thus but few men are added to the old regiments. It is producing very great demoralization."[28] Substitutes deserted in high numbers even though they were often closely guarded.[29] The Enrollment Branch of the Provost Marshal General's Bureau was surprisingly even-handed in its treatment of substitutes in its end-of-the war report. "Substitution is . . . doubtless the most practical and equitable way of avoiding personal service by those who, from inclination, business interests, or other causes, were unwilling to give personal response to the calls of the Government. The services rendered by a large number of substitutes have been valuable, while in some instances the reverse of this is true."[30] The safety-valve role of substitution in mitigating the impact of the draft on the local economy and society may have underlain the thinking.

The relatively low desertion rate for draftees understates the true picture. Desertion under the military code can occur only after the man has been mustered into the service. Desertion under the draft should be viewed more broadly to include men who avoided enrollment in the system to begin with and men who failed to report for examination after their names were drawn. Roughly one hundred thousand men fled their local communities to avoid enrollment in the system.[31] This represented about 2.5 percent of the white male military age population of the Union. More significantly, on average roughly 20 percent of the men called failed to report for each of the four drafts—a total of 160,000 men (see Table 5.3). As a result, the desertion rate for men subject to the draft arguably starts out at 20 percent-plus before considering desertion by draftees actually mustered into military service. On that basis, the overall desertion rate for draftees would approach the desertion rate for substitutes.

Drafted men would seem to be prime candidates for desertion because they had been brought into the service against their will. However, after being mustered in, drafted men generally deserted less frequently than substitutes and even later-enlisting volunteers in some regiments. Ties with their local community may have limited any propensity of draftees to desert. A man could be drafted only if the authorities had enrolled him. He probably had some permanence in the local community if the authorities had found him. The transient men who often appeared to claim a high local bounty or substitute fee as volunteers may have had such weak ties to whatever local community that they were last from that they would have been missed by (or could have avoided) the enrollment net. In his postwar report on recruiting, Fry noted that "the large floating population of the country, and the disposition and right of our people to go from place to place without let or hindrance, rendered it exceedingly difficult to perfect [the draft enrollment]."[32] In an April 1865 letter to Stanton, a committee of New York City officials noted that of the men drafted in New York City, "75 per cent. of the number are composed of mechanics and middling classes of trades people, whose personal and most continuous efforts are required to supply the wants of their large families and to protect and make lucrative their business." Strong ties to the local community that received credit for the soldier generally indicated a lower tendency to desert.[33]

Differences among Old Regiments

Because much can potentially be learned about desertion from the differences among regiments, the desertion rates of large cohorts of volunteers, draftees, and substitutes for individual old Pennsylvania and New Jersey regiments are also considered.

There is wide variation in the desertion rates among the old Pennsylvania regiments studied for later-enlisting volunteers—from 1.5 percent in the 105th Pennsylvania and the 145th Pennsylvania to nearly 75 percent in the Fifty-Seventh Pennsylvania. The low end is more typical—two-thirds of the cohorts are below the 7 percent average. There are also wide variations in the desertion rates for substitutes and draftees in old regiments from both states.[34] The wide variations indicate that regiment-specific factors were present, most likely the failure of unit cohesion at the company and regiment levels.

The Late-War New Regiments

The average desertion rate for the thirty-four late-war new regiments in the Army of the Potomac was only 9.6 percent (not including the Not Taken Up Factor).[35] Looking beneath the average, there were substantial differences among the

Table 5.7: Desertion Rates: Late-War New Regiments

	Rate (%)		Rate (%)
31st ME	7.1	60th OH	0
32nd ME	4.3	183rd PA	19.9
56th MA	15.1	184th PA	3.2
57th MA	10.9	187th PA	10.6
58th MA	10.5	198th PA	6.1
59th MA	17.9	200th PA	10.9
61st MA	1.0	205th PA	7.7
18th NH	7.7	207th PA	5.2
39th NJ	5.6	208th PA	9.2
40th NJ	32.5	209th PA	11.8
179th NY	13.7	210th PA	31.9
184th NY	1.0	211th PA	1.2
185th NY	4.6	17th VT	19.8
186th NY	6.5	36th WI	2.2
187th NY	9.9	37th WI	2.4
188th NY	11.1	38th WI	5.8
189th NY	0.9		
193rd NY	29.3		
		Organized	
	All regiments	Spring 1864 (15)	Fall 1864 (18)
Average	9.6	9.6	9.6

Source: HIBO Database. For a fuller discussion, see Methodology–Desertion in Late War Regiments, at latewarunionsoldiers.org.

Note: The 0 percent desertion for the Sixtieth Ohio seems unlikely. The 193rd New York was organized in March and April 1865 and is not included in the computed averages.

Table 5.8: Desertion Rates: Late-War Pennsylvania Regiments

Unit	Total	Within 30 Days	After Arriving in the Field
Dec. 1863–May 1864			
183rd	21.0	9.6	11.4
184th	3.7	1.5	2.2
187th	10.6	3.2	7.4
Regimental average	11.8	4.8	7.0
Vol. cohorts in old regiments, Jan. to June 1864	6.8		
198th	6.2	5.9	0.3
200th	11.0	11.0	0
205th	7.7	7.5	0.2
207th	5.2	5.1	0.1
208th	9.2	8.5	0.7
209th	11.9	10.9	1.0
210th	34.0	33.6	0.4
211th	1.2	0.9	0.3
Regimental average	10.8	10.4	0.4
Vol. cohorts in old regiments, July to Dec. 1864	8.2		
Overall average	11.1	8.9	2.2

Source: Compiled from HIBO Database.

Note: Desertions within thirty days were significantly higher for the new regiments (average 93.6 percent of all desertions) than for the "old" regiments (average 38.8 percent of all desertions).

desertion rates in the late-war new regiments (which were generally comprised almost exclusively of later-enlisting volunteers) both among states and within states. The differences should not be surprising. As Costa and Kahn have demonstrated, a wide range of factors influenced desertion and they could hardly be expected to come together in the same way in every regiment. For example, differences in the degree of unit cohesion are likely.

The desertion rate for the late-war new Pennsylvania regiments averaged 11 percent. As previously discussed, a soldier who deserted within thirty days of enrollment probably was a bounty jumper. For the eight Pennsylvania regiments organized in the fall of 1864, roughly 10 percent of the recruits probably were bounty jumpers. What is striking is that after the bounty jumpers left, desertion in these regiments largely ended.

*Late-War New Regiments Compared to the Original Complement
of Old Regiments*

The desertion rate for the original complement of the old Pennsylvania regiments and the desertion rate for the late-war Pennsylvania regiments were similar (without consideration of the Not Taken Up Factor)—10.0 percent on average for the old regiments and 11.1 percent desertion rate for the late-war new regiments. However, the timing of desertion was different between old regiments and late-war new regiments. As posited above, a later-enlisting volunteer who deserted within thirty days of enlisting probably was a bounty jumper. Bounties were not a significant factor in 1861 and were lower in 1862 than in 1864 and 1865. For men enlisting in 1861 and 1862 in the seventy-one Pennsylvania regiments selected, the average percentage of men deserting within thirty days was only 1.5 percent, with the average being slightly lower for the regiments organized in 1861 and higher for the 1862 regiments. Desertion within thirty days by these men could be attributable to second thoughts about volunteering. However, 8.5 percent deserted after thirty days, making desertion an ongoing problem with the 1861 and 1862 volunteers for the old Pennsylvania regiments.[36]

For the late-war Pennsylvania regiments in the Army of the Potomac, the percentage deserting within thirty days was much higher—8.9 percent. (If 1 percent is subtracted to represent other causes of early desertion based on the experience with the soldiers joining in 1861 and 1862, roughly 8 percent could be viewed as likely bounty jumpers.) At the same time, only 2.2 percent deserted after thirty days, making desertion much less of an ongoing problem in the late-war new Pennsylvania regiments.

One-Year Term versus Three-Year Term

For Pennsylvania volunteers in the Army of the Potomac under the July 1864 call, there was no real difference in desertion rates between the one-year term and the three-year term with its higher bounties. For the December 1864 call, the three-year volunteers also deserted in the 10 percent range, but only 5 percent of the one-year volunteers deserted (Table 5.9).

The Pennsylvania volunteers apparently were more interested in a short term of service than the money—90 percent enlisted for only one year under the July 1864 call and 80 percent enlisted for only one year under the December 1864 call.[37] Considering the financial motivation of substitutes presumed by historians, it is surprising that the percentage of Pennsylvania substitutes who opted for a three-year enlistment was not higher. Only about 60 percent of the substitutes under the July 1864 call opted for three years. Moreover, nearly three-quarters of the substitutes under the December 1864 call actually chose the one-year term

Table 5.9: Desertion: Pennsylvania One-Year and Three-Year Volunteers and Substitutes

Muster-in from July 19, 1864, to December 18, 1864

	Volunteers	Substitutes
One-year term (%)	91.6	42.1
Deserted	10.9	10.2
Three-year term (%)	8.2	57.3
Deserted	11.2	28.9

Muster-in from December 19, 1864, to April 13, 1865

	Volunteers	Substitutes
One-year term (%)	81.8	72.2
Deserted	4.6	12.3
Three-year term (%)	17.8	27.5
Deserted	10.9	36.3

Sources: HIBO Database.
Notes: See introduction, note 25. Totals for one-year and three-year enlistment terms do not add to 100 percent because of other small categories.

with its lower bounty payment. This suggests that substitutes may have been less interested in maximizing financial gain than previously thought. And even more surprising still is that only 10 percent of the one-year substitutes from the July 1864 call and 12 percent from the December 1864 call deserted. This suggests that the one-year substitutes generally intended to serve their full term rather than being bounty jumpers. The Pennsylvania substitutes who chose a three-year term performed more in line with traditional expectations—29 percent and 36 percent from the July 1864 and December 1864 calls, respectively, deserted.

Causes of Desertion

In the leading study of desertion during the Civil War, Ella Lonn grouped the causes of desertion from the Union army into nine "heads": (1) opposition to "coercion of the South by military force"; (2) the "hardships of war," both in terms of shortages of food and equipment and of exposure to the extremes of weather; (3) extended delays in pay and the consequent inability of the soldiers to support their families at home; (4) "an utter absence of a realization of the obligation incurred by enlistment"; (5) lax discipline, particularly with respect to sick leave and furloughs; (6) "war weariness and discouragement" with the lack of progress toward Confederate defeat; (7) "Probably the most serious cause producing desertion was the caliber of the recruits, noticeably inferior after 1862.

Reinforcements were constantly being sent to the armies, but they were for the most part mercenaries, immoral and cowardly"; (8) the "large and numerous bounties given to volunteers proved undoubtedly an inducement to desert for the purpose of reenlisting, or to enlist when the recruit knew that he had no intention of remaining in the field"; and (9) "the cowardly or traitorous encouragement of desertion by civilians," which could take forms as different as inciting the draft riots and encouraging soldiers not to return from furlough.[38] Apart from describing the inferior caliber of recruits after 1862 as probably the most serious cause of desertion, Lonn did not attempt to assess the relative percentages of desertion caused by the individual "heads." The lack of computer technology (and possibly the lack of the necessary statistical methodology as well) would have prevented such an effort.

With respect to the "noticeably inferior" quality of recruits after 1862, Lonn specifically referred to substitutes and noted that "they were pretty generally felt to be worthless material." Lonn also included foreign-born men as part of "the inferior quality of recruits after 1862."[39] Lonn's distinction between substitution and high bounties as causes of desertion is important because the problem of substitution is independent of bounties. As long as a person was permitted to hire a substitute, market forces would have created a premium for the substitute even if no bounties at all were offered to volunteers.

Fry discussed the causes of desertion in multiple sections of his end-of-the-war report in 1866. Discussing desertion as a component of "Casualties in the military forces" (part VI), Fry pointed to three factors: (1) "the crime of desertion is especially characteristic of troops from large cities"; (2) "desertion is a crime of foreign rather than native birth"; and (3) "in general, those States which gave the highest local bounties are marked by the largest proportion of deserters." Reflecting the first two factors, Fry further noted that "In general, the manufacturing States . . . rank high in the column of desertion."[40] Fry was certainly a severe critic of the bounty system as implemented by the state and local governments, but the foregoing observations make it clear that he, like Lonn, did not believe that bounties were necessarily the primary cause of desertion.

With respect to Fry's conclusion that "In general, those States which gave the highest local bounties are marked by the largest proportion of deserters," the Eastern States generally had higher desertion ratios than the Western States and did pay higher bounties than the Western States. However, the Western States had much higher percentages of farmers in their workforces and farmers were the least likely occupation to desert. Moreover, the correlation between high bounties and high desertion rates is less clear among the Eastern States. Delaware had the highest desertion rate but offered the lowest state and local bounties. (The high desertion rate in Delaware might be explained by the "Southern sympathies" in parts of Delaware.) Maine had the lowest desertion rate, but over the course of the war, offered the third highest state and local bounties. Massachusetts offered the highest state and local bounties over the course of the war but had the third lowest desertion rate among the Eastern States.[41]

Considering this chapter's heavy reliance on data from Pennsylvania and New Jersey, the desertion rates in Pennsylvania and New Jersey warrant further discussion. Over the course of the war, the Pennsylvania infantry regiments in the Army of the Potomac had a much lower desertion rate than the New Jersey regiments—11 percent versus 20 percent (Table 5.10).

Bounties were in fact higher in New Jersey than in Pennsylvania, but the answer is not that simple. The desertion rate for volunteers in New Jersey was already somewhat higher than in Pennsylvania in 1861 when there were no bounties of significance. In 1862, New Jersey was still somewhat higher (see Table 5.2). That suggests that factors other than bounties should also be considered. Costa and Kahn determined that farmers were less likely to desert than laborers. New Jersey had about one-third fewer farmers in its work force than Pennsylvania—14 percent versus 20 percent. That would suggest a higher desertion rate for New Jersey apparently unrelated to bounties.[42] Costa and Kahn also determined that foreign-born men in general were more likely to desert than native-born men in general. The percentage of foreign-born males in 1860 was greater in New Jersey than in Pennsylvania—24 percent versus 16 percent. That would also suggest a higher desertion rate for New Jersey. These demographic factors would account for part of the greater desertion rates for New Jersey later-enlisting volunteers and substitutes.[43]

There may also have been a political dimension. Lincoln carried Pennsylvania with 52 percent of the popular vote but received only 47 percent of the popular vote in New Jersey.[44] That also suggests a higher desertion rate for New Jersey. Local governments in New Jersey also seem to have been more concerned about limiting the impact of the draft on their communities than local governments in Pennsylvania. In 1864, New Jersey relied much more heavily on substitutes than Pennsylvania did—37 percent versus 10 percent (see Table 5.10). That would result in a higher desertion rate for New Jersey. Thus, there are factors in addition to local bounties that may have led to the higher desertion rate in New Jersey.[45]

There were also significant differences in the desertion rates among regiments from the same state. For example, the late-war Thirty-Ninth New Jersey and the Fortieth New Jersey were both recruited around the same time but had significantly different desertion rates—nearly 30 percent for the Fortieth New Jersey, but only 5 percent for the Thirty-Ninth New Jersey.[46] Differences in local bounties is a natural

Table 5.10: Recruitment Categories and Desertion: Pennsylvania and New Jersey

Period	Category	Pennsylvania		New Jersey	
		Recruits	Desertion	Recruits	Desertion
		% sample	%	% sample	%
1861–65	Volunteers	87.6	10.2	82.5	15.1
	Draftees	7.1	11.8	1.7	4.6
	Substitutes	5.3	20.9	15.8	37.4
	Combined	100	10.9	100	20.1
1861	Volunteers	100	9.9	100	11.5
1862	Volunteers	100	12.4	100	13.9
1863	Volunteers	31.2	19.8	100	34.7
	Draftees	60.2	18.5	–	
	Substitutes	8.5	17.9	–	
	Combined	100	18.8	100	
1864	Volunteers	84.4	8.4	59.5	18.5
	Draftees	6.1	3.8	3.0	6.7
	Substitutes	9.5	24.3	37.5	42.2
	Combined	100	9.6	100	27.0
1865	Volunteers	38.2	5.8	59.0	19.6
	Draftees	25.1	3.5	5.4	2.8
	Substitutes	36.7	17.6	35.6	29.8

Source: HIBO Database.
Note: See introduction, note 25.

first consideration. The bounties paid to the Fortieth New Jersey were claimed to be the highest in the state in February 1865.[47] However, the bounties offered to the volunteers for Thirty-Ninth New Jersey were also substantial. The Newark men in the Thirty-Ninth New Jersey received a $500 bounty from Essex County and $100 from the city.[48] Still, there was one bounty-related difference. All of the men in the Thirty-Ninth New Jersey enlisted for only one year, which indicates less of a concern for financial gain. In contrast, nearly 30 percent of the men in the Fortieth New Jersey enlisted for three years—and the significantly higher bounty. Nearly half of the three-year volunteers in the Fortieth New Jersey deserted compared to the nearly 30 percent rate for the regiment as a whole.[49]

The primary reason for the Thirty-Ninth New Jersey's lower desertion rate seems to be the regiment's implementation of strict discipline. The Thirty-Ninth New Jersey's initial commander, Lieutenant Colonel Close, who had served as a major in the Second New Jersey, planned on "inaugurating strict military discipline, holding drills & c." His successor, Colonel Wildrick, a West Point graduate who had been serving in the regular army in California, focused on preventing desertion when he took command while the Thirty-Ninth New Jersey was still in camp.[50]

Better cohesion as a regiment is also a likely explanation. Like many late-war new regiments, the Thirty-Ninth New Jersey was sent to the front in detachments, but they were closely spaced. As a result, the Thirty-Ninth New Jersey operated in the field as a full regiment almost from the outset. That would have provided the opportunity to build regimental cohesion. The Thirty-Ninth New Jersey performed well as the lead regiment in the Ninth Corps' attack at Fort Mahone on April 2, 1865.[51] Thus, the experience of the Thirty-Ninth New Jersey indicates that the potential impact of high bounties on desertion could be successfully managed.

In contrast, the Fortieth New Jersey was sent to the front one company at a time over a five-month period. The first five companies joined the Fourth New Jersey when they each arrived in Virginia. The Fortieth New Jersey did not operate as a separate command until the sixth company arrived in mid-February. Each company also received new recruits in March. That undoubtedly impaired development of regimental cohesion.[52]

The Fortieth New Jersey lost nearly two hundred men to desertion from camp and en route to the front.[53] The numerous desertions before the Fortieth New Jersey even reached the field apparently had already given it a bad reputation. At the end of February 1865, a soldier noted that the Fortieth New Jersey had long been "talked of as a failure," but he was happy to report that it was then in a flourishing condition "after all its trouble and trials."[54] Assuming that that were true, there still would have been legitimate concerns about the Fortieth New Jersey's potential performance in battle. As discussed in chapter 1, historian A. Wilson Greene has criticized the Fortieth New Jersey's performance in the April 2, 1865, assault.[55]

Care must be taken when trying to generalize about desertion because it was not a uniform phenomenon. Not only were there differences among foreign-born men and native-born men as Fry and Lonn noted and Costa and Kahn found, but there were also differences among states; differences among occupations; differences among drafted men, substitutes, and volunteers; differences among regiments; and even differences among the ten companies comprising a particular infantry regiment.[56]

Accordingly, high desertion rates require more explanation than just state and local bounties. Indeed, high bounties and substitutes were not the only causes of desertion that Lonn identified that impacted the Army of the Potomac in 1864. All nine causes did. Arguably some of the causes were more intense in 1864 than earlier in the war—notably "War weariness and discouragement" with the lack of progress toward Confederate defeat. The importance of the other causes is underscored by the fact that the Union soldiers deserting in 1864 and 1865 were not just the late-war replacements. Some of the deserters in 1864 and 1865 had enlisted in 1861 and 1862.[57] Nonetheless, as a general proposition, increasing bounties probably did increase desertion over the course of the war. While there are exceptions and qualifications as discussed in this chapter, desertion rates generally were higher in the states with higher bounties.

The real challenge is answering the question "by how much" did higher bounties increase desertion compared to other factors. The substantial differences in desertion rates among late-war new regiments from the same state, as well as among old Pennsylvania regiments with large numbers of late-war replacements, suggest that regiment-specific factors played a significant role.[58] Failure of unit cohesion at the regimental level probably was a significant cause of high desertion rates. Unfortunately, the statistical techniques necessary to identify the relative impact of high bounties and the other factors are beyond the resources of this project.[59]

CHAPTER 6

Late-War Union Soldiers in Battle

The contention that the late-war replacements made poor soldiers has multiple facets. The high rate of desertion discussed in the previous chapter is one facet. Avoiding combat and leaving the risk of death and injury to the veterans is another. When the late-war replacements did engage in combat, they supposedly fought poorly. And they allegedly adversely impacted the veterans' ability to fight, "wrecking" the Second Corps at the Battle of Second Reams's Station. Each of these facets of the poor soldier contention must be tested by the facts.

Historians have charged the late-war replacements with "skulking" and "shirking" to avoid combat, while praising the veterans from 1861 and 1862 for carrying the burden. James McPherson has counseled that "The best way to tell who fought is to look at casualty figures. The fighting regiments were those with the highest casualties; the fighting soldiers were those most likely to get killed." The casualty numbers for Pennsylvania soldiers in the Army of the Potomac suggest that the later-enlisting volunteers were as much "fighting soldiers" as the veterans from 1861 and 1862. The later-enlisting volunteers from Pennsylvania died in combat with roughly the same frequency as the volunteers from 1861 and 1862 when their shorter time in the field is factored in. The casualty numbers also suggest that Pennsylvania substitutes and conscripts, who represented less than 20 percent of the late-war replacements, did not engage in combat as actively as both the later-enlisting volunteers and the volunteers from 1861 and 1862. This is by no means conclusive. More refined analysis and broader data would be necessary to resolve the issue, but Table 6.1 indicates that an allegation that later-enlisting volunteers shirked combat requires more than anecdotal support.[1]

Table 6.1: Battle Deaths: Pennsylvania Soldiers in the Army of the Potomac

	Soldiers	Killed/MW	
Volunteers			
10/63–5/64	13,597	1,044	7.7%
6/64–12/64	12,022	335	2.8%
1861	41,496	3,977	9.6%
1862	23,761	2,169	9.1%
Substitutes			
10/63–5/64	223	10	4.5%
6/64–12/64	2,746	55	2.0%
Draftees			
10/63–5/64	368	23	6.3%
6/64–12/64	1,687	36	2.1%

Source: Compiled from HIBO Database. See also Methodology–HIBO Database, latewarunionsoldiers.org.

Note: Data for draftees and substitutes for 10/63 to 5/64 may be too sparse for meaningful analysis. Data for New Jersey volunteers suggest the same conclusion. Data for New Jersey substitutes and draftees may be too sparse for meaningful analysis.

The late-war new regiments in the Army of the Potomac proved to be "fighting regiments." Public recognition as a "fighting regiment" was a great honor during and after the war.[2] As Lesley Gordon writes, "The higher the casualties, the more proudly heroic the regiment's claim."[3] In 1888, William F. Fox published his list of "Three Hundred Fighting Regiments" as part of his compilation of Union casualty data. Fox's list sanctioned bragging rights for veterans of the three hundred regiments and canonized the regiments for future generations.[4] Michael Musick has noted that "it became a matter of intense pride to say that one had served in one of 'Fox's 300 Fighting Regiments.'"[5] Debates occurred in the *National Tribune* about the strong "fighting quality" of regiments that did not make the three hundred.[6] A veteran of the Fifty-Seventh Massachusetts recalculated the loss percentage for the regiment to show that the Fifty-Seventh Massachusetts should have been tied for second rather than in third place.[7] Authors of regimental histories often cite inclusion in Fox's Three Hundred in their introduction as justification that the regiment warrants the attention.[8]

Fox's standard—one hundred thirty or more men killed or mortally wounded in battle—was objective but worked against inclusion of the late-war new regiments because they had served in the field for only a year or less, while older regiments had incurred casualties over three to four years. Nonetheless, seven of the late-war new regiments in the Army of the Potomac qualified for Fox's Three

Hundred—the Thirty-First Maine, the Fifty-Sixth Massachusetts, the Fifty-Seventh Massachusetts, the Fifty-Eighth Massachusetts, the Thirty-Sixth Wisconsin, the Thirty-Seventh Wisconsin, and the Seventeenth Vermont.[9] Fox noted that "although the Seventeenth [Vermont] was in service only one year, yet it saw more fighting and sustained greater losses in action than three-fourths of the regiments in the whole Union Army," and that the Fifty-Seventh Massachusetts "was in active service less than a year, and yet its percentage of killed was one of the highest of the war."[10] Eight other late-war new regiments in the Army of the Potomac were more than halfway toward qualifying for Fox's Three Hundred by the end of the war, even though they were in the field for only a year or less and engaged in fewer battles. The Sixtieth Ohio and the 184th Pennsylvania, which both served in the Overland Campaign, each had 113 combat deaths. Table 6.2 demonstrates that most of the late-war new regiments in the Army of the Potomac saw a good deal of combat while they were in the field.

While casualty numbers may be useful in evaluating whether the late-war replacements and late-war new regiments tried to avoid fighting, they are not useful in determining whether the late-war replacements and late-war new regiments in the Army of the Potomac fought well, as even Fox would acknowledge.[11] Historians have approached this question by using variants of the theme of "effectiveness." There are two dimensions to assessing the effectiveness of a military unit: (1) performance (whether the unit accomplished its mission) and (2) capability (the factors that enabled the unit to accomplish its mission).[12] The two are quite distinct. War makes for harsh grading. If a unit fails to accomplish its mission, the operation cannot be deemed a success no matter how well it was performed by objective standards. However, even the most capable units may fail to accomplish their mission on occasion. Extenuating circumstances, such as particularly strong enemy positions or unusually harsh weather conditions, may explain a failure to achieve the assigned mission. Or the mission may have been extremely difficult to achieve for other reasons.[13] When a unit succeeds in accomplishing its mission, particular capabilities may stand out that increase the confidence of senior commanders. For example, the unit's officers may have departed from the battle plan to take advantage of an unexpected opportunity arising during the battle.

Historians writing on the effectiveness of military units have generally focused their study on the capability side of combat effectiveness rather than the performance side. They generally begin by selecting for study a unit with an acknowledged record of success and then concentrate on assessing the reasons for that success. For example, Edward J. Coss selected Wellington's army, which achieved "a series of unbroken battlefield victories in Spain and Portugal." Similarly, John

Table 6.2: Battle Casualties: Late-War New Regiments Not in Fox's Three Hundred

	Killed/MW	Wounded		Killed/MW	Wounded
32nd ME	85	112	60th Ohio	113	129
59th MA	90	290	183rd PA	96	82
61st MA	6	29	184th PA	113	104
18th NH	5	9	187th PA	66	64
39th NJ	32	24	198th PA	73	191
40th NJ	2	6	200th PA	30	141
179th NY	68	88	205th PA	40	107
184th NY	11	38	207th PA	54	138
185th NY	56	199	208th PA	21	79
186th NY	48	59	209th PA	19	90
187th NY	15	51	210th PA	40	74
188th NY	37	94	211th PA	44	111
189th NY	9	28	38th WI	57	171
193rd NY	0	0			

Sources: Fox, *Regimental Losses,* passim (for "Killed/MW"); compiled from HIBO Database (for "Wounded"). See also Methodology–HIBO Database, latewarunionsoldiers.org; Phisterer, *New York in the War of the Rebellion,* passim.
Note: Phisterer shows significantly higher numbers of wounded for the 179th New York (182) and the 186th New York (126). Phisterer, *New York in the War of the Rebellion,* 4029, 4067. This illustrates the difficulty in compiling casualty data at the regimental level. Regimental casualty data may be compiled from the individual soldier up to the regimental total, as with the HIBO database, or from contemporary regimental casualty reports by battle, which provided only the total number. Because of differences in the accuracy with which individual regiments maintained their personnel records, these two approaches will not necessarily yield the same number.

Lynn chose the Army of Revolutionary France from 1791 to 1794.[14] Successful performance was taken as the starting point for assessing the reasons for their success. In contrast, for this project determining whether the late-war new regiments and the late-war replacements accomplished their missions in battle must be the first step in assessing their effectiveness because historians and many in the military have accused them of being poor soldiers. More generally, a focus on whether the mission was accomplished is necessary to assure the completeness of the assessment of capability. If a unit that scores well on quality repeatedly failed to accomplish its mission with no extenuating circumstances, something is probably missing in the capability analysis and the historian must dig deeper.[15]

As to capability, John Lynn provided the leading model for assessing the factors that enable a unit to fight effectively in *Bayonets of the Republic,* written in 1984. There are two "systems" comprising Lynn's model of "combat effectiveness," which he defines as "the quality of performance in combat."[16] The Motivational System examines "the motive force that drives [an army]." The Military System comprises the mechanisms of operation, including such factors as tactics, training, and weapons.[17]

Civil War historians have generally focused on motivation rather than the military system.[18] Historians generally follow Steven Westbrook's model that three different forces can generate a soldier's motivation—coercion (the ability to inflict physical punishment for disobedience), remuneration (often but not necessarily money), and normative (the values of the larger group that the soldier identifies with).[19] Lynn further breaks down motivation into three chronological phases: (1) "Initial Motivation," explained by McPherson as "the reasons why men enlisted"; (2) "Sustaining Motivation," "the factors that kept them in the army and kept the army in existence over time"; and (3) "Combat Motivation," "what nerved them to face extreme danger in battle."[20] The critique by Civil War historians that the late-war volunteers and substitutes were motivated by money expressly addresses the first phase using the remunerative force. The critique also implicitly addresses the second and third phases. The bounty presumably had little positive motivating impact in these phases because the bulk of the bounty was paid in advance.[21] A man motivated by money would likely desert or at least do the minimum possible duty while in service. And a man who had been motivated by money to enlist would do what he could to avoid combat. McPherson described the late-war replacements as "soldiers [who] wanted nothing so much as to go home or at least to stay as far away from combat as possible."[22] Civil War historians have not considered the possibility that the lost remunerative motivation could be replaced during the second and third phases by positive normative motivation, such as the development of unit cohesion.[23] As Lynn concluded, "Within soldier groups, cohesiveness seems to be a natural, even unavoidable, response to the conditions of army life. Shared labor, shared discomfort, and shared danger unite men when it is clear they can achieve their goals better through association."[24] For example, payment of high bounties did not ultimately impede development of the fighting capability of the six late-war new regiments in Hartranft's Division and the two late-war new regiments in Chamberlain's Brigade because normative motivating force prevailed in those regiments.

In Lynn's model, morale and primary group cohesion are the most important bases of motivation. McPherson states that a Civil War soldier's primary group "may have been as large as his company but was likely to be smaller: his messmates, the men from his town or township with whom he enlisted, the squad commanded by his sergeant." The Civil War soldier's "regiment, brigade, army, country, even community and family as long as he remained in the army" were all secondary.[25] Primary group cohesion provides important insight as a building block, but Union soldiers were not deployed in groups of messmates or men from the same hometown. Effectiveness in combat depends on the extension of strong cohesion, which John Guilmartin defines as "the social force that makes the difference between a combat-effective unit and a mob," into the higher units in which soldiers were deployed—notably the regiment for Union soldiers. If cohesion does not extend beyond the primary group, conduct antithetical to combat effectiveness may develop, such as stopping to help a wounded comrade to the rear or desertion in small groups.[26]

Unit cohesion cannot be assessed quantitatively. It is best assessed by observation and by talking with unit personnel at all levels.[27] Personal observation and interviews are not possible one hundred and fifty years after the fact. The historian must search for contemporary observations and indicia of unit cohesion.[28] For example, in an old Union regiment from 1861, a high rate of reenlistment would indicate strong unit cohesion—an individual decision to remain with the group rather than returning home.[29] The veteran furlough would have reinforced regimental cohesion as the local community celebrated the soldiers' homecoming as a group before they dispersed to visit their families and friends. Designation as a veteran regiment also would have reinforced cohesion at the regimental level. The degree of cohesion at the regimental level may also be reflected in a soldier's letters to his family and friends. Did the soldier write only about the men from his hometown and his messmates? Or did he also write about the activities of his regiment? The familiarity of the language used by the soldier may also reflect the degree of cohesion. If the soldier recounted the activities of "the 185th New York" or "the regiment," that suggests a low level of identification with his regiment. The use of "we" to recount the actions of the regiment indicates a somewhat higher level. The use of the familiar phrase "the boys" as opposed to "the men" or "the regiment" to recount the actions of the regiment indicates very strong cohesion at the regimental level.[30] The progression of training may also promote cohesion at higher levels. Bell Wiley noted that as a unit advanced in its training, it emphasized brigade and battalion drill over squad and company drill.[31]

The introduction of replacement troops into a veteran unit creates a difficult challenge for primary group cohesion and unit cohesion in general.[32] The replacements may make up for casualties on paper, but if the replacements are not accepted by the veterans, the cohesion and fighting effectiveness of the unit will suffer. The tension between battle-hardened veterans and newly arriving raw recruits is a reality of warfare. Generally, that tension dissipates as the recruits prove themselves in battle. The old Pennsylvania regiments with a majority of late-war replacements in their ranks faced this challenge in 1863 and 1864. The late-war new regiments generally did not have to face this challenge because they received few if any replacements.[33] The increase in bounties over time potentially introduced an additional dimension of tension.[34] In fact, the high bounties may not have been as much of a threat to unit cohesion as might at first appear. The later-enlisting volunteers and substitutes entering old Union regiments from the end of 1863 through the end of the war did receive much higher bounties than those offered to the veterans in 1861. However, the reenlistment program at the end of 1863 and the beginning of 1864 offered the veterans from 1861 the same bounties as those offered to the later-enlisting volunteers and substitutes joining the army at that time. Indeed, the federal government offered the reenlisting veterans an additional $100 and special chevrons in recognition of their service. The reenlisting veterans were also often personally involved in recruiting later-enlisting volunteers from their hometowns during their veteran furlough. George Uhler described recruiting during the Ninety-Third Pennsylvania's veteran furlough in his 1898 regimental history: "The liberal bounties, the jollity and roystering of 'the boys' and great stories of the good times in the field over-persuaded many, and enlistment papers by the score were signed." The veterans may have had some harsh words for the late-war replacements, but they also recognized that their arrival restored the fighting force of the regiment before the spring campaign. Oliver Norton wrote to his friends in August 1863 that the replacements "are all armed and equipped now and doing full duty and the Eighty-three [Pennsylvania] looks something like a regiment again."[35] Thus, the reenlisting veterans from 1861 may have been more welcoming to the later-enlisting volunteers than would be expected.

The three-year regiments recruited in the summer of 1862 would seem to have faced a more difficult replacement challenge. The reenlistment program with its higher bounties was never offered to the veterans in those regiments. Thus, they never had a chance to receive the higher bounties available in 1864 and 1865. However, there does not appear to be a difference in fighting capability between the Pennsylvania three-year regiments from 1862 and the Pennsylvania three-year regiments from 1861 with roughly a majority of late-war replacements in their ranks (although the research was not deep enough to validly test the proposition). The benefit of restoring force levels in seriously depleted regiments may also have had a favorable impact on integrating late-war replacements into regiments raised in 1862. The 148th Pennsylvania, after heavy losses at Chancellorsville and Gettysburg, received four hundred late-war replacements in late 1863 and early 1864, restoring their force level. Draftee Simon Shuman wrote to a friend that "The regiment was glad to see us coming. They went to work and made us some coffee and gave us a good dinner of hard tack and meat."[36]

Lynn's model for motivation provides unquestionable insights for assessing the performance of units large and small, but his model for the military system is unnecessarily complex for assessing the performance of a much smaller unit like a regiment. The model includes factors that are not relevant at the regimental level. For example, "tactics" is an element of Lynn's military system, and Lynn concluded that the French army's "tactical system" "best explains [its] combat effectiveness." However, Union regiments were not responsible for the development of the tactical system. For a Union regiment, the relevant factors are how well they trained their soldiers in the tactical system and their experience in following it in combat.[37]

Writing shortly before Lynn, Martin van Creveld applied a much less complicated model to compare the performance of the German and American armies during World War II. He posited that "within the limits of its size, the military worth of an army equals the quantity and quality of its equipment multiplied by its fighting power." While recognizing that a successful army must have both "moral" and "material" capabilities, he focused on the former. He defined "fighting power" as the "sum total of mental qualities that make armies fight. . . . The mixture, in one combination or another, of discipline and cohesion, morale and initiative, courage and toughness, the willingness to fight and the readiness, if necessary, to die." In his view, "an ideal fighting army . . . should consist of men who are born fighters, are held in high esteem by their society, are well trained, well disciplined, and well led." He acknowledged that the German Army lost the war but concluded that it "was a superb fighting organization. In point of morale, elan, unit cohesion, and resilience, it probably had no equal among twentieth century armies."[38] Thus van Creveld's view of "fighting power" is similar to Lynn's view of "motivation."

The "military effectiveness" model developed by Allan R. Millett, Williamson Murray, and Kenneth H. Watman, which was followed by Carol Reardon in her study of the Battle of Spotsylvania, is also designed for large units but also offers insights for smaller units. They define military effectiveness as "the process by which armed forces convert resources into fighting power. A fully effective military is one that derives maximum combat power from the resources . . . available. . . . Combat power is the ability to destroy the enemy while limiting the damage he can inflict in return."[39] A focus on factors key to developing fighting power facilitates assessment of what enables regiments to achieve their missions in battle.

The concept of "readiness" is like "effectiveness," but the difference offers key insights. The US Department of Defense currently defines readiness as "the ability of military forces to fight and meet the demands of assigned missions" and uses readiness to evaluate small as well as large units. The Department of Defense approach focuses on what advances a unit's ability to fight as opposed to Lynn's less direct approach of defining combat effectiveness in terms of quality. The American military and Congress have used the term "'readiness' since at least the eighteen thirties to discuss the state of military personnel, training, equipment, and other related activities."[40] Readiness also presents the perspective before combat—the same perspective as Union commanders deciding when and how to deploy late-war new regiments or old regiments with a majority of late-war replacements.

Drawing on these resources, this project measures "regimental effectiveness" with a two-step process.[41] First, comparing performance in the field to the assigned mission, including identification of elements of success (or failure) such as rapid (or slow) deployment and extenuating circumstances, such as an unexpectedly large enemy force or bad weather. Inflicting heavy enemy casualties or capturing significant amounts of important enemy equipment, in addition to accomplishing the mission, would be an element of success. However, even if the mission were accomplished, suffering unnecessary casualties would be an element of failure. Second, assessing the following essential readiness capabilities to explain that performance:

(1) motivation (morale and unit cohesion)[42]
(2) leadership[43]
(3) training and discipline[44]
(4) experience in the field[45]
(5) actual versus authorized strength[46]
(6) supply (food, arms, and equipment)[47]
(7) demographics (occupation, nationality at birth and age)[48]

These factors are not equal in weight. Motivation and leadership are the most important by far (see page 106). These factors are also interrelated. Strong leadership can have a positive effect on morale, while weak supply capability can have a negative effect on morale. Strong motivation and strong leadership can maximize the benefit of experience in the field. Kreidberg and Henry noted that because "the War Department never developed a comprehensive training program, [w]hatever training was given in the Union Army was due to the foresight and initiative of individual officers." Assessments under these factors also are not static. Assessments can change significantly over even short periods of time, for example, with the introduction of large numbers of new recruits or the loss of a key officer.[49]

This framework is applied in detail to assess the performance of the six late-war new regiments in Hartranft's Division at Fort Stedman and of the two late-war new regiments comprising Chamberlain's Brigade in the Five Forks Campaign. It is used more generally in discussing the performance in the Overland Campaign and the Petersburg Campaign of late-war new regiments and the old Pennsylvania regiments with roughly a majority of late-war replacements in their ranks.

Regimental Effectiveness

CHAPTER 7

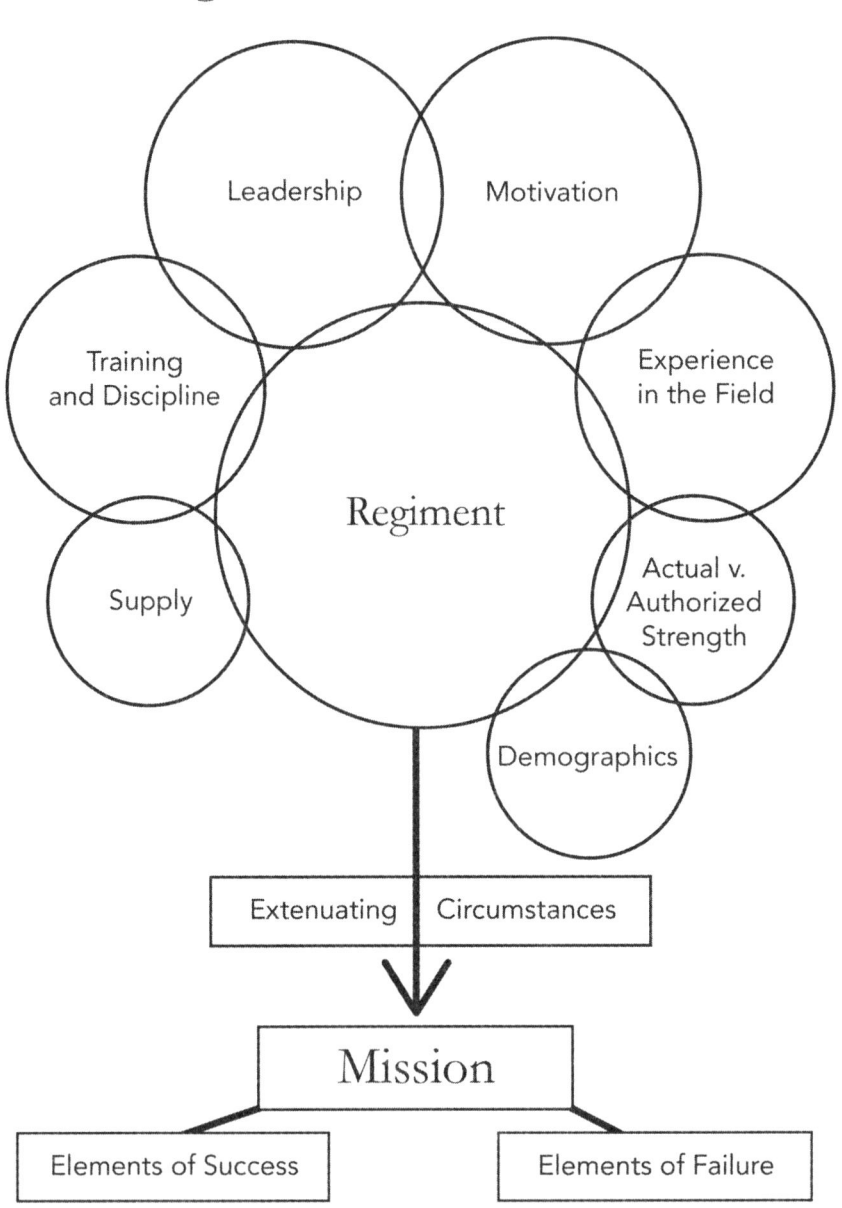

The Overland Campaign

May 4 to June 12, 1864

As noted, James McPherson has written that "While the conscription-substitute-bounty system produced three-quarters of a million new men, they did little to help with the war. This task fell mainly on the pre-bounty veterans of 1861 and 1862."[1] These numerous "new men" obviously did not contribute to the Union's progress toward victory through Gettysburg and Vicksburg in July 1863. But the Union had not yet defeated the Confederacy as the campaign season began in 1864. The late-war Union soldiers played an important role in the Overland Campaign. They not only provided much needed numbers of new troops, but they also generally fought well.

At first glance it might appear that the veterans of 1861 and 1862 constituted the overwhelming majority of the men in the Army of the Potomac at the beginning of the Overland Campaign. Two-thirds of the white regiments were from 1861 with an additional 30 percent from 1862. However, the regiments from 1861 and 1862 suffered heavy casualties from battle and disease. By late 1863 their force levels were well below their original strength. As a result of the combat losses, nearly three-quarters of these regiments from 1861 ultimately qualified for Fox's Three Hundred Fighting Regiments.[2]

To offset the tremendous losses from combat and disease, many of these regiments remained operational through the infusion of new recruits—later-enlisting volunteers, substitutes, and conscripts—in late 1863 and early 1864. A. Wilson Greene estimates that "barely half" of the nearly one hundred twenty thousand men in the Army of the Potomac and the then independent Ninth Corps were veterans as of April 30, 1864.[3] Gen. Ambrose Burnside, who commanded the Ninth Corps during the Overland Campaign and the beginning of the Petersburg Campaign, had a positive view of the late-war replacements. He noted that when the Ninth Corps returned from Tennessee, it was comprised of fewer than six thousand veterans, but then recruited eighteen thousand new men, "thus making the preponderance of raw troops very large, . . . The new infantry regiments . . . soon became as steady and reliable as the older regiments, displaying a courage which rendered them honorable associates of the veterans."[4]

In the Second Corps, three-quarters of the Irish Brigade—the Sixty-Third, Sixty-Ninth, and Eighty-Eighth New York; the Twenty-Eighth Massachusetts; and the 116th Pennsylvania—were recruits. (To be clear, *recruit* means any new soldier in the regiment, whether volunteer, substitute, or draftee.) And Hancock praised these recruits for their "great steadiness and gallantry" in the Battle of the Wilderness. After his brigade (Fourth of the Second Corps' First Division) repelled three Confederate charges by Heth's Division on May 10, 1864, Brig. Gen. John Brooke reported that the battle was "the first in which most of the men were ever in," and that the men "behaved with great gallantry."[5]

Of the sixty-one Pennsylvania infantry regiments in the Army of the Potomac at the beginning of the Overland Campaign, not quite half received one hundred or more volunteer replacements from December 1863 through April 1864. (Thirteen Pennsylvania regiments also received one hundred or more draftees or substitutes as replacements during the summer and early fall of 1863.) One fifth received three hundred or more volunteer replacements and three received more than six hundred volunteer replacements. The distribution was uneven among the Army of the Potomac's four corps. Half of the Pennsylvania regiments in the Second and Sixth Corps received one hundred or more replacements, while only a quarter of the Pennsylvania regiments in the Fifth Corps did. All five of the Pennsylvania regiments in the Ninth Corps received more than three hundred replacements.[6]

The following eighteen old regiments from Pennsylvania in the Army of the Potomac received large enough infusions of replacements that roughly half or more of their force was comprised of late-war replacements as they headed into the Overland Campaign. Morale among the veterans was generally strong as evidenced by the high reenlistment rates. These regiments generally performed well during the Overland Campaign and thereafter.[7] The late-war replacements did not "ruin" these regiments—the late-war replacements kept them going. Rare was the instance of these regiments "breaking without cause" (see Table 7.1).

By the standards of the day, there was ample time for training in drill before the Overland Campaign began for the late-war replacements from the fall of 1863 and even for many of the later-enlisting volunteers from early 1864.

Table 7.1: Old Pennsylvania Regiments with a Majority of Late-War Replacements

	Reenlisting Veterans	Late-War Replacements		Time Period
		Volunteers (V)	Draftees (D)	
11th	276 (over 3/4)	388		Spring 1864
45th	420 (all)	348		Spring 1864
48th	230 of 275	632		Spring 1864
49th	260	159	255	V: Spring 1864 D: 2nd half 1863
50th	300 (almost all)	351		Spring 1864
51st	–	442		Spring 1864
53rd	More than 3/4	619	140	V: Spring 1864 D: 2nd half 1863
57th	170 (all eligible)	458		Spring 1864
63rd	discontinued 9/64	100	203	V: Dec. 1863–Mar. 1864 D: July–Sept. 1863
82nd	half	340	213	V: Spring 1864 D: July–Sept. 1863
83rd	169	231	375	V: Spring 1864 D: 2nd half 1863
93rd	284 (3/4)	389		Spring 1864
95th	250	220		Spring 1864
100th	366	392		Spring 1864
116th	organized 9/62	580		Spring 1864
143rd	organized 10/62	69	275	V: Spring 1864 D: 2nd half 1863
145th	organized 9/62	143	198	V: Spring 1864 D: 2nd half 1863
148th	organized 9/62	120	283	V: Spring 1864 D: 2nd half 1863

Source: Compiled from HIBO Database. See also Methodology–HIBO Database, latewarunionsoldiers.org.
Notes: There are additional sources for all regiments except the 51st and 143rd Pennsylvania in Methodology–Old Pennsylvania Regiments on latewarunionsoldiers.org. There were no substitutes in these Pennsylvania regiments.

Moving from late-war replacements to late-war new regiments, the latter were barely visible in the Army of the Potomac's ranks as it crossed the Rapidan to begin the Overland Campaign. Late-war new regiments comprised only nine of the 233 infantry regiments in the Army of the Potomac at that time—the Thirty-First and Thirty-Second Maine; the Fifty-Sixth, Fifty-Seventh, Fifty-Eighth, and Fifty-Ninth Massachusetts; the Sixtieth Ohio (reorganized); the 183rd Pennsylvania; and the Seventeenth Vermont. Except for the 183rd Pennsylvania, they were all in the Ninth Corps.[8]

These nine regiments and the two additional new regiments that arrived during the Overland Campaign—the 184th Pennsylvania and the Thirty-Sixth Wisconsin—generally shared eight important characteristics that affected their capability in battle—some positive, some negative. First, their field grade and company officers generally had previously served in the army, although often in nine-month regiments or as enlisted men. Second, as high as a quarter of the enlisted men also had previously served, again often in nine-month regiments. Third, the Union army rarely assigned draftees and substitutes to new regiments—volunteers overwhelmingly predominated. Fourth, their demographics were generally consistent with the overall Union army profile. Fifth, because of the Army of Potomac's pressing need for troops, the War Department often sent new regiments to the front before they had filled the standard ten companies. As a result, they often operated as battalions, with much smaller numbers than a standard regiment. Sixth, because a colonel was not authorized to take the field until the full ten companies had been organized, late-war new regiments often initially operated in the field without their senior officer. Seventh, the Army of the Potomac often sent these regiments into battle three weeks or less after they left their home state, which limited training in drill, discipline, and live fire. Eighth, notwithstanding the heavy casualties they often incurred, new regiments received only a smattering of replacements beyond completion of their ten companies.

Strong as the Army of the Potomac had been when it crossed the Rapidan, the heavy casualties from the very beginning of the Overland Campaign quickly caused the need for even more replacements. In the middle of the campaign, Grant's chief of staff, Gen. John Rawlins, wrote that "It is of the greatest importance to get to the front every available man possible."[9] General Halleck looked everywhere throughout the Union army to find replacement troops and was able to forward fifty-five thousand more men to the Army of the Potomac between May 1 and the middle of June 1864. The late-war replacements and late-war new regiments accounted for more than a quarter of the fifty-five thousand new troops. (The largest single source of additional troops was ten old heavy artillery regiments that were converted from garrison troops to frontline infantry—sixteen thousand men and 29 percent of the total).[10]

Halleck wrote Grant that he was unaware of the casualties suffered by the Army of the Potomac, but "presume[d] that these re-enforcements will make that army as strong as at the beginning of the campaign."[11] They did not. Disease as well as battle had an impact. By June 30, which included the beginning of the Petersburg Campaign, the force levels for the Second, Fifth, and Sixth Corps were down by as much as 40 percent (although the Ninth Corps was down by only 6 percent; see Table 7.2). Grant must have been quite concerned by Halleck's statement that

Table 7.2: Army of the Potomac Force Levels (Present for Duty)

	April 30, 1864	June 30, 1864
Second Corps	28,675	17,201 (-40%)
Fifth Corps	26,007	17,947 (-31%)
Sixth Corps	24,048	18,311 (-24%)
Ninth Corps	17,008	16,014 (-6%)

Sources: For April 30, 1864: OR 33, 1036; OR 36:1, 198. For June 30, 1864: OR 40:2, 542.

Notes: For April 30, 1864, Ninth Corps numbers are staff and infantry only. OR 33, 1045. The "starting" number for the Ninth Corps as of this date may be underinclusive.

"Nearly all our resources for supplying the losses of our armies in the field are now exhausted." However, Lee's manpower situation was far more dire.[12]

However, the increase in the Army of the Potomac's numbers provided by the late-war replacements leading up to the Overland Campaign and as the campaign progressed would have been immaterial if the late-war replacements had proven to be poor soldiers. To test how well the late-war replacements fought, this project created a sample consisting of the late-war new regiments in the Army of the Potomac and the old Pennsylvania regiments with roughly a majority of late-war replacements in their ranks at the beginning of the Overland Campaign (see Table 7.1). For each regiment, comments on their performance in battle in the after-action reports of officers in the Army of the Potomac were compiled. These comments were generally taken at face value. Comments by several leading historians were also considered. For the late-war new regiments, a discussion of their formation is included to provide insight into their capability in the field. The performance of the late-war Union soldiers is presented by battle to show their overall contribution to the Overland Campaign.

The Wilderness (May 5–6)

Pvt. Gideon Mellin of the Ninety-Third Pennsylvania wrote his sister on April 27, 1864, about what lay ahead for the Army of the Potomac: "Where we will go I can't tell, but I suppose to some slaughter shop."[13]

The Seventeenth Vermont, reduced to slightly more than three hundred men by measles and several days of long, hard marches, fought well in the Battle of the Wilderness. Its brigade commander, Simon Griffin, said that "The Seventeenth Vermont did nobly though it was their first baptism of fire." Fox wrote: "Though without drill or necessary preparation the regiment moved steadily under fire, its colors waving on the line of the farthest advance." Pvt. Mark Slayton wrote to his friends at home that they took "the field of danger" on May 5 "and ever since then we have been exposed to an enemy fire night and day. We have been two day's in a hot fire where we lost considerable over 100 men killed & wounded." The Seventeenth Vermont also fought well at Cold Harbor, "commanding the willing praise of their superiors and associates of the other regiments engaged." At the end of the Overland Campaign, Gen. Robert Potter is reputed to have said that the Seventeenth Vermont is "a god-d—m good fighting regiment."[14]

Governor Holbrook authorized the Seventeenth Vermont in August 1863. Recruiters had expected that the men recently discharged from the nine-month regiments would be a prolific source of recruits, but that was not to be. Still, the Seventeenth Vermont had nearly two hundred veterans in its ranks.[15] Experienced officers also led the men of the Seventeenth Vermont. Col. Francis Randall had commanded the Thirteenth Vermont (a nine-month regiment); Lt. Col. Charles Cummings had held the same rank in the Sixteenth Vermont (also a nine-month regiment); Maj. William Reynolds had been a company commander in the Sixth Vermont (a three-year regiment from 1861); and the adjutant, Lt. James Peck, had also served in the Thirteenth Vermont. All the company commanders had also previously served in the field.[16]

Vermont was the most heavily reliant on agriculture of the Eastern States. Thirty-nine percent of the workforce was reported as "farmers" and another 14 percent as "farm laborers," a total of 53 percent. Sixty-three percent of the men in the Seventeenth Vermont were listed as "farmers." However, it appears that the vast majority of these men probably would have been classified as "farm laborers" in the 1860 Census. Thus, the Seventeenth Vermont had an even more dominant percentage of men from agriculture than the work force for the state, but the men of the Seventeenth Vermont probably were predominantly laborers rather than owner/operators.[17] For the leading nonagricultural occupations, the percentages for the Seventeenth Vermont were generally close to the 1860 Census numbers.[18] Senior Union commanders probably would not have been concerned about the Seventeenth Vermont's occupational profile. Seventy-seven percent of the original complement of the Seventeenth Vermont was native-born—basically the same as the percentage for the Union army overall.[19]

The Seventeenth Vermont left the state on April 18, 1864, with seven companies with nearly six hundred men. Recruiting had been slow due to competition with old regiments. Lieutenant Colonel Cummings had written his wife in March that "Extraordinary efforts are now making to fill the regiment; and for that purpose many officers are detailed and over a hundred enlisted men now furloughed for the purposes of each securing a recruit." Delays in recruiting had also limited training for large unit maneuvers. Cummings was glad that the Seventeenth Vermont was initially held in reserve after arriving in Virginia "for I could not take such undrilled troops into the field without some misgivings." Major Reynolds noted that the Seventeenth Vermont "had been drilled as a battalion but twice" before engaging in the Battle of the Wilderness.[20] Although it was short of the full ten companies and short on training, the Seventeenth Vermont did have experienced officers and a decent number of experienced enlisted men.

The Seventeenth Vermont suffered seventy-four casualties at the Battle of the Wilderness, seventy more at Spotsylvania, another seventy-two at North Ana, and twenty-seven at Cold Harbor. Those heavy casualties had reduced the Seventeenth Vermont to under two hundred men by June 8, 1864, when Company H arrived with another fifty-seven men.[21]

The Fifty-Seventh Massachusetts left for the front with 928 men on April 18 and joined the Ninth Corps in Annapolis.[22] General Hancock commended the Fifty-Seventh Massachusetts for its performance at the Battle of the Wilderness and Brigadier General Webb from the Second Corps praised the Fifty-Seventh Massachusetts as "particularly gallant" when he worked with them at the Battle of the Wilderness. However, the price of gallantry was quite high—245 casualties out of 545 men engaged. During the Spotsylvania phase of the Overland Campaign, the Fifty-Seventh Massachusetts suffered 115 casualties in two days of battle and then another forty-six at North Anna.[23] Emory Thomas observed that "The 57th Massachusetts had the misfortune usually to be in the wrong place at the wrong time. Cold Harbor excepted, the regiment was in the thick of the fighting in every major battle on the Eastern front during 1864 and 1865." As a result, it is not surprising that Fox made special note that the Fifty-Seventh Massachusetts, another one of his Three Hundred, "was in active service less than a year, and yet its percentage of killed was one of the highest of the war."[24]

The organization of the Fifty-Sixth, Fifty-Seventh, Fifty-Eighth, and Fifty-Ninth Massachusetts Volunteers was a long time coming. At the end of June 1863, the provost marshal general authorized the governor of Massachusetts to raise four new three-year regiments of Veteran Volunteer Infantry, but active recruiting did not get underway until August and September. The recruiting officers of the Fifty-Sixth Massachusetts were admonished in October that "It is not sufficient to remain quietly in an office and wait for men to enlist; they must be talked to, reasoned with, and inducements in the way of promotion to noncommissioned officers should be held out to deserving men."[25]

Under army regulations, "new organizations will be officered only by persons who have been in service and have shown themselves properly qualified." Enlisted men were required to have served at least nine months. The initial advertising was directed at veterans of specific regiments such as the "old 3rd" and the Forty-Ninth Massachusetts. A bounty of $727—$400 cash before leaving the state—was advertised. However, recruiting proceeded slowly and the regiments ultimately were filled primarily with new men.[26]

The Fifty-Seventh Massachusetts' first commander, William Francis Bartlett, had previously served in the Twentieth Massachusetts and would command a division by the end of the war. Almost all of the other officers had also served previously, although many as enlisted men. Just under a quarter of the men of the Fifty-Seventh Massachusetts had previously served. However, many of these veterans had seen little combat, having served as garrison troops in North Carolina.[27] The prior service of the officers and enlisted men would have been a plus for readiness.

The Fifty-Seventh Massachusetts was recruited in central Massachusetts. The regiment was about ten percentage points less American-born than the Union army in general. Roughly 40 percent were Massachusetts-born, with not quite another quarter being native-born. Nearly a fifth were Irish and 10 percent Canadian.[28] Farmers made up nearly a quarter of the force. At 16 percent and 15 percent respectively, both laborers and shoemakers were well above the 9–10 percent average for both in the Massachusetts workforce. Occupations like carpenter and clerk were very close to the state averages.[29]

The Fifty-Sixth Massachusetts had left home with roughly 850 men on March 21, 1864. On May 6, the Fifty-Sixth Massachusetts suffered seventy-two casualties, including the death of its colonel, in a "short" and "indecisive" action. Lt. Col. Stephen Weld, who had joined the army in 1861, recorded in his diary that "The firing to-day was the heaviest I have ever known or heard. I think the regiment did remarkably well considering that they were a new regiment, and that the old troops whose terms of enlistment were expiring did not behave very well . . . I have every reason to feel proud of the regiment." James Carlyle was proud of himself: "I was not a bit friten behaved myself so brave that I was made corporal." On May 18, John Osborn wrote his family that "I have now been in four battles and have not got a single scratch with the exception of one on the shoulder caused by a spent ball . . . We have lost many men since we came out as we cannot now muster more than 380 men in the Regt. and of 31 we have only thirteen officers left." Despite the heavy casualties, Osborn had "no desire to get home until this cruel war is over and every Rebel in our hands an humble supplicant for our mercy. . . . [They] wish to make . . . their own [government] which we cannot allow." Osborn was killed in action a week later.[30]

Osborn was not exaggerating the casualty numbers. The Fifty-Sixth Massachusetts lost 245 men in the Wilderness, another 100 men in two days of unsuccessful assaults at Spotsylvania and 74 at North Ana and Bethesda Church.[31]

At Cold Harbor, the Fifty-Sixth Massachusetts was just engaged in skirmishing, losing only half a dozen men.[32]

Fox described the Fifty-Sixth Massachusetts as "a steady, reliable, fighting regiment" Its two senior commanders had seen prior service—Colonel Griswold had served in the Twenty-Second Massachusetts, while Lieutenant Colonel Weld had served as a captain in the Eighteenth Massachusetts. Company B's Albert Cook described Griswold and Weld, as well as the major and adjutant, as "good Ofesers" and his company officers as "all good men." (He also described Burnside as "the best General in the field.") In the ranks, roughly a quarter of the men had previously served.[33]

The Fifty-Sixth Massachusetts was recruited in eastern Massachusetts. While nearly half of the men in the Union army had been farmers before the war, only about 9 percent of the men in the Fifty-Sixth Massachusetts had been farmers, roughly the same percentage as in the Massachusetts work force. A leading occupation in the regiment was mariner—an occupation inured to hard work but of questionable discipline in the minds of many civilians—at 13.5 percent compared to only 3 percent for the Massachusetts labor force. Laborers constituted 17 percent, compared to 10 percent for both the Union army and the Massachusetts work force.[34]

As opposed to most late-war new regiments, the Fifty-Ninth Massachusetts had a full ten companies when it joined the Army of the Potomac. At the beginning of the Battle of the Wilderness, the Fifty-Ninth Massachusetts was held back to guard the road but still lost fifty-five men by the end of the battle. The Fifty-Ninth Massachusetts suffered fewer casualties during the Overland Campaign than its fellow new Massachusetts regiments—sixty-three at Spotsylvania, forty-four at North Ana, and thirty-two at Cold Harbor, but it was actively engaged.[35]

The Fifty-Ninth Massachusetts was recruited in Boston and its environs. Shoemaker was the leading occupation at 20 percent (compared to only 9 percent of the state workforce), closely followed by laborer at 16 percent (10 percent of the state work force). Farmers comprised nearly 13 percent, somewhat more than the state work force.[36]

The Fiftieth Pennsylvania was in contact with the Confederates virtually every day of the Overland Campaign. At the Battle of the Ny River on May 9, the Fiftieth Pennsylvania played a prominent role in seizing a key bridge over the river against a superior force, suffering sixty casualties. Four companies of the Fiftieth Pennsylvania made a bayonet charge against counterattacking Confederates, the former of whom General Willcox wrote (after the war) "probably saved the day." By May 9, their effective strength had already fallen to fifteen officers and 301 enlisted men.[37]

The veterans in the Fiftieth Pennsylvania had reenlisted "almost without exception," but as they headed home on furlough in January 1864, they numbered only about three hundred men. However, they recruited over three hundred new volunteers, doubling their ranks.[38]

Fox noted that the 116th Pennsylvania participated in all the Second Corps' battles from the Wilderness to Appomattox and "proved itself worthy of a place in the [Irish] brigade."[39]

The 116th Pennsylvania's losses early in the war had been so severe that it was consolidated into a battalion of four companies after Fredericksburg. In the spring of 1864, the 116th Pennsylvania was authorized to recruit six new companies, as well as to fill up the four companies. As a result, the 116th Pennsylvania entered the Wilderness Campaign eight hundred strong—roughly three-quarters of them new volunteers.

The 143rd Pennsylvania's brigade commander, Colonel Stone, blamed it for the failure of an attack on May 5, but there were extenuating circumstances. There was a gap between Stone's and Cutler's brigades, which the Confederates exploited. Moreover, the 143rd and 149th Pennsylvania, which were the leading regiments, were maneuvering through a swamp and got separated. When they came under Confederate fire, the 149th Pennsylvania sent friendly fire into the 143rd Pennsylvania.[40] The 143rd Pennsylvania's new brigade commander, General Bragg, reported that the 143rd Pennsylvania (along with the 149th Pennsylvania) "distinguished themselves for endurance and cool conduct in a night attack and under a galling fire" in coming to the aid of the Sixth Corps on May 11 at Spotsylvania.[41]

The 143rd Pennsylvania had lost nearly half of its men at Gettysburg. In August and September 1863, it received roughly three hundred fifty replacements—two-thirds of whom were draftees—to bring its strength up to five hundred men.

The morning of May 5, the Sixty-Third Pennsylvania had "a severe engagement with the enemy," losing 40 percent of the 485 men engaged. The Sixty-Third Pennsylvania later captured the colors of the Twenty-Eighth North Carolina at Spotsylvania.[42] The afternoon of May 5, the Eighty-Third Pennsylvania was part of Bartlett's brigade, which advanced too far without support after their initial success. They were forced into a retreat that "disintegrated into a rout." The Eighty-Third Pennsylvania "ran almost every step of the way back."[43]

Spotsylvania Court House (May 7–12)

The Thirty-Second Maine had not been engaged at the Battle of the Wilderness, instead being tasked with building fortifications. But the Thirty-Second Maine was engaged at Spotsylvania, losing fifty-seven men. Pvt. Michael Kennedy, an eighteen-year-old, wrote his father from the battlefield: "I have seen more than I ever expected in such a short time since I left home. . . . We were under the most galling fire that has been known during the war. I saw and talked to men of old regiments and they said it beat Antietam and Gettysburg."[44]

The Thirty-Second Maine apparently proved itself to the veterans in its brigade during the Overland Campaign. Henry Clarence Houston, who enlisted in the Thirty-Second Maine at age seventeen, recounted a textbook version of how veterans and new recruits should interact in his regimental history, published in 1903. "The veterans questioned somewhat indignantly whether these new troops, who had never been under fire, deserved to stand side by side with them . . . [But] when our behavior under fire had shown them that we deserved their respect and confidence, [they] unhesitatingly and fully accepted us."[45]

Recruiting for the Thirty-First Maine and the Thirty-Second Maine was authorized on February 8, 1864, at which time they were assigned to the Ninth Corps. Maine's adjutant general specified that "It is both desirable and practicable that two-thirds of the commissioned officers of these regiments shall be those who have heretofore held commissions in active service. One lieutenant of each company may be a civilian." The expectation was also that a large proportion of the recruits would be veterans. As with the Seventeenth Vermont, the hope was that men from Maine's nine-month regiments whose terms of service had expired in 1863 would be a strong recruiting source for the Thirty-First and Thirty-Second Maine. However, as with the Seventeenth Vermont, that did not prove to be the case.[46]

Senior Union commanders could reasonably have expected that the Thirty-Second Maine would perform well in the field. The Thirty-Second Maine had an experienced contingent of officers. Col. Mark Wentworth had commanded the Twenty-Seventh Maine, a nine-month regiment. Lt. Col. John Marshall Brown had been a company commander and the adjutant in the Twentieth Maine and served on the staff of General Ames. He had seen combat at Antietam, Fredericksburg, and Gettysburg. Maj. Arthur Deering had been a company commander in the Twenty-Fourth Maine. The adjutant, the quartermaster, the sergeant major, and the commissary sergeant had all previously served. Five of the company commanders had led companies in other Maine regiments. Four had previously served as lieutenants, noncommissioned officers, or enlisted men. Only one company commander had not previously served. Two-thirds of the lieutenants had previously served. In contrast, not quite 15 percent of the men in the ranks were veterans, although most of the noncommissioned officers were veterans.[47] The men of the Thirty-Second Maine were relatively young. One third of the enlisted men reported their age as eighteen, while only a small proportion were older than thirty.[48]

Letters home from two soldiers suggest that morale was reasonably good. However, there was some soon-to-be disappointed optimism. Eighteen-year-old

Henry Sproul wrote his mother that "this cruel war won last long. I hope Mother we will git Richmond [this time?]. They say we shall come home this fall."[49]

Six companies of the Thirty-Second Maine joined the Ninth Corps on April 20, 1864, with about four hundred fifty men. The Thirty-Second Maine was sent to the field before completion because of the pressing need for troops as forces were being mobilized for the Overland Campaign.[50]

Experienced officers led the Thirty-Second Maine, but company and battalion drill before leaving for the front unfortunately had been hampered by the snow, which fell as late as April. The Thirty-Second Maine did have a week at Bristoe Station at the end of April and the beginning of May for drilling and their first live-fire training. The experience of the officers and, to a lesser extent, the enlisted men would have been a plus for readiness, but the lack of time for training would have been a concern. The incomplete organization was cured relatively quickly with the arrival of the final four companies with somewhat more than three hundred men on May 26.[51]

On May 8, the 183rd Pennsylvania "suffered considerable loss" in defending against a Confederate attack at Laurel Hill before withdrawing. Gordon Rhea recounted that the 183rd Pennsylvania "folded," then "rallied," but then tried to run again.[52] The 183rd Pennsylvania lost 161 more men on May 12 in a successful attack, 36 at North Ana on May 30 and 95 at Cold Harbor on June 3, 1864, in the unsuccessful daybreak charge.[53] The 183rd Pennsylvania had started out with 28 officers and 654 men when it was assigned to the Second Corps at the end of March 1864.[54]

The 183rd Pennsylvania had leadership problems. In a dispute with their brigade commander, Nelson Miles, the field grade officers and adjutant of the 183rd Pennsylvania resigned in May—as officers could do. Because the company officers lacked experience, the 183rd had a serious deficit in leadership. Capt. John McCullough from the 140th Pennsylvania was appointed colonel, but he was killed on May 31. J. C. Lynch was promoted from captain in the 106th Pennsylvania to lieutenant colonel in the 183rd on June 21, 1864, and colonel on July 19, 1864. Another concern was the "large proportion of very young men."[55]

Also at Laurel Hill, the Eighty-Third Pennsylvania was in the first line of an unsuccessful attack by Bartlett's Brigade (Fifth Corps). A few men of the Eighty-Third Pennsylvania reached the Confederate barricades, but the brigade "buckled under blistering volleys" and "fell back without much regard for order." Company A's Capt. Amos Judson recalled that the day "did a great deal towards impairing, for the time, the *morale* of the men: for they all knew that it was a badly managed affair, and that they were rushed into the fight without any display of skill or foresight on the part of their commanding generals."[56]

Shortly after arriving in the field, the Sixtieth Ohio went into action on May 9 in the battle of Ny River. The Sixtieth Ohio's brigade commander praised them for "maintain[ing] its position with creditable determination, especially considered that they were just organized and quite undrilled." The Sixtieth Ohio's division commander, Orlando Willcox, reported that the Sixtieth Ohio, a "new regiment," and three other regiments "distinguished themselves" in the attack. The Sixtieth Ohio's effective strength as of May 9, 1864, was only 14 officers and 279 men. They suffered 89 casualties at Spotsylvania.[57]

The Sixtieth Ohio had been raised from February through April 1864 and left Ohio for the front on April 21.[58] As the Ninth Corps moved toward the Wilderness, the Sixtieth Ohio was initially held back (along with the Seventy-Ninth New York) as a garrison force. Burnside had expressed some concern about the Sixtieth Ohio to Willcox on April 30, 1864, suggesting that an "older" regiment should be placed at Cedar Run.[59]

Also on May 9, the 148th Pennsylvania was the first regiment across the Po River and "clawed up a steep and heavily wooded bank and secured a lodgment" with the help of the 145th Pennsylvania. The 148th Pennsylvania also shared in General Brooke's praise for his brigade for repelling Heth's Division on May 10. On May 12, the 148th Pennsylvania participated in the Second Corps' successful attack on the Mule Shoe. Pvt. John Miller described the assault as "one of the greatest charges that was ever made." Colonel Beaver accepted the surrender of Confederate Gen. George Steuart. Later in the Overland Campaign, the 148th Pennsylvania captured a small Confederate camp on May 21 and led a successful attack on June 2. The 148th Pennsylvania suffered three hundred casualties in the Overland Campaign.[60]

The Forty-Ninth Pennsylvania was one of the twelve regiments selected for Upton's charge on May 10. Rhea referred to the twelve regiments as "the cream" of the Sixth Corps. The Forty-Ninth Pennsylvania lost 260 men in Upton's charge. John Arnold, a later-enlisting volunteer who was slightly wounded in the attack, wrote to his wife that "As soon as we got a little ways up the hill . . . the bullets came as thick as hale. But we run up to [the Confederate] entrenchments and charged on them with our bayonets."[61] The Forty-Ninth Pennsylvania lost heavily again two days later. Barely a week into the Overland Campaign, the regiment had already lost half its men. The Forty-Ninth Pennsylvania had suffered such heavy casualties early in the war that its original ten companies were consolidated into four in January 1863. The resulting supernumerary officers, including Colonel Irwin and Major Miles, were sent back to Pennsylvania to recruit the regiment back to full strength. By the end of 1863, the Forty-Ninth Pennsylvania had received over two hundred fifty replacements, primarily draftees and substitutes. The Forty-Ninth also received around one hundred fifty later-enlisting volunteers in the spring of 1864. The late-war replacements enabled the Forty-Ninth Pennsylvania to begin the Overland Campaign with 32 officers and 668 enlisted men present for duty.[62]

Rather than dispersing the late-war replacements among the four existing companies, the Forty-Ninth Pennsylvania placed them in five new companies officered by the Forty-Ninth's supernumerary officers along with "old line" noncommissioned officers from the Forty-Ninth. This different approach worked. The new troops were heavily drilled and regularly inspected throughout the fall and winter. The muster roll ratings for discipline and instruction show that the late-war replacements were successfully integrated into the Forty-Ninth Pennsylvania. The company ratings were good or better as of April 30, 1864, on the eve of the Overland Campaign. The ratings for "Military Appearance" were similarly strong.[63]

The veterans did subject the late-war replacements to the usual hazing, but there at least was some recognition that it could go too far. Sgt. Robert Westbrook, who had enlisted in February 1862, commented in February 1864 that "our new men are doing fine, but the old men are playing too many tricks on them in camp, such as knocking the barrels off the tops off [sic] their chimneys, throwing a handful of powder when they are having prayer meeting in their tents . . . [W]e have to laugh, but it is a shame and should be stopped." The Forty-Ninth Pennsylvania had an unusual form of teambuilding for the day—football. Nearly all the regiment was involved, officers as well as men, and they occasionally played "nearly all day."[64]

Westbrook thought that the men of "new Company H" and old Company D deserved special mention in Upton's charge because "they did more hard fighting than any of the other companies." He thought that "new Company G" "deserves much credit for the way it advanced while on the skirmish line on May 19, 1864. No old men could have done better."[65]

The Fifty-Third Pennsylvania shared General Brooke's praise for repelling Heth's troops on May 10. On May 12, the Fifty-Third Pennsylvania was one of the regiments in Wheaton's brigade that he reported had all "behaved excellently well and fought with great spirit, although holding ground most disadvantageously opposed to an enemy strongly intrenched and close in our front."[66] They suffered 177 casualties at Spotsylvania.[67]

The Fifty-Third Pennsylvania had been reduced to about two hundred seventy men by the time they returned home for their veteran furlough in January 1864, but they returned to the field with nearly seven hundred new volunteers. Thus later-enlisting volunteers made up about three-quarters of the regiment heading into the Wilderness Campaign.[68]

North Ana River (May 13–25)

The Thirty-Sixth Wisconsin lost 166 men at North Ana and several days later, four companies made what Fox called a "dashing charge" at Bethesda Church, where more than half of the 240 men engaged became casualties. Lt. James Aubery recalled that "While this seemed like a useless sacrifice of life, it fully accomplished the object proposed. . . . This was one of our 'busiest' days and cut into our numbers, bringing the regiment down to compare with the veteran regiments." The Thirty-Sixth Wisconsin lost another seventy-five men at Cold Harbor, ultimately qualifying for Fox's Three Hundred.[69]

The Thirty-Sixth Wisconsin—nine hundred strong—had joined the Second Corps on May 16 at Spotsylvania, where it was initially held in reserve. The officers were short on experience. Colonel Haskell had been the adjutant in the Sixth Wisconsin and had served with distinction at Gettysburg, but Lieutenant Colonel Warner not only had no prior service but had paid the $300 commutation fee to avoid service in 1863. Only a handful of the company-level officers had prior service and most of those who did had served as enlisted men. The Thirty-Sixth Wisconsin also had limited time for training. By April 9, the Thirty-Sixth Wisconsin was training six hours a day, but when the regiment arrived in the field it was "utterly unpracticed" in the battalion and skirmishing drill, which Aubery considered "essential" for "modern warfare." Moreover, the Thirty-Sixth Wisconsin did not receive its arms until May 5. There probably was no live-fire training before their first battle.[70]

The Fifty-Seventh Pennsylvania drove Confederate forces out of prepared positions on May 17. The Fifty-Seventh Pennsylvania had performed well earlier, helping drive back the Confederates on May 6, falling back in good order when commanded to do so on May 7, and driving Confederate troops out of prepared positions on May 8. However, the Fifty-Seventh Pennsylvania suffered heavy casualties—so large that it was consolidated into six companies. The Fifty-Seventh Pennsylvania had started out the war with about eight hundred fifty officers and men, but by the time it returned home for its veteran furlough in January 1864, more than two-thirds of the men having reenlisted, the Fifty-Seventh Pennsylvania was down to a little more than two hundred men. Roughly four hundred fifty volunteers were recruited between the end of 1863 and April 1864, resulting in replacements constituting nearly three-quarters of its numbers.[71]

On May 23, the Eighty-Third Pennsylvania helped check a "sudden and vigorous [Confederate] attack . . . that would probably have caused a perfect rout" and captured a Confederate brigade commander. Captain Judson recalled that the Eighty-Third Pennsylvania "and the leading regiment of the rebel brigade pitched into each other, like two rams, and the Eighty-third proved to have the hardest head of the two."[72]

Cold Harbor (May 26–June 3)

The Fifty-Eighth Massachusetts "moved against the works at Cold Harbor . . . with a line whose steadiness and precision elicited praise from all who saw it, winning the compliments of both brigade and division commanders" in the words of Fox. The Fifty-Eighth Massachusetts lost 125 men.[73]

The Fifty-Eighth Massachusetts was recruited in southeastern Massachusetts and Cape Cod. Like the Fifty-Sixth Massachusetts, mariner was the lead occupation at 17 percent. Farmers and shoemakers followed at 14 percent and laborers at 13 percent.[74] The average age was a couple of months older than for the Union army.[75]

Recruiting began in September 1863, but only eight companies had been raised by the time the Fifty-Eighth Massachusetts left for the front at the end of April 1864. (The ninth company arrived at Cold Harbor in June, but the tenth did not arrive until February 20, 1865.)[76]

Having been assigned to the Ninth Corps' Second Division after arriving at the front on May 2, the Fifty-Eighth Massachusetts was engaged in a different sector from its fellow Massachusetts regiments during the Wilderness and suffered fewer casualties—forty-five. A week later it was engaged at Spotsylvania, where it suffered another 105.[77]

The Thirty-First Maine fought with such gallantry at Cold Harbor that its brigade commander, Brig. Gen. Simon Griffin, complimented it.[78] The Thirty-First Maine lost eighteen killed and fifty-two wounded. Only three weeks after leaving Maine with nine companies, the Thirty-First Maine had been engaged in the Battle of the Wilderness, suffering thirty-one casualties. A week later, it suffered another hundred casualties at Spotsylvania. In just three months—May to July 1864, the Thirty-First Maine lost well over three hundred men in combat, setting the stage for consolidating the Thirty-Second Maine, which also lost heavily, into the Thirty-First Maine in December 1864.[79]

The Thirty-First Maine fell far short of the "desire" for late-war new regiments that two-thirds of the officers have prior service as officers. Col. Thomas Haight had prior service as a lieutenant colonel in the Seventh Maine and Maj. Stephen Talbot had served as a lieutenant in the First Maine Heavy Artillery, but only half of the company commanders had prior service as captains and only three of the twenty lieutenants had previously served as officers. Most of the other lieutenants did have prior service, but usually only as corporals or privates.[80]

As to readiness, the primary concerns about the Thirty-First Maine would have been the lack of experience of its officers and the lack of time for training.

The 184th Pennsylvania was heavily engaged at Cold Harbor, leading its brigade in two assaults on June 3 and was commended by its brigade commander.[81] The 184th Pennsylvania had earlier gone into battle at Totopotomy Creek the day after it arrived in the field with seven companies totaling five hundred fifty men.

Overall, in its first twenty-five days in the field (which included the beginning of the Petersburg Campaign), the 184th Pennsylvania suffered 70 percent casualties—"a loss unprecedented" in the words of Samuel Bates.[82] However, the 184th Pennsylvania ultimately did not qualify as one of Fox's Three Hundred.

The Fifty-First Pennsylvania attacked under heavy fire and took an advanced line of rifle pits, suffering nearly ninety casualties but was unable to penetrate any further.[83] Fox noted that the Fifty-First Pennsylvania had "achieved historic prominence at Antietam by its charge across the stone bridge" under then Col. John Hartranft.[84] Antietam, Fredericksburg, and other battles, not to mention disease, greatly reduced the Fifty-First Pennsylvania's numbers. But the Fifty-First Pennsylvania was very popular at home and received nearly four hundred fifty later-enlisting volunteers in the first four months of 1864.[85]

Gordon Rhea recounted that at Cold Harbor the Eighty-Second Pennsylvania and another "novice" regiment supported another brigade by "stepping out, . . . [and] dr[iving] Rebel skirmishers through a narrow strip of woods" and carried on after receiving heavy fire.[86] Only about half of the veterans from 1861 had re-enlisted in the regiment, suggesting concerns about morale. The Eighty-Second Pennsylvania had received nearly three hundred draftees in the late summer and early fall of 1863 and four hundred later-enlisting volunteers from December 1863 through April 1864, so its numbers had been significantly augmented before the Overland Campaign. When it left Belle Plain for the Army of the Potomac, it had a little over five hundred men.[87]

While the Army of the Potomac was still maneuvering after the Battle of Cold Harbor, Potter criticized the Forty-Eighth Pennsylvania for falling back from a hill he was trying to fortify. Although an officer from Willcox's staff said that the attacking Confederates were "a very heavy force," Potter reported that "my force . . . was some 300 or 400, and there was no excuse for not holding it." However, at Totopotomy Creek, the Forty-Eighth Pennsylvania had taken the Whitlock Farm from the Confederates after a "vigorous firefight."[88]

Over three-quarters (two hundred thirty men) of the veterans in the Forty-Eighth Pennsylvania from 1861 reenlisted—a sign of good morale—and they left for home to recruit, with the support of the *Philadelphia Inquirer*: "it is to be hoped that this veteran body will speedily be raised up to the standard of a full regiment." With the addition of over six hundred fifty later-enlisting volunteers, the Forty-Eighth Pennsylvania pretty much got there.[89]

The Forty-Fifth Pennsylvania suffered three hundred casualties during the Overland Campaign, but its performance did not stand out one way or the other. "Veteran" wrote in his local newspaper on June 8 that "Our boys, (or rather what is left of them,) are in good spirits, but badly worn out. . . . When we are not fighting or skirmishing, we are fortifying or marching." Lt. Samuel Haynes, who had not reenlisted, wrote that "Our army has been almost constantly under fire for the last 30 days and the end is not yet. When will it be? [T]his campaign is destined to be the death blow to the Rebellion and also . . . to many thousands of brave men. . . . Truly the cost of preserving the Union is great. Is it too great?"[90]

The late-war replacements in the eleven old Pennsylvania regiments specifically discussed made a significant contribution to restoring the force levels in their old regiments in preparation for the Overland Campaign. But the late-war replacements—and the late-war new regiments—did not just contribute numbers. They were no mere bystanders in the Overland Campaign. They fought hard alongside the veterans and suffered heavy casualties just as the veteran regiments did. More importantly, the late-war new regiments and the old Pennsylvania regiments with a majority of late-war replacements generally fought effectively during the Overland Campaign.[91]

CHAPTER 8

The Petersburg Campaign during 1864

June 15 to December 11

Grant caught Lee by surprise with his brilliant change of front from Cold Harbor to Petersburg in June 1864, but the Army of the Potomac bungled the opportunity to seize a very lightly defended Petersburg. General Smith, commanding the Eighteenth Corps (on loan from the Army of the James) breached the northern sector of the Petersburg defenses with "astonishing ease" late in the day on June 15. However, due to ineffectual communication with General Hancock, commander of the Second Corps, which had just arrived, Smith decided not to enter Petersburg until the following day. Confederate General Beauregard took advantage of the intervening night to cobble together the forces for a successful defense.[1] The Army of the Potomac failed to take Petersburg during the next week in assaults by the Second, Fifth, and Ninth Corps, which led to the nearly year-long siege. The common soldier understood the change. On June 27, Pvt. Michael Kennedy of the Thirty-Second Maine wrote his father that "we are in a siege now instead of a battle."[2]

Eighteen late-war new regiments joined the Army of the Potomac after the Overland Campaign through the end of 1864. However, only four arrived in June. Union commanders quickly threw them into battle. The other fourteen did not arrive until the fall and had little impact in 1864. However, they did have the advantage of the winter for additional training. Their contribution would come in the spring of 1865 as illustrated by the six new regiments comprising Hartranft's Division at Fort Stedman and the five new regiments in Griffin's Division in the Five Forks Campaign. Like their predecessors from the Overland Campaign, these new regiments often arrived at the front in battalions before completion of the full ten regiments. As with their predecessors, the Army of the Potomac assigned most of the new regiments to the Ninth Corps, with the Fifth Corps receiving seven. The Sixth Corps received only one and the Second Corps none. The officers and enlisted men in the fall arrivals generally had less prior service than the earlier new regiments.

The late-war new regiments joining the Army of the Potomac during the Overland Campaign generally continued to fight effectively during the Petersburg Campaign. As during the Overland Campaign, mounting casualties required replacements. Sometimes the arrival in the field of the balance of their ten companies augmented their forces. Occasionally the newest late-war regiments increased their forces with late-war replacements, in which case the new regiment faced the same challenge of integrating replacements that the old regiments did. And sometimes new recruits never came in significant numbers at all.

The Initial Assaults (June 1864)

The subtitle of Thomas J. Howe's book on the June 15 to 18 battles at Petersburg aptly describes the sacrifice of the troops engaged—"Wasted Valor."[3]

The day that they arrived at Petersburg, the Fifty-Third Pennsylvania participated in the Second Corps' unsuccessful June 16 attack against well-defended Confederate positions. The Fifty-Third Pennsylvania pushed right up to the Confederate lines before the Confederates forced them to withdraw under a "murderous fire." They lost nearly one hundred men.[4] The Fifty-Seventh Pennsylvania also participated in the attack. Lieutenant Colonel Neeper reported that the Fifty-Seventh Pennsylvania "fought well, repeatedly advancing and falling back. Our force was insufficient to scale the works."[5] The Sixty-Third Pennsylvania took position on the right of the Fifty-Seventh Pennsylvania and suffered fifty casualties.[6] The 116th Pennsylvania lost seventy men in the June 16 assault.[7] The Confederates also repulsed the 148th Pennsylvania.[8]

The 184th Pennsylvania lost heavily in the Second Corps' assaults on June 16 and June 18. On June 22, the Confederates outflanked the 184th Pennsylvania's brigade after an initially successful Union attack. The 184th Pennsylvania lost fifty-two killed and wounded and one hundred fifteen prisoners. Starting out with five hundred men in May, the 184th had lost three hundred fifty by the end of June.[9]

The Ninth Corps arrived outside of Petersburg the afternoon of June 16. Each of the Ninth Corps' first three divisions attacked the Confederate positions on June 17. The predawn attack by Potter's Division on June 17 was "one of the most remarkable successes of the war" in the opinion of Edwin Bearss, taking a mile of the Confederate front. Both Meade and Burnside complimented Potter's Division for the attack.[10]

The Seventeenth Vermont led the assault for the Second Brigade of Potter's Division on June 17. They captured "2 canon, a caisson, 6 horses, 70 prisoners, and the colors and adjutant of the Seventeenth Tennessee" and were "warmly complimented" by their brigade and division commanders. Noting that the Seventeenth Vermont had attacked with only 135 men, Lieutenant Colonel Cummings proudly wrote his wife that "if I had 800 such men I could do almost anything."[11] Fox related that the Fifty-Eighth Massachusetts was "conspicuous for its gallant action in the June 17 assault." The Forty-Eighth Pennsylvania captured the flag of the Forty-Fourth Georgia as well as two cannons. The Thirty-First Maine and the Forty-Fifth Pennsylvania also joined in Potter's attack.[12]

Willcox's Division failed in an afternoon attack. Capt. R. C. Eden of the Thirty-Seventh Wisconsin described the strong Confederate positions: "Though not very strongly manned, the work was a heavy one, and from its commanding position and the heavy enfilading fire that could be brought to bear on almost any part of it, not by any means an easy one to carry."[13] Fox described the Thirty-Seventh Wisconsin's charge on June 17 as "gallant," although it was unsuccessful. The Thirty-Seventh Wisconsin lost very heavily in the unsuccessful attacks by Willcox's Division on June 17 and again on June 18—250 casualties out of 400 men engaged.

The Thirty-Seventh Wisconsin had joined the Ninth Corps at Cold Harbor on June 10 with eight companies of 521 men just as the change of front to Petersburg was about to begin.[14] The officers of the Thirty-Seventh Wisconsin had limited experience. Arms apparently had not been issued until May 17, so the men may not have taken any live-fire training before battle. Battalion drill had also been limited.[15]

General Willcox commended the Fiftieth Pennsylvania and Fifty-First Pennsylvania for "behav[ing] like veterans, meeting with bloody losses without discouragement, and always fighting gallantly" during the beginning of the Petersburg campaign, notwithstanding the large number of late-war replacements in their ranks. At that point, the Fiftieth Pennsylvania was down to only six officers and one hundred fifty enlisted men fit for duty.[16] The Fifty-First Pennsylvania suffered one hundred casualties in the first six weeks of the Petersburg Campaign.[17] The Sixtieth Ohio was also part of Willcox's unsuccessful attack, losing nearly half of the men engaged.[18]

Later in the evening, Ledlie's Division attacked the same Confederate positions as Willcox's Division had. The Fifty-Sixth, Fifty-Seventh, and Fifty-Ninth Massachusetts and the 179th New York formed the center of the first line of attack, while the 100th Pennsylvania served as skirmishers. The Confederates initially also repulsed Ledlie's Division, but they regrouped to take the Confederate works. Fox stated that the Fifty-Seventh Massachusetts "made a brilliant charge . . . carrying the works at the point of the bayonet." The 179th New York's William Larzalere wrote that the attack "was done under a mushroom fire of grape canisters, shells and musketry." Lt. Col. Franklin Doty wrote a friend that "I am proud of my men. They charged like veterans." Ledlie's Division repulsed several Confederate counterattacks but fell back at night. The Fifty-Seventh Massachusetts's Lt. George Barton wrote home that "We had the works until our ammunition gave out—and then we were obliged to fall back."[19] Ledlie reported that "Too much praise cannot be accorded the men making this charge, subject as they were not only to a terrible fire of shell and cannister . . . , but to heavy and continuous volleys of musketry."[20]

The 179th New York had only five companies when it joined the Army of the Potomac at Cold Harbor on June 3, 1864, just as the battle was ending. A sixth company arrived several days later, bringing the total to just under four hundred fifty men. The seventh regiment arrived the day before the Battle of the Crater and the remaining three companies shortly before the Battle of Poplar Spring Church, at which point Colonel Gregg was authorized to take the field. Although the 179th New York did eventually reach ten regiments, it never came close to having the nine hundred to one thousand men of a standard regiment in the field at any one time.[21]

Gregg, who had served as a major in the Twenty-Third New York, a two-year regiment that was mustered out in May 1863, drew heavily from the ranks of his former comrades. Franklin Doty, a captain in the Twenty-Third New York, became lieutenant colonel; James Bowker became adjutant; and John Prentiss and Moses Van Benschoten became company commanders. Two sergeants and a private from the Twenty-Third New York became company commanders in the 179th New York by the end of the war—Martin Doty, Levi Force, and Samuel G. H. Musgrave. Another sergeant from the Twenty-Third New York, William Norton, helped make up for the fact that none of the officers in his company in the 179th New York had prior service.[22]

Two combat veterans initially led the 179th New York in the field—Lieutenant Colonel Doty and Maj. J. Barnett Sloan, who had served as major in the Thirty-First New York, another two-year regiment from 1861. In addition, all five company commanders had previously served, as had roughly 10 percent of the enlisted men.[23] The June 17 assault was the 179th New York's first battle. Already only a battalion with limited training, a detachment of one hundred men sent to Cumberland Heights further reduced the 179th New York's numbers. Forty percent of the men of the 179th New York engaged became casualties. Just as seriously, Doty and Sloane were both wounded (Sloane mortally).[24] The 179th's deep roster of veteran officers provided a capable captain, John Barton, for promotion to major.

Little could be expected of the Thirty-Eighth Wisconsin, a battalion of only four companies officered by men of limited experience. Nonetheless, Ledlie stated that the Thirty-Eighth Wisconsin (from Willcox's Division) "rendered important service" in supporting his June 17 assault.[25] After Wisconsin met its quota, recruiting for the Thirty-Eighth Wisconsin all but dried up. As a result, the recruiters were only able to forward the battalion of four companies—280 men. After a month at Arlington Heights, the Thirty-Eighth Wisconsin arrived at White House Landing at the beginning of June and joined the Ninth Corps.[26] The officers of the Thirty-Eighth Wisconsin had limited experience—both in the first four companies sent to the field and the later six companies. Only one of the company commanders and none of the lieutenants had previously served as an officer.[27]

On June 18, Potter's and Willcox's Divisions advanced across the Petersburg and Norfolk Railroad through difficult terrain. Burnside reported that "No better fighting has been done during the war than was done by the divisions of generals Potter and Willcox during this attack."[28] The Fifty-Eighth Massachusetts had performed well the day before, but Lieutenant Colonel Whiton believed that on June 18: "Our Regiment never showed greater bravery than on that day advancing over an open field. Exposed to a severe musketry fire it is surprising that so many escaped uninjured." The Fifty-Eighth Massachusetts lost forty-four men in these two actions.[29]

The Fifth Corps' attack on June 18 was unsuccessful. The 143rd Pennsylvania, a "seasoned" "veteran"—but "depleted" regiment in the words of A. Wilson Greene, attacked in the first line of Chamberlain's Brigade on June 18. Chamberlain's troops faced a "daunting task." Not only were they attacking well-prepared and supported positions in the Dimmock Line, but they had to descend into a valley, cross a creek, and attack uphill. Their chances of success were "slim," according to Greene. The 143rd Pennsylvania lost fifty men.[30] By the time the 143rd Pennsylvania reached Petersburg, it was probably down to about two hundred fifty men.

The 187th Pennsylvania was in the second line of Chamberlain's attack. The 187th initially broke, "although some of them rallied, [but] their hesitance robbed the brigade of whatever slim chance it enjoyed of breaking the Rebel line," according to Greene. The 187th Pennsylvania lost nearly two hundred men. The 187th had arrived at Cold Harbor on June 6 with between nine hundred and a thousand men.[31] A unit referred to as the "First Battalion," which had been recruited for six months in June and July 1863 to respond to the threat of invasion by Lee's forces, formed the nucleus of the 187th Pennsylvania. The 187th Pennsylvania recruited these men after their terms of enlistment expired. After organizing in Philadelphia in early May 1864, the individual companies of the 187th Pennsylvania were "scattered throughout the department, on duty at the different draft rendezvous and district provost-marshal's headquarters and coal regions." But the manpower needs of the Army of the Potomac took precedence and the War Department ordered the companies to gather in Harrisburg and then head to the front.[32] The 187th Pennsylvania served in the field for only a short time. After the June 18 attack, the 187th served in reserve in July and early August. They were ordered back to Philadelphia in September 1864 and spent the rest of the war performing garrison, escort, and provost duty in Pennsylvania.[33]

Deep Bottom (July 27–29, 1864)

The 183rd Pennsylvania performed well at Deep Bottom on July 27. Hancock stated that the 183rd Pennsylvania (along with the Fifth New Hampshire and the Twenty-Eighth Massachusetts) "merit[ed] particular mention" "for their gallantry in the capture of the enemy's battery [four twenty-pounder Parrotts]" and had done so "by a well-executed movement." Their division commander reported that the three regiments, under the command of the 183rd Pennsylvania's Col. J. C. Lynch, had been sent across an open field as skirmishers "without indication of the enemy . . . when [they were] met by a fire from a force partially entrenched . . . Colonel Lynch moved his line by the right flank around the flank of this force in the road, and by a vigorous push drove it from its position and captured the pieces, with caissons and ammunition chests." The 183rd Pennsylvania lost only four men killed and eight men wounded in the assault.[34]

The 184th Pennsylvania lost a quarter of the men engaged at Deep Bottom. The Confederates later routed the 184th Pennsylvania at Second Reams's Station on August 25. The 184th Pennsylvania was part of Miles' Division's reserves. "The reserves could do nothing, as the First Division, apparently panic-stricken, were passing to the rear over our men, which made it impossible for them to fire on the enemy, and shortly after the panic spread to them, and they also left the field."[35]

The Battle of the Crater (July 30, 1864)

The Ninth Corps led the Union attack—brilliant in concept, but horrendous in execution—at the infamous Battle of the Crater. All of the late-war regiments in the Ninth Corps participated to varying degrees. The causes of the disaster lay not with a lack of courage or motivation among the individual soldiers but rather with the senior commanders—notably Burnside, the corps commander, and Gen. James Ledlie, who commanded the First Division, which led the attack. Burnside drew lots to choose the division to lead the attack and Ledlie, with the short straw, headed to the rear under the influence of alcohol. Given the failures of Burnside and Ledlie, the disaster at the Battle of the Crater does not mean that the Union troops did not fight hard.

The Forty-Eighth Pennsylvania dug the "mine" under no man's land, which enabled the Union to blow up the Confederate positions at Elliott's Salient. While Burnside exempted the Forty-Eighth Pennsylvania from participating in the attack as a reward for digging the mine, the excellence of their work on the mine should not be overlooked. Not only did they overcome numerous practical obstacles in digging the tunnel, but they also protected the element of surprise by carefully disposing of the construction debris so as not to attract attention of the Confederates. The work required nearly all four hundred enlisted men. General Meade gave "highest praise" to the Forty-Eighth Pennsylvania for "the willing endurance by the officers and men of the regiment of the extraordinary labor and fatigue involved in the prosecution of the work to completion."[36]

In Ledlie's Division, the Fifty-Sixth Massachusetts was one of the few regiments "working their way north from the Crater." The Fifty-Sixth Massachusetts lost another fifty men at the Battle of the Crater.[37] Along with the Third Maryland, the 179th New York also advanced somewhat north of the crater.[38] Company G of the 179th New York had arrived at the front with eighty more men the day before the Battle of the Crater. However, the first five companies had been so badly depleted in the beginning of the Petersburg Campaign that 40 percent of the men of the 179th New York who went into the Battle of the Crater were from Company G. The Fifty-Seventh Massachusetts suffered a comparatively low fifty casualties in the Battle of the Crater, but after the battle it was commanded by a lieutenant who began the campaign as a private.[39]

General Hartranft in Willcox's Division gave an "honorable mention" to the Fifty-First Pennsylvania and the Thirty-Seventh Wisconsin (as well as other regiments) for their work.[40] The Thirty-Seventh Wisconsin entered the Battle of the Crater with only 250 men and lost another 158.

In Potter's Division, the Forty-Fifth Pennsylvania's effective strength had been reduced to two hundred ten men by the time of the Battle of the Crater and it charged with only one hundred ten. The Forty-Fifth Pennsylvania claimed to have advanced beyond the Crater, falling back for lack of support. It did capture a Confederate flag. Lt. Samuel Haynes described the explosion as "the most terribly magnificent sight I ever witnessed." Cpl. Homer Thompson wrote his sister that "The fight . . . proved to be a grand failure—nothing short of a perfect butchery."[41] The Thirty-First Maine charged in the first line of the attack by Griffin's Brigade to the right of the Crater. Amid the confusion of the crammed Union troops, the Thirty-First Maine and Griffin's Brigade could not advance. In the rebel counterattack, the Thirty-First Maine "fought heroically" for its colors and lost eighty-six men.[42] Pvt. Henry Sproul of the Thirty-Second Maine wrote his mother at the end of June that they "had nine hundred men when we came out hear but now we hante got but . . . two hundred men left."[43] The Battle of the Crater made things worse for the Thirty-Second Maine—only twenty-seven men commanded by the adjutant returned from the battle. The Thirty-Second Maine and the Seventeenth Vermont in Griffin's Brigade may have been able to advance further beyond the Crater than Ledlie's Division did, but the difference was not significant.[44] Charles Caruthers of the Sixtieth Ohio spoke for many a Union soldier: "the day was lost much to our chagrin."[45]

Weldon Railroad (August 18–21, 1864)

By August 1864, casualties had significantly reduced the force levels in the late-war new regiments in the Ninth Corps. General White, who succeeded Ledlie as commander of the Ninth Corps' First Division, commended the performance of the Thirty-First Maine, regretting that "decimated ranks prevented their accomplishing more."[46] After the battle on August 19, 1864, the effective strength of the Fifty-Seventh Massachusetts was only thirty-nine, augmented a bit in early September by sixty men returning from convalescence and detached duty.[47] The Fifty-Sixth Massachusetts had an effective strength of only seventy-one men as did the Fifty-Ninth Massachusetts.[48] On August 21, the Thirty-Second Maine helped repel attacks by Confederate generals Hill and Mahone, but the cost was high. At the end of August, the Thirty-Second Maine had only four officers and 114 men present for duty. Over four hundred men were sick.[49]

After Weldon Railroad, the operational readiness of the 179th New York was low. Only seven officers and 128 enlisted men were available for duty, and forty of the enlisted men were on detached duty. Two-thirds of its complement were sick—eight officers and two hundred fifty enlisted men. Lieutenant Colonel Doty, who had returned to the field from his June 17 wound, rated the 179th as "Fair" in discipline, "Good" in instruction, "Fair" in military appearance, "Good" in arms and accoutrements, and "Poor" in clothing.[50]

The old regiments were also suffering. The 100th Pennsylvania and its brigade repulsed "the enemy . . . with heavy loss," but after the battle, the 100th Pennsylvania was down to an effective strength of only 149 men.[51] The Fifty-First Pennsylvania lost fifty-five men when Hartranft's Brigade came to the aid of the Fifth Corps at Weldon Railroad.[52] The Fiftieth Pennsylvania performed particularly well at Weldon Railroad and suffered few casualties. They went head-to-head with the

Forty-Seventh Virginia, a veteran regiment tested in thirteen engagements going back to Bull Run and emerged with one of the Forty-Seventh Virginia's flags and a large number of prisoners, while losing only twenty-two of their own men.[53]

Second Reams's Station (August 25, 1864)

The next chapter discusses the Second Battle of Reams's Station in detail.

Poplar Spring Church (September 30, 1864)

Like most of the regiments in Potter's Division, the Thirty-Second Maine in Griffin's Brigade was overwhelmed by the Confederate attack. As Henry Houston recalled, "the unfortunate overlapping of our line and enveloping of our flank by the enemy resulted in our being thrown into considerable confusion, which rendered it easy for the enemy to capture so large a number of our men." The Thirty-Second Maine had only about one hundred men available at Poplar Spring Church and 40 percent of them became casualties, mostly prisoners of war.[54] The Thirty-First Maine was the last to fall back when the Confederates turned Griffin's Brigade's right flank. After Poplar Spring Church, the Thirty-First Maine had only about sixty men reporting for duty and was briefly commanded by a sergeant.[55]

The 179th New York had approximately four hundred men present for duty on September 30—not a bad number for a Union regiment at that point in the war. But roughly 60 percent of the men were from the three new companies that had been in the field for only two weeks. Another 15 percent were replacements who had arrived just that morning, the vast majority without weapons.[56] The predominance of truly raw recruits may have led General Griffin to hold back the 179th New York when he moved the rest of his second line forward, but shortly thereafter overwhelming numbers of Confederates took the 179th New York by surprise on its right flank. Lieutenant Colonel Doty almost immediately called for retreat and the 179th broke in "confusion." Arguably the 179th New York should have tried to stand their ground and possibly slow the Confederate advance. However, Maj. John Hudson from the nearby Thirty-Fifth Massachusetts saw the 179th New York's situation and concluded that they had "wisely made no attempt at resistance." The 179th New York lost twelve men dead, twenty wounded, and twenty-six captured.[57] Had they resisted, hundreds could have been captured. Instead, the 179th New York remained operational, and with the opportunity to train over the winter, was ready for the 1865 campaign season. They led the attack on Confederate Battery 28 on April 2, 1865.

Despite having been routed at Poplar Spring Church, the 179th New York received a huge boost to morale in October. With the arrival of the last three companies, the 179th New York became a full regiment entitled to colors and a full colonel. When Col. William Gregg arrived, Lt. John Andrews wrote in his journal "the boys went out in front of his tent and gave him twice six rousing cheers—they appeared pleased at the idea of having a colonel at last." When the 179th New York received its colors at a dress parade on October 13, 1864, the men responded "with hearty cheers." This evidences strong unit cohesion at the regimental level. And the men of the 179th New York were ready to put Poplar Spring Church behind them. William Lamont, one of the new men, wrote a friend that they "had broke and run in every direction" on September 30, but "we are in hopes to do better next time."[58]

The Confederates also overwhelmed the Fifty-Eighth Massachusetts, taking nearly its whole force prisoner. By the time of Poplar Spring Church, the Fifty-Eighth Massachusetts had already been reduced to only about one hundred men. Lieutenant Colonel Whiton reported to the Massachusetts adjutant general that "The Enemy taking advantage of [the Fifth and Ninth Corps'] failure to connect, came down on us in overpowering numbers."[59] The Forty-Fifth Pennsylvania, also in Curtin's Brigade, was overwhelmed. Beauge recalled that "Attacked by superior numbers in front, flank and rear and practically surrounded, seven-eighths of what was left of the Forty-fifth were obligated to surrender or be shot down." The day after the battle, the Forty-Fifth Pennsylvania had only ninety-two men present for duty, most of whom were veterans from 1861 who had been excused from battle because their terms of enlistment were about to expire.[60]

The Fifty-Eighth Massachusetts and the Forty-Fifth Pennsylvania each lost one of their battle flags at Poplar Spring Church. Loss of colors in battle was not only extremely embarrassing to a regiment's reputation but could also result in punitive action such as loss of furlough privileges. Potter defended both regiments, stating that they and two other regiments had been lost "by holding on too long to their positions; the order for their withdrawal could not be got to them in season." Potter specifically noted that "The Fifty-eighth Massachusetts (not a fully organized regiment) joined the division a day or two before crossing the Rapidan; has lost very heavily and shown great bravery." Potter referred to the Forty-Fifth Pennsylvania as a "veteran regiment" holding "as high a reputation as any organization in this corps for uniform valor and good conduct." Meade subsequently confirmed the regiments' right to carry colors because the colors "were lost under circumstances that reflect no dishonor upon those regiments."[61]

The Thirty-Seventh Wisconsin in Willcox's Division played a role in containing the Confederate advance after the Confederates routed Potter's Division. General Willcox reported that "the Thirty-seventh Wisconsin, Eighth and Twenty-seventh Michigan, retired in good order to a fence on the left of the Pegram house, where these regiments halted, faced about, checked the farther advance of the enemy, and threw up hasty breast-works of rails, where they remained."[62] Colonel Harriman, commander of the Thirty-Seventh Wisconsin as well as the brigade, stated that these regiments "did good service in keeping the enemy at bay."[63] Hartranft himself commended his regiments, including the Thirty-Eighth Wisconsin: "They behaved nobly . . . , especially when the brigade was almost surrounded by the enemy . . . All the regiments displayed a steadiness under trying circumstances, which speaks well of their discipline."[64]

Burgess's Mill (October 27, 1864)

The Confederates attacked the right flank and rear of the Fifty-Seventh Pennsylvania and forced them to fall back in confusion, "but after falling back . . . [the Fifty-Seventh] formed line of battle and advanced, driving the enemy before us in great confusion" as reported by Captain Bumpus, then commanding the regiment. The Fifty-Seventh Pennsylvania took two hundred prisoners.[65] Some of the replacements who joined the Fiftieth Pennsylvania on October 12 did skulk at Burgess's Mill.[66]

A New Round of Reinforcements

The losses in the Overland Campaign and the beginning of the Petersburg Campaign greatly reduced the numbers in the late-war new regiments, many of which had been sent to the front before completion of the standard ten regiments. Fortunately, ongoing recruiting enabled these late-war regiments to complete their organization, with more men in the field, in the fall of 1864.

After the rout at Poplar Spring, the Seventeenth Vermont had about one hundred fifty men left and was commanded by a captain. The tenth company of the Seventeenth Vermont mustered in on October 8, 1864, with ninety-five officers and men and reached the Ninth Corps in the field at the end of the month. With the completion of ten companies, Colonel Randall was authorized to take the field. Company K plus additional recruits and the return of convalescent veterans brought the Seventeenth Vermont back to 316 officers and men by mid-November, a respectable force level for a regiment at that time.[67] The Seventeenth Vermont had been a rare exception to the federal policy that substitutes were not assigned to new regiments. One hundred fifty substitutes joined the Seventeenth Vermont in July and August 1864. However, 80 percent of them deserted—almost all before being sent to the front.[68]

The Fifty-Eighth Massachusetts was relieved from active duty after Poplar Spring because of its heavy losses. The arrival of fifty-four recruits in November and the tenth company in January 1865—nearly one hundred strong, as well as a number of replacements did enable the Fifty-Eighth Massachusetts to participate in the final assault on Petersburg in April 1865.[69] The heavy casualties incurred by the Fifty-Eighth Massachusetts in the Overland Campaign and the beginning of the Petersburg Campaign necessitated promotions to fill vacancies. Promotions were normally based on seniority, but the Fifty-Eighth Massachusetts took a different approach. Lacking a roster showing seniority, Lieutenant Colonel Whiton instead recommended to the Massachusetts adjutant general promoting "those whom I think most worthy and capable or best qualified."[70]

The Thirty-First Maine received two new companies—L and M—of recruits in October.[71] Consolidation of the Thirty-Second Maine into the Thirty-First Maine on December 12 further strengthened the Thirty-First Maine. The Thirty-First Maine gained an additional 15 officers and 470 enlisted men on paper. However, the Thirty-Second Maine had only 6 officers and 175 men present for duty. By mid-March 1865, the Thirty-First Maine was back up to nearly 600 men present for duty.[72]

A correspondent for an Ohio newspaper visiting the Sixtieth Ohio in October reported that "The boys as far as I seen, and could learn, were feeling well; but the regiment needs recruiting. . . . One hundred sick, well and wounded, is all it can muster now." The Sixtieth Ohio's numbers had fallen below two hundred by mid-August. The Sixtieth Ohio did receive some new troops. Company K arrived by the end of the year and two independent companies of sharpshooters joined the Sixtieth Ohio as companies G and H. Still, in mid-December the Sixtieth Ohio had only five officers and 171 men present for duty.[73]

Five new companies, along with Colonel Bintliff, arrived for the Thirty-Eighth Wisconsin on October 1, boosting the Thirty-Eighth Wisconsin's numbers over five hundred. The new troops had been recruited as one-year men under the July 1864 call. The original battalion of five companies had fallen to only forty men fit for duty by the Fourth of July.[74] The 184th Pennsylvania received three new companies in October to bolster its badly depleted ranks.[75] However, in December, the 184th Pennsylvania was cited as the regiment in the "worst order" of the nine regiments (including the Thirty-Sixth Wisconsin) in the First Brigade of the Second Corps' Second Division.[76] The 183rd Pennsylvania received a different source of replacements—one hundred fifty transfers who had reenlisted or whose terms had not expired when the Seventy-Second Pennsylvania was mustered out.[77]

The old regiments, which had been replenished before the Overland Campaign, also suffered heavy losses in the beginning of the Petersburg Campaign. Seven of the old regiments studied here received large numbers of replacements in the fall of 1864 and early 1865.[78] There was ample time for training most of these new arrivals for operations in 1865.

1864 Election (November 8, 1864)

In August 1864, someone reputedly asked the Sixtieth Ohio's commanding officer if the Union would ultimately have to compromise with the Confederacy. He responded, "If the President hints ever at 'compromise'" all his men would storm the White House. In the November election, the Sixtieth Ohio voted nearly 70 percent for Lincoln.[79] While there is a legitimate dispute whether a soldier's vote for Lincoln can be properly interpreted as support for Lincoln's policy of emancipation, a soldier's vote for Lincoln as opposed to McClellan can legitimately be interpreted as a vote to continue the war until the Confederacy surrendered on the battlefield as opposed to negotiating a peaceful end to the war. A soldier's vote to continue the war until victory rather than for negotiating a peace treaty that would bring him home sooner without the risk of further casualties suggests strong morale. A vote to continue the war could also be viewed as a patriotic act.

Jonathan White has written that "Soldier support for Lincoln . . . rose and fell as the prospects for victory rose and fell." After the fall of Atlanta on September 1, "victory and honorable peace again seemed attainable [and] northern voters rejected the Democratic Party, lock, stock and barrel."[80] Seventy-eight percent of the Union soldiers who voted cast their ballot for Lincoln, compared to 55 percent for all voters.[81] The late-war new regiments and old Pennsylvania regiments studied here for which data are available voted more heavily for Lincoln than the overall vote for Lincoln in their home states.[82] However, the percentages for Lincoln were not as high as for the Union army overall (see Table 7.1). The fact that the soldiers generally cast their votes for Lincoln at markedly higher rates than their civilian counterparts suggests that the normative motivating forces in their regiments predominated over those of their home states. The high percentages in favor of continuing the war also cast doubt on the proposition that the late-war replacements were mercenaries lacking in patriotism. Even if the men had been motivated by the bounty to enlist, the normative motivating forces within their regiments apparently prevailed.

Table 8.1: Support for President Lincoln in the 1864 Election

	For Lincoln (Percent)					For Lincoln (Percent)		
	Unit Total					Unit Total		
	Votes	Regiment	State			Votes	Regiment	State
Maine					Pennsylvania			
31st	129	84	59		11th	279	53	52
32nd	99	69			45th	116	84	
					48th	290	83	
New York					50th	234	65	
185th	580	89	50.5		51st	398	64	
187th	221	96			53rd	193	61	
188th	545	93			83rd	149	79	
189th	558	86			100th	253	84	
					116th	112	48	
Ohio					143rd	286	65	
60th	134	69	56		145th	99	79	
					148th	199	64	
Vermont					183rd	105	55	
17th	102	71	76		184th	254	63	
					198th	599	59	
Wisconsin					200th	606	63	
36th	137	63	56		207th	643	69	
37th	168	87			208th	680	59	
38th	358	79			209th	565	55	
					210th	447	58	
					211th	571	75	

Source: OR 42:3, 561, 565–66, 569, 576–77, 594; *New York Daily Reformer* (Watertown), November 5, 1864, 2; *Albany Evening Journal,* October 31, 1864, 1. The state percentages for Lincoln are from Wikipedia, 1864 United States Presidential Election.

Voter participation data can provide additional insight. High voter participation indicates strong voter interest in the outcome. As high as 80 percent of eligible soldiers voted.[83] Combined with the high percentage of soldiers voting to continue the war until the Confederacy surrendered, the high voter participation further indicates strong morale among the Union soldiers in the field.

Warren's Hicksford Raid (December 7–11)

While not a battle, the Hicksford Raid is important because the successful mission of destroying more track on the Weldon Railroad further stressed Confederate supply capabilities, and the operation itself provided the most recent late-war new regiments the opportunity to maneuver as units under difficult circumstances outside of the Union lines.

The Fifth and Second Corps had destroyed the Weldon Railroad up to a point just below Reams's Station in August, but Grant and Meade wanted to push the destruction further south. On December 7, Warren moved out with a force of three divisions from his Fifth Corps, Mott's division from the Second Corps, Gregg's cavalry division, four batteries of artillery, and two hundred fifty feet of canvas pontoon equipment. Their objective was Hicksford—forty miles south of Petersburg. Meade—undoubtedly remembering Second Reams's Station— was concerned about the safe return of Warren's troops and sent a relief force from the Ninth Corps under Potter to meet them. The rumored Confederate force never appeared, and the Union troops returned safely. Warren reported to Meade that "I have completely destroyed the track from the Nottoway [River] to Hicksford." William Shackleton from the 198th Pennsylvania wrote that "we destroyed every thing that we com to. We burnt houses and barns and [farms?] and toar up railroad."[84]

The mission was arduous. New recruits in the 179th New York Volunteers recounted the harsh conditions. Abram Meyer recalled that "it snowed, rained and hailed the first night. The next day it was cold and the snow was about three inches deep." Henry Ap Rees claimed "that trip alone was worth a pension."[85]

The manpower provided in 1864 by late-war new regiments and the late-war replacements for the old regiments was critical to the Army of the Potomac's capability to maintain unrelenting pressure on the Army of Northern Virginia. But as with the Overland Campaign, their contribution was not just a matter of numbers. During the first six months of the Petersburg Campaign, the late-war replacements (as represented by the old Pennsylvania regiments studied here) and the late-war new regiments generally fought well.

CHAPTER 9

Second Reams's Station

August 25, 1864

The Battle of Second Reams's Station stands out because it was a blot on the reputation of the Union's vaunted Second Corps—and the reputation of its commander, Gen. Winfield Scott Hancock. The Confederates overran the Union defenses and took more than seventeen hundred Union prisoners. For Lincoln, the Confederate rout of Union forces could not have come at a worse time. Civilian morale in the North reached its low point in August 1864. Two days before Second Reams's Station, Lincoln had written that "it seems exceedingly probable that the Administration will not be re-elected" in November.[1] Lincoln desperately needed victories on the battlefield. Somebody had to be blamed for the defeat at Second Reams's Station.

Hancock himself singled out the high-bounty men in three of his regiments, and historians have followed his lead. Richard Sommers wrote in *Richmond Redeemed* that the high-bounty men "wrecked" the Second Corps at Second Reams's Station.[2] However, the causes of the defeat went beyond the simple presence of high-bounty men in the Second Corps' ranks. Moreover, the performance of the veterans from 1861 and 1862 at Second Reams's Station was little, if any, better than that of the high-bounty men.

The mission of the Second Corps, as Miles's and Gibbon's divisions exited from the Union lines on August 22, 1864, was to destroy the Weldon Railroad, a critical supply line for the Confederate troops at Petersburg, down to Rowanty Creek.[3] The Fifth Corps was also destroying track in the vicinity of Yellow Tavern.[4] Destruction of Confederate supply logistics was a critical element of Grant's strategy. By the end of the day on August 24, the Second Corps had destroyed

General Winfield Scott Hancock
(Library of Congress)

track to a point about three miles south of Reams's Station—five miles short of its objective.[5] The Second Corps' mission had not specifically been to engage Confederate troops. However, when Confederate troops arrived in force on August 25, Hancock decided that he could not safely withdraw that day and instead would remain and defend, consolidating his troops in existing fortifications that the Sixth Corps had built adjacent to Reams's Station in July 1864. While the Second Corps repulsed the initial Confederate attacks, a stronger Confederate attack beginning around 5:30 P.M. broke through the main Union line at several points. Despite the ensuing chaos and the heavy loss of prisoners, the Second Corps regrouped to the east and held fast, even retaking some of its lost ground. The Second Corps withdrew from Reams's Station during the night and reached the Union lines on August 26.[6]

In his after-action report, Hancock singled out the Seventh, Thirty-Ninth, and Fifty-Second New York for criticism, noting that they were "largely made up of recruits and substitutes" and "compare[d] very unfavorably with the veterans" they had replaced. These three regiments were not the only regiments that retreated. At the same time as these three regiments fell back, "a break occurred" in the 125th and 126th New York.[7] The Seventh, Thirty-Ninth, Fifty-Second, 125th, and 126th New York were five of the ten regiments comprising the Consolidated

Brigade, which had brought together the decimated regiments of the Second and Third Brigades in June 1864.[8]

Was Hancock's and Miles's criticism of these regiments justified? Did they "break without cause," as Gibbon reported? They did in fact break. Indeed, Confederate observers commented on the weakness of the Union soldiers' defense when the last Confederate attack hit the Union line.[9] However, the Confederates attacked vigorously. Union officers variously described the Confederate attack, which was preceded by a "fierce cannonade," as "a powerful assault," "a heavy column," and a "heavy force." Capt. T. Fred Brown of the First Rhode Island Light Artillery reported that the Confederates attacked "en masse, and with as reckless determination as was ever seen." Earl J. Hess concluded that Confederate general MacRae's "fierce determination to lead his Tar Heels into the Union position at any cost was a watershed in the course of the battle."[10]

Moreover, the Seventh, Thirty-Ninth, and Fifty-Second New York had helped repulse three Confederate attacks against their sector earlier in the day.[11] Second Corps memoranda described the Confederate attack at 2 P.M. as "quite a heavy assault," although it only lasted ten minutes.[12] Miles described it as a "vigorous" attack on the Fourth Brigade, to the left of the Consolidated Brigade, which was "handsomely repulsed" with "the assistance of . . . the Consolidated Brigade, firing to the right and left oblique, the troops fighting with determination."[13] The Second Corps repulsed a repeat attack at 3 P.M. and a "brisk dash" at 5 P.M.[14]

The Confederates may also have outnumbered somewhat the Seventh, Thirty-Ninth, and Fifty-Second New York. The three Confederate Brigades making the assault—MacRae's (right), Cooke's (center), and Lane's (left)—comprised about seventeen hundred fifty soldiers. As John Horn recounts, "the main impact of Cooke's right and MacRae's brigade fell on . . . the 7th, 39th and 52nd New York."[15] A Confederate officer speculated that the Union defenders "must have smiled as they beheld the small force advancing against them" but the attacking Confederates may have been equally surprised by the small number of defenders awaiting them. The three Union regiments had somewhat less than a thousand men—about two hundred fifty in four companies in the Seventh New York, about three hundred in six companies in the Thirty-Ninth New York, and about four hundred in six companies in the Fifty-Second New York. They formed only a single line with the men a pace apart in some places, contrary to standard doctrine, which required two ranks for a "vigorous" defense. Moreover, the fact that the Union parapet was only about three feet high in many places undercut the normal advantage of troops in prepared positions. MacRae's Brigade faced no Union abatis and may have followed Upton's tactic at Cold Harbor of not firing until they reached the enemy lines. The Consolidated Brigade's after-action report, written by its new commander, Lt. Col. William Wilson, stated that "the thin line in the works, flanked on the right and left, was obliged to fall back," noting that the Confederate broke through at the gaps at Depot Road and where the railroad passed through the Union positions.[16]

The Seventh, Thirty-Ninth, and Fifty-Second New York also did not have effective artillery support as the Confederate troops closed. The Tenth Battery, Massachusetts Light Infantry had run so low on ammunition at that point that it had to reserve fire until short range. Other batteries could not fire at all for fear of hitting Union troops or because of physical obstructions.[17]

Hancock noted that the Seventh New York was "entirely new." Indeed, the Seventh New York did not arrive at City Point until July 19, only five weeks before Second Reams's Station. The Seventh New York was only a battalion of four companies, which had been performing garrison duty in New York Harbor after having been mustered in from March 29 through July 15. They did not receive their arms until July 26, which provided little, if any, time for live-fire training. A Confederate officer derisively recalled that the Union defenders "sent their shots into the tops of the trees" during the final attack. That certainly could be the mark of nervousness under fire, but it could also reflect a lack of live-fire training.[18] For Hancock to say that a battalion of four companies that had only been in the field for just over a month with hardly any training "compares very unfavorably with the veterans absent" is hardly surprising—or fair. Moreover, there is a threshold question—how could the Second Corps' commanders position a unit as clearly inexperienced as the Seventh New York at or near what was obviously one of the most vulnerable points in the Union lines—the ten-yard gap at Depot Road? That just does not make sense.[19]

Moreover, it is important to remember that the late-war replacements did not suddenly appear in the Second Corps' ranks for the first time at Second Reams's Station. Late-war replacements provided a sorely needed increase in numbers for many of the regiments in the Second Corps in the fall of 1863 and the spring of 1864. For example, as the Overland Campaign began, the Second Corps' First Division had three thousand new recruits in its ranks. The inspector general reported that "considering this fact [the First Division] is in admirable condition."[20] These new recruits fought alongside the veterans throughout the Overland Campaign and into the Petersburg Campaign.

Hancock did not criticize the late-war replacements then. Indeed, he praised the First Division's Irish Brigade for fighting with "great steadiness and gallantry" at the Battle of the Wilderness even though "four-fifths of its numbers were recruits."[21] All five regiments of the Irish Brigade qualified for Fox's Three Hundred.[22] At Second Reams's Station, the Sixty-Third, Sixty-Ninth, and Eighty-Eighth New York were part of the Consolidated Brigade.[23] Similarly, on July 31, 1864, just a month before Second Reams's Station, Hancock "express[ed] to the troops his gratification with their conduct during the late movement across the James River. . . . The spirit exhibited by the command shows that they are determined to maintain the high reputation they have heretofore acquired."[24]

Most of the late-war replacements in the Thirty-Ninth New York and the Fifty-Second New York were veterans of the Overland Campaign and the beginning of the Petersburg Campaign. Their commanding generals had not criticized their performance then.

The Fifty-Second New York was a three-year regiment from 1861. Heavy casualties at Fair Oaks, Fredericksburg, Chancellorsville, and Gettysburg had seriously depleted its strength by the end of the summer of 1863.[25] Recruits replenished its ranks in July, August, and September 1863. The Fifty-Second New York's regimental (and brigade) commander, Col. Paul Frank, was pleased with the Fifty-Second's performance at Bristoe Station: "numbering about 85 old men, [the regiment] had been filled up with nearly 600 recruits, most of them substitutes . . . [C]ontinual marches . . . prevented all drills and instructions of this regiment. In consideration of all these circumstances, I must state that the men . . . behaved well."[26] An unidentified observer recounted that the Fifty-Second New York, "a conscript regiment, . . . wavered and were falling back on the old regiments, when Col. Frank . . . rallied them. . . . In a moment the panic subsided, and the men stood cooly in their lines, though the shot and shell of the enemy were knocking them over pretty fast."[27]

With new recruits predominating in its ranks, the Fifty-Second New York actively participated in the Overland Campaign and the beginning of the Petersburg Campaign, losing 164 men at Spotsylvania and fifty-four in the June assaults at Petersburg. Somewhat more than half the men of the Fifty-Second New York on the field at Second Reams's Station were replacements from 1863 and an additional 15 percent or so were from 1864, some of whom had only arrived earlier in August.[28]

Nor should one assume that the veterans from 1861 and 1862 in the Fifty-Second New York all performed appropriately. Shortly after the battle, two sergeants in Company D were reduced to the ranks, one as "unfit" for his position and the other "on account of cowardice," as were two sergeants in Company G as "unfit" and "as absent without authority."[29] The Fifty-Second New York also had perhaps fifty short-timers on the field—men who had enlisted for three years in 1861, but who had decided not to reenlist at the end of 1863 and early 1864. They would leave the army in September and October 1864.[30] They may have broken just as quickly.[31]

The Thirty-Ninth New York was a three-year regiment from May 1861. As a result of casualties, the remaining soldiers were consolidated into four companies in May 1863 that were mustered out on June 24, 1864, upon expiration of the original term of service. Six new companies were formed in December 1863 and January 1864. The reconstituted Thirty-Ninth New York lost heavily at the Wilderness and Spotsylvania.[32] It lost one hundred men or more the day before Cold Harbor when the veterans from 1861 who had not reenlisted were discharged. On August 25, 60 percent of the men present had joined the regiment in 1863 and a quarter in 1864.[33]

The 125th and 126th New York were three-year regiments organized in August 1862. They had surrendered at Harpers Ferry in September 1862, but the Confederates paroled them. At Gettysburg, the 126th New York suffered over two hundred casualties and the 125th over one hundred.[34] Despite these losses, only twenty-six replacements joined the 126th New York. At Second Reams's Station, veterans from August 1862 comprised the 126th New York, not high-bounty men. Roughly one hundred late-war replacements joined the 125th New York before the Overland Campaign. They comprised about half of its force at Second Reams's Station.[35]

Looking at the Second Corps as a whole, Lawrence Kreiser noted that "In placing the blame on draftees, the volunteers of 1861 and 1862 avoided some hard truths. Many of them streamed away from the fighting as quickly as had replacement soldiers." As noted, the Confederates captured over seventeen hundred Second Corps soldiers. The casualties suffered by the Seventh New York, the Thirty-Ninth New York, and the Fifty-Second New York were in line with the casualties suffered by other Second Corps regiments. By far the largest number of casualties was suffered by a regiment organized in 1861—the Fourth New York Heavy Artillery (forty-five killed or wounded/three hundred thirty captured)—and a regiment organized in 1862—the Eighth New York Heavy Artillery (thirty-four killed or wounded/two hundred ten captured or missing), although they also had large numbers of men engaged.[36]

Miles also criticized a late-war new regiment. The Thirty-Sixth Wisconsin was one of the regiments in Rugg's Brigade that were held in reserve and criticized by General Miles for not counterattacking when the Confederates broke through the Consolidated Brigade's line. However, the Thirty-Sixth Wisconsin did not retreat and 134 of its men were captured.[37] The Thirty-Sixth Wisconsin also suffered the indignity, along with a dozen old regiments, of losing its colors to the enemy. The Union command punished the Thirty-Sixth Wisconsin and the other regiments by depriving them of the right to carry colors. However, the men of the Thirty-Sixth Wisconsin redeemed themselves at Burgess's Mill two months later, "having behaved with distinguished bravery," and the Union command restored their colors.[38]

Miles did praise one regiment in his division—the Sixty-First New York, which he observed "fighting with determination. It had changed front after the rifle-pits had been flanked, and with its right resting on the works was contesting every foot of ground gained by the enemy." The Sixty-First New York anchored the makeshift line that blunted the Confederate attack.[39] However, most of the men in the Sixty-First New York on the field that day were late-war replacements, not veterans from 1861. The Sixty-First New York was a three-year regiment raised in 1861. By the time of Second Reams's Station, it had already suffered the casualties that would qualify it as one of Fox's Three Hundred. But it was because of heavy casualties that only about seventy-five of the men of the Sixty-First on the field at Second Reams's Station had enlisted in 1861. Another forty or so had enlisted in 1862. Late-war replacements from earlier in 1864 comprised the substantial majority of the men on the field. From the beginning of 1864 through the end of April 1864, roughly one hundred fifty replacements joined the Sixty-First New York and these replacements fought with the Sixty-First through the Overland Campaign and into the Petersburg Campaign. In the last half of July, another 60 replacements joined the Sixty-First New York and in the beginning of August about another 275 joined, many of whom apparently arrived in time for the Battle of Second Reams's Station because some of them became casualties.[40] The predominance of high-bounty men apparently did not adversely impact the Sixty-First New York at Second Reams's Station. Indeed, their development as soldiers over time puts in question Miles's reaction in August 1863 when they began arriving. Back then, Miles viewed "nearly all" of the recruits as "miserable surly rough fellows . . . without any patriotism or honor."[41]

The inspector general's August 1864 report noted that "The 148th Pa. and 61st N.Y. Vols. are reported to have behaved remarkably well."[42] The 148th Pennsylvania was a three-year regiment organized in October 1862. The 148th lost heavily at Chancellorsville and Gettysburg, with nearly three hundred casualties in the two battles. At the end of 1863, nearly three hundred conscripts joined the 148th Pennsylvania, followed by one hundred twenty recruits in the spring of 1864. The high proportion of late-war replacements in the ranks of the 148th Pennsylvania apparently did not adversely affect its performance at Second Reams's Station.[43]

Hancock also criticized the performance of Gibbon's Division. The men in the detached regiments held in reserve from the Second Division to back up the First Division "could neither be made to go forward nor fire."[44] The rest of Gibbon's Division "offered very little resistance, though the attack was feeble."[45] Hancock specifically criticized the 152nd New York, which "was reported to have behaved very badly here, running away without firing more than one or two shots" when called from reserve to reinforce the front line.[46] The 152nd was a three-year regiment from October 1862. The 152nd New York was actively engaged at the Wilderness, Spotsylvania, North Ana, Cold Harbor, and in the June 1864 attacks at Petersburg.[47] Some new recruits did join the 152nd New York in the spring of 1864, but at Second Reams's Station, 80 percent or more of the men of the 152nd on the field had enlisted in 1862. Thus, as with 126th New York, high-bounty men apparently did not cause the poor performance of the 152nd New York at Second Reams's Station.[48]

The performance of the Sixty-First New York (and perhaps the 148th Pennsylvania) at Second Reams's Station demonstrated that late-war replacements could fight well. The performance of the 126th and 152nd New York demonstrated that there were also veterans who "behaved badly." Hancock's explanation that some of his troops performed poorly at Second Reams's Station because of "their great fatigue, owing to the heavy labor exacted of them and to their enormous losses during the campaign" certainly seems to apply to the 126th and 152nd New York. But that explanation also applies to the Thirty-Ninth and Fifty-Second New York, whose "substitutes and recruits" had been fighting for nearly a year and had just finished two and a half days of hard labor tearing up railroad tracks.[49]

Both Hancock and Gibbon emphasized the loss of large numbers of officers in the recent campaigns as an explanation for the defeat. Gibbon noted that his division had lost forty regimental commanders and that the brigades had had seventeen different commanders. In his view, the heavy loss of officers as well as men "show why it is that the troops, which at the commencement of the campaign were equal to almost any undertaking, became toward the end of it unfit for almost any."[50] Similarly, the inspector general's July 1864 report noted that "The very great losses sustained by the Corps, especially in commanders . . . have most materially impaired its efficiency."[51]

The lack of field-grade officers and the resulting organizational problems hit the Consolidated Brigade the hardest of the seven brigades in Miles's and Gibbon's divisions. At the end of July 1864, none of the ten regiments in the Consolidated Brigade was commanded by a field-grade officer—eight were commanded by captains and two by lieutenants. The other six brigades had at least one regiment commanded by a field-grade officer and as many as five regiments commanded by a field-grade officer.[52]

When the Consolidated Brigade arrived at Reams's Station on August 23, Lt. Col. Levin Crandall was in command. However, the next day Miles put Crandall in command of the First Division's picket line and command of the Consolidated Brigade devolved on Maj. John Byron from the Second Brigade. At some point in the battle, Byron was captured and Capt. Nelson Penfield from the 125th New York took command of the Consolidated Brigade.[53]

Captain Nelson Penfield (125th New York Volunteers) (Courtesy of the New York State Military Museum)

Matters became more complicated during the battle around 1 P.M., when Lt. Col. Oscar Broady commanding the Fourth Brigade of the First Division (positioned to the left of the Consolidated Brigade) took command of the Third Brigade of the Consolidated Brigade without officially advising the Consolidated Brigade headquarters. Under Broady's orders, Penfield advanced the 111th, 125th, and 126th New York as skirmishers into the woods. The remainder of the Third Brigade in the main line—including the Seventh, Thirty-Ninth, Fifty-Second, and Fifty-Seventh New York—was separated from Broady's position by the ten-yard gap in the fortifications at Depot Road.[54]

As a result of Penfield having moved the 111th, 125th, and 126th New York forward as skirmishers, the main position was thinned, as noted, to a single line with the men a pace apart in some places. Captain Penfield's failure to return his troops to the main line after being warned that Confederate troops were approaching in force aggravated the situation. The Confederates "advanced with the utmost silence" and "suddenly broke with full force on the skirmish line, which soon became mingled with the pursuing column." Both the troops in the main line and the supporting artillery had to withhold their fire to allow the skirmishers to disengage and return to the main line.[55] Disengagement of the skirmishers cost both firepower and separation at a critical moment. A field-grade officer might have made the correct decision to immediately withdraw the skirmish line, which Captain Penfield had not. Moreover, because Confederates quickly moved through the ten-yard gap between the Third (Consolidated) and Fourth Brigades, it is highly unlikely that Lieutenant Colonel Broady was able to provide any field-grade leadership to the Third Brigade. At this critical time, the Seventh New York, the Thirty-Ninth New York, and the Fifty-Second New York had only the three captains commanding them to rally the troops.[56]

Finally, it is noteworthy that Hancock's analysis of the causes of the defeat at Second Reams's Station did not include his own decisions as the commander of the Second Corps. Hancock was humiliated by his defeat at Second Reams's Station.[57] His failure to consider his own role in the defeat is understandable, but two critical mistakes on his part were at least as significant in the defeat as the performance of his troops—choosing to defend from the pre-existing fortifications and failing to make the organizational changes necessitated by the heavy casualties during the Overland Campaign and the beginning of the Petersburg Campaign.

First, Hancock and his division commanders unanimously—and legitimately—criticized the layout of the fortifications built by the Sixth Corps at Reams's Station back in July. Hancock believed that the works were "very poorly located, the bad location contributing very materially to the subsequent loss of the position." But Hancock chose to defend from those fortifications without significant modification. Miles stated that "I did not consider the position strong, but was obliged to occupy the works as I found them."[58]

The rectangular shape with a short face on the west side made it easy for the Confederates to concentrate their forces on that short face. While the senior commanders of the Second Corps incorrectly claimed that they had been heavily outnumbered at Second Reams's Station, the rectangular layout of the Union fortifications may have enabled Confederates to bring superior numbers to bear against the Consolidated Brigade defending the west face. The elongated works also gave the Confederates the opportunity to position their artillery for enfilading fire into the Union ranks, an opportunity that Col. John Pegram seized.[59] As a result, the Union troops defending the northern and southern sides were able to bring only limited fire to bear to support the Consolidated Brigade.[60]

In addition, the front of the Sixth Corps' fortifications was built west of the Weldon Railroad and Halifax Road, with gaps for the railroad and road to pass through. That gap separated the Consolidated Brigade's right from the First Brigade's left and Confederate troops flooded through that gap. The opening where Depot Road ran through from the west allowed Confederate troops to flood through on the Seventh New York's left flank.[61] Had Hancock located his troops

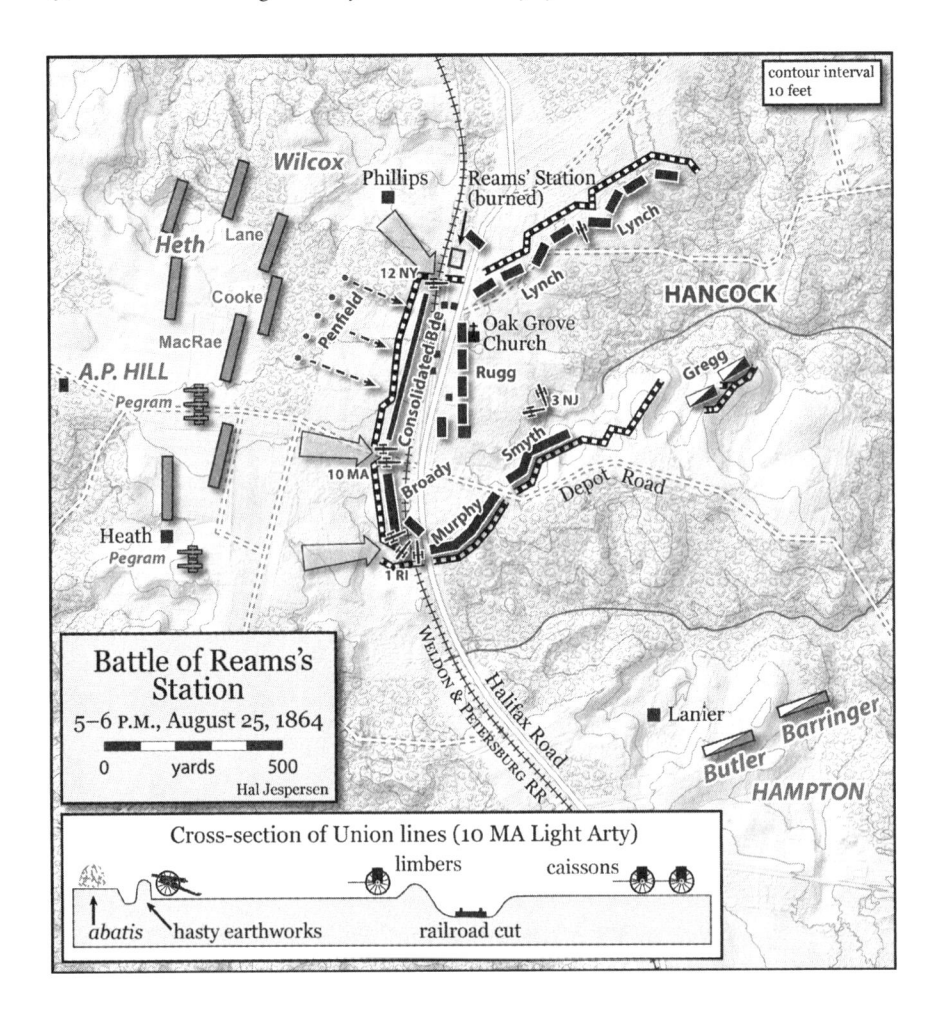

on the east side of the Weldon Railroad, his defensive position would have been considerably stronger. For the southern half of that sector, the six-foot embankment built for the railroad could have served as the line. For the northern half, the railroad ran through a cut as much as thirteen feet deep and the natural lay of the land would have been the choice.[62]

Second, as commander of the Second Corps, Hancock was responsible for the organization of his forces. In his after-action report, Gibbon—as mortified as Hancock by the defeat—could "only account for the unsteadiness shown by my men by the fact that so many of my very best officers and men have been lost on this campaign, that the command is in a great measure disorganized."[63] Gibbon returned to the impact of disorganization in his memoirs. He recalled that shortly after Second Reams's Station he had raised with Hancock the "absolute necessity of a complete reorganization of the corps by which commands should be consolidated and placed under efficient leaders." Hancock reacted quite an-grily and suggested that Gibbon should leave the Second Corps, which he did soon thereafter.[64] Hancock bears the responsibility for not reorganizing his com-mand to reflect its depleted state. The ineffective organizational structure cer-tainly had an impact on the Consolidated Brigade, as discussed above.

There is no basis to claim that all the late-war replacements in the Second Corps performed well at Second Reams's Station. However, the evidence shows that factors beyond their control caused their shortcomings. Moreover, the evidence also shows that the veterans from 1861 and 1862 did not perform any better. The evidence is even stronger that poor decisions by senior and junior officers com-ing on top of the debilitating impact of the constant fighting since the beginning of the Overland Campaign undercut the performance of the troops in general, the veterans from 1861 and 1862, as well as the late-war replacements. As Gibbon succinctly wrote in his memoirs, the men of the Second Corps were just "fought out" at Second Reams's Station.[65]

In his history of the Second Corps, Francis Walker, assistant adjutant general of the Corps, recounted that after Second Reams's Station, the Second Corps "was yet again to rise, under the healing touch of time, powerful, valiant and victori-ous" in its pursuit of Lee toward Appomattox. Walker attributed the change in large part to wounded veteran officers and enlisted men's return to the field, but he also pointed to the benefit of "the wholesome discipline of the camp for the recruit."[66] Rather than "wrecking" the Second Corps, the late-war replacements were a critical resource—first for sustaining it—and then for rebuilding it.[67]

Finally, while there is no dispute that the Confederates badly defeated the Sec-ond Corps on August 25, 1864, the question whether the Second Corps achieved its assigned mission should not be overlooked. The Second Corps' original mis-sion was to destroy railroad track, not to engage Confederate troops. The Second Corps destroyed track three miles beyond Reams's Station but five miles short of its objective. The combined efforts of the Second Corps and the Fifth Corps im-paired Confederate supply logistics enough that Grant and Meade were generally pleased with the operation, but the impairment was not decisive.[68]

CHAPTER 10

Fort Stedman

March 25, 1865

By the end of 1864, the Confederacy had little chance for survival. Lincoln's victory in the November election dashed Confederate hopes that McClellan would win and negotiate a peace treaty.[1] As the spring campaign season approached in 1865, both the Union and the Confederacy knew that it would be the last of the war. In the east, Grant's Overland Campaign in late spring of 1864 and the following offensive at Petersburg had not yet worn down Lee's forces to the breaking point, but the Army of the Potomac clearly had the necessary forces to defeat the Army of Northern Virginia in a matter of months.[2] Moving from the west, Sherman's forces had taken Atlanta in September 1864 and would take Charleston in February 1865. They were unstoppable.

But Lee was not ready to surrender. Lee tasked Gen. John Gordon with developing a plan of attack that would so disrupt Grant's forces and supply capabilities that Grant would have to significantly curtail his lines, which had been doggedly extending to turn Lee's flank. If the attack succeeded, Lee could split his forces, one part defending shorter lines around Petersburg while holding Grant's forces in place and the other disengaging to unite with General Johnston's forces in North Carolina to defeat Sherman.[3] Gordon saw a weak point in the Union positions around Fort Stedman, manned by General Willcox's Division of the Ninth Corps, and planned to open a hole large enough to send troops sweeping through into the Union rear. Gordon thought that by capturing Fort Stedman and the Union positions in the rear, "the disintegration of the whole left wing of the federal army" might be possible. Lee approved the plan and authorized Gordon to deploy nearly half of the available Confederate forces.[4]

The Engagement

The mission of Hartranft's Division as the Ninth Corps' reserve force was to work with the frontline troops to defeat any Confederate assault. If the Confederates broke through the front lines, Hartranft's Division would be responsible for initially containing and ultimately repulsing them. Pvt. Charles Hemphill, a later-enlisting volunteer in Hartranft's Division, believed that the Ninth Corps would hold "the position against three times their number of Johnnies for I think we have an impregnable position."[5] Events proved him correct, but not without some perilous moments.

The attack began auspiciously for the Confederates around 4 A.M. on the morning of March 25, 1865. Willcox's Division bore the brunt of the attack. Confederate soldiers deceived Union pickets by claiming that they were deserters. The Union picket lines fell without sounding the alarm, and the Confederates quickly carried the Union line between Battery IX and Fort Haskell, including Fort Stedman and Batteries X, XI, and XII. The Confederates then headed—albeit slowly— toward Meade Station on the military railroad and the Union rear.[6] However, after the initial surprise, the Union forces responded quickly and decisively, just as the Confederate forces had after the explosion of the mine at the Battle of the Crater. Willcox's forces held at Battery IX and Fort Haskell. Hartranft's Division contained the Confederate thrust toward the Union rear and then forced the

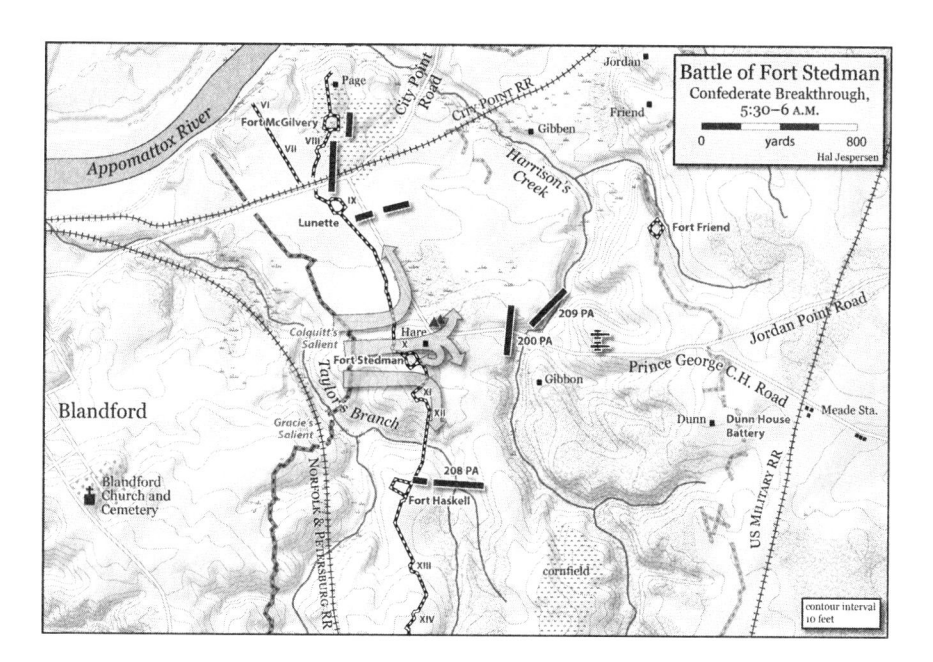

Confederates to retreat. By 8 A.M., the Union troops had forced the Confederates back to their original positions.[7]

The six regiments comprising Hartranft's Division were all late-war new regiments from Pennsylvania—the 200th, 205th, 207th, 208th, 209th, and 211th Pennsylvania Volunteers. The six regiments did not arrive in the field until the end of September.[8] Apart from picket duty, they had not yet been in combat. As J. M. of the 207th Pennsylvania wrote home, the Battle of Fort Stedman gave them "an opportunity to test their courage."[9] Hartranft praised his men for their "gallant and heroic conduct": "You have won a name and reputation of which veterans might feel proud, and have proved yourselves worthy of being the associates of the brave soldiers of the old 9th corps."[10] General Parke, the commander of the Ninth Corps, reported that Hartranft's troops, "the vast majority of them new men, for the first time under fire, charged with great spirit and resolution."[11] General Meade commended their "conspicuous gallantry . . . for the first time under fire."[12]

What exactly did these six regiments do to earn such lofty praise? More importantly, how was it that new, inexperienced soldiers were able to perform in a way that would make even veterans feel proud?

Movement to Contact

The six late-war new regiments met their first challenge by moving into position quickly and effectively to seal off the Confederate breakthrough. As the reserve, they were spread out behind the entire extent of the Ninth Corps' front-line positions—the 200th Pennsylvania between Dunn House Battery and Fort Friend (one mile behind Fort Stedman); the 209th Pennsylvania about two hundred yards in front of Meade Station on the US Military Railroad (another half mile further east of Fort Stedman); the 208th Pennsylvania to the right of Hartranft's headquarters at Avery House (two miles southeast of Fort Stedman); the 205th and 207th Pennsylvania on the military railroad near Fort Prescott (about three miles south of Fort Stedman), and the 211th Pennsylvania near the railroad about halfway between forts Howard and Alexander Hays (about four to five miles south of Fort Stedman). From Dunn House Hill, where the Dunn House Battery and Fort Friend were located, "an excellent view of Petersburg could be obtained, the tantalizing steeples of the 'Cockade city' being especially conspicuous."[13]

Firing awakened Union troops shortly after 4 A.M.[14] Hartranft "heard the alarm" of the Confederate attack around 4:30 A.M.[15] He immediately sent forward a staff officer, Capt. Prosper Dalien, to investigate and alerted his two brigade commanders, who put their men "under arms ready for any emergency."

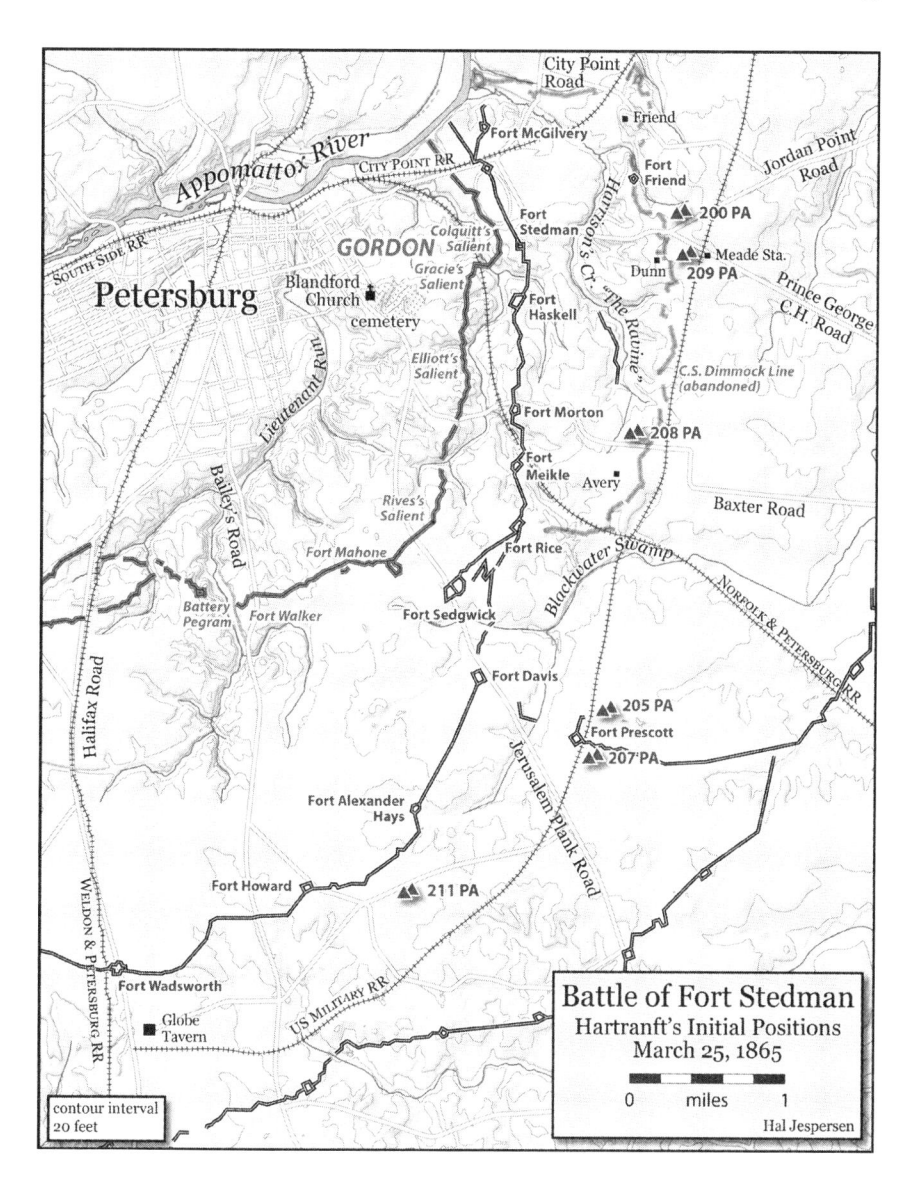

Battle of Fort Stedman
Hartranft's Initial Positions
March 25, 1865

0   miles   1

contour interval
20 feet

Hal Jespersen

Dalien returned shortly after 5 A.M., reporting that the Confederates had carried Fort Stedman and Battery XI and were moving north toward the Appomattox River. At 5:15 A.M. General Parke ordered Hartranft to move his troops near Meade Station—the 200th and 209th Pennsylvania—to reinforce General Willcox.[16] Hartranft ordered the 208th Pennsylvania to report to the Third Brigade (General McLaughlen) of Willcox's Division near Fort Haskell, and then Hartranft rode off to Willcox's headquarters at Friend House, two miles from Avery House, to confer with him.[17]

The Union defensive response depended on the initial movements of the 200th and 209th Pennsylvania as the reserve regiments closest to Fort Stedman. While the particular day of March 25 came as a surprise, the Union command anticipated the possibility of a predawn Confederate attack and put in place certain precautionary measures, such as loading artillery with canister at nightfall. As one of these precautionary measures, Hartranft and Willcox had agreed that in the event of an emergency, Willcox would direct the 200th and the 209th Pennsylvania because he could more quickly and effectively direct them to respond to the needs of his troops in the front lines.[18] Thus, even before Hartranft could execute the orders from Parke to send the 200th and the 209th Pennsylvania to reinforce Willcox, Willcox had already set the two regiments in motion. He ordered the 200th Pennsylvania to move north to his headquarters at Friend House and the 209th Pennsylvania to move to the signal station in the rear of Dunn House Battery.[19] The 200th Pennsylvania began moving toward Friend House—about three-quarters of a mile away, but about halfway there, Lt. Col. William McCall, commanding the 200th, "saw a number of men retreating from the front, when I immediately halted my regiment" and moved it back to Dunn House Battery.[20] At that point, Hartranft arrived on the scene after conferring with Willcox and took command. It was then "sufficiently light [around 6 A.M.] to see the enemy's skirmishers advancing" up Prince George Court House Road from Fort Stedman.[21]

When they arrived at Dunn House Battery, Hartranft and the 200th Pennsylvania found the remnants of the Fifty-Seventh Massachusetts, which the Confederates had driven back from their camp located about one hundred yards behind Fort Stedman and Battery X. The Fifty-Seventh Massachusetts had counterattacked at the rear of Fort Stedman, but the Confederate forces outflanked them and forced them to fall back. The Fifty-Seventh Massachusetts tried to hold, but the Confederates forced them to retreat back up the road toward Meade Station four times. The Fifty-Seventh Massachusetts suffered heavy losses all along the way. They finally fell back to Dunn House Battery at the top of the ridge, the Confederates having reduced them to "a small party."[22]

Hartranft ordered an attack back down the road toward the 57th Massachusetts's camp, deploying the Fifty-Seventh Massachusetts as skirmishers.[23] The 200th Pennsylvania advanced to the camp of the Fifty-Seventh Massachusetts without sustaining significant casualties, but heavy Confederate fire from Fort Stedman and the road running north from Fort Stedman forced the 200th Pennsylvania to withdraw forty yards to an old line of works to the right of the Fifty-Seventh Massachusetts's camp.[24] Hartranft feared that the Confederates seeing the 200th Pennsylvania retreat "would take advantage of it and attack," so he attacked again and "gained quite a good position."[25] The 200th Pennsylvania "held this position for about twenty minutes, losing very heavily (the loss being about one hundred men at this point), when the line wavered and fell back and was rallied on the old line of works" it had just left.[26]

In the meantime, Hartranft had ordered the 209th Pennsylvania forward. The 209th Pennsylvania moved into position on the right of the 200th Pennsylvania. With troops from Willcox's Division covering the position from the 209th Pennsylvania back to Battery IX on the Union front line, Hartranft decided to go on the defensive.[27]

An officer in Ransom's Brigade, part of the Confederate force advancing from Fort Stedman, described the persistence of the 200th Pennsylvania: "A solid column of blue appears upon the rising ground to our front and right. Their alignment is perfect, and down they dash only to be repulsed by the steady volleys from our line. Over again they come, and again they are driven back. The third time they meet with no better success."[28] However, as William Wyrick notes: "Even though they had repulsed Hartranft's counterattack, Ransom's Carolinians were no longer on the attack. Instead, they were now using their bayonets to dig in where they were—stalled between Battery No. IX on the north and Fort Stedman on the south. The attack was beginning to bog down."[29]

In his 1889 history of the battle, Capt. William Henry Hodgkins, one of Hartranft's staff officers, recounted the maxim attributed to the Duke of Wellington that the "test of a soldier was not whether he would run, but whether he would run and come back."[30] The 200th Pennsylvania passed that test. In Hartranft's words, the 200th Pennsylvania made "two stubborn attacks on the enemy, and when compelled to retire it fell back in good order."[31]

A week after the battle, Company D's Pvt. Charles Dellinger wrote to a friend that "we had a very hevy fight." Noting that the Union had taken Charleston and Savannah, he commented that "I guess next we will walk into Petersburg."[32]

In the 209th Pennsylvania, Company A's Capt. John Landis recalled that "a sudden rattle of musketry, quick, angry and sharp awakened me at about four o'clock in the morning. . . . Just what had taken place we did not know."[33] Quickly changing orders directed the 209th Pennsylvania. Following General Willcox's initial order, the 209th Pennsylvania—camped in front of Meade Station—first moved several hundred yards to a point near the signal station in the rear of Dunn House Battery and then double-quicked to the front and right of the battery.[34] They then marched toward Friend House and westward down the road to the left of Friend House.[35] They "suddenly . . . heard a heavy volley just to the left and in front of us, and hurrying over the little hill in our front, . . . saw the 200th Regiment had engaged the enemy."[36]

The 209th charged down the hill at the double-quick and reformed at Harrison's Creek.[37] The Seventeenth Michigan was on their right. Willcox had ordered the Seventeenth Michigan forward from Friend House to oppose Confederate skirmishers advancing between Batteries IX and X. The Seventeenth Michigan had only about one hundred men—the 209th had over six hundred.[38] The 209th Pennsylvania and the Seventeenth Michigan advanced across a field "under a very heavy fire of musketry and artillery" to the same line of old works entered by the 200th Pennsylvania, moving into position on the 200th's right. The old works extended north to the Petersburg & City Point Railroad. The Confederates were in force and not far away in a parallel section of the Prince George Court House Road running between Batteries IX and X.[39] The 209th briefly halted and then advanced, gaining a ditch—nearly breast deep—near the hill.[40] As noted, Hartranft decided to go on the defensive and the 209th remained in that position until the final assault.

Hartranft had ordered the 208th Pennsylvania to report to General McLaughlen (Third Brigade, Willcox's Division) near Fort Haskell around 5:30 A.M., just before he left Avery House headed for Willcox's headquarters at Friend House.[41] The lay of the land favored the 208th Pennsylvania's movement into position. A ravine with an established path ran northeast along Harrison Creek from Avery House to McLaughlen's headquarters, located about eight hundred yards east of Fort Haskell.[42] The ravine not only facilitated movement but also served as a covered way so that the Confederates did not see the 208th for the first time until just as it arrived.[43] However, the Confederates "immediately opened a heavy fire" when they saw the 208th.[44]

The 208th Pennsylvania arrived on the scene by 6 A.M. By that time, Fort Haskell's defenders had fought off three Confederate charges.[45] The 208th linked up with several small detachments from the Third Brigade of Willcox's Division numbering about two hundred men—the 208th Pennsylvania itself numbered over six hundred. The 208th moved into an old line of works in the rear of the camp of the One Hundredth Pennsylvania. The 208th had initially taken position too far to the left, but Capt. Prosper Dalien from Hartranft's staff directed a flank movement with filing to the right to create the new battle line lying between Fort Haskell and McLaughlin's headquarters.[46]

The 208th's initial volleys drove the advancing Confederates back to a ravine for cover. The 208th then advanced on the ravine, taking one hundred prisoners and forcing the remaining Confederates back to Battery XII and the lines connecting to Fort Stedman. The 208th remained there until about 7:30 A.M. when the final Union counterattack began.[47] The 208th's regimental scribe reported that they had been under fire for about two hours.[48]

Hartranft initially ordered his Second Brigade—the 205th, 207th, and 211th Pennsylvania—to stand ready to move to the right if needed.[49] Around 6 A.M., with the three regiments of the First Brigade already engaging the Confederates, Hartranft ordered the Second Brigade to report to Avery House.[50] The 205th and 207th Pennsylvania moved out from Fort Prescott at the double-quick, led by Maj. John D. Bertolette from Hartranft's staff, while the 211th started out from two miles further south.[51] At Avery House, the 205th and 207th Pennsylvania slowed to a quickstep and moved down the ravine toward Fort Haskell, as the 208th had earlier done. However, Hartranft held the 205th and 207th Pennsylvania in support and they did not engage the Confederates at that time. "Entirely unobserved by the enemy, [they] took position under an abrupt bank which, though near the enemy, completely sheltered them from fire" in the words of Captain Hodgkins.[52] They remained there for about an hour until the final Union counterattack.[53]

With the 205th and the 207th Pennsylvania in position, there was still a gap of three hundred yards—with Prince George Courthouse Road running through it—between the 200th Pennsylvania and the 207th Pennsylvania. Parke had ordered Hartranft to move his Second Brigade (the 205th, 207th, and 211th Pennsylvania) to Dunn Hill to protect the road to Meade Station. However, Hartranft believed that the Confederates could not advance any further due to "the concentrated infantry fire from the [200th and 209th Pennsylvania] and Batteries 9 and McGilvery on the right, and the [205th, 207th, and 208th Pennsylvania] and Fort Haskell on the left, and from the field artillery in position on the hills in rear of Stedman."[54] Concluding that Parke's objective had already been accomplished, Hartranft left the 205th and 207th Pennsylvania in position. However, he did move the 211th Pennsylvania to Dunn Hill.[55]

The fortuities of war left the 211th Pennsylvania under the command of a captain, William A. Coulter, on the morning of March 25. Two of the field-grade officers were absent and the third was sick in the hospital.[56] The 211th Pennsylvania had the farthest to come—four to five miles. The 211th had double-quicked to Avery House, arriving around 6:30 A.M.[57] The 211th then moved into position on the high ground in front of Meade Station to be ready to counterattack along the road from Meade Station back to Fort Stedman. The ridge between Fort Stedman and Meade Station masked the 211th's movement into position. The 211th Pennsylvania had over six hundred fifty men for the counterattack.[58]

The Final Union Counterattack

Hartranft had ordered his other regiments to be ready to attack when the 211th Pennsylvania appeared at the top of the ridge above Meade Station. The fully coordinated counterattack began around 7:45 A.M. The 209th charged Battery X and the line north of it; the 200th the northeast angle of Fort Stedman and the contiguous lines; the 208th Batteries XI and XII and the lines into Fort Stedman; the 205th directly at Fort Stedman, and the 207th at the west angle of Fort Stedman. Colonel Cox of the 207th cheered his troops on: "Boys, let's take that fort!"[59]

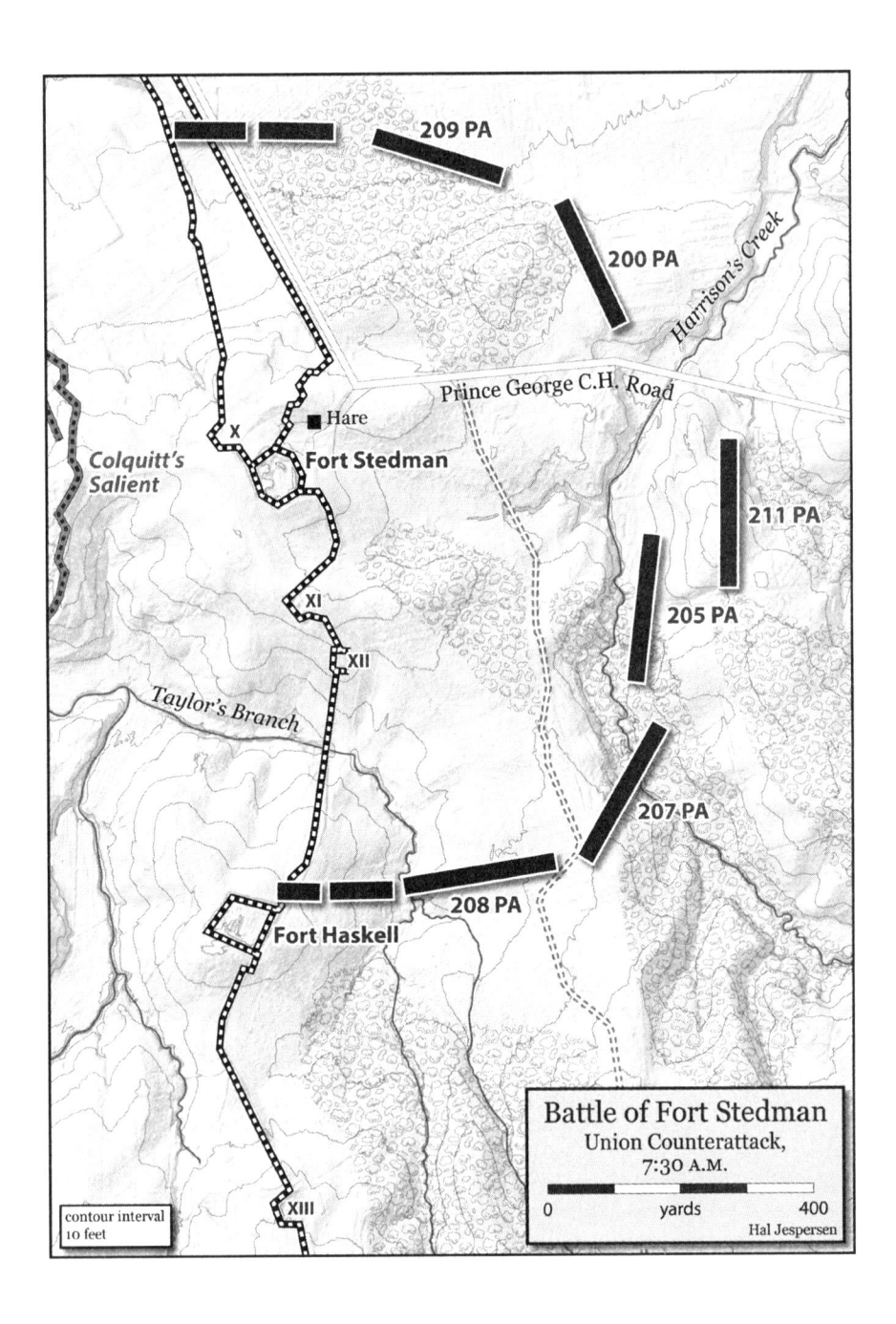

Battle of Fort Stedman
Union Counterattack,
7:30 A.M.

0   yards   400

Hal Jespersen

contour interval
10 feet

The 211th formed what Captain Landis of the 208th Pennsylvania described as a "tidal wave" to support them all. The 211th Pennsylvania, under the direction of Capt. Richard Watts from Hartranft's staff, completed the envelopment of the Confederate forces as the 211th advanced down Prince George Courthouse Road toward Fort Stedman by filling in the three-hundred-yard gap between the 200th and the 205th Pennsylvania.[60] Hartranft noted the effect of the 211th's size on the Confederate attackers: "The enemy, seeing the advance of this regiment, numbering about 600 muskets, in such handsome manner, commenced to waver, when the balance of the division charged with a will, in the most gallant style."[61] Samuel Bates wrote that the 211th Pennsylvania "had nearly full ranks, and when drawn out in line, it showed like a brigade."[62] Cpl. Nelson Statler from Company E wrote his wife that after arriving at the battlefield, "we was halted, ordered to load at will & formed in line of battle. Then we was ordered to charge. We fixed bayonets & and then we started on a run yelling as we advanced. . . . We was very lucky—the way the bullets flew around our heads—but we made the Johnnies suffer."[63] The Union forces took nineteen hundred prisoners as the Union counterattack forced the Confederates back across the field to their original lines.[64]

After Hartranft had ordered the attack, Parke ordered him to wait for reinforcements coming from the Sixth Corps, but Hartranft did not believe the attack could be called off at that late point and that it would succeed without reinforcements: "I saw that the enemy had already commenced to waver, and that success was certain."[65] Hartranft's assessment was correct and his division drove the Confederates back to their lines. The battle was over by 8:15 that morning, four hours after it started.[66]

In Hartranft's Division 200th Pennsylvania suffered the highest casualties (122), followed by the 209th at 55 and the 208th with 41. The regiments in the Second Brigade, which arrived later in the battle, suffered significantly lower casualties—17 in the 207th Pennsylvania, 11 in the 211th, and 10 in the 205th.[67]

Mission Accomplished

The six late-war new regiments from Pennsylvania in Hartranft's Division fully accomplished their mission of helping to initially contain and ultimately repulse the Confederate breakthrough. The notable elements of their success were: (1) Hartranft and his staff were directly involved throughout the battle; (2) the regiments deployed quickly and decisively; (3) the regiments used their large numbers to advantage; and (4) the 200th Pennsylvania transitioned effectively from offense to defense and back to offense. The relatively small number of casualties incurred was reasonable under the circumstances. These regiments of later-enlisting volunteers performed like veterans in shutting down the Confederate attack because they had achieved a high state of readiness for combat by March 25, 1865.

The Union army did not formally evaluate the elements of a unit's readiness during the Civil War era, but it did regularly inspect its regiments. Edmund Schriver, the Army of the Potomac's inspector general, required that an inspector be designated for every brigade, division, and corps. He had about seventy-five inspectors reporting to him.[68] The standard inspection form for a regiment began with the usual report of the numbers "present" and "absent" by company, followed by inventories and the condition of arms and ammunition, horses, and clothing and camp equipment. The form then called for evaluation on forty separate factors, ranging from the fundamental (for example, "Discipline," "System of military instruction," efficiency of officers," whether the troops are "properly fed," "Accommodations for Sick," and "What has been the general sanitary condition") to whether the regiment was going by the book, for example, whether Articles of War were "frequently read," whether "Morning Reports made regularly," and whether "Company Officers, Quartermasters, Commanders &c. account for public property regularly."[69] An "Inspector and Mustering Officer"—usually the regimental commander—also evaluated the regiment every two months on six criteria: discipline, instruction, military appearance, arms, accoutrements, and clothing.[70]

The initial inspector general reports did not augur well for future performance of the regiments in battle. At the end of November 1864, when the 200th, 207th, 208th, and 209th Pennsylvania were still assigned to the Army of the James's Provisional Brigade, the inspectors reported their officers as "inefficient." The inspectors also cited the four regiments as "indifferently" instructing officers and men in drill. They specifically criticized the 207th Pennsylvania: "Line officers generally ignorant of duties. Non-commissioned officers not selected with care—appearance of men untidy. Men not drilled in use of arms."[71]

Inspectors also cited these four regiments on numerous points in the October 1864 inspection reports. They criticized the 200th Pennsylvania particularly harshly: "Men allowed to do as they wish. Line officers with a few exceptions totally incompetent for the position. . . . Accoutrements dirty. Officers and men think they have too much duty to do and have not time to keep clean." But the inspectors did see potential in the 208th Pennsylvania—"Personal appearance good . . . the men seem willing and anxious to learn and will make a fine regiment when properly instructed," and the 211th Pennsylvania—"The men present a fine appearance, with proper drill would make a good regiment."[72]

After they joined the Army of the Potomac (third division of the Ninth Corps), things improved. The 200th, the 208th, and 209th Pennsylvania (comprising the first brigade) apparently passed inspection in December 1864 (or at least were not included in the "Summary of Irregularities"). Inspectors cited the 205th, 207th, and 211th Pennsylvania, comprising the second brigade, for "System of military instruction loose," "Officers & men indifferently instructed in drill," "Officers & men not well instructed in guard and picket," "Commanding officers indifferent to being informed about the condition of the regiment," and "wants of command not reasonably anticipated," among others. The inspectors found the books and records of the 207th and 211th Pennsylvania to be "very incomplete." They also reported that the 211th did not enforce orders.[73]

The 200th, 208th, and 209th also basically passed inspection in January and February 1865. The 205th, 207th, and 211th showed some improvement, although they were still cited for things like lax discipline and indifferent instruction in drill.[74] Thus, by the end of February 1865, the Inspector General's Office was essentially giving the 200th, 208th, and 209th Pennsylvania a passing grade. They "especially praised [the 200th Pennsylvania] as the best drilled Regiment in the Brigade" (the 200th, 208th, and 209th Pennsylvania) and the 211th as the "most soldierly in appearance." The 207th Pennsylvania was not too far off the mark.[75]

Based on the inspectors' findings in the January and February inspections of the 205th Pennsylvania—among other things, "discipline lax," "system of military instruction loose," "officers and men instructed in drill indifferently," and "orders not enforced"—their brigade commander (and former regimental commander) Colonel Mathews concluded that considering the limited duty assigned and the ample time for training, he was "compelled to cast censure upon the commanding and other officers of the Regiment for this evident neglect of their Duties."[76] Colonel Mathews had come down hard on the 205th before. In October 1864, as regimental commander, he called attention to his company commanders "again and for the last time" to follow the schedule for drill.[77] On March 4, 1865, a soldier in the 205th wrote home that Mathews had reported the 205th as "Condempt."[78]

Unit Readiness

Consideration of the capabilities identified in chapter 6 provides a detailed and focused assessment of the unit readiness of these six regiments on March 25, 1865.

1. Motivation (Morale and Unit Cohesion)

Morale and unit cohesion were strong in the six regiments.

John Lynn wrote in *The Bayonets of the Republic* that "Some observers go so far as to say that good food, sufficient rest, efficient equipment, proper medical care, and frequent mail guarantee high morale. Experience does not always bear out this view, but such conditions are unquestionably important."[79] Letters home from the soldiers suggest that morale was generally strong in all six regiments from the time they arrived in Virginia through the end of the war. The soldiers also were generally optimistic that victory was at hand.[80]

The fact that soldiers were able to communicate with home itself boosted morale. In the fall of 1864, letters from home could reach the front in a week. Service was even quicker in the spring of 1865.[81] "Gamma" from the 209th Pennsylvania wrote that when a soldier receives a letter from home, "a new fire lights up the eye, a new vigor starts the blood to quicker action, the soul receives new life, and joy fills the heart."[82] Richard Bohn from the 205th Pennsylvania wrote his parents: "You Dont know how glad I feel when I hear from home."[83] In November, Gamma reported the receipt of "packages of almost every description, and for almost every body." In the 207th Pennsylvania, John Shell wrote home that "nearly all get boxes in our regiment."[84] Gamma recounted that the hometown newspaper "was received, and attained a high degree of importance and interest. It contained the news 'from home,' and hence was eagerly sought for, eagerly read and eagerly listened to by the boys."[85]

At the end of September, the *Philadelphia Press* reported that the six regiments had arrived at Bermuda Hundred, and that "the boys are all in the best of spirits."[86] Pvt. Henry H. Otto of the 205th Pennsylvania wrote that "The army is . . . in good spirits and hoping the war will be over till spring."[87] As the new year began, the 207th Pennsylvania's J. V. L. optimistically referred to "the glorious peace now evidently fast approaching."[88] Another soldier from the 207th wrote his father that "all the boys from home are well."[89] In mid-January, J. S. Lemmon of the 209th Pennsylvania wrote home that "The *morale* of this regiment is good in comparison with that of many others."[90] Musician Henry C. Staily described the men of Company K of the 208th Pennsylvania as being in "their usual . . . buoyant spirits." He said Company H was "feel[ing] that the war cannot be successfully prosecuted without having something to do in the matter themselves."[91]

Samuel Maynard from the 207th Pennsylvania wrote his father with words of determination in February 1865: "The peas meting has gone up so we wil have to fight the jonies another year if we cant whip them sooner but I hope we can whip them in a month but there is no use of talking about that for this war is a big thing. It cant be settled and let the South have their independence after they have bin so much blood shed."[92] In the 200th Pennsylvania, Charles Dellinger wrote a friend at the beginning of March that "I think we will all com home in a few monse. I think thay wose is all most over."[93] In the middle of March, Cpl. Nelson Statler of the 211th Pennsylvania wrote that "The Spring campaign is now opened

& we will give the rebs Hail Columbia if they don't give it to us. But I rather think they can't." The day before the attack at Fort Stedman, Statler presciently wrote that "if the rebs don't give up, we are ready for them at any time."[94]

With respect to physical comfort, J. S. Lemmon wrote that "the 209th occupies a most beautiful site for a camp, and if it was not for the scarcity of wood it would be one of the most desirable of situations. . . . A bubbling spring nearby supplies us with an abundance of pure, fresh water."[95] Richard Bohn of the 205th Pennsylvania wrote that "I have a Bulley Loghouse here."[96] When the 211th Pennsylvania moved into winter quarters, Cpl. Nelson Statler wrote that "We have a very good and warm house. We have built a splendid chimney . . . and cooked supper in it. . . . We will live gay and happy."[97]

While morale was generally good, it was not universally so. The 205th's Richard Bohn had earlier written home that "I am reddy for them any times" and "I ain't afraid about fighting," but three weeks before the Battle of Fort Stedman, Bohn praised Colonel Mathews as "the Best cornal in the hole army" because Mathews had reported the 205th Pennsylvania as "Condempt" (Condemned) and "they can't put us in a fight if our Regt is condempt." An unidentified soldier in Company C of the 207th Pennsylvania bitterly wrote after the November election: "I hope that every man who supported this Lincoln Administration may be drafted and sent to the front . . . they will then have to stand fire for days and nights, without rest or sleep, and then on half rations." He was also skeptical about the Union's prospects for success at Petersburg: "The rebel works look rough, but we cannot take them with all the men we can get."[98]

Soldiers' letters can indicate the morale of the individual soldier, but they are not necessarily representative of the morale of his comrades. Joseph T. Glatthaar has cautioned that "If a scholar searches long enough, he or she will find evidence [in soldiers' writings] to justify virtually any argument the scholar may pose, regardless of its representativeness. For this reason, valid statistics may break that scholarly logjam."[99] A variety of broader, objective criteria is helpful in assessing morale. Desertion rates can certainly reflect morale for the entire regiment. As noted, none of the six regiments lost any men to desertion from the field. Only a handful of men failed to return from furloughs in the spring of 1865 and were absent without leave. This supports a conclusion that morale was fairly strong in all six regiments. While somewhat removed in time, how the regiments voted in the 1864 presidential election also has some probative value on morale at the time. Soldiers knew that if Lincoln were reelected, the war would be pursued to Confederate surrender. If McClellan were elected, peace negotiations would be pursued with the Confederacy to end the war.[100] For the five regiments in Hartranft's division reporting results, 64 percent voted for Lincoln and 36 percent for McClellan. This was only slightly less than the 68 percent voting for Lincoln in the forty Pennsylvania regiments in the Army of the Potomac.[101] The election results indicate good morale.[102]

How a soldier was recruited may also have affected morale in Union regiments. While the prospect of the draft meant that even volunteers were not necessarily entirely willing to serve, volunteers presumably would have higher morale than conscripts or substitutes. The fact that the men in these six regiments were almost all volunteers would be consistent with good morale.

Finally, the state of morale may also be reflected in the soldiers' "military appearance" as evaluated by their officers every two months. Unfortunately, the data for these six regiments is limited. The evaluating officers for the 200th Pennsylvania generally rated the companies as "good" from October 1864 through February 1865. The 205th Pennsylvania fell to "fair" in February 1865 from "good" in October and December 1864, but that may just reflect a change in the evaluating officer.[103]

The best evidence that there was strong unit cohesion in these six regiments comes from Hartranft's personal observation. The six regiments did not engage in combat at Hatcher's Run in February 1865, but they did perform strenuous duties, including building fortifications and roads. After the battle, Hartranft concluded that "although the command did not become engaged with the enemy, yet they performed all labors and marches with the utmost promptness, each and all seeming willing and anxious to do what was required of them."[104] Other officers made similar observations of strong unit cohesion. At the beginning of November 1864, the 207th Pennsylvania's Lt. Peter Blanchard, a veteran of the Thirty-Fifth Pennsylvania, had written that "I never saw men more willing to perform the duty of soldiers than the men of this regiment."[105] After returning from the Hicksford Raid in the beginning of December, Lt. A. B. Cloos wrote that "the boys were several days getting over their lameness; but they are now all right and ready for any work General Grant may have for them to do."[106] Evidence of strong unit cohesion at the regimental level also comes from the way that the men referred to their regiments. George Aumiller endearingly referred to "our Old 208th" in describing the regiment's actions at Hatcher's Run in a letter to his sister and mother.[107] The six late-war Pennsylvania regiments did not have to face the difficult challenge to unit cohesion of integrating replacements.

2. Leadership

Leadership was strong at all levels of command.

Five of the six regiments mustered in roughly one thousand men, while the 211th Pennsylvania mustered in over nine hundred. Those large numbers presented a leadership challenge. As Earl J. Hess has noted, during the Civil War the military generally believed that an infantry regiment at or near full strength of one thousand men or more was "too large for one man to assuredly control." Smaller numbers around three hundred were easier to control.[108] That consideration put a premium on effective leadership for these six regiments.

DIVISION LEADERSHIP. Before assessing regimental leadership, it is important to remember that Hartranft and his division staff officers personally directed the movement of the six regiments at key points during the battle. That reduced, but certainly did not eliminate, the importance of regimental leadership. Hartranft himself was an experienced combat commander. In Richard Sommers's opinion, Hartranft was "the best combat officer the IX Corps ever produced."[109] A lawyer before the war, he led one of Pennsylvania's ninety-day regiments at the beginning of the war, volunteering to serve at Bull Run after his regiment was mustered out. He then commanded the Fifty-First Pennsylvania and subsequently rose to brigade and division command. His combat service included Antietam, Fredericksburg, Spotsylvania, and the Wilderness. After the war, he served as governor of Pennsylvania from 1872 to 1878.[110]

Hartranft also had an experienced staff. Maj. John D. Bertolette, who brought up the 205th and 207th Pennsylvania, had enlisted in April 1861 at the age of twenty-two, serving as a lieutenant and adjutant in the Sixth Pennsylvania. He

General John Hartranft
(Library of Congress)

became the adjutant in the Forty-Eighth Pennsylvania (one of Fox's Three Hundred and the unit that dug the mine that led to the Battle of the Crater) and moved to brigade staff in 1862. He was breveted major in December 1864 for "gallant and distinguished service" at Poplar Spring Church and Hatcher's Run and later breveted to lieutenant colonel.[111] Maj. George Shorkey, who guided the 209th Pennsylvania into position, had served with the Fifty-First Pennsylvania, also one of Fox's Three Hundred. Capt. Prosper Dalien, who repositioned the 208th Pennsylvania, was a French native and graduate of St. Cyr, the French West Point, and had been decorated for gallantry during the Italian campaign. Capt. Richard Watts, who directed the final assault by the 211th Pennsylvania, had served in the Seventeenth Michigan, another one of Fox's Three Hundred. Capt. William H. Hodgkins, who advanced the Second Brigade in the final assault, had enlisted in the Thirty-Sixth Massachusetts in July 1862 and risen through the ranks.[112]

REGIMENTAL LEADERSHIP. The field-grade officers generally had solid experience. Five of the six colonels had previously served as field-grade officers in other units, although only one as a full colonel. Overall, roughly three-quarters of the field-grade officers had previously served.[113] Prior service of course does not guarantee competence. All three field-grade officers and most of the company officers of the 205th Pennsylvania were veterans, but Brigadier General Benham still concluded in early November 1864 that the 205th was "very poorly officered and very inefficient, at least for the fatigue duties" while assigned to the Engineering Brigade.[114]

As to the officers in command on March 25, 1865, Col. C. W. Diven, commanding the First Brigade, had served as a major in the Twelfth Pennsylvania Reserves and Col. J. A. Mathews, commanding the Second Brigade, had served in the Forty-Sixth Pennsylvania (one of Fox's Three Hundred) and the 128th Pennsylvania. In the 200th Pennsylvania, Lt. Col. W. H. H. McCall had served as a captain in the Fifth Pennsylvania Reserves, one of Fox's Three Hundred; in the 205th Pennsylvania, Maj. B. M. Morrow had served in the Eighty-Fourth Pennsylvania, another one of Fox's Three Hundred; in the 207th Pennsylvania, Col. R. C. Cox had been a major in the 171st Pennsylvania, a nine-month regiment that apparently did not see combat; in the 208th Pennsylvania, Lt. Col. George M. T. Heintzelman had served in the Tenth, Seventy-Sixth (one of Fox's Three Hundred), and 172nd Pennsylvania; in the 209th Pennsylvania, Lt. Col. George W. Frederick, a recent college graduate, had not previously served; and in the 211th Pennsylvania, Capt. W. A. Coulter also had not previously served.[115] Thus, at the Battle of Fort Stedman, the combat experience of the brigade and regimental commanders varied significantly.

Even though an officer may be competent, he still needs the confidence of his men to be effective. Speaking about Hartranft's Division as a whole, Isaac Brown of the 211th Pennsylvania recalled in 1891 that "The one thing that gave us great assurance was that the men who commanded our regiments, our companies, and marched in the line of the file closers, were already veterans of the war. . . . [M]uch was due to those veteran officers who so faithfully advised, led and commanded us."[116] In the 207th Pennsylvania, "the boys say 'Dad' [Colonel Cox] will take us through all right. They have all confidence in him."[117] In the 208th Pennsylvania, the first sergeant of Company K described Maj. Alexander Bobb "as a man worthy to fill the position he occupies." The enlisted men of Company H had presented Major Bobb with a horse, saddle, and bridle valued at $325 in November.[118] In the 209th Pennsylvania, Col. Tobias B. Kaufman "was considered by all as a kind, competent and brave commander." Kaufman had served in seventeen battles with the Pennsylvania Reserves, including Antietam, Gettysburg, the Wilderness, and Spotsylvania, but the regiment lost the benefit of his experience when the Confederates captured him in November 1864 by surprising the Union picket line in the 209th's sector.[119] However, in the 200th Pennsylvania, Pvt. George Aughenbaugh had a decidedly negative view of Colonel Diven—"our colonel is not fit to have command of a regiment and I believe that a great many of the men would rather shoot him than look at him." Aughenbaugh did not explain the basis for his animus.[120]

COMPANY LEADERSHIP. Two-thirds of the company commanders and two-thirds of the company-level officers had previously served. Many of the noncommissioned officers had also previously served—roughly 60 percent of the sergeants and 45 percent of the corporals. As noted above, the early inspection reports had expressed concern about some of the officers and noncommissioned officers, but these concerns lessened over time. Evidence of the opinions among the troops of the company-level officers and noncommissioned officers is limited but largely positive. In the 200th Pennsylvania, Company H's Pvt. George Aughenbaugh "lik[ed] our company officers." Hiram Robyler in Company A of the 207th Pennsylvania wrote his parents that "we have a bully good captain [and] we have to bully good lieutenants."[121] In Company K of the 208th Pennsylvania, "Captain Weaverling and Lieutenants Bessor and Sparks are constantly exercising a vigilant and scrutinizing care for the morals, health and general welfare of the company; in consequence of this supervision have become warmly attached. The sergeants also are very attentive to every duty enjoined upon them."[122] However, Richard Bohn in Company C of the 205th Pennsylvania complained at the end of October that his company commander "is drunk near all the time" and later that his fifth sergeant was drunk.[123]

While privates do not have command authority as such, veteran privates can have a mentoring role with new recruits. Thus, the percentage of privates in a new regiment who have prior service is a relevant factor. Roughly a quarter of the privates in the 205th, 208th, and 209th Pennsylvania had previously served, while roughly a fifth in the 200th, 207th, and 211th Pennsylvania had previously served. However, well over half of these men had served in nine-month regiments or in militia regiments briefly called up when Lee invaded Pennsylvania in 1863. The three most frequent regiments for prior service were the 158th, 165th, and 166th Pennsylvania, nine-month regiments that saw only limited combat.[124]

3. Training and Discipline

The subjective muster roll ratings for "discipline" and "instruction" varied in the six regiments from "fair" to "good" at the end of February 1865.[125]

For training, the facts on the ground provide a basis for assessment in addition to these subjective ratings.[126] The six regiments arrived at the front in late September and joined a provisional brigade in the Army of the James at Bermuda Hundred. They had had little time for drill before they left Pennsylvania.[127] Training initially fared better in Virginia. "Veritas" wrote his hometown newspaper that the 207th Pennsylvania was being put "through all the preliminaries of a camp of instruction, on double quick."[128] However, picket duty and detached duty for assignments such as building fortifications soon took the lion's share of the time of many of the soldiers in the six regiments. J. Howard Wert, orderly sergeant and later first lieutenant in Company G of the 209th Pennsylvania, recalled that "with September 29th began for our Pennsylvania regiments two months of the most severe and exhaustive duty that soldiers ever performed. . . . Drills and inspections became almost obsolete."[129] Gamma from Company C of the 209th Pennsylvania wrote home that "We are so unfortunate as to be cut up into a good many detachments," including one to build hospitals at Point of the Rocks. These various details left only forty men in Gamma's company "present for duty."[130] During September, the 205th Pennsylvania did picket duty and built forts, "nearly the entire regiment being called to duty daily."[131] Work on fortifications was hard. The 205th's Richard Bohn wrote home in mid-December that they were working like "[slaves]."[132]

The six regiments joined the Army of the Potomac at the end of November 1864. They reported to the Ninth Corps and comprised a provisional brigade, which became the Third Division under Hartranft.[133] After the forced march in support of the Fifth Corps in early December, the daily regimen of the six regiments focused more on training. At the beginning of January 1865, Hartranft emphasized to his regimental commanders "the importance of devoting every moment of time during the present season of inactivity to Drills and discipline of their Commands. The present may be the only opportunity . . . At least two companies should be drilled in skirmishing and if possible the whole Command."[134] The regimental commanders apparently followed Hartranft's directive. The schedule recorded by Company I of the 200th Pennsylvania shows an almost daily combination of drill, inspection, and/or dress parade interrupted only by the Battle of Hatcher's Run.[135] J. Howard Wert from the 209th Pennsylvania recalled that "Hours were spent daily in squad, company, regimental and brigade drills, the men soon becoming quite proficient in the duties of a soldier . . . This was the first time since we had been in Virginia that we had had the opportunities for systematic drill."[136] Bates wrote that the 211th Pennsylvania was "thoroughly drilled" during the winter.[137]

Union soldiers rarely had the opportunity for live-fire training.[138] While the six regiments had no experience firing under battle conditions, it seems likely that they did have more target practice than new units generally. Company B of the 200th Pennsylvania engaged in "target shooting" on October 19 to 21, 25, and 27, 1864. Company H and I also reported "target firing" on October 19. Company H of the 208th Pennsylvania reported "target practice" on the mornings of October 24 and 26. The other regiments may have done so as well on these days. On January 18, 1865, the Ninth Corps ordered target practice with ten rounds per man. Company I of the 200th Pennsylvania reported target practice on January 31, but there is no confirmation in the regimental books that the other units of Hartranft's Division complied with the Ninth Corps' order.[139]

The veterans presumably had had at least some live-fire experience during their prior service. Some men also had experience with firearms in civilian life. After the battle of Fort Stedman, J. M. of the 207th Pennsylvania wrote that "woodsmen of Potter and Tioga [had shown they] know how to handle guns." Similarly, Bates wrote that "the men of the [208th] were of hardy habits, and were skilled in the use of the rifle." The 209th had "many hardy mountaineers . . . who were accustomed to bringing a squirrel from the top of a lofty tree."[140]

Veritas from the 207th had noted on arriving in Virginia in September that "there are so many veterans among these new troops that I think we shall soon be ready for active service."[141] He was not alone in observing the benefit of training with veterans. In his write-up on the 209th Pennsylvania, Bates noted that a "considerable number" of the officers and men had previously served in other units and that that experience was "of great advantage in disciplining the raw recruits."[142]

While close-order drill lost out to picket duty and detached duty when the six regiments first arrived at the front, the six regiments did undergo two to three months of solid training before the Battle of Fort Stedman.

4. Experience in the Field

Although not tested in battle as units, the six regiments comprising Hartranft's Division had valuable experience in the field prior to Fort Stedman. By the time of the Confederate attack, the six regiments had been in the field for nearly six months. They potentially had been under fire on picket duty, but picket duty is no substitute for experience in maneuvering as a large unit under fire. Some of the detached duty, such as building fortifications, had been hard work, but it also did not involve maneuvering as a regiment.[143] Still as John Lynn has written, "how well a unit performs in combat will depend heavily on how well it performed its duties before combat."[144] These six regiments performed those prebattle duties very well.

While the six Pennsylvania regiments were new regiments, they still included in their ranks men who had previously been in combat in other units. Approximately a quarter of the men in the 205th, 208th, and 209th Pennsylvania had previously served, while about a fifth of the men in the 200th, 207th, and 211th had previously served (although not necessarily in combat). In some companies, nearly 40 percent of the men had previously served.[145]

The first time that the six regiments maneuvered as regiments came in early December. Warren's Fifth Corps undertook the Hicksford Raid that reached thirty miles south of Petersburg to destroy track on the Weldon Railroad. The six regiments of Hartranft's Division were part of the relief force sent to assure the Fifth Corps' safe return.[146] The relief force marched twenty miles out to the Nottoway River to meet up with the Fifth Corps. The march was hard—"mostly in the night, amid snow and mud to our knees and often through creeks. . . . Our blankets and clothes being wet, our load was heavier than usual and the boys were completely worn out in marching the distance in ten hours."[147] The march back was equally difficult, although it turned out that the Fifth Corps was not in danger and the relief force did not engage the Confederates. Nonetheless, Lt. A. B. Closs believed that "the 207th regiment has won the respect of the veterans by its conduct in passing through dangers and hardships."[148]

During the Battle of Hatcher's Run in February 1865, Hartranft's division played a supporting role for Humphrey's Second Corps. Hartranft's division joined the Second Corps line the evening of February 5 and entrenched a line of one thousand yards overnight. Hartranft reported that the division had arrived "in good order, having made the march very rapidly, and . . . without a straggler." The 200th Pennsylvania went out on reconnaissance the morning of February 6 but did not encounter any significant Confederate forces. On February 6 and 7 large details slashed timber in front of their lines. Pvt. George Aumiller wrote home that "We made ourselves good entrenchments to lay behind and made ourselves little holes to shoot through. Oh, we had it fixed first rate. All we wanted was the Rebs to come. We would have showed them what our Old 208th could do." On February 8, 9, and 10 the division built roads before returning to the Ninth Corps.[149]

While the six regiments did have some experience maneuvering in the field as a unit, they had no experience conducting close order drill under fire, which would have raised concerns about their readiness for combat.

However, there is not necessarily a continuous correlation between amount of combat experience and combat effectiveness. A US Army study of combat exhaustion in World War II concluded that "There is no such thing as 'getting used to combat' . . . The general consensus was that a man reached his peak of effectiveness in the first 90 days of combat, that after that his efficiency began to fall off, and that he became steadily less valuable thereafter until he was completely useless."[150] While Civil War soldiers did not endure the extent of continuous combat that the infantry did in France and Italy or in the Pacific during World War II, Carol Reardon has pointed to the change for both Union and Confederate soldiers that came with the "seemingly endless quality" of the fighting in the battles of the Wilderness and Spotsylvania.[151] Deploying fresh troops could be advantageous. In the aftermath of the controversy over whether untested but fresh African American troops should have led the charge at the Battle of the Crater, Col. Henry Thomas, a white officer commanding the Second Brigade in Ferrero's division of African American troops, commented that "it is an axiom in military art that there are times when the ardor, hopefulness and enthusiasm of new troops, not yet rendered doubtful by reverses or chilled by defeat, more than compensate, in a dash, for training and experience."[152] Veterans were much more wary in 1864 about attacking strong positions than they had been earlier in the war—the so-called "Cold Harbor syndrome."[153]

5. Actual versus Authorized Strength

The six regiments in Hartranft's Division were significantly below authorized strength at the Battle of Fort Stedman, but still had roughly twice as many men available as the typical old regiment in the Army of the Potomac.

Authorized strength for a Union infantry regiment was ten companies of eighty to one hundred enlisted men with three officers each and about a dozen field and staff officers and enlisted men.[154] The 211th Pennsylvania mustered in with slightly over nine hundred enlisted men. The other five regiments all had around one thousand.[155]

On March 24, 1865, the day before the attack at Fort Stedman, the six regiments each had between 654 and 771 men present for duty.[156] While significantly below the regiments' original strength, these were exceptionally high numbers at a time when some old regiments in the field had fallen below 100 men. In March 1865, the average "effective strength" of an infantry regiment in the Army of the Potomac was 279 in the Second Corps, 389 in the Fifth Corps, 380 in the Sixth Corps, and 412 in the Ninth Corps, for an average of 354.[157] Indeed, as noted, Samuel Bates commented that the 211th Pennsylvania "when drawn out in line, showed like a brigade" at Fort Stedman.

The four main causes of losses from authorized strength for the old regiments in the Army of the Potomac had been battle casualties, sickness, desertion, and expiration of term of service. Battle casualties and expiration of term of service were not then factors for these six new regiments. Desertion and sickness did impact the regiments' strength but not significantly.

Desertion was a problem for these six regiments in varying degrees, but the rates were not out of line with old Pennsylvania regiments in the Army of the Potomac.[158] The rates were 12 percent or less in all six regiments—only 1 percent and 5 percent in the 211th Pennsylvania and 207th Pennsylvania. Particularly significant is the fact that all but a handful of the desertions occurred in August and September 1864 before the regiments arrived in Virginia. Once the six regiments reached the field, desertion all but ended.[159]

Sickness was generally a problem for new regiments when they reached the field because they had to learn the techniques for maintaining proper sanitary conditions necessary to protect the health of large numbers of men living so close together.[160] These six regiments followed that pattern. "Fully thirty percent" of the provisional brigade they comprised were in hospital in November 1864, according to J. Howard Wert of the 209th Pennsylvania.[161]

The public knew the dangers of sickness in the army camps, so soldiers' letters to their hometown newspapers frequently reported that the local "boys" were in good health. For example, in late October 1864, a soldier in the 209th Pennsylvania reported that "the health of the regiment is extraordinarily good. Not a single death has yet occurred."[162] The actual numbers of sick men seem higher than what was reported to home. The morning reports for March 24, 1865, show roughly fifty men "present-sick" or "absent-sick" for each regiment except for the 211th Pennsylvania with seventy-six.[163] Nonetheless, the six regiments were manned and healthy enough for each to field six hundred-plus men on March 25, 1865.

6. Supply (Food, Arms, and Equipment)

The six regiments had appropriate rations, arms, and equipment leading up to Fort Stedman. The muster roll ratings on "arms" were generally "good" for the three two-month rating periods from October 31, 1864, through February

28, 1865.[164] The 200th Pennsylvania carried Springfield rifles and the other regiments probably did as well. The ratings were also generally "good" for "accoutrements" and "clothing."[165]

The men generally believed they were well fed. Nelson Statler from the 211th Pennsylvania wrote his wife in January 1865 that "We get plenty to eat. We get fresh bread and fresh beef every other day and hard bread and pork the balance of the time." In February, George Aumiller from the 208th Pennsylvania wrote his mother and sister that "I have as much to eat as I want."[166] The men also often received boxes from home with food and clothing that supplemented what the army issued.[167]

7. Demographics (Occupation, Nationality at Birth, and Age)

There were no indications of weakness in the demographics of the six regiments.

The average Union soldier was 25.8 years old when he enlisted.[168] The men in Hartranft's Division were only slightly older. The proportion of troops eighteen years old or younger was generally about one-sixth; the age of the troops would not have been a concern.

As to birthplace, the six regiments were significantly more homogeneous than the Union army as a whole. Language or cultural differences would not have been expected to be a problem as they were in some regiments.[169] More than three-quarters of Union soldiers were born in the United States.[170] The six regiments far exceeded that percentage, falling within a narrow band of 92 percent to 95 percent native-born. Of the native-born, high percentages were born in Pennsylvania, ranging from 92 percent in the 208th Pennsylvania to 78 percent in the 211th Pennsylvania. Of the roughly 7 percent in the six regiments who were foreign-born, about two-thirds were German-born and one-third Irish-born with a small number of English and Canadians.

Table 10.1: Hartranft's Division: Ages, Farmers, and Laborers

	200th	205th	207th	208th	209th	211th
	Average Age					
	25.9	26.2	26.1	27	26	26.8
	Eighteen or Younger (%)					
	16.1	15.9	17.3	9.5	15.0	12.9
	Occupations (%)					
Farmers	21	18	52	36	25	52
Laborers	29	40	18	23	33	19
Total	50	58	70	59	58	71

Source: Compiled from the regimental descriptive books. Regimental Books, RG 94, NARA.

Men in certain occupations were viewed as more fit to be soldiers than others. The nature of their work arguably better prepared farmers and laborers for the hardships of the field than white-collar occupations or even the trades. Nearly half of Union soldiers had been farmers before the war, while more than 10 percent had been common laborers.[171] The 207th and the 211th Pennsylvania were close to that pattern, but the 205th, 209th, and 200th Pennsylvania had more laborers than farmers. The 208th Pennsylvania was in between. For the two occupations combined, the six regiments ranged from 50 percent to 71 percent. Building trades averaged about 9 percent; while white collar ranged from 2 percent to 5 percent.[172]

One can never really know how effective a unit will be in its first battle. However, the six late-war new regiments in Hartranft's Division gave the Army of Potomac's senior commanders good reason to believe—with the possible exception of the 205th Pennsylvania—that they were as ready as a new regiment reasonably could be expected to be. They had strong morale and unit cohesion. They were well led. Most of the officers had previously served, as had about half of the noncommissioned officers. Overall, between a fifth and a quarter of the men in the six regiments had previously served. Two to three months of uninterrupted training in close order drill disciplined the men as well as trained them to maneuver as a unit. The march to the Nottoway River and the battle at Hatcher's Run hardened the men and their ability to operate as units. All six regiments had strong force levels—twice the size of the average Union regiment in the Army of the Potomac at the time.

The purpose of recounting the critical role that these six late-war new regiments played on March 25, 1865, and evaluating their unit readiness in detail is *not* to suggest that their excellent performance was typical of all late-war new regiments. Rather, the purpose is simply to demonstrate that late-war new regiments and late-war replacements should not be presumed as a group to have been poor soldiers. More discriminating analysis is necessary.

CHAPTER 11

The Five Forks Offensive

March 29 to April 1, 1865

In early February 1865, the Second Corps and the Fifth Corps had seized two key crossings of Hatcher's Run at the Vaughn Road and at Armstrong's Mill. However, the Fifth Corps failed to reach the South Side Railroad, the Confederates having stopped them at Dabney's Mill. Nonetheless, the Union held an advantageous position for another attempt to turn the Confederate right flank.[1]

Several days after the Ninth Corps repulsed the Confederate attack at Fort Stedman, the infantry in the Fifth Corps and four divisions of cavalry under General Sheridan set out to swing west and turn Lee's right flank and/or sever the South Side Railroad. The Fifth Corps prevailed in its initial contact with the Confederates at the Lewis Farm on March 29. On March 31, the Confederates initially succeeded in driving back the Fifth Corps from White Oak Road, but the Fifth Corps ultimately held and regained all lost ground and somewhat more. A combined Confederate force of infantry and cavalry successfully attacked Sheridan's cavalry in front of Dinwiddie Courthouse the same day. The Union cavalry regained some lost ground, but the Confederate forces still threatened them. On April 1, the Fifth Corps and Sheridan's cavalry decisively defeated the Confederate forces at Five Forks, at long last turning the Confederate right flank, which enabled them to reach the South Side Railroad.[2]

Only seven of the forty-four regiments in the Fifth Corps at the end of March 1865 were late-war new regiments. Late-war new regiments did comprise the entirety of the first and second brigades of Gen. Charles Griffin's Division—the 185th New York and the 198th Pennsylvania (an unusually large regiment of fourteen companies) in the first brigade under Joshua Chamberlain and the 187th,

188th, and 189th New York in the second brigade under Edgar Gregory, but there were none in the third brigade.[3] There were only two late-war new regiments in General Ayres's Division—the 210th Pennsylvania and the Eighth Delaware (only three companies) and none in Crawford's Division.[4] The five late-war new regiments in Griffin's Division played a key role in the Fifth Corps' victories in the Five Forks offensive despite their small number.

Lewis Farm (March 29, 1865)

The Fifth Corps moved out on March 29 with nearly sixteen thousand men—sixty-five hundred in Griffin's Division, four thousand in Ayres's Division, and fifty-three hundred in Crawford's Division. Within Griffin's Division, Chamberlain's Brigade and Gregory's Brigade each had about seventeen hundred fifty men, while Bartlett's Brigade had about three thousand. Sheridan's cavalry force had about nine thousand men.[5]

To avoid detection, the Fifth Corps swept widely to the southwest as it left the Union lines. Ayres's Division took the lead, leaving at 3 A.M. and clearing the Stage Road after the Fiftieth New York Engineers built a pontoon bridge over Rowanty Creek to replace the bridge that the Confederates had destroyed. Griffin's Division, led by Chamberlain's Brigade, started out around 6 A.M. Moving along the Vaughn Road, Griffen's Division initially marched past the intersection with Quaker Road toward Dinwiddie Courthouse and stopped at the Chappell Farm, about two miles east of Dinwiddie Courthouse. Around 11:30 A.M., General Warren ordered Griffin back to Quaker Road to proceed northward toward the Confederate positions at Burgess Mill.[6]

The 198th Pennsylvania led Griffin's Division as it moved up Quaker Road. The Confederates had destroyed the bridge over Gravelly Run and dug in on the other side, so the advance was already in jeopardy after only a mile and a half's march. Chamberlain placed Sickel's Battalion (eight companies) of the 198th Pennsylvania on the right of Quaker Road and the 185th New York under Lt. Col. Gustavus Sniper on the left to provide supporting fire for Major Glenn's Battalion (six companies) of the 198th Pennsylvania as it forded the waist-deep water and attacked the Confederate rifle pits. Glenn's Battalion "pushed forward vigorously and drove the enemy's skirmishers out of their works without any difficulty."[7]

The crossing of Gravelly Run by Union forces presented a sufficient threat for Confederate General Anderson to order Gen. Bushrod Johnson's Division to move down Quaker Road, "attack them, and drive them back to the Vaughn

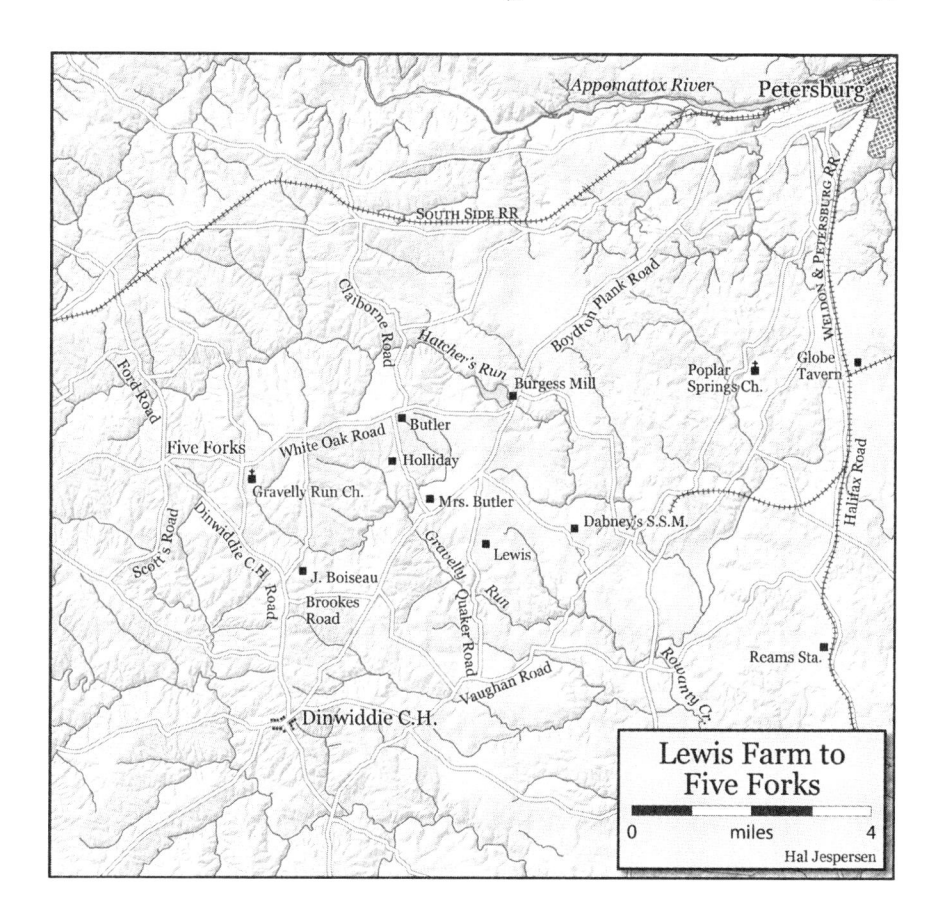

road." With as many as six thousand men available, the Confederates heavily outnumbered Chamberlain's forces.[8]

Major Glenn's Battalion took the lead as skirmishers and the rest of the 198th Pennsylvania and the 185th New York continued up the Quaker Road through dense forest for another mile to the Lewis Farm, located in the midst of a clearing one thousand yards wide and long. With Confederate forces strengthening breastworks in the woods beyond Lewis Farm, Chamberlain prepared his line of battle with the 185th New York on the left of Quaker Road and the 198th Pennsylvania on the right. A company from the 185th New York strengthened Glenn's Battalion of skirmishers in the center.[9]

Chamberlain reported that the 185th New York and the 198th Pennsylvania advanced "with great steadiness and drove the enemy from their position and far into the woods." However, shortly thereafter, the gathering Confederate troops counterattacked in superior numbers "and we became completely enveloped in a withering fire." Over the course of half an hour, the 185th New York "gradually gave way" on the left. The Confederates drove them from the woods back to Quaker Road.[10]

As the situation rapidly deteriorated, Griffin assured Chamberlain "that if we would hold on five minutes he could bring up the artillery."[11] Inspired by the promise of artillery support, Sniper and the 185th New York halted the Confederate advance and pushed them back into their breastworks in the woods. And as promised, Battery B of the Fourth US Artillery arrived and "opened a most effective fire."[12] The Confederates counterattacked, but the vigorous defense by the 185th New York prevented them from capturing the battery. *Harper's Weekly* later published a sketch captioned "Gallant Action of Colonel Sniper," as he rallied the 185th New York.[13]

Chamberlain's left was now holding, but then the Confederates "fell heavily on our right and center." Almost out of ammunition, the 198th Pennsylvania fell back to the Lewis Farm buildings. In response to Chamberlain's plea for help, Gregory sent up the 188th New York. As Chamberlain's Brigade moved up Quaker Road, Gregory's Brigade had moved up on Chamberlain's left. However, the "swampy and difficult grounds" slowed their advance.[14] Griffin also sent three regiments from the Third Brigade. Chamberlain concluded that "this assistance and the

General Joshua Chamberlain
(Library of Congress)

admirable service of the artillery compelled the enemy to abandon their position; otherwise I must have been driven from the field." The Confederates finally withdrew back toward White Oak Road in the face of these reinforcements.[15]

Chamberlain congratulated the 185th New York and the 198th Pennsylvania for "their admirable conduct . . . , the steadiness of their advance, the gallantry of their attack, the courage with which they withstood the repeated assaults of a largely superior force of the enemy for nearly two hours without support, . . . the good order which they maintained when compelled to yield ground only by the exhaustion of their ammunition."[16]

By tenaciously holding at Lewis Farm, the 185th New York and the 198th Pennsylvania bought enough time for the engineers to build a passable bridge for the rest of the Fifth Corps to cross Gravelly Run. They defeated Anderson's objective of driving the Fifth Corps back to the Vaughn Road.

Both regiments lost heavily—the 185th New York suffered 180 casualties and the 198th Pennsylvania suffered 228, including many of its officers. Among them were Colonel Sickel, whose arm was shattered, and Major Maceuen, who was mortally wounded. Major Glenn took command of the first battalion, and Capt. John Stanton from Company A took command of the second battalion. Chamberlain himself was wounded and almost captured.[17]

By the end of the day on March 29, Griffin's Division had moved up Quaker Road from Lewis Farm to the junction with Boydton Plank Road. Crawford's Division took position along the Boydton Plank Road, below Griffin's Division. Ayres's Division served as the reserve, located on the Quaker Road between Gravelly Run and the Lewis Farm.[18]

The success of Griffin's late-war new regiments at Lewis Farm, combined with the Second Corps' movement past Dabney Mill, led Grant to rethink the objective of the Union offensive. He wrote Sheridan after Lewis Farm that "I now feel like ending the matter if it is possible to do so before going back. I do not want you, therefore, to cut loose and go after the enemy's roads at present. In the morning push round the enemy if you can and get onto his right rear."[19]

White Oak Road (March 31, 1865)

It rained very heavily the night of March 29, rendering the roads impassable for artillery the next day. As a result, there was little movement. Griffin's Division advanced a little further up Boydton Plank Road to occupy abandoned Confederate rifle pits, its right flank connecting with Miles's Division of the Second Corps. Crawford's Division remained along the Boydton Plank Road and Ayers's

Division moved up from Quaker Road and crossed the Boydton Plank Road partway to White Oak Road.[20]

For the morning of March 31, Warren planned to "mass" Ayres's Division near "S. Dabney's"; Griffin's Division near "Mrs. Butler's"; and Crawford's Division halfway between. Later in the morning, Meade directed Warren to reconnoiter the area in front of him and "should you determine by your reconnaissance that you can get possession of and hold the White Oak road you are to do so, notwithstanding the order to suspend operations to-day."[21] Ayres's Division began the reconnaissance with Winthrop's Brigade around 10:30 A.M. and reached a point about fifty yards shy of White Oak Road, when a large Confederate force attacked them. Ayres thought that the Confederates "had four or five to my one." Ayres's Division fell back, unable to hold.[22] The 210th Pennsylvania was on Ayres's right. They initially helped check the Confederate advance, but then "broke and fled" when the superior Confederate force flanked them. The 210th Pennsylva-

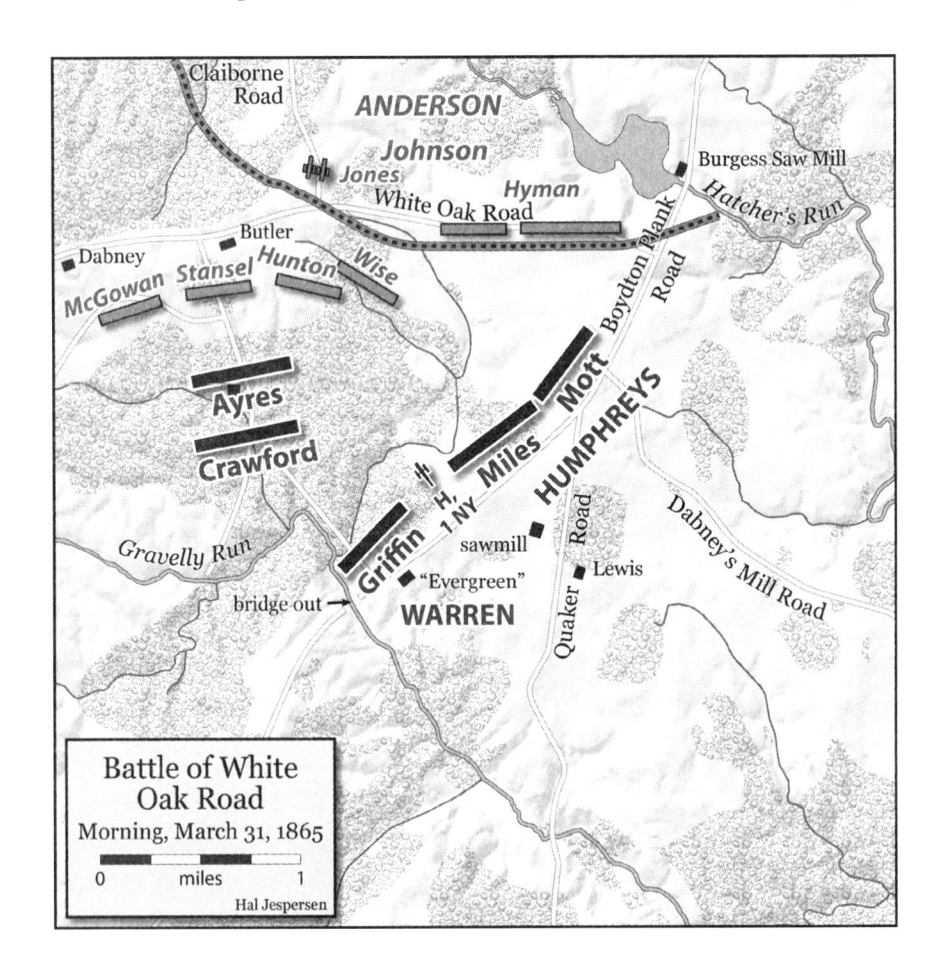

nia retreated for a mile. They lost heavily—thirty-five killed, 115 wounded, and 150 missing in action.[23] The Confederates also forced back Crawford's Division. Griffin described Crawford's Division as "running to the rear in a most demoralized and disorganized condition, soon after followed by [Ayres's] Division."[24]

Warren directed Griffin's Division into a blocking position behind a branch of Gravelly Run and Ayres's and Crawford's retreating divisions fell in behind Griffin's Division. Griffin's Division then stopped the Confederate advance.[25]

The Second Corps occupied positions to the right of the Fifth Corps. General Miles ordered Ramsay's Brigade to attack a Confederate force in the vicinity of Gravelly Run and the Adams's Farm that was advancing as Fifth Corps units were falling back. Ramsay's attack failed, which he attributed in part to the 148th Pennsylvania's "[giving] way unceremoniously and in confusion." Captain Sutton of the 148th Pennsylvania did acknowledge that they had in fact fallen back "in some confusion" after "a sharp fight," but he also reported that they "soon rallied and pushed forward, driving the enemy out."[26]

While Ramsay's attack failed and he criticized the 148th Pennsylvania, he did praise the "admirable" conduct of the other regiments in his brigade, including the Fifty-Third Pennsylvania, the 116th Pennsylvania, and the 183rd Pennsylvania.[27]

Notwithstanding the rout of Ayres's and Crawford's divisions, once Griffen's Division halted the Confederates, Warren saw the opportunity to counterattack. "The prospect of fighting the enemy outside of his breast-works, instead of having to assail him behind his defenses and through his obstructions, was one sufficiently animating to our hopes to more than compensate for the partial reverse we had sustained."[28]

Fording the waist-deep stream, Major Glenn's Battalion of the 198th Pennsylvania led the counterattack. Captain Stanton's Battalion provided covering fire. The 198th Pennsylvania and the 185th New York reformed on the opposite bank and steadily moved forward, driving the enemy back to prepared works near where Ayres's and Crawford's divisions had started out the day.[29]

Warren ordered a halt to the advance so that he could reconnoiter the ground, but Chamberlain found his brigade in a precarious position. Chamberlain assessed the situation: "As it appeared that the enemy's position might be carried with no greater loss than it would cost us merely to hold our ground, and the men were eager to charge over the field, I reported this to General Griffin, and received permission to renew the attack."[30]

On the left, the "impetuous 185th New York roll[ed] over the enemy's right, and seems to swallow it up" in Chamberlain's words. In the center, the 198th Pennsylvania attacked Hunton's Brigade. Hunton later recalled that "The 198th Pennsylvania wavered under the fire very decidedly, and a portion of it broke and ran.

The balance of the line reformed under my fire, advanced, and drove us back. I thought it was one of the most gallant things I had ever seen." The 198th Pennsylvania captured much of the Fifty-Sixth Virginia. Gregory's Brigade (the 187th, 188th, and 189th New York) took the Confederate positions in the woods on the right while under heavy artillery fire.[31]

Chamberlain's Brigade ultimately took the Confederate rifle pits on White Oak Road and advanced three hundred years beyond. "The battle of White Oak Road, which had begun so disastrously for Warren's Corps, had ended in victory," in the words of Edwin Bearss.[32]

With the victory at White Oak Road, the Union commanders had two main options for achieving Grant's directive "to push around the enemy . . . and get onto his right rear." Sheridan, who now commanded the Fifth Corps as well as the cavalry, could build on the Fifth Corps' victory and deploy his infantry and cavalry to turn the Confederate flank on Claiborne Road. Or he could attack the Confederate positions at Five Forks. In either case, his forces could then move north and interdict the South Side Railroad.[33]

The primary disadvantage of attacking the Confederate fortifications along Claiborne Road was that the Confederates could reinforce their troops in significant numbers with relative ease. Because of the declining numbers of Confederate forces and the increasing length of the opposing lines, Lee faced a constant problem of "robbing Peter to pay Paul" in moving troops to address the latest Union threat, but he had succeeded in doing so quite well throughout the Petersburg Campaign.

Lee would have much more difficulty reinforcing the troops at Five Forks. Lee's directive to Pickett to hold Five Forks at all costs implicitly recognized that reinforcement would be problematic.[34] However, any Union attempt on the left flank of the Confederate positions at Five Forks would risk a counterattack on the Union rear by Confederate forces from Claiborne Road (although they would face the same risk in reverse if they attacked the Claiborne Road positions). In any event, the ample Union cavalry forces could protect their rear and flanks.

That logic, plus the fact that the combined Confederate force of cavalry and infantry threatened Sheridan's cavalry in front of Dinwiddie Courthouse, counseled in favor of moving against Five Forks.[35]

Five Forks (April 1, 1865)

Sheridan's objective was to force the Confederate troops back to their positions at Five Forks, "crush the whole force, if possible, and drive westward those who might escape, thus isolating them from Petersburg." Sheridan's plan of attack had three elements as his forces moved toward Five Forks from the vicinity of Dinwiddie Courthouse. First, General Merritt would push his dismounted cavalry-men up to the Confederate works at Five Forks and drive in the skirmishers in a manner to "make the enemy believe that our main attack would be made on their right flank." Second, the Fifth Corps would move up to the White Oak Road along the Gravelly Run Church Road and attack the Confederate left flank and rear. Mackenzie's cavalry division—one thousand strong—would protect the rear of the Fifth Corps from attack along the White Oak Road from the Confed-erate positions at Claiborne Road. (During the battle, Mackenzie's Division also seized the Ford Road crossing of Hatcher's Run, cutting off a potential avenue of Confederate retreat from Five Forks.) Third, as soon as the Fifth Corps at-tacked, the cavalry would attack the front of the Confederate lines.[36] Although the Fifth Corps initially came into position on White Oak Road further east than intended, the combined Union forces executed the attack plan effectively, with Sheridan reporting "the complete rout of the enemy with a loss of 5 pieces of artillery and caissons, a number of their wagons and ambulances, and I think at least 5,000 prisoners and several battle-flags."[37]

Relieving the pressure on Sheridan's cavalry in front of Dinwiddie Court-house and forcing the Confederates back to their positions at Five Forks was the first priority for Union forces. Sheridan held a precarious position in Meade's view: "Sheridan cannot maintain himself at Dinwiddie without reinforcements." Based on the receding sound of battle to the southwest late in the afternoon on March 31, Warren himself already believed that the "enemy was driving our cav-alry." Warren ordered Bartlett's Brigade from Griffin's Division to move "directly across the country" to support Sheridan. Bartlett did not attack but reached a position on the Crump Road close to the Confederates by the end of the day. This movement and the anticipation of further Fifth Corps movements forced the Confederates back to Five Forks. The following morning, the rest of the Fifth Corps moved down the Boydton Plank Road toward Dinwiddie Courthouse. Sheridan put the Fifth Corps in a holding pattern until the early afternoon, when he started them off toward Five Forks.[38]

As the Fifth Corps moved up Gravelly Church Road, Ayres's Division took the left of the road and Crawford's Division the right, with Griffin's Division in the rear of Crawford. Warren ordered his divisions to move forward until they reached White Oak Road and then to "swing around to the left perpendicular to the White Oak Road." The cavalry would charge the main line "as soon as the in-fantry get engaged." Warren also gave them a diagram, which unfortunately con-fused matters.[39] The diagram incorrectly showed the Gravelly Church Road as intersecting White Oak Road, where the Confederate fortifications turned north (referred to as the "return" or "angle"). In fact, Gravelly Church Road intersected White Oak Road seven to eight hundred yards east of the return.[40]

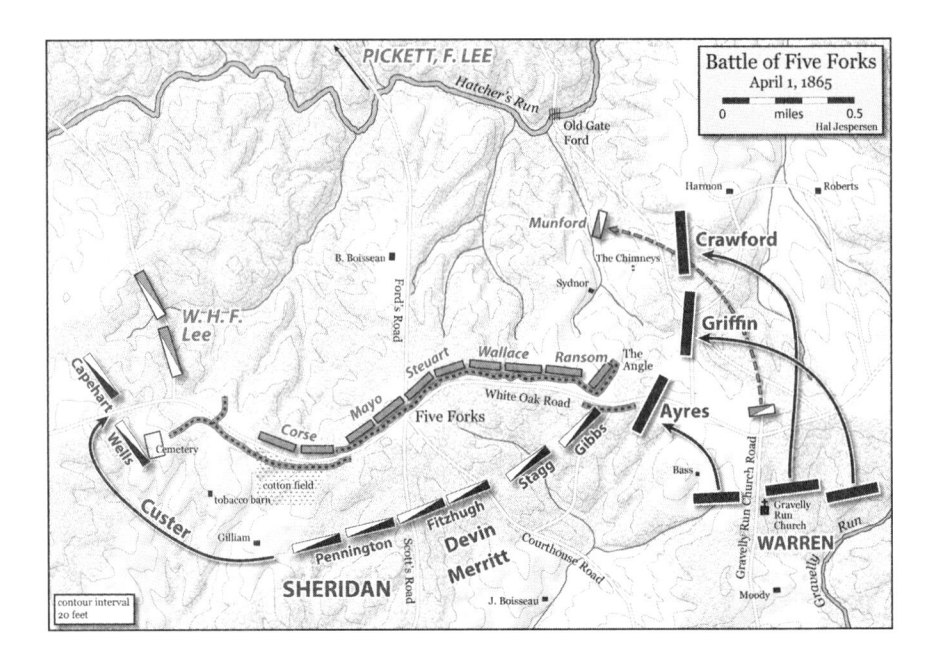

The Fifth Corps divisions crossed White Oak Road shortly after 4 P.M. but did not encounter the Confederate "return" as expected. Warren reported that they realized "for the first time that we were too far to our right of the enemy's left flank." "Finding the enemy's fire to come from the left," Ayres's Division immediately pivoted left and moved down White Oak Road toward the Confederate positions, while Crawford's and Griffin's divisions continued moving north for a time before moving to the left. Crawford described the terrain as "bogs, tangled woods, and thickets of pine, interspersed with open spaces here and there." Ayres's Division and Crawford's Division lost connection with each other. Fortunately, Crawford's and Griffin's divisions faced only skirmishers. Neither division was moving enough to the left and as a result, neither division could support Ayres's Division until Warren's orders to move left caught up with them in the vicinity of the Chimneys.[41]

Around 4:30 P.M., Ayres's Division had turned to the left and moved along White Oak Road to engage Ransom's Brigade defending the return at the far left of the Confederate positions.[42] At that point, Crawford's Division was well beyond White Oak Road but was moving to the left. Munford's cavalry was the only Confederate force in their front. A gap had developed between Ayres's Division and Crawford's Division, and Griffin's Division moved in to fill it. Mackenzie's cavalry continued to cover the Fifth Corps' right flank.[43]

By 5 P.M., Ayres's Division had forced Ransom's Brigade from the return. Lieutenant Colonel Whitman of the 210th Pennsylvania succinctly reported that "we were ordered forward, and drove the enemy from his works, whom we followed for about two miles, until the regiment became scattered." Sheridan then ordered Ayres's Division to halt briefly. By taking the return, Ayres's Division forced Ransom's Brigade and the two brigades west of it in the White Oak Road line, Wallace's Brigade and Steuart's Brigade, to fall back and establish a new line perpendicular to White Oak Road in the woods west of Sydnor's farm to protect Ford's Road—only temporarily, as it turned out. Time permitted construction of only light fieldworks.[44]

Griffin's Division attacked this new Confederate position, with Chamberlain's Brigade (supplemented by the 188th New York) on the left, Bartlett's Brigade (only three regiments available) on the right, and the 187th and 189th New York of Gregory's Brigade in the rear. Within Chamberlain's Brigade, the 185th New York and Major Glenn's Battalion of the 198th Pennsylvania were on the right and Stanton's Battalion of the 198th Pennsylvania and the 188th New York were on the left.[45] The 185th New York and Glenn's Battalion of the 198th Pennsylvania broke through and moved toward White Oak Road. The 188th New York captured roughly four hundred Confederates and a four-gun battery. General Gregory reported that despite "uneven and unfavorable ground" and "oblique fire," the 188th New York "advanced in perfect order," changing formation twice. "The fighting here was desperate, but the courage and bravery of the troops carried the day and decided its fortunes."[46] The 187th and 189th New York covered the right of Griffin's Division.[47]

Bartlett's Brigade faced heavy resistance. The Confederates forced back Bartlett's exposed right flank, placing Griffin's entire division at risk. Chamberlain slid the 185th New York and the 188th New York behind Bartlett's Brigade to meet the Confederate attack on Bartlett's right flank. The combined force ended the threat and the Confederates fell back west of Ford's Road. Griffin's Division then moved westward and southward to Five Forks, where it connected with the cavalry, which had achieved its own breakthrough.[48]

In the meantime, Crawford's Division had reached Ford's Road by 5 P.M., cutting off that lane of potential Confederate retreat, and proceeded south and southwest from the Boisseau Farm toward the rear of the Confederate lines. Crawford referred to "the enemy fleeing before us, though keeping up a desultory firing."[49] In Sheridan's words, the Fifth Corps "burst on the enemy's left flank and rear like a tornado."[50] The Eleventh Pennsylvania captured a Confederate flag in the assault.[51]

By 6 P.M., Sheridan's forces had completely routed the Confederates, sending them in full flight to the west. The Army of the Potomac had finally turned the Confederate right.

Mission Accomplished

The 185th New York and the 198th Pennsylvania fully accomplished their missions throughout the Five Forks Campaign. At Lewis Farm, they protected the Fifth Corps' bridgehead over Gravelly Run, which enabled the advance toward White Oak Road. At White Oak Road, they halted the Confederate advance and initiated the Union counterattack. At Five Forks they took their assigned portion of the Confederate works. The key elements of success were: (1) Chamberlain's personal involvement at the points of engagement, including his decision to continue their advance at White Oak Road; (2) the fierce determination of the two regiments, notably at Lewis Farm, where they defeated a larger Confederate force of veterans; and (3) the resilience of the officers in the 198th Pennsylvania after the loss of Colonel Sickel and other officers at White Oak Road. Casualties were heavy but commensurate with the circumstances.

Unit Readiness

The high state of unit readiness achieved by the 185th New York and the 198th Pennsylvania since arriving in the field in September 1864 explains their excellent performance during the Five Forks Campaign.

185th New York

1. Motivation (Morale and Unit Cohesion). The 185th New York had strong morale and unit cohesion.

Lynn has written that "wartime opinion has considerable influence on morale [and] the most critical wartime opinion is . . . appreciation of soldiers' sacrifices and triumphs. [Appreciation] is the most potent transmitter of values from the homefront to the front line. Appreciation is recognition of value."[52] The 185th New York had strong support from their community. A "very large and respectable audience" of Syracuse citizens showed their support for the 185th New York in a ceremony presenting a battle flag to the regiment before they left for the front. After the 185th New York had left home, another "large audience assembled at City Hall" for the dedication of a banner with the New York State seal to be sent to the regiment in the field. At the end of October, a local pastor traveled to the field to preach to the regiment. W. G. wrote that "the regiment was very much pleased . . . as many were well acquainted with him." The Syracuse newspapers regularly reported on the actions of the 185th New York throughout the war. The soldiers knew this and frequently sent letters to the newspapers to update the community on everything from the weather to battles. E. W. F. sent a letter to the *Syracuse Standard,* understanding that "a word from 'the boys' is always acceptable." The men of the 185th New York valued the respect and interest of their community. LEW promised in a letter to the *Standard:* "My word for it, the regiment will be an honor to the counties from which they came."[53]

The men of the 185th New York were confident. They were also apparently healthy.[54] Lieutenant Phillips wrote home in late October that "The troops were never in better condition and spirits, and were never more confident of certain victory. . . . It is now nothing but advance on our side and fall back on theirs. Won't it be fine for our regiment to help in taking Petersburg and Richmond?"[55] In November, the 185th New York gave Lincoln nearly a 90 percent majority, which indicates strong morale. Pvt. W. L. Winslow had predicted that "We are going to give the Union ticket two-thirds of the vote in our Regiment at least." An unidentified soldier had said that "Our regiment is almost unanimous for Lincoln." Pvt. Alburtus Peckham wrote home that Confederate deserters said that "if Lincoln was elected, they would have but little hope and it would be a hard matter to get many of them to fight anymore."[56]

The 185th New York's muster roll ratings on "military appearance" also indicate strong morale. From October to December 1864, most of the companies improved, with four companies rated as excellent at the end of the year.[57]

The volunteers for the 185th New York did receive high bounties, but that did not mean that they had no patriotic motivation. While acknowledging that they had received a $1,000 bounty, T. S. M. still viewed himself and his fellow recruits as "good, patriotic volunteers." As further evidence that the men of the 185th New York held patriotic concerns, E. W. F. closed a letter to an unidentified newspaper with "Yours, for our Glorious Union" and LEW closed a letter to the *Syracuse Standard* with "Yours for an undivided country." Some men did desert en route to City Point. The 185th New York lost twenty-three deserters soon after leaving Binghamton and after arriving in New York City was "marched down Broadway to the Battery where we were put under double guard." However, the overall desertion rate was less than 5 percent and only one man deserted after the 185th New York reached the field.[58]

As discussed in chapter 6, unit cohesion cannot be assessed quantitatively. It is best assessed by observation and by talking with unit personnel at all levels.[59]

The 185th apparently made a good impression as a unit on a general who traveled with them from Fortress Monroe to City Point. He told their brigade commander at the time, General Baxter, that he liked their appearance so much that he thought they could be put in the field at once.[60]

The language used by soldiers in their letters to family and friends can reflect the degree of unit cohesion. The informality of using the term *the boys* to refer to the men in the regiment as a group rather than *the regiment* or *the 185th New York* reflects strong cohesion at the regimental level. Use of the term *the boys* in this context occurred with some frequency in the 185th New York. LEW used "the boys" to refer to the support that the regiment was receiving from the regimental quartermaster, as did TSM. An unidentified soldier used "the boys" to describe the experience of the regiment during the Hicksford Raid. W. G. used the term to refer to the regiment's camp. Similarly, E. W. F. referred to the regiment as "her," another indication of personal attachment to the regiment.[61]

2. LEADERSHIP. An unidentified soldier wrote to a local newspaper that many of the regimental officers "are men of no experience."[62] The 185th's officers did indeed have limited experience. Twenty-four-year-old Col. Edwin Jenney had been a major in an artillery unit and Lt. Col. Gustavus Sniper had been the lieutenant colonel in the 101st New York, but the 185th's major had not previously served, nor had its adjutant and its quartermaster. Only one of its company commanders had previously served (as a lieutenant) and only one of its lieutenants had previously served (as a sergeant).[63] Nonetheless, the officers worked hard. LEW wrote that "Colonel Jenny and the other field officers of the regiment are doing all in their power to make the regiment a good one."[64] The brigade commander praised Colonel Jenney for his "great coolness on the field and ability in the management of [his] troops." However, Jenney resigned his commission for personal reasons shortly thereafter. Sniper was promoted to full colonel to succeed him.[65] The officers of the 185th New York earned the confidence and respect of their men.[66] DRAUGHTGILSIVAD wrote that the company officers "are all, to a man, doing their best to bring their commands to an efficient standard."[67] The confidence of the men extended to the regimental quartermaster (as discussed below) and the chaplain. TSM wrote that the chaplain was "ready on every occasion to grant spiritual relief."[68]

3. TRAINING AND DISCIPLINE. The officers of the 185th New York were committed to strong training and discipline. The enlisted men recognized and respected that and so became committed themselves. As the 185th New York left for Virginia, DRAUGHTGILSIVAD wrote that "thanks to the untiring energy

and thorough discipline of Col. Jenny and Lieut. Col. Sniper, those men who left this morning to guard our front are as well drilled as three-fourths of the forces in the field."[69] Another soldier wrote home in early December 1864: "The regiment is making rapid strides in discipline and drill, . . . [N]o pains are spared by the officers of the regiment to make it a good and effective regiment in every sense of the word. With the material that the 185th possesses, . . . in a short time it will be second to none in the service, if indeed it is not now as good as the best."[70] DRAUGHTGILSIVID noted that while "there are some growlers . . . [t]he greater portion of the regiment . . . are anxious to become skilled in the tactics."[71]

The bimonthly ratings by the inspecting officers show that the level of discipline and instruction generally improved from the end of October to the end of December 1864 and reached high levels by the end of the war. Companies E and H were the exceptions, reaching only "ordinary" levels by the end of the war.[72]

4. EXPERIENCE IN THE FIELD. The men of the 185th New York lacked experience when they arrived in the field. Only 10 to 15 percent of the enlisted men had previously served. One soldier wrote home that "our men are all green in military tactics, and I cannot say how they will stand fire."[73]

Lynn observed that the French Army of the North had successfully used "petite guerre" (small-scale combat) to introduce new units to combat.[74] While the

"General Warren's Raid–Soldiers Making a Greek Cross (The Fifth Corps Badge) out of the Heated Rails of the Weldon Railroad [sketch by A. W. Warren]" (*Harpers Weekly Journal of Civilization,* December 31, 1864, 837)

185th New York missed the Fifth Corps involvement in the Peebles Farm actions at the end of September, the 185th New York was lightly engaged at Burgess Mill at the end of October, suffering six casualties. The 185th New York suffered another sixteen casualties at Hatcher's Run in February 1865, when it came to the aid of Winthrop's Brigade. Company G's Capt. Albern Barber recounted that "In about three minutes we were double quicking to the left. . . . Formed our line and with some of the tallest yelling you can imagine in we went on a dead run."[75]

Just as important, Warren's Hicksford Raid in December to destroy track hardened the 185th New York, as it had other new units not yet fully tested in battle. A soldier in the 185th New York wrote to his brother: "I . . . never suffered so much a night in my life. Being nearly exhausted from long marches, . . . this terrible storm of wind, hail and rain was awful to bear. But it was wonderful to perceive with what courage the brave boys . . . , stood up against this storm, in some respects more terrible than a storm of bullets." Another soldier wrote the *Syracuse Standard* that "The boys worked with a will, and it was really surprising to see with what rapidity and how effectually the road was destroyed."[76]

5. Actual versus Authorized Strength. Recruiters had raised the 185th New York within four weeks in August and September 1864. The 185th New York arrived at City Point on September 29, 1864, with about eight hundred men, somewhat on the low side for a regiment of ten companies. The 185th Pennsylvania left camp for the Five Forks Campaign with sixteen officers and six hundred men present for duty—a strong number for a Union regiment at that time of the war.[77]

6. Supply (Food, Arms, and Equipment). The 185th New York had arrived at Globe Tavern on October 1 without tents, rations, or ammunition.[78] Nonetheless, the men apparently were comfortable that the regimental quartermaster was doing the best he could. LEW wrote the *Standard* that "Quartermaster Gilbert is supplying the boys with as good rations and clothing as can be procured under the circumstances." Later in October, DRAUGHTGILSIVAD wrote that "Especially are the men indebted to Quartermaster Gilbert, for the perfect manner in which he conducts his department." He also reported that Commissary Sergeant Morey "has done his duty well."[79]

The muster roll ratings for Arms, Accoutrements, and Clothing indicate some supply problems at the end of 1864, which were generally resolved by the end of the war.[80]

7. Demographics (Occupation, Nationality at Birth, and Age). The men had the standard demographics for an Onondaga County regiment.[81]

In summary, Union commanders could have been concerned about the 185th New York's readiness for battle when it arrived in the field, primarily because of the lack of experience among both officers and men. However, both the officers and men had a strong commitment to training and the success of the regiment. The time available for training over the winter, building on the limited combat experience at Burgess's Mill and the hardening provided by the Hicksford Raid against the Weldon Railroad in December augured well for the 185th New York's performance in the 1865 campaign. Indeed, the 185th New York once again performed well in harsh weather in the February 1865 Hatcher's Run offensive. LEW proudly wrote the *Syracuse Standard* that "The 185th Regiment has been tried and found itself worthy of all that has been predicted in its favor."[82]

198th Pennsylvania

1. MOTIVATION (MORALE AND UNIT COHESION). The 198th Pennsylvania also had strong morale and unit cohesion.

The 198th Pennsylvania was the sixth infantry regiment raised by Philadelphia's Union League Club. When it was time to move to the front, the 198th Pennsylvania marched from camp into the city for a ceremony at the Club for the presentation of the unit colors, and the public showed its support.[83] The muster roll ratings for military appearance suggest good morale heading into the Five Forks Campaign. Twelve of the fourteen companies were rated as "Good" at the end of February 1865.[84]

In November, only 59 percent of the men of the 198th Pennsylvania voted for Lincoln, but the 198th was raised in Philadelphia, which gave Lincoln a nearly identical 56 percent majority. Pvt. Jacob Wilson had thought that the "majority was for Little Mac." Wilson believed that if McClellan were elected, "this war will soon be over but if Old rail splitter goes in then look out . . . they can stand it to fight as long as we can."[85]

At the beginning of 1865, the men of the 198th Pennsylvania were optimistic that the war would end soon. James Daily wrote his sister at the end of February that "Reble deserters ar coming in our lines every day and they say that the South is about gone." Three weeks before the Five Forks Campaign began, Morgan Shaffer wrote his father that "The Confederacy is about played out. Old Sickels says we will all be home by the first of may."[86]

The men of the 198th Pennsylvania did receive large bounties. Advertisements promoted "One Year's Income" of $742 (including $400 Philadelphia bounty and $50 Ward bounty) "Besides Fuel, Clothing and Subsistence." Despite the high bounty, only 6 percent of the recruits for the 198th Pennsylvania deserted, and only two men after they reached the field.[87]

SIXTH UNION LEAGUE

REGIMENT!

FOR

ONE YEAR'S SERVICE.

Colonel H. G. SICKEL,

(Late of the 3d Regiment, Pennsylvania Reserve Corps, Commanding.)

HEAD QUARTERS,

NATIONAL GUARD'S HALL

RACE STREET BELOW SIXTH.

City Bounty Cash,	. .	$400
Ward, " "		50
Gov. " "		33
Gov. Bounty at end of Year,	.	67
Pay for One Year,	. . .	192
One Year's Income,	. .	$742

☞ Besides Fuel, Clothing and Subsistence furnished by the United States Government.

☞ **Recruits will be mustered in singly, or in squads, and
sent to camp immediately.**

In order to avoid unnecessary delay, the Military Committee of the Union League, have
made arrangements to ADVANCE THE LOCAL BOUNTIES to Recruits, as soon as they are
mustered in.

King & Baird, Printers, 607 Sansom Street, Philadelphia

Sixth Union League Regiment [198th Pennsylvania Volunteers] for One Year's Service (Reproduced by
permission from the New-York Historical Society)

Colonel Horatio Sickel (198th Pennsylvania Volunteers) (National Archives)

As evidence of strong unit cohesion, Henry Dieble was proud of his regiment and his own service. In February 1865, he sent his mother his "Solger's memorial." "There you can see the names of our Company and the Regement and the battles and Wen and Ware it Was and git it frame and take good care of it till I git home."[88]

2. Leadership. The 198th Pennsylvania had a solid, experienced field commander in Horatio Sickel, a coach maker and lamp maker before the war, as well as a militia soldier. He joined the Third Pennsylvania Reserves as a captain in 1861 and quickly rose to colonel. Meade, who had been Sickel's brigade commander earlier in the war, thought so highly of Sickel that when he learned that the 198th had arrived in the field, he asked Grant to assign the 198th to the Army of the Potomac rather than the Army of the James as originally planned and Grant did so.[89] Almost all of the other line officers in the 198th Pennsylvania had previously served, although some only in nine-month or militia units or as enlisted men.[90]

3. Training and Discipline. The 198th Pennsylvania drilled every other day or so in September and October, including skirmish drill on two days, but picket duty and operations took up most of November and December. More frequent drilling resumed in mid-January. Lieutenant Colonel Murray was concerned about the regiment's early progress. In mid-October, he wrote that "The Regiment is already a month old; and yet but very few men have been observed on post that appear to be acquainted with the simple duties of a sentry." He blamed the company commanders.[91]

The muster roll ratings for Discipline and Instruction indicate that the 198th Pennsylvania improved from the end of October to the end of December, with all but two of the fourteen companies being rated good in both categories. The same was true at the end of February, the last rating period before the Five Forks Campaign.[92]

4. EXPERIENCE IN THE FIELD. Roughly a quarter of the enlisted men had previously served, although some men had served only in nine-month or militia units.[93] The 198th Pennsylvania saw combat fairly soon after arriving at the front in a charge on September 30, losing ten men. At Burgess's Mill at the end of October, the 198th Pennsylvania was "held in readiness," losing only three men.[94] The 198th Pennsylvania participated in the Hicksford Raid in December. In the February 1865 Hatcher's Run offensive, the 198th Pennsylvania and the 185th New York, with Colonel Sickel as their brigade commander, came to the aid of Winthrop's Brigade of the Fifth Corps' Second Division when it was under attack by a superior force and "retiring" due to lack of ammunition. Colonel Sickel "at once ordered a charge upon the enemy's line, whose numbers, I believe, were equal, if not superior . . . This was executed in a most gallant style and with great steadiness, both officers and men conducting themselves in a manner which would have done credit to the best veteran troops."[95] Sickel commended Major Glenn of the 198th Pennsylvania (as well as Colonel Jenney of the 185th New York) for display[ing] great coolness on the field and ability in the management of their troops." Pvt. Jordan Lear wrote his friends that "the balls flew as thick as hail" and that he had "used up . . . fifty rounds." Pvt. Josiah Shuman simply wrote in his diary that "we were marched into a fight with the Rebs and drove them into their works." The 198th Pennsylvania suffered twenty-one casualties.[96]

5. ACTUAL VERSUS AUTHORIZED STRENGTH. Heading into the Five Forks Campaign, the 198th Pennsylvania had twenty-four officers and nearly seven hundred fifty enlisted men present for duty (thirty-five officers and one thousand enlisted men present). This was well below the 198th Pennsylvania's original strength, but quite a large number for a Union regiment at that point in the war.

Philadelphia's Union League had raised five regiments before the 198th Pennsylvania. The League recruited over eleven hundred fifty men for the 198th Pennsylvania in ten companies by the time it reached the field in late September 1864 and another three hundred-plus in four more companies in October 1864. The recent muster-out of the three-year Third and Fourth Pennsylvania Reserves (Thirty-Second and Thirty-Third Pennsylvania Volunteers) provided a good pool of potential volunteers. The 198th Pennsylvania was unusually large at fourteen companies. As previously noted, a regiment this size was too large to be effectively led by one commander. At the time of Five Forks, the 198th Pennsylvania was divided into two battalions, one led by Sickel (who was succeeded by Joshua Chamberlain as brigade commander before Five Forks), the other by Major Glenn, a veteran of the Third Reserves.[97]

6. Supply (Food, Arms, and Equipment). The ratings for the supply of arms, accoutrements, and clothing were generally "good" from the time the regiment was mustered in until the spring of 1865 but fell to "fair" at the end of April 1865.[98] Enough enlisted men complained about short rations in November 1864 that Colonel Sickel issued a circular addressing the problem, which apparently resolved the concerns.[99]

7. Demographics (Occupation and Nationality at Birth). Reflecting the fact that the 198th Pennsylvania was raised in Philadelphia, although not all recruits resided there, twice as many men in the 198th Pennsylvania were laborers compared to the Army of the Potomac as a whole and only a quarter as many were farmers (see Table 11.1).

Table 11.1: 198th Pennsylvania Occupations (Percent)

Laborer	20.0
Farmer	14.1
Shoemaker	6.1
Carpenter	5.7
Blacksmith	3.7
Miner	3.0
Clerk	2.8
Machinist	2.4

Source: Compiled from Descriptive Book, 198th Pennsylvania
    Regimental Books, RG 94, NARA.

In summary, Colonel Sickel's strong reputation gave credibility to the 198th Pennsylvania when it arrived in the field. That credibility was solidified as it performed well during the fall of 1864 and the spring of 1865.

187th New York

Recruits for the 187th New York came primarily from New York's four westernmost counties—Niagara, Erie, Cattaraugus, and Chautauqua. Roughly half the men came from Buffalo. Three-quarters enlisted for one year, with the remainder enlisting for three years. Bounties were relatively high. Overall, just under 10 percent of the men deserted, but few men deserted after the 187th New York reached the field.[100]

Union commanders might have been concerned that there were not enough good men in the 187th New York. The occupational profile of the 187th New York differed substantially from the profile of the Union army as a whole. Farmers made up only 15 percent of the regiment, while laborers comprised 32 percent. Other unskilled occupations took that category to 40 percent. The 187th New York was also significantly more diverse than the Union army as a whole. Nearly 60 percent of the men in the 187th New York were foreign-born—including 30 percent from Germany, 11 percent from Canada, and 8 percent from Ireland. Only 32 percent were born in New York.[101]

The 187th New York arrived in the field in late October as a battalion of only six companies with five hundred men under Lt. Col. Daniel Myers. The seventh company arrived at the end of November, but the eighth and ninth companies did not arrive until February and May 1865 respectively, and a tenth company was never recruited. Many of the men came from the Sixty-Fifth New York National Guard, which had served for thirty days in the summer of 1863.[102]

A local newspaper wrote that the 187th New York was "officered by experienced soldiers, men who have seen service and are willing to endure more."[103] In fact, that was not true. Half of the officers, including Lieutenant Colonel Myers, had not previously served, and most of the officers who had previously served had been in the Sixty-Fifth New York National Guard.[104] Lieutenant Colonel Myers singled out for praise Captains Loeb (Company I) and Wagner (Company E) "to whom I am indebted . . . for the good behavior of the regiment on the march and while under fire" and Adj. Carl Zentz without whom "my duties would have been much more laborious" in his last after-action report following Lee's surrender. However, Loeb had served for only a year in the Seventy-Second New York and Wagner for only thirty days in the Sixty-Fifth New York Militia, while Zentz had not previously served, so even they were short on experience.[105] In the enlisted ranks, roughly 15 percent of the men had served previously in nonmilitia units.[106]

Recognizing the inexperience of the 187th, 188th, and 189th New York, their brigade commander placed them in the battle lines at Burgess's Mill behind experienced skirmishers from the Ninety-First Pennsylvania and the 155th New York.[107] But that did not mean they did not suffer casualties. D. K. N. described the seventy-two casualties suffered by the 187th New York out of four hundred forty men engaged as "a severe introduction for a regiment three weeks old."[108] The regiment's many moves after arriving in the field "left us no time to drill or learn the manual of arms; in fact, I venture to say, three-fourths of the men had never loaded or fired a musket until the morning we went into the fight. But they stood to their work bravely and showed that the material was there, all it needed was cultivation."[109]

Over 90 percent of the men of the 187th New York voted for Lincoln. That indicates good morale. However, "scarcely half" the regiment voted.[110]

188th New York

The 188th New York arrived at a key moment and performed well at the Battle of Lewis Farm, but Union commanders could have been concerned about its readiness before the battle.

The recruits for the 188th New York came primarily from Rochester and the surrounding area of Monroe County. Monroe County may have had a bounty as high as $1,000. Eleven percent of the men deserted.

A battalion of six companies comprised of 430 men and twenty officers arrived at City Point on October 18, 1864, and joined the Fifth Corps on October 21 and Griffin's Division on October 24.[111] The officers of the 188th New York had limited field experience. The field commander, Lt. Col. Isaac Doolittle, had served as lieutenant and captain in the Ninety-Fourth New York and 105th New York, and had been wounded at both Antietam and Fredericksburg, but the major, adjutant, and quartermaster had not previously served. Only one of the company commanders had previously served as a captain. Five company commanders had not previously served and two had served as sergeants. Two-thirds of the lieutenants in the companies had not previously served.[112]

Understrength, inexperienced officers and limited opportunity for training were not good indicators for combat readiness. However, combat veteran Lieutenant Colonel Doolittle did recognize four officers for "exceeding coolness and gallantry under heavy fire" in his last after-action report: Capt. James Reilly (Company F), who had not previously served; Lt. John Marks (Company I) and Lt. Edward Martin (Company H), who had served as lieutenants in the two-year Thirteenth New York; and Lt. Patrick Sweeney (Company B), who had served as a private in the Thirty-Third New York.[113]

Only three days after arriving in the field, the 188th New York engaged at Burgess's Mill suffering fifty-four casualties. The *Jamestown Journal* reported that "The regiment, with very little drill or experience, was sent into a disastrous charge and lost heavily."[114] Pvt. William Whitlock wrote home: "I have seen the elephant. . . . we drove in the Reb pickets and stoud and fought about two hours and then fel back. . . . [T]he bulits whistled right smart. . . . i was perfectly cool all through the fight. I dont feel a bit as I expected i should. I was not a bit scaird."[115]

Over 80 percent of the men of the 188th New York voted for Lincoln, which indicates strong morale.[116]

189th New York

The 189th New York came primarily from four different counties: Steuben (four companies); Allegany (two companies); Oneida (one company); and Oswego (three companies), but the individual companies were relatively homogeneous. Companies A and H were recruited entirely in the town of Bath (Steuben County), Company E entirely in Oswego, and Company F in Constantia (Oswego County). The local governments generally offered high bounties. Steuben did not offer a county bounty, but the towns offered from $200 to $1,000, with Bath at $500. Oswego offered a county bounty of $600, with town bounties ranging from $100 to $300 and Constantia at $300. Allegany offered a county bounty in an undetermined amount, with town bounties ranging from $300 to $1,000. Oneida offered a county bounty of $300 with town bounties ranging from $300 to $1,000. Despite these high bounties, only 1 percent of the men in the 189th New York deserted.[117]

Like so many late-war new regiments, the 189th New York left for the front in battalions—four companies in mid-September 1864 and another five in mid-October. The nine companies totaled about eight hundred men and were briefly assigned to the Engineering Brigade before joining the Fifth Corps on November 2.[118]

The officers of the 189th New York had limited experience. The three field-grade officers had previously served only as captains. Only one of the company commanders had previously served as a captain. One had previously served as a second lieutenant, two as noncommissioned officers, one as a private, and five had not previously served. Only four of the lieutenants in the companies had previously served as lieutenants and another four as sergeants—half had not previously served and three had served only as privates.[119]

Shortly after the 189th New York joined the Fifth Corps, Pvt. Henry Bull, a nineteen-year-old son of a farmer, wrote his father: "I will try and do my duty the best I know how and if I am draw into Battle I shall fight for my Country the best I know how to. I have got so I can handle my gun first rate." He also understood the importance of military discipline: "I will look on the bright side of it and do as I am told and make everything pass off as smoothly as I can. I find that is the Best way for to do in the army for we enlisted for to obey all orders given us by those that was appointed over us and obey them. That is the only way we can get along." And he was learning how to work together as a team: "I know more about helping work now than I did before I came away from home."[120]

As general indicators of morale, over 80 percent of the men of the 189th New York voted for Lincoln in the 1864 election and only 1 percent deserted.[121]

210th Pennsylvania

The 210th Pennsylvania was "760 strong" when it joined the Fifth Corps at the end of September. Almost one-third of the men had deserted by then, but few deserted after reaching the field.[122] According to Bates, most of both officers and men "had experience in military duty." Col. William Sergeant had served as a captain in the Twelfth US Infantry and Lt. Col. Edward Whitman had served as a captain in the Forty-Sixth Pennsylvania.[123]

Hatcher's Run in October 1864 is included in the 210th Pennsylvania's record of engagements, but the 210th did not report any casualties. The 210th Pennsylvania participated in the Fifth Corps' December 1864 raid on the Weldon Railroad.[124] Bates states that the 210th Pennsylvania "displayed great gallantry" at Dabney's Mill in February 1865, but that has not been confirmed. The 210th Pennsylvania did suffer thirty-three casualties.[125]

Fifty-eight percent of the men of the 210th Pennsylvania voted for Lincoln—a definite majority, but a relatively low percentage for a Union regiment.[126]

While not seriously tested in battle, the 210th Pennsylvania looked reasonably good on paper except for the high desertion rate en route to the front.

Eighth Delaware

Three companies of the Eighth Delaware—254 men and nine officers—reported to the Engineering Brigade at City Point on October 11, 1864. The men received new weapons because the weapons issued in Delaware were "worthless."[127] In addition to work in the Engineering Brigade, the Eighth Delaware performed garrison duty and served in the Army of the Potomac's Provost Guard over the next several months.[128] Still only a battalion of three companies, the Eighth Delaware joined the Fifth Corps on March 18, 1865. As a battalion, the Eighth Delaware contributed little because of its size, but Capt. John Richards was recommended for promotion to brevet major for "great bravery" at White Oak Road and Five Forks.[129]

The 185th New York and the 198th Pennsylvania truly proved themselves to be effective fighting regiments at Lewis Farm. Not only did they stand their ground in a two-hour seesaw battle to protect the Fifth Corps' bridgehead over Gravelly Run, but they also defeated a larger force of Confederate veterans. At White Oak Road, they literally saved the day for the Fifth Corps after Ayres's and Crawford's divisions had been routed. At Five Forks, many parts of Sheridan's forces performed well. For their part, the 185th New York and the 198th Pennsylvania, along with the other regiments of Chamberlain's Brigade, broke the Confederate's back in their sector.

Union commanders could have expected great things of the 198th Pennsylvania given the solid experience of Colonel Sickel, as well as the prior service of many of the other officers and roughly a quarter of the enlisted men. However, the performance of the green 185th New York probably surprised them. The commitment of Colonel Jenney and Lieutenant Colonel Sniper to discipline and training and the willingness of the men to learn deserve the credit. The 185th New York and the 198th Pennsylvania also benefited from having Joshua Chamberlain as their brigade commander and Charles Griffin as their division commander.

The 188th New York also performed well in the Five Forks offensive. While not standing out throughout the three battles like the 185th New York and the 198th Pennsylvania, the 188th New York arrived at a key moment at Lewis Farm. The 187th New York and the 189th New York did not stand out, but they consistently performed their assigned duty. In contrast, the performance of the 210th Pennsylvania was only mediocre.

As the six late-war new regiments in Hartranft's Division had demonstrated at Fort Stedman, the five late-war regiments of Chamberlain's and Gregory's brigades showed during the Five Forks offensive that Union commanders could generally rely on late-war new regiments to develop the readiness necessary to perform effectively in battle.

Conclusion

The long-standing division of Union soldiers between the recruits of 1861 and 1862 as "patriots" and the late-war replacements of 1863 through 1865 as "mercenaries" is not a useful approach to understanding how the Union Army was raised and replenished. Gary Gallagher has counseled that: "It is always worth asking whether new interpretive frameworks would make sense to the historical actors who lived through an era."[1] However, the old interpretive framework of patriot versus mercenary may not have made sense to the Union citizenry at large during the later part of the war.

There is certainly strong evidence that the men who enlisted in 1861 and 1862 viewed the later-enlisting volunteers as unpatriotic mercenaries. However, a man weighing his personal responsibilities against his obligations as a citizen with the prospect of being drafted in the background probably would not have considered himself a mercenary because he chose to enlist and receive a large bounty. And depending on his family circumstances, he may not have considered a decision not to enlist earlier as unpatriotic. Most of the men in the Eastern States during the Civil War probably saw themselves within J. Matthew Gallman's framework as "people who wished to do their duty but who were often unsure about precisely what that meant." Their family members and neighbors likely would have seen it that way as well.[2] Similarly, while many people used the word *high* during the Civil War to describe the amount of the bounties, many others used the word *liberal*. The former implies that the later-enlisting volunteers were paid too much. The latter implies that the amount was generous rather than unwarranted. Many citizens believed that liberal bounties were fair compensation for men who volunteered to face the risks of war and the hardships of separation from family, while other men stayed at home and prospered in the booming civilian economy.

A more productive approach to understanding the process of raising and replenishing the Union army is to see it as a series of pragmatic responses to changing political and battlefield realities. To begin with, a strict division between *patriot* and *mercenary* is not justified by the facts. The economic benefits of volunteering in 1862 and to a lesser degree in 1861 were sufficiently great for large enough numbers of men that an economic motivation for volunteering early in the war cannot be dismissed out of hand. Many of the volunteers in 1864 and 1865 were too young in 1861 and 1862 to have enlisted without parental consent. Historians should not presume them to have been unpatriotic. Older men who enlisted later in the war may have believed that their family responsibilities precluded them from volunteering in 1861, but that the time had come in 1864 to step up and volunteer (or that the draft left them no choice).

A division between patriots and mercenaries also overlooks the reality that patriotism alone has never been a sufficient motivator in the United States for a prolonged, large-scale war. The early volunteers are critical to be sure, but prolonged, large-scale wars are won with the men who can be drawn upon to maintain the necessary troop levels. Patriotism was no longer viable as the primary motivating force for maintaining, much less augmenting the Union army by the summer of 1862. At the same time, a stand-alone draft was politically unacceptable for both philosophical and economic reasons for the Union public at large. The citizenry widely acknowledged the weaknesses—indeed the evils—of the bounty system at the time. But compared to a stand-alone draft, the consensus was that the bounty was preferable—the lesser of two evils in the eyes of many. The public also recognized that high bounties alone would not generate enough recruits. The pragmatic compromise of combining bounties and the conditional draft as a "carrot and stick" was necessary to raise enough men—most of whom hopefully would be good. Historians can legitimately criticize the bounty system on a wide variety of grounds—it was costly, inefficient, provided opportunity for corruption, and encouraged desertion, but it worked well enough in conjunction with the conditional draft to raise enough good men for the Union army to win the war.

The conclusion that the combination of bounties and a conditional draft "worked" is not original with me. Where I differ with Eugene Murdock is his focus on the primacy of conscription. Use of the bounty to induce volunteering preceded conscription. Recognition that increased bounties were necessary to stimulate recruiting occurred in July 1862 before the conditional draft was adopted in August 1862. Competition among towns for recruits to meet their quotas by using local bounties as the key means was deeply entrenched prior to

the Enrollment Act. Murdock contended that the failure to equalize local bounties was a major failing. However, the inability to use local bounties as a means
to compete for recruits would have been anathema to most towns. States that
tried to limit local bounties generally failed. Bounties without the threat of the
draft would not have worked after 1862, but the draft without bounties (and commutation and substitution) was politically unacceptable. Union leaders failed to
adopt increases in enlisted men's wages beyond the $3 a month increase in 1864.
Moreover, higher wages would not have addressed the recognized need for a
large advance payment.[3] Combining bounties and the conditional draft was a
classic American compromise.[4]

Two lesser components of the bounty/conditional draft structure also warrant
discussion. Commutation played an important role as a safety valve for the harsh
impact of the draft on local economies, but its continued viability was doomed
because it allowed too many men to escape military service. Regardless of the
actual impact of commutation, the "rich man's war, poor man's fight" accusation facilitated its demise politically. The $300 statutory fee for commutation
had provided a check on the fees for substitutes, but once the check of commutation was removed, the law of supply and demand drove substitute fees upward.
Unregulated substitution became the real evil in the system. Men volunteering
as substitutes—who by law could not be subject to the draft—deserted at much
higher rates than the later-enlisting volunteers who were subject to the draft.
However, appropriate regulation of substitution was also politically unacceptable
both because substitution became the ultimate safety valve for protecting a local
economy and because substitute brokers had powerful political connections.

The bounty system should not be dismissed as just the lesser of two evils.
There were broader benefits that the Union realized from the fact that the bounty
system worked in addition to the numbers of men brought to the field. Three are
worth further consideration.

First, bounties served as the means for state and local governments to work
an unacknowledged compromise with the federal government on the extent to
which the civilian economy would be sacrificed to win the war. James McPherson recently wrote that "the Civil War Still Matters" because it is fundamental to
understanding issues that we still struggle with today such as "the relative powers
and responsibilities of federal, state and local governments."[5] Effective action in
the United States generally requires cooperation at all three levels of government. During the Civil War, bounties played a key role in how the three levels
of government worked out the conflict between conscription and volunteering.
Separate local bounties were the means for local governments to mitigate the
impact of the federal draft on their community's economy and social structure

Second, the country's recent experience has demonstrated that appropriate compensation is a critical element of national defense. While World War II seemingly confirmed the primacy of conscription over volunteering for raising a large-scale army for a prolonged war, the Vietnam War reopened the debate. Today, America's military needs—offensive or defensive—are pursued with a professional force of volunteers. Forever gone are the days before the Civil War and World War II when a minimal standing army would suffice. In 2022, 1.3 million volunteers were on active duty in the five branches of service. Another 750,000 were on reserve status.

A professional military requires a compensation structure that can compete with civilian demands for labor. A private in the army today earns over $25,000 a year. Today's medical, housing, and other benefits for service members and their families did not exist during the Civil War. And just as the Union recognized the importance of enlistment "bounties" during the Civil War, today's army offers significant enlistment "bonuses."[6] While today's volunteers are professional soldiers, we would hardly call them mercenaries. We respect them as men and women dedicated to serving their country, thinking of them as both patriots and professionals.

With the benefit of hindsight, the Union's reliance on well-compensated volunteers does not look so bad. Indeed, both Fry and Sherman recognized the potential need for increased military compensation in order to raise the needed troops. In November 1863, Fry recommended increasing the federal bounty from $100 to $300, noting that: "the present pay and bounty of the soldier do not compete with the wages paid throughout the country." In his memoirs, Sherman opined that when recruiting becomes difficult, "the pay should be raised by Congress, instead of tempting new men by exaggerated bounties. I believe it would have been more economical to have raised the pay of the soldier to thirty or even fifty dollars a month than to have held out the promise of [large bounties]."[7] With monthly pay at only $16, it was bounties that raised military compensation to the needed levels.

Third, taking compensation a step further, the Civil War bounties may have served as the equivalent of the education and other benefits in the GI Bill for World War II veterans in funding the expansion of the middle class.[8] The criticism that bounties were too high has never gone a step further and inquired how the bounty money was spent. Among the handful of examples of how soldiers spent their bounty money encountered in the research for this book, buying a new farm or paying down the mortgage on an old one was the most common. The possibility of buying a farm with the bounty money was promoted by many newspapers. While education was the pathway to middle-class wealth during the twentieth century, farm ownership was a major pathway in the nineteenth century. Starting a small business was another. The proceeds of the bounty may have promoted both. Studying changes in Union soldiers' occupations and wealth from 1860 to 1870 could produce interesting results.[9]

Just as the reputation of the bounty system deserves a more favorable light, the reputations of the late-war Union soldiers deserve a more balanced treatment. Criticized as mercenaries in entering the army, the later-enlisting volunteers and substitutes, as well as the draftees, have been further discredited as deserters and shirkers in combat. The desertion issue has to be placed in perspective. The typical later-enlisting volunteer definitely was not a deserter.[10] A desertion rate in the range of 20 percent (including the Not Taken Up Factor) is not a number to be proud of, but the desertion rate for the original complement of the old Pennsylvania regiments was in the range of 10 percent—too high to ignore. Addressing the "shirking" in battle accusation on a comprehensive statistical basis is challenging, but the casualty percentages for the Pennsylvania late-war volunteers in the Army of the Potomac are similar to the percentages for the veterans from 1861 and 1862. Even if the late-war volunteers-were motivated by bounties rather than patriotism to join the army, the normative influences of army life in the field still generally turned them into good soldiers. There is also the fact that half the veterans from 1861 in the Army of the Potomac chose to return home when their term of service expired before the Union defeated the Confederacy (although some did return as late-war replacements).

The subject of Union desertion itself needs reappraisal. Despite Ella Lonn's view that Union desertion was "the more to be deplored," historians have given Confederate desertion far more attention, although even that has been limited.[11] Lonn's nine "heads" are nearly one hundred years old—far too long a period not to be tested by new ideas. For example, the wide variation in the desertion rates of the Pennsylvania regiments in the Army of the Potomac suggests that new insights are to be gained by studying the internal dynamics of individual regiments. Failure to develop unit cohesion, which historians did not study when Lonn was writing, seems like a probable cause of desertion. Reorganizations also may have destroyed unit cohesion. For example, a veteran of the Thirty-Second Maine concluded in his regimental history that the consolidation of the Thirty-Second Maine into the Thirty-First Maine in December 1864 led to desertion by soldiers from the Thirty-Second Maine.[12] Lonn's discussion of a lack of discipline as a cause of desertion might be expanded by looking at regiments—and companies within regiments—with a history of desertion.[13]

Lonn based her research primarily on the *Official Records,* which had been available only for a generation at the time she published *Desertion during the Civil War* in 1928. Soldier's letters were theoretically available but not practically accessible in large numbers.[14] It would be another generation before Bell Wiley would use soldiers' letters to write the social history of the Civil War in *The Life of Johnny Reb* and *The Life of Billy Yank*. Today, the internet makes soldiers' letters readily accessible. There likely are important causes of desertion not addressed by Lonn that a broad examination of soldiers' letters might reveal. For example, a soldier's concern about the welfare of his family back home may have had a broader impact on desertion than Lonn considered. In his end-of-the-war report, Fry attributed the relatively high desertion rate in Kansas in part to the fact that the Kansas contingent "contained an unusually large percentage of men whose presence was necessary to the subsistence and protection of their families." Family crises also may have called Union soldiers to return home. The 179th New York's George Cross deserted from Mower Hospital in Washington, DC, to visit his sick wife in upstate New York. He was arrested just before reaching home and sent back to the hospital. He then received a letter from his mother telling him that his wife had come down with typhoid fever. "We thought she was getting better and the fever turned and she now by spells is crazy. . . . [Doctors] said they thought she would not get well . . . [W]hen Mary Ann is in her right mind she says all she wants is to see George." Cross deserted again—and was caught again.[15]

Another possibility is that the perception by an unknown percentage of Union soldiers that the North's objective in pursuing the war had changed from simply preserving the Union to also freeing the slaves may have caused desertion. The additional objective of ending slavery was certainly widely—and heatedly—discussed. Indeed, Jonathan W. White has concluded that "many common soldiers deserted rather than fight in a war for abolition."[16]

In 1928, the possibility of using "massive data and statistical analysis" to study desertion probably did not occur to Lonn. Using the "Early Indicators" database, Costa and Kahn have provided numerous insights about desertion in *Heroes & Cowards* and their earlier work.[17] Some of their conclusions support Lonn's analysis of causation. For example, Costa and Kahn concluded that foreign-born soldiers were more likely to desert than native-born soldiers.[18] Their discussion of unit cohesion suggests the possibility that desertion resulting from impaired unit cohesion may go beyond the specific causes identified by Lonn.[19]

Because Costa and Kahn were seeking to answer a different set of questions related to "how social networks affected men's decisions to sacrifice their lives" during the Civil War, they "control[led] for the receipt of a bounty," rather than testing for the impact of the bounty.[20] However, in the context of raising an army during the Civil War, the impact of bounties on desertion is a fundamental question. Perhaps someone will someday utilize sophisticated statistical modeling techniques, like those employed by Costa and Kahn, to determine the quantitative impact of bounties on desertion. (Further research will not minimize the impact of bounties on desertion. The percentage of late-war Pennsylvania volunteers deserting within thirty days of enlistment is strong support for that impact.)

One of the original hypotheses of this project was that the late-war new regiments more effectively integrated the later-enlisting volunteers than the old regiments in the field did because of the antipathy of the veterans over the large bounties on top of the traditional disdain of veterans for new recruits. The late-war new regiments in the Army of the Potomac did generally perform well in battle. However, the Army of the Potomac's old Pennsylvania regiments with half or more of their ranks comprised of late-war replacements also generally performed well. Despite the anecdotal evidence of the veterans' animosity toward the late-war replacements, these old Pennsylvania regiments integrated their late-war replacements well enough to perform their assigned missions. Similarly, my hypothesis that the heavy casualties of the Overland Campaign may have deprived the old regiments of the numbers of experienced officers and noncommissioned officers necessary to do the training of the new recruits received for the Petersburg Campaign also is not correct for these regiments.

Even though there was no significant difference in performance between new regiments and old regiments with large numbers of late-war replacements, there was still justification for creating new regiments late in the war. The primary contribution of the late-war new regiments was that they provided an alternative vehicle for recruiting men—both returning veterans and new recruits—who might not have joined an old regiment. Moreover, they were generally effective as fighting regiments. Bringing back experienced officers into the army was particularly important. The prospect of higher rank in a new regiment was certainly an inducement.

There also may have been a benefit from the late-war new regiments as fresh units. Studies of World War II soldiers have found that the combat effectiveness of soldiers deteriorated over time to the point where they became ineffectual. While Civil War soldiers may not have been subject to the stress of prolonged day-to-day combat to the same degree as World War II soldiers, Carol Reardon has written that "the fighting at the Wilderness and especially Spotsylvania . . . set apart May 1864 from all previous campaigns for the seemingly endless quality of the fighting," and that "the intensity of the fighting brought many Union soldiers to the limits of their endurance." That the late-war new regiments often fought effectively in their first battle likely reflects the fact that they were fresh units. General McClellan reputedly said in 1862 that "More than once have battles, nearly lost by veterans, been restored by the intrepid obstinacy of new soldiers." Similarly, Col. Henry Thomas, who had commanded a brigade in Ferraro's Division of African American troops at the Battle of the Crater, remarked: "It is an axiom in military art that there are times when the ardor, hopefulness and enthusiasm of new troops, not yet rendered doubtful by reverses or chilled by defeat, more than compensate, in a dash, for training and experience."[21] A secondary benefit of the late-war new regiments was that desertion generally ended when the regiment arrived in the field. Desertion in old Pennsylvania regiments generally continued after the regiment reached the field.

Moreover, not all old regiments were worth saving by sending them late-war replacements. Thomas Livermore, who enlisted in 1861 as a private and rose through the ranks to ultimately become the colonel of the late-war Eighteenth New Hampshire, noted that "it was sometimes the case that regiments which took the field with inefficient officers never recovered from that misfortune, . . . [N]ew regiments, well officered, were sometimes preferable."[22] An old regiment could become a failed regiment for other reasons as well. For example, an old regiment with a low percentage of reenlisting veterans not only likely had low morale but would also be entrusting the training of the late-war replacements to short-timers. Late-war new regiments were fresh and potentially more energetic.

Combat effectiveness as an analytic tool is all but absent from Civil War historiography. As a result, historians are missing potential insights. Regimental histories that do not include an assessment of the unit's combat effectiveness—including my own history of the 179th New York Volunteers—are incomplete. Fox's thesis with his "Three Hundred Fighting Regiments" that the worth of a regiment is measured by the amount of blood spilled on the battlefield is the product of a different era. Indeed, large casualties may indicate that the regiment was ineffective in combat. The author who moves beyond Fox to write a book along the lines of "Twenty Combat Effective Regiments" will make an important contribution to the study of the Civil War.

It is striking that the well-earned glory from the Union army's victory has not been accorded to all who served. Historians have justifiably given the lion's share of the credit to the men who enlisted in 1861 and 1862. But proper recognition of the contributions to the Union victory made by the volunteers of 1861 and 1862 does not necessitate demeaning the character or minimizing the contributions of the late-war replacements. The record of the volunteers from 1861 and 1862 undeniably stands on its own. However, as stated in the Introduction, their contribution to the Union victory was indispensable, but it was not sufficient. There should still be room for recognition of the contributions of the late-war replacements, particularly the later-enlisting volunteers. In celebrating America's triumph in World War II, we take pride in America's "Greatest Generation"—civilians as well as soldiers, not just the men and women who volunteered in 1941 and 1942.[23]

It is also not clear that the fighting effectiveness of the Army of the Potomac in the spring of 1865 was less than it had been earlier in the war. While Grant was hardly an objective observer and his judgment may have been clouded by the passage of time, it is still worth noting his proud statement in his *Memoirs* about the capability of the Union army at the time of the Grand Review: "The troops . . . appeared in their respective camps as ready and fit for duty as they had ever been in their lives. I doubt whether an equal body of men of any nation, take them man for man, officer for officer, was ever gotten together that would have proved their equal in a great battle."[24] Grant apparently saw no need to qualify his opinion due to the fact that the late-war replacements probably comprised more than half of the Union army at that time.

The answer to the question "Who won the war?" is not "The veterans of 1861 and 1862." The answer is that the veterans of 1861 and 1862 and the late-war replacements all did.

Notes

Abbreviations

In citing works in the notes, short titles have generally been used. Works frequently cited have been identified by the following abbreviations:

CMSR   Compiled Military Service Record (National Archives and Records Administration)
HIBO   HIBO Database on latewarunionsoldiers.org
NARA   National Archives and Records Administration
NYSMM   New York State Military Museum and Veterans Research Center
OR   *War of the Rebellion: A Compilation of the Official Records of the Union and Confederate Armies,* Washington, DC: Government Printing Office, 1880–1901. (All references are to Series I unless otherwise indicated.)
RG   Record Group (NARA)
USAHEC US Army Heritage and Education Center, Carlisle, Pennsylvania

Introduction

1. Rhodes, *History of the United States from the Compromise of 1850,* 4:430–32; Rhodes, *History of the Civil War, 1861–1865,* 331; Lonn, *Desertion During the Civil War,* 138; Catton, *A Stillness at Appomattox,* 23, 25; McPherson, *Battle Cry of Freedom,* 606; Foote, *Red River to Appomattox,* 129–30; Newsome, *Richmond Must Fall,* 20; Wiley, *Life of Billy Yank,* 343; Robertson, "Re-enlistment Patterns of Civil War Soldiers," 15n1.

2. Men enlisting in 1864 and 1865 have also been referred to as "eleventh-hour soldiers." Hickox, "The Civil War's 11th-Hour Soldiers," *National Tribune,* May 15, 1890, 4. A veteran who had enlisted in 1864 at the age of sixteen used the terms *new-comers* or *late-comers. National Tribune,* Oct. 1, 1903, 2.

3. Catton, *A Stillness at Appomattox,* 23; Marvel, *Lincoln's Mercenaries,* xiii.

4. McPherson, *Battle Cry of Freedom,* 606. See also Gallagher, *Enduring Civil War,* 124–25; Hess, *Union Soldier in Battle,* 91.

5. See generally Rutan, *179th New York Volunteer Infantry.* My great-great-grandfather, James C. Rutan, served in the 179th New York. I do not know the origin of the phrase "high-number" regiments. As I recall, my first encounter with the term was in Bruce Catton's *A Stillness at Appomattox,* 30. John D. Wright defines "high-number regiment" as "A Union regiment that was formed later in the war and therefore had a higher number. The higher number indicated the regiment comprised relatively inexperienced troops— young men or older ones finally caught by conscription. Such regiments were looked down upon by older low-number regiments." Wright did not define "high-bounty" men. Wright, *Language of the Civil War,* 146.

The numbers that qualify as "high" under the "high-number" rubric vary by state. Regiments were generally numbered sequentially as they were organized. In New York, the 179th New York was the first new regiment raised after the October 1863 call, while in New Hampshire, the Eighteenth New Hampshire was the only one. Fox, *Regimental Losses,* 481, 468.

6. See generally Lincoln's "Opinion on the Draft," Basler, *Collected Works of Abraham Lincoln,* 6:444–49; Gallman, *Defining Duty in the Civil War,* 3.

7. Gallman, *Defining Duty in the Civil War,* 12, 137. See also Sandow, "Limits of Northern Patriotism," 177, 186, 194; *Philadelphia Public Ledger,* July 24, 1862, 1 ("it is no reflection on a man's patriotism to know that he cares thoughtfully for his family").

8. Rutan, *179th New York Volunteer Infantry,* 31; McPherson, *For Cause and Comrades,* viii; Gallman, *Defining Duty in the Civil War,* 8.

9. OR III:5, 626, 636–37, 639, 720, 733–37; III:4, 927–28. The specific numbers are: Commutation (86,724); Substitutes (116,188); and Drafted, but failed to report (161,244). McPherson correctly states that 74,000 drafted men provided substitutes (*Battle Cry of Freedom,* 605), but in addition, 40,000 enrolled men provided substitutes before the draft. OR III:5, 637, 639. See also Boggs, *Patriotism by Proxy,* 7.

10. See Noe, *Reluctant Rebels,* 8, 10, passim. The Enrollment Act permitted a drafted man to provide a substitute to serve in his stead—a man who himself was not subject to the draft (e.g., foreign-born or under the age of twenty-one) but was otherwise eligible for military service.

11. With respect to the relative importance of the Eastern and Western theaters, see Gallagher, *Enduring Civil War,* 117–18. I do not discuss the Army of the James, which coordinated closely with the Army of the Potomac, nor do I discuss the corps, which were temporarily assigned to the Army of the Potomac. I have limited this reappraisal to infantry regiments because there may have been different motivations for enlisting in the other branches of military service. I also do not discuss the important role played by the African American volunteers because their differences in circumstances likely affected their motivations for volunteering. Achorn, *Every Drop of Blood,* 180.

There were many numerically high-number regiments that served in organizations other than the Army of the Potomac. I say "numerically" because most of these other high-number regiments were recruited under different bounty and conditional draft circumstances from those discussed in this book. A list of all the numerically high-number regiments by state, along with a brief description of their service, is provided on the latewarunionsoldiers.org website.

12. Eugene C. Murdock used the term *unrestricted draft* (*One Million Men,* 335). I prefer the term *stand-alone draft* because it conveys more clearly the idea of a draft operating on its own without complementary measures.

13. *Rochester Daily Democrat,* July 18, 1862, 2; McPherson, *Battle Cry of Freedom,* 606; Boggs, *Patriotism by Proxy,* xiii, 13.

14. Murdock, *One Million Men,* 333, 335–37, 344–45, 7, x–xi; McPherson, *Battle Cry of Freedom,* 605. See also Geary, *We Need Men,* 75 ("Local bounties unquestionably were the key factor in recruiting men after the federal draft arrived, but they also helped undermine confidence in the combined system of drafting and recruiting"); Nevins, *War for the Union,* 145. Murdock uses the phrase "it worked" to refer to the 1863 Enrollment Act (xi), while I use it to refer to the combination of bounties and the conditional draft—the so-called "carrot" and "stick." I disagree with Murdoch's concentration on the Enrollment Act because his characterization of the Enrollment Act as a "semidraft" to "spur enlistments" would not have worked without the additional "spur" of the bounty. The "threat of the draft" by itself was not sufficient to induce early enlistment and the complementary relationship of substitution and commutation could not have generated the number of volunteers that bounties did. Moreover, as discussed in chapter 2, the bounty system with state and local as well as federal components was already well established in the summer of 1862, seven months before adoption of the Enrollment Act (although only shortly before the August 1862 conditional draft).

15. Shannon, *Organization and Administration of the Union Army,* 2:49, 69, 80. Shannon titled his chapter "The Mercenary Factor."

16. *Brooklyn Daily Eagle,* Dec. 24, 1864, 2. See also *Waltham Sentinel* (MA), Sept. 9, 1864, 2; *Rochester Daily Democrat and American,* Aug. 11, 1862; *New York Reformer* (Watertown), Aug. 2, 1862, 2. Fry noted the difficulty in enrolling men for the draft stemming "from the opposition encountered in almost every house, if not to the [Enrollment] act itself, at least to its application to the particular persons whose names were sought for enrollment." OR III:5, 618.

17. For example, after reporting that the board of supervisors had voted to double the county bounty, the *Ontario County Times* (NY) commented that "the bounties now offered are generous, and not yet too generous to meet the approval of the patriotic citizens who have them to pay" (Aug. 31, 1864, 3) Similarly, Oswego County, NY, was already heavily in debt for bounties paid for prior calls, but the citizens voted 775 to 75 in favor of a $600 bounty to aid recruiting for the December 1864 call. Churchill, *Landmarks of Oswego County,* 209.

18. Marvel, *Lincoln's Mercenaries,* xii.

19. Table 3.5, Tables, latewarunionsoldiers.org. For further explanation of "economically compelling," timing of local bounties and more sources on the anticipated short duration of the war, see "Methodology" and "Methodology—Duration of the War," latewarunionsoldiers.org. As to the anticipated duration of the war, a soldier in the 148th New York, which was organized in September 1862, wrote that "when we enlisted we supposed the war would be ended, and what was left be at home in less than a year." Letter from B. to the Editor, Sept. 12, 1864, *Geneva Daily Gazette* (NY), Sept. 23, 1864, 2.

20. See chapter 3, note 63.

21. Murdock, *One Million Men,* 7. Murdoch seems to base his assessment of "quality" solely on a propensity to desert. However, most of the later-enlisting volunteers did not desert.

22. Kautz, *Customs of Service,* 11, para. 7.

23. OR III:2, 236.

24. Kautz, *Customs of Service,* 11, para. 7.

25. The data available in the HIBO Database point to trends that can be verified (or not) with more focused studies using a more complete database. Some of the functionality

of the HIBO Database may be directly accessed on the latewarunionsoldiers.org website. I chose Pennsylvania for further study because of the richness of the desertion data available in two independent compilations—Bates's *History of Pennsylvania Volunteers* and Penn State's Civil War Deserters Database based on records from the Provost Marshal General's Office. Pennsylvania also provided the second largest number of troops for the Union army. I selected New Jersey for further analysis because William Stryker, the adjutant general of New Jersey, compiled individual and regimental desertion data and identified individual soldiers as original complement, recruit, substitute, unassigned substitute, or draftee in a way that facilitates analysis in his two-volume *Record of Officers and Men of New Jersey in the Civil War, 1861–1865* (1876). New Jersey also had the fourth largest military-age population of the Eastern States. For further discussion, see Methodology—HIBO Database and Methodology—Desertion—HIBO Database on the latewarunionsoldiers.org website.

26. Table 5.1 and Table 5.2; OR III:5, 676; Gallagher, *Enduring Civil War,* 40.

27. Table 6.1. See also note 25.

28. Fox, *Regimental Losses,* 122.

29. Sommers, *Richmond Redeemed,* 234; rev. ed., 231.

30. Lynn, *Bayonets of the Republic.*

31. *Paterson Daily Press* (NJ), Sept. 1, 1864, 2. See also *Brooklyn Daily Eagle,* Dec. 24, 1864, 2; *Hartford Courant,* Aug. 11, 1864, 2; *Newburyport Morning Herald,* Aug. 1, 1864, 3.

1. Demonization of the Late-War Replacements

1. For example, Ramold, *Across the Divide,* 1131, 1323.

2. OR III, 5: 674, 675.

3. McPherson, *Battle Cry of Freedom,* 492.

4. Rhodes, *History of the United States from the Compromise of 1850,* 4:432; Rhodes, *History of the Civil War,* 331; Lonn, *Desertion During the Civil War,* 138.

5. Shannon, *Organization and Administration of the Union Army,* 2:49.

6. Murdock, *Patriotism Limited,* 16. With respect to the "love of country boys" of 1862, Murdock had earlier noted that it was recognized by the spring of 1862 "that the previous years' enlistment of 700,000 represented the full, hard core of patriotic citizenry. Response to Lincoln's July 2, 1862 call was so feeble that in two weeks' time Congress was compelled to pass a new law drafting men for military service." Murdock, *Patriotism Limited,* 5. Thus it is not clear why Murdock put the 1862 volunteers in the same class as the 1861 volunteers. It is also important to point out that Murdock concentrated on New York State, commenting that "we need only change the names of a few people and places and this book could well be a review of bounty affairs in Massachusetts, Pennsylvania or Illinois. The pattern set forth here was repeated throughout the North." Murdock, *Patriotism Limited,* viii. My own research has gone beyond New York State to include the New England and Mid-Atlantic states, but I have not researched the Midwestern states. I would qualify Murdock's generalization based on New York State by pointing out that a number of New England and Mid-Atlantic states offered a state bounty in 1861, whereas New York did not, and that local bounties in the New England and Mid-Atlantic states were higher earlier than in New York (although not ultimately as high). The interaction of the state government in either trying to encourage or limit bounties adopted by local governments also varied by state. See chapter 3 and Union Bounties (Eastern States), latewarunionsoldiers.org.

7. Murdock, *One Million Men,* xi.

8. Shannon, *Organization and Administration of the Union Army,* 2:49–50, 1:39; McPherson, *Battle Cry of Freedom,* 492, 605.

9. McPherson, *Battle Cry of Freedom,* 605; *Bridgton Reporter* (ME), Aug. 29, 1862, 2.

10. See Table 3.2.

11. See Table 3.5 and Table 3.6, latewarunionsoldiers.org.

12. For example, Catton, *Grant Takes Command,* 368; Wiley, *Billy Yank,* 343; Lonn, *Desertion,* 138.

13. Catton, *A Stillness at Appomattox,* 23, 25.

14. Catton, *A Stillness at Appomattox,* 30–31. Catton did note that the Ninth Corps "does not seem to have lost its old fighting quality with the transfusion" of late-war replacements. Catton, *A Stillness at Appomattox,* 30–31.

15. Catton was even more critical in *Grant Takes Command,* written fifteen years later: "Replacements this year [1864] tended to be of deplorable quality; the army contained too many men who did not particularly want to fight and never had wanted to, human refuse sent to camp by the substitute broker and the high bounty system." Catton, *Grant Takes Command,* 368.

16. Wiley, *Billy Yank,* 343–44.

17. Murdock, *One Million Men,* 342. See also Foote, *Red River to Appomattox,* 129–30.

18. Krick, "Repairing an Army," 47; *Burlington Weekly Free Press,* Aug. 1, 1862, 2; *Spirit of the Times* (Batavia, NY), Feb. 13, 1864, 5. See Holberton, *Homeward Bound,* 31–32; Rutan, *179th New York Volunteer Infantry,* 239–40.

19. Ramold, *Across the Divide,* 97. See also *Vermont Journal* (Windsor), Aug. 2, 1862, 1, 2, republishing *Burlington Free Press*); *Farmer's Museum* (Keene, NH), Aug. 6, 1862, 2, republishing the *Boston Herald.* Ramold also wrote that "The Enrollment Act provided the army only angry draftees or 'volunteers' who enlisted merely to collect large bounties." Ramold, *Across the Divide,* 113.

The bounty men who were scorned by the veterans of 1861 were not limited to the volunteers who enlisted in 1864 and 1865. Catton recounted the "cold and savage hostility" that the Twenty-Fourth Michigan received in late 1862 from the 1861 volunteers in the Iron Brigade: "A damning word had come to camp ahead of this new regiment. Here, said camp rumor—unsubstantiated, but accepted as gospel—here were bounty men." Catton, *Glory Road,* 12–13.

20. *Altoona Tribune* (PA), Aug. 28, 1862, 3. Interestingly, the officers neither "know nor care nothing about" "sums donated by private citizens." They based their claim on the fact that the bounties would be funded by taxes—which property owners in the Seventy-Sixth Pennsylvania would have to pay along with everyone else.

21. *Geneva Daily Gazette* (NY), Sept. 23, 1864, 2 (emphasis in original).

22. Letter dated Mar. 2, 1865, in Greene, *Final Battles of the Petersburg Campaign,* 62, 416n57; HIBO Database, 139th Pennsylvania, latewarunionsoldiers.org.

23. Compiled from the Roster in Lord, *History of the Ninth Regiment.*

24. Greene, *Final Battles of the Petersburg Campaign,* 208, 232–33. See also Bilby, *Three Rousing Cheers,* 225–26. See also Baquet, *First New Jersey Brigade,* 282. The data do provide a factual basis for the Fortieth New Jersey's reputation for desertion. From January 1, 1865, up to the April 2, 1865, assault, fifty men in the Fortieth New Jersey deserted from the field. Greene, *Final Battles of the Petersburg Campaign,* 208; Compiled from Stryker, *New Jersey in the Civil War,* vols. 1 and 2.

25. Greene, *Final Battles of the Petersburg Campaign,* 233.

26. Baquet, *First New Jersey Brigade,* 188; OR 46:1:2, 924–25.

27. OR 46:1:2, 917.

28. Stryker, *New Jersey in the Civil War,* 1:267; OR 46:1, 571; *Camden Democrat* (NJ), Oct. 6, 1864, 2.

29. Greene, *Final Battles of the Petersburg Campaign,* 208; Baquet, *First New Jersey Brigade,* 201; Stryker, *New Jersey in the Civil War,* 1:182–225 (Fourth New Jersey); Stryker, *New Jersey in the Civil War,* 1:488–541 (Tenth New Jersey); Bilby, *Three Rousing Cheers,* 219; Stryker, *New Jersey in the Civil War,* 1:697–739 (Fifteenth New Jersey). The strength of the Fourth New Jersey is unclear. The Table of Organization for the Army of the Potomac at the end of March 1865 reports the First and Fourth New Jersey combined as a battalion. OR 46:1, 571. The history of the Fifteenth New Jersey written in 1883 states that the Fourth New Jersey had been recruited to more than six hundred men present for duty. Haines, *History of the Fifteenth Regiment,* 294. See also Stryker, *New Jersey in the Civil War,* 1:182–225. The Tenth New Jersey had 450 men at the time of the Grand Review. Baquet, *History of the First Brigade,* 201. The Second New Jersey and the Third New Jersey, which were also assigned to Penrose's Brigade, had only two companies and one company respectively and were commanded by captains. OR 46:1, 571.

Greene suggests that Colonel Truex's decision to place the Eighty-Seventh Pennsylvania last in his line because "it was composed almost entirely of raw troops, five companies having joined within two weeks of this movement" supports the argument that Penrose was punishing the Fortieth New Jersey. Greene, *Final Battles of the Petersburg Campaign,* 209–10, 464n56. However, the Fortieth New Jersey had been in the field for several months, not two weeks. It was the Fifteenth New Jersey that had the really raw troops— two hundred who had arrived in late March—and Penrose placed the Fifteenth New Jersey last in his line. Greene, *Final Battles of the Petersburg Campaign,* 62; see Stryker, *New Jersey in the Civil War,* 1:697–739.

30. OR 46:1, 2, 909.

31. OR 46:1, 2, 927.

32. OR 46:1, 2, 927.

33. For example, *Brooklyn Daily Eagle,* Sept. 11, 1861, 3; *Philadelphia Inquirer,* Sept. 19, 1864, 4; *Rutland Weekly Herald,* Aug. 25, 1864, 3; *Troy Daily Whig* (NY), Aug. 18, 1864; *Waterville Times* (NY), Aug. 1, 1862; *Ellsworth Advocate* (ME), July 31, 1862, 2; *Manchester Journal* (NH), July 29, 1862, 4; *New York Times,* Aug. 20, 1863, 2; *Elmira Daily Advertiser* (NY), July 27, 1864, 3; *Boston Morning Herald,* Aug. 26, 1864, 3; *Boston Evening Transcript,* Aug. 19, 1864, 3; *Boston American Traveler,* Sept. 24, 1864, 2; Adjutant General of the State of Connecticut, *Annual Report,* Apr. 1, 186, 20.

The most detailed accounting of serial bounty jumping that I have seen was provided by Samuel W. Downing (alias "John W. Ball") after he was arrested. He admitted to deserting in July 1863 and reenlisting seventeen times. He provided dates, places, and amounts of the bounties. He was executed in September 1864. *Philadelphia Inquirer,* Sept. 19, 1864, 4.

34. OR III:5, 725; Rhodes, *History of the Civil War,* 4:301, 431; Shannon, *Organization and Administration of the Union Army,* 2:71; Foote, *Red River to Appomattox,* 130; Ward, *Civil War,* 243.

35. McPherson, *Battle Cry of Freedom,* 606.

36. See Rutan, *179th New York Volunteer Infantry,* 26, 131; Wilkenson, *Fifty-Seventh Massachusetts Veteran Volunteers,* 24.

37. *The American Annual Cyclopedia and Register of Important Events of the Year of 1864,* 37. The New Hampshire Regiment was not identified, but it may have been the Second New Hampshire (see Fox, *Regimental Losses,* 468–69) or the Fifth New Hampshire (see Fox, *Regimental Losses,* 468–69; Pride and Travis, *My Brave Boys: To War with Col. Cross and the Fighting Fifth,* 254).

38. Rhodes, *History of the Civil War,* 301; Lonn, *Desertion,* 142, 161; Foote, *Red River to Appomattox,* 130.

39. *Brooklyn Daily Eagle,* Sept. 11, 1861, 3.

40. Foote, *Red River to Appomattox,* 129; OR 3, 5: 636–37.

41. Table 5.6 below.

42. OR III:4, 995.

43. OR II:7, 614 (emphasis added). Grant's "one-in-eight" estimate to Seward included the subjective test of "doing good service." Thus qualified, Grant's statement could mean that more than one in eight substitutes were received in the field, but that regardless of the number arriving, the army netted only one good soldier out of every eight substitutes. In Ramold's view, Grant "believed that bounty money furnished only a soldier of lesser physical ability and patriotic motivation." Ramold, *Across the Divide,* 107. In his memoirs, Sherman asserted that "the men who voluntarily enlisted at the outbreak of the war were the best, better than the conscript, and far better than the bought substitute," but did not comment on the later-enlisting volunteers. Sherman, *Memoirs,* 328.

44. OR III:4, 706. Fry, who apparently had discussed the matter with Grant (see OR II:7, 614), wrote the local provost marshal in Albany on September 12, 1864, that "There is a wide discrepancy between the number of men mustered in the service and the number received at the various general rendezvous. This may result . . . from neglect . . . in forwarding safely through rendezvous the men mustered in. See that the proper precautions are taken." *Fort Edwards Ledger* (NY), Sept. 16, 1864, 2.

45. OR III:4:2, 709–10.

46. Grant's letters to Seward and Stanton likely were generated by statements they made about the numbers of volunteers, which were much greater than the numbers that Grant was seeing arrive in the field as reinforcements. Seward had said in a speech that there would be no draft "because the army is being reinforced at the rate of 5000 or 10,000 men per day by volunteers." *Buffalo Morning Express,* Sept. 8, 1864, 1. Similarly, Stanton had written Grant that "The recruiting returns show an average of about 5,000 mustered in per day for the last week." OR III:4:2, 699. Grant probably was seeing the results in the field from an earlier enrollment period when far fewer than five thousand men a day may have been volunteering.

The lengthy time that it often took to complete organization of a new regiment also caused shrinkage unrelated to desertion. For example, the first eight companies of the Fifty-Eighth Massachusetts Infantry reached Virginia on May 2, 1864. The ninth company arrived in June, but the tenth company did not arrive until January 1865. As of September 28, 1864, Company K "in formation" had sixty men back in Massachusetts. In Grant's terms, these men would have been "reported north" as enrolled several months before, but not yet received at the front, even though they were not deserters. Fox, *Regimental Losses,* 176; Letter dated Sept. 28, 1864, from Lieutenant Colonel Whiton, RG 94, Fifty-Eighth Massachusetts Volunteer Infantry Regimental Books, NARA.

47. OR III:5: 675 (emphasis added). One political challenge coming with the draft, which I do not address here, was the almost constant complaints by the states that their quotas under each call were unfair and/or wrongly calculated.

48. Eaton, *Army Paymaster's Manual,* 127; Marvel, *Lincoln's Mercenaries,* 198, 226; George Carpenter, CMSR, NARA; Stewart and Brown, *History of Wages,* 160. See also McPherson, *Battle Cry of Freedom,* 493. The average daily wage for a carpenter in New York in 1864 was $2.70. However, on a monthly basis (twenty-six days) the rate was probably only two-thirds of that and the work was seasonal. Stewart and Brown, *History of Wages,* 160; Lebergott, *Manpower in Economic Growth,* 143, 245; Methodology, Comparison of military and civilian compensation, 8, latewarunionsoldiers.org.

49. Sherman, *Memoirs,* 329; Nevins, *The War for the Union: The Organized War to Victory 1864–1865,* 146; Costa and Kahn, *Cowards and Heroes,* 58. There was also a point at which a regiment's numbers fell so low as to render it ineffective. Sherman, *Memoirs,* 329; Nevins, *The War for the Union: The Organized War to Victory 1864–1865,* 146; Costa and Kahn, *Cowards and Heroes,* 58. James Geary notes that the military also was concerned about the section of the Enrollment Act that called for the consolidation of understrength units, with surplus officers being discharged. Geary, *We Need Men,* 67.

50. OR II:4, 210; Lerwill, *Personnel Replacement System,* 88. Lincoln was convinced by McClellan (or was already of the same view) and wrote Stanton on July 22: "It is a very important consideration, too, that one recruit into an old regiment is nearly or quite equal in value to two in a new one. We can scarcely afford to forgo any plan within our power, which will facilitate the filling of the old regiments with recruits." Basler, *Works of Abraham Lincoln,* 5:338.

51. OR III:2, 225; Lerwill, *Personnel Replacement System,* 88. The War Department had earlier advised Morgan that New York was required to raise twenty-eight infantry regiments under the July 1862 call, which Morgan could well have understood to mean new regiments. OR III:2, 208. The New York Agency of the US Sanitary Commission also wrote Lincoln in July 1862 recommending against creating new regiments. "If all the 300,000 men . . . were recruited [for old regiments], it would save the country . . . thousands of lives and millions of dollars. . . . They would have a thorough medical inspection, and every man would soon cease to be a raw recruit when absorbed into a veteran regiment." OR III:2, 237.

52. See Fox, *Regimental Losses,* 479–81; Lerwill, *Personnel Replacement System,* 90.

53. See Fox, *Regimental Losses,* 471, 486–88, 472, 481, 488. The comparisons are not entirely "apples to apples." Not as many troops were raised in 1863 as in 1862.

54. OR III:3, 386; Lerwill, *Personnel Replacement System,* 93.

55. Sherman had expressed similar views in an earlier letter to Grant, which Grant attached. OR III:3, 387. But see Livermore, *History of the Eighteenth New Hampshire Volunteers,* 13 (old regiments with ineffective officers not worth saving).

56. OR 45:2, 344–45; OR 42:3, 1068. Stanton and Vincent sought Thomas's comments because "applications are made by Governors of States to raise new regiments of volunteers under the recent call for 300,000 men by new regiments." OR 45:2, 330. Grant and Meade received the same inquiry. OR 42:3, 1068.

57. OR 42:3, 1068.

58. OR III:3, 415, para. V.

59. Rutan, *179th New York Volunteer Infantry,* 288–92, 21–22; *Hornellsville Tribune* (NY), Feb. 25, 1864, 3.

60. Livermore, *History of the Eighteenth New Hampshire Volunteers,* 20–21, 25, 28.

61. Livermore, *History of the Eighteenth New Hampshire Volunteers,* 15; Rutan, *179th New York Volunteer Infantry,* 12–13.

62. Compiled from Stryker, *New Jersey in the Civil War,* 1:300–365.

63. For example, in the Ninety-Fourth New York, the late-war replacements apparently were not distributed throughout the regiment with the result that the "three right companies being mostly new men surrendered without any effort to repulse the assault . . . They became panic stricken at the first fire from the enemy." OR 42:1, 510. Because they were new troops, their brigade commander said that "they must be considered with some degree of allowance." OR 42:1, 511.

64. OR III:5, 609; *Ellsworth American* (ME), Aug. 1, 1862, 2; *Sentinel of Freedom* (Newark, NJ), Aug. 16, 1864, 2. See also *Ellsworth American* (ME), Feb. 26, 1864, 3; *Herkimer Democrat* (NY), Nov. 25, 1863, 2.

65. Henry Bull to Father, Sept. 24, 1864; copy in author's collection.

66. *Hornellsville Tribune* (NY), Feb. 25, 1864, 3. See also recruiting advertisements for the Seventeenth Vermont, *Lamoille Newsdealer* (Hyde Park, VT), Feb. 23, 1864, 3, and the 179th New York Volunteers. *Ithaca Journal,* Aug. 17, 1864. Volunteers with prior service may have had the inside track on promotion to corporal or sergeant.

67. Livermore, *History of the Eighteenth New Hampshire Volunteers,* 14.

68. Livermore, *History of the Eighteenth New Hampshire Volunteers,* 14. In January 1865, Gov. John Andrew of Massachusetts advised Stanton that discharged veterans considering reenlistment "are averse to being placed with conscripts, substitutes, &c." OR III:4, 1055. Conscripts and substitutes generally were not assigned to late-war new regiments. The facts on the ground do not fully support Gilmore's statement. For the July 1864 call, two-thirds of New Hampshire's volunteers selected the three-year term (as he himself had suggested).

69. OR 42:1, 226.

70. OR 42:1, 227. However, Hancock did assess some blame beyond the late-war replacements. OR 42:1, 227. See also Humphreys, *Virginia Campaign of '64 and '65,* 280–83.

71. Humphreys, *Virginia Campaign of '64 and '65,* 283n1. Humphreys added the following in a footnote: "The large bounties paid . . . had a very injurious effect upon the army, for it brought to its ranks many men who were actuated by very different motives from those that had influenced the men who had voluntarily filled the ranks before, and the veterans that now re-enlisted."

72. Livermore, *History of the Eighteenth New Hampshire Volunteers,* 16. Gibbon referred to the replacements in his own division as "a mass of newly drafted men, many of whom, it had been reported to me, had in the battle huddled behind their breastworks without firing a piece and allowed themselves to be captured en masse." Gibbon, *Personal Recollections,* 259–60. See also Mulholland, *116th Regiment, Pennsylvania Volunteers,* 297. ("The veterans . . . had been largely replaced by recruits and substitutes who had but little heart in the work.")

73. Sommers, *Richmond Redeemed,* 234. See also the second edition, 230. See also Foote, *Red River to Appomattox,* 129–30 ("[Replacement] would be done by the conscripts and substitutes who were now arriving as a result of Lincoln's February call. . . . [T]hey were a mixed blessing at best. At worst they were considerably less. . . . [T]he outsized bounties had created a new breed of soldier: the bounty jumper.") Similarly, James McPherson wrote that "many three year veterans who had mustered out in the spring [of 1864] re-enlisted in the fall. . . . [and] helped restore the Army of the Potomac's tone, which had all but disappeared during the summer under the weight of conscripts, substitutes and bounty-jumpers." McPherson. *Battle Cry of Freedom,* 780, 719. However, McPherson did also note the adverse impact on morale during the summer of 1864 of the veterans who did not reenlist and remained in the army as short-timers. McPherson, *Battle Cry of Freedom,* 720.

74. Sommers, *Richmond Redeemed,* 9. Sommers referred to the new recruits in more neutral terms at other points in the book. "Fresh (though inexperienced) troops also became available." Sommers, *Richmond Redeemed,* 3. Even Hancock attributed in part "the bad conduct of some of my troops" at Second Reams's Station "to their great fatigue, owing to the heavy labor exacted of them and to their enormous losses during the campaign, especially in officers." OR 42:1, 227.

75. Hess, *Union Soldier in Battle,* 90.

76. OR 42:1, 579. For the poor performance of the Thirty-Fifth Massachusetts, two-thirds of whose men were newly arrived recruits with many speaking German, see Sommers, *Richmond Redeemed,* 1981 ed., 283.

77. OR 42:1, 547–48.

78. OR 42:1, 579.

79. OR 42:1, 567.

80. Fox, *Regimental Losses*, 474, 494.

81. Compiled from Forty-Sixth Infantry Roster, NYSMM Unit History website; Phisterer, *New York in the War of the Rebellion 1861–1865*, 3:2320; 83; Compiled from HIBO Database, Fiftieth Pennsylvania, latewarunionsoldiers.org and *Philadelphia Age*, Jan. 26, 1864, 2.

82. Under the Pension Act of 1890, only ninety days of service was required for eligibility, so the "hundred days" men qualified. Glasson, *Federal Military Pensions*, 234, 237. While one hundred days regiments were uncommon in the Eastern States, the Western States created them in some number. Ohio created over forty. Fox, *Regimental Losses*, 467–520.

83. Glasson, *Federal Military Pensions*, 181.

84. In *Pittsburgh Daily Post*, July 12, 1887, 4. See *Des Moines Register*, July 14, 1887, 4.

85. *Bismarck Weekly Tribune*, Mar. 4, 1887, 4.

86. Hyde, *Following the Greek Cross or, Memoirs of the Sixth Army Corps*, 254.

87. Hyde, *Following the Greek Cross or, Memoirs of the Sixth Army Corps*, 254–55. Greene wrote that "cowardice more than confusion robbed the 61st Pennsylvania of three-fifths of its strength during the attack." Greene, *Final Battles of the Petersburg Campaign*, 224. Greene relied on the account in Hyde's 1894 memoirs but did note that Hyde said nothing at all about the alleged cowardice in the Sixty-First Pennsylvania in his after-action report in 1865 and that the regimental history of the Sixty-First Pennsylvania stated that the new men performed appropriately. Greene, *Final Battles of the Petersburg Campaign*, 466n20. Hyde apparently meant that the men temporarily "disappeared" during the battle, and that they "were never heard from" only during the rest of the day, not that they had deserted. See Hyde, *Following the Greek Cross*, 254. The Sixty-First Pennsylvania's Descriptive List of Deserters does not show any deserters on or about April 2, 1865. Regimental Books, RG 94, NARA.

88. Bates, *History of Pennsylvania Volunteers*, 1:443–44, 446–47, 449–50.

89. OR III:3, 386–87.

90. In Company H, Capt. Horatio K. Tyler had served as the major in a hundred days regiment, the 193rd Pennsylvania; as a first lieutenant in the three-month Seventh Pennsylvania and as a captain in the nine-month 123rd Pennsylvania. 2Lt. William J. H. Tyler had served as a private in the 123rd Pennsylvania. I have not found whether 1Lt. Samuel B. McKowen had previously served.

In Company I, Capt. Isaac Wright had served as a sergeant in the three-month Seventh Pennsylvania and as a captain in the one-hundred days 193rd Pennsylvania. 2Lt. Frank Bowen had not previously served. I have not found whether 1Lt. William Graham had previously served.

In Company K, Capt. Henry Scriba served for two years as a private in the Thirty-Eighth Pennsylvania (Ninth Pennsylvania Reserves) and neither 1Lt. Jeremiah R. Murphy nor 2Lt. Charles Weaver had previously served. Civil War Collection, Ancestry.com.

91. Greene, *Final Battles of the Petersburg Campaign*, 224; OR 46:1:2, 976; Hyde, *Following the Greek Cross*, 251, 254; OR 46:1:2, 954. See also OR 46:1:2, 963 (General Warner, commanding the First Brigade, reported that the space between the Confederate picket line and the main works "was passed over in great confusion" "owing to the darkness, the uneven and swampy character of the ground, and the artillery fire"); OR 46:1:2, 911. General Wheaton reported that "During the advance in the dark each command became more or less disordered." OR 46:1:2, 910.

92. Bates, *History of Pennsylvania Volunteers,* 2:411–12; HIBO Database, Sixty-First Pennsylvania, latewarunionsoldiers.org. The Sixty-First Pennsylvania also received one hundred later-enlisting volunteers in the spring of 1864. Bates, *History of Pennsylvania Volunteers,* 2:411–12; HIBO Database, Sixty-First Pennsylvania, latewarunionsoldiers.org.

93. *New York Times,* May 24, 1865, 1. The order of procession is provided in the *Times* article. There was nothing in the order that appeared intended to give old regiments prominence over late-war new regiments.

94. Eden, *Sword and the Gun,* 5. In 1903, Clarence Wilson, a later-enlisting volunteer, made a plea to the editor of the *National Tribune* for more balanced treatment, noting a "disposition of some comrades to make light of the newcomers or the late-comers who enlisted in the last years of the war." *National Tribune,* Oct. 1, 1903, 2. He said that his regiment "lost heavily in its brief service. But it, also, aided in saving the Union."

95. Marten, *Sing Not War,* 260; Rutan, *179th New York Volunteer Infantry,* 262.

96. Marten, *Sing Not War,* 206–7.

97. McPherson, *Battle Cry of Freedom,* 606.

98. Wiley, *Billy Yank,* 344.

99. Hess, *Union Soldier in Battle,* 90–91.

100. Newsome, *Richmond Must Fall,* 19–20.

2. Raising the Union Army

1. Basler, ed., *The Collected Works of Abraham Lincoln,* 5:98; McPherson, *Tried by War,* 70. Paul Escott noted that "although Abraham Lincoln was unschooled in military matters, he read and studied military texts and deserves the credit historians have given him for grasping [this] crucially important point." Escott, *Rethinking the Civil War Era,* 71.

2. Kennedy, *Population of the United States in 1860,* xvii.

3. McPherson, *Battle Cry of Freedom,* 312–13; Kreidberg and Henry, *History of Military Mobilization,* 90; *Union Army: A History of Military Affairs in the Loyal States 1861–65,* 1:21 (Maine); 71–73 (New Hampshire); 96 (Vermont); 137 (Massachusetts); 322 (Pennsylvania); 509 (Delaware). But see 1:232 (Rhode Island). Even including those "absent," the army had only 16,402 men. OR III:5, 604–5.

4. Grant, *Memoirs,* 2:502, 503.

5. OR III:5, 636–37; OR III:5, 387. The October 1863 draft and the February and March 1864 calls sought 700,000 troops, but that was adjusted down to 407, 092. The July 1864 call sought 500,000 troops, but that was adjusted down to 272,463. OR III:5, 636–37.

6. de Tocqueville, *Democracy in America,* 260; McPherson, *Battle Cry of Freedom,* 605.

7. de Tocqueville, *Democracy in America,* 260. See also Gallman, *Defining Duty in the Civil War,* 255, and Fry's postwar report, OR III:5, 611. Fry argued that conscription in fact was "truly republican" and that the "security of republican governments mainly depends . . . [on] the principle that every citizen, not incapacitated by physical or mental disability, owes military service to the country in the hour of extremity." OR III:5, 611, and 610.

8. Gallagher, *Union War,* 27, 3, 69, 124; McPherson, *Battle Cry of Freedom,* 605; Widmer, *A History of the Civil War,* 87; Baier, *Three Days in January: Dwight Eisenhower's Final Mission,* 197–98; Rutan, *179th New York Volunteer Infantry,* 1–2. For example, in his introduction to *Massachusetts in the War, 1861–1865,* Sen. Henry Dawes wrote of the debt owed by the country "to the valor and sacrifice of their citizen soldiery." Bowen, *Massachusetts in the War, 1861–1865,* vii. See also Phisterer, *New York in the War of the Rebellion,* 1:36 ("citizen soldiery").

9. OR III:5, 605; OR III:1, 22.

10. OR III:1, 67–68, Statutes at Large 12:1258; Statutes at Large, I:264. The term *militia* can be confusing. At the time of the Militia Act of 1792, the *militia* meant all able-bodied males between the ages of eighteen and forty-five as a group. See *District of Columbia v. Heller,* 554 US 570 (2008), slip opinion, 7. The term was not necessarily referring to organized military units, although such units existed in most Union states.

11. McPherson, *Battle Cry of Freedom,* 333.

12. OR III:4:2, 1264.

13. OR III:5, 606; Lerwill, *Personnel Replacement System,* 85.

14. OR III:1, 301.

15. Kreidberg and Henry, *History of Military Mobilization,* 93. Act of July 22, 1861.

16. OR III:1, 775. The aggregate number present and absent for the Union army as a whole was 527,804 at the end of 1861. Comparisons over time for the Army of the Potomac are not entirely apples to apples because of the creation of new organizations in the Eastern Theater, such as the Army of the James, and the transfer of troops between armies, such as the transfer of the Ninth Corps to the west in the fall of 1863 and subsequent return in 1864.

17. Kennedy, *Population of the United States in 1860,* xvii; OR III:4, 1264.

18. OR III:5, 608; Kreidberg and Henry, *History of Military Mobilization,* 102. See also *Rochester Daily Union and Advertiser,* July 5, 1862; *Monmouth Democrat* (NJ), July 24, 1862, 2.

19. The Union army as a whole was up to 501,663 present from 477,193 at the end of 1861. Table 2.2; OR III:1, 775, OR III:2, 185.

20. OR III:2, 180; OR III:2, 187–88; OR III:5, 608.

21. *Oxford Democrat* (Paris, ME), Aug. 1, 1862, 2; *Troy Weekly Times* (NY), Aug. 9, 1862, 3.

22. OR III:5, 672.

23. OR III:5, 608; *New York Evening Post,* July 25, 1862, 2. See also Sandow, "Limits of Northern Patriotism: Early Civil War Mobilization in Pennsylvania," 175–76.

24. *Columbia Spy* (PA), July 19, 1862, 2; Marvel, *Lincoln's Mercenaries,* 97, 180.

25. See Murdock, *Patriotism Limited,* 5.

26. *Albany Atlas & Argus,* reprinted in *Elmira Advertiser and Republican* (NY), July 19, 1862; *New London Weekly Chronicle,* Aug. 28, 1862, 4. Compiled from *Report of the Adjutant General of the State of Maine for the Years 1864 and 1865,* 38–61 (many towns did not report); Ford, *A History of the Bounty System,* 106; *Second Annual Report of the Chief of the New York Bureau of Military Statistics,* 109–54; Bounties, latewarunionsoldiers. org; Kennedy, *Population of the United States in 1860,* 328. At least half of the counties in New Jersey and Pennsylvania and the towns in Connecticut and New Hampshire offered bounties in 1862. At least a third of the towns in Vermont offered bounties. Compiled from Bounties, latewarunionsoldiers.org. See also *Philadelphia Inquirer,* July 23, 1862, 5; *Ontario (County) Repository and Messenger* (Canandaigua, NY), July 16, 1862, 2; *Frontier Palladium* (Malone, NY), Aug. 28, 1862, 2; *Portland Daily Press* (ME), Aug. 26, 1862, 4; *Boston Liberator,* Sept. 2, 1864, 4; *New York Evening Post,* July 24, 1862, 2; *Northern New York Journal* (Watertown), July 29, 1862, 3.

The Union Bounties (Eastern States) database documents bounties for eleven hundred local governments during the summer of 1862. Bounties, latewarunionsoldiers.org. McPherson significantly understated the use of local bounties in the Eastern States for the July and August 1862 calls. See McPherson, *Battle Cry of Freedom,* 605.

27. OR III:4:2, 1265; OR III:2, 957; OR III:2, 185. For a discussion of the Confederate version of the "carrot and stick," see Noe, *Reluctant Rebels,* 104–9. The Confederate

bounty started at fifty dollars. Local bounties apparently were also provided. The Confederacy adopted a draft in April 1862. Noe concluded that only 11 percent of the men in his sample of later enlisting Confederate soldiers volunteered "at least in part for the Confederate bounty [and wages]." "The vast majority of later-enlisting Confederates sampled for this study volunteered for other reasons [than financial gain], with ideology and hatred of the enemy providing more motivation and slavery proving more central still." Noe, *Reluctant Rebels,* 106, 120–21. A dearth of wage data would prevent an income-based analysis of the financial attractiveness of volunteering for Confederate men.

28. The aggregate number of men present and absent as of December 31, 1862, was 868,591 for the Union army as a whole and 267,379 for the Army of the Potomac, which meant that substantial numbers of men were absent.

29. OR III:5, 612; Chernow, *Grant,* 250.

30. OR III:5, 611–12; Kreidberg and Henry, *History of Military Mobilization,* 104; Noe, *Reluctant Rebels,* 104–5.

31. OR III:5, 717–18.

32. Governor's Message, Assembly Document No. 2, Jan. 5, 1864, 18–19, 21.

33. *Poughkeepsie Eagle,* Aug. 16, 1862, 6. See also Gallman, *Defining Duty,* 139; *Newport Daily News* (RI), Aug. 14, 1862, 2; *Havana Journal* (NY), Aug. 16, 1862; *Berkshire County Eagle* (MA), Aug. 28, 1862, 2; *New York Reformer* (Watertown), Aug. 6, 1862, 2; *Hornellsville Tribune* (NY), Aug. 21, 1862, Sept. 4, 1862; *Livingston Republican* (Geneseo, NY), Aug. 21, 1862, 2. But see *Rochester Daily Democrat and Advertiser,* Aug. 25, 1862 (if necessary to resort to a draft, it would not be a "disgrace.")

34. *Brooklyn Daily Eagle,* Aug. 13, 1862, 2; *Ontario Repository and Messenger* (Canandaigua, NY), July 23, 1862. See also *Gardiner Home Journal* (ME), July 17, 1862, 2 (the draft "should be reserved as a last resort and every possible means should be taken to secure voluntary enlistment from the classes best situated to leave their homes").

35. *New York Times,* Jan. 6, 1864, 1.

36. *Hartford Courant,* Aug. 11, 1864, 2; *Poughkeepsie Daily Eagle,* Feb. 9, 1864, 3. Just what that "sorrow and suffering" would be was not specified. The thought may have been the same as expressed by the *Brooklyn Daily Eagle* (Aug. 13, 1862, 2) that the longer-term, more stable men of the community would be caught by the draft's net, while the more transient men would have avoided enrollment for the draft. See also *Brooklyn Daily Eagle,* July 15, 1862, 2, and July 22, 1862, 2; *Ontario Repository and Messenger* (Canandaigua, NY), July 23, 1862; *Yates County Chronicle* (Penn Yan, NY), Feb. 4, 1864, 2; *Hartford Courant,* July 30, 1864, 2.

37. *Lewistown Gazette* (ME), Aug. 3, 1864, 3; *Hartford Courant,* Aug. 11, 1864, 2. See also *Columbia Democrat and Bloomsburg General Advertiser* (PA), Aug. 13, 1864, 2; *Manufacturers' and Farmers' Journal* (Providence, RI) Aug. 8, 1864, 2; *Vermont Phoenix* (Montpelier), July 29, 1864, 3.

38. *Delaware Gazette* (Delhi, NY), Aug. 13, 1862, 2; *Ontario Repository and Messenger* (Canandaigua, NY), July 23, 1862; *Philadelphia Inquirer,* July 23, 1862, 1; *Mexico Independent* (NY), Aug. 28,1862, 1; Bounties, latewarunionsoldiers.org. See also Gallman, Review of *Patriotism by Proxy,* 331.

39. *Wellsborough Agitator* (PA), July 30, 1862, 2 (loss of Tioga County, PA, men to Elmira and Corning, NY); *Portland Daily Press* (ME), July 18, 1862, 3; *Delaware Republican,* Aug. 11, 1862, 2.

40. Miller, *States at War,* 3:293; *Pennsylvania Daily Telegraph,* July 24, 1862, 2.

41. Union Bounties (Eastern States), latewarunionsoldiers.org; calculated from Kennedy, *Population of the United States in 1860,* 499. While the draft quotas were in theory neu-

tral among the states because they were based on enrolled numbers of military-age men, the pools were not necessarily uniform—there were differences among the states that could affect the likelihood of men to volunteer. For a farm owner or operator, there were significant practical limitations on his ability to leave the farm behind and go off to war. Farmers represented different percentages of the workforce in the Eastern States—39 percent in Vermont, 31 percent in Maine, and 30 percent in New Hampshire, but only 20 percent or less in the other Eastern States (10 percent in Massachusetts). Calculated from Kennedy, *Population of the United States in 1860,* passim. Thus Vermont, Maine, and New Hampshire had a supply constraint that the other Eastern States did not, and there is no doubt that the law of supply and demand was very much in play in setting state and local bounties.

42. Miller, *States at War,* 1:591–92; *Rutland County Herald* (VT), Sept. 1, 1864, 4; *Burlington Weekly Free Press,* Nov. 27, 1863, 2; *Burlington Weekly Sentinel,* Aug. 26, 1864, 3; *Report of the Adjutant and Inspector General of the State of Vermont for October 1, 1863 through October 1, 1864,* 15. See also Union Bounties (Eastern States), latewarunionsoldiers.org; *Vermont Phoenix* (Brattleboro), Aug. 12, 1864, 2. The *Burlington Weekly Free Press* noted that it had "been decided to give towns a fair chance to show their patriotism, without any interference on the part of the State," Nov. 20, 1863, 2. The *Rutland County Herald* viewed the $7 per month as "virtually a bounty of eighty-four dollars a year" (July 31, 1862, 7). The Legislature did provide a $125 advance payment as an option to the additional $7 in monthly pay, which had been in effect since early in the war (Nov. 11, 1863, Miller, *States at War,* 1:677.

43. Calculated from Kennedy, *Population of the United States in 1860,* 311.

44. *Manchester Daily Mirror* (NH), Nov. 5, 1863, 4; *New Hampshire Patriot and State Gazette* (Concord), Feb. 10, 1864, 2; "F. F." to Editor of the *Boston Journal in Boston Morning Herald,* July 27, 1864, 2. See also *Daily Mirror* (Manchester, NH), Dec. 11, 1863, 2; *Mirror and Farmer* (Manchester, NH), Aug. 13, 1864, 2; *Newburyport Morning Herald* (MA), Aug. 11, 1864, 2, *Manchester Weekly Union,* July 26, 1864, 3; *Mirror and Farmer,* Aug. 27, 1864, 2. The *Manchester Union Democrat* expressed concern about high bounties in New York because "most of our conscripts have secured their subs in New York," Nov. 24, 1863, 1. The *Union Democrat* cynically commented: "Certainly we would rather pay a New York rough any sum to fight in such a war as this, than take a hand in it ourselves," Feb. 16, 1864, 1.

45. *Farmer's Museum* (Keene, NH), Aug. 24, 1864, 2; *Farmer's Cabinet* (Amherst, NH), Sept. 1, 1864, 2; Miller, *States at War,* 1:415. The intent apparently was only to allow cities and towns to offer their residents up to $300 for one year, but the cities and towns apparently took even greater advantage of this loophole. See Miller, *States at War,* 1:410, Aug. 24, 1864; Union Bounties (Eastern States), latewarunionsoldiers.org. The $1,000 bounties caught the attention of the *Newport Mercury* in Rhode Island, Sept. 3, 1864, 2. Nonresidents were offered substantially less. Union Bounties (Eastern States), latewarunionsoldiers.org.

46. Union Bounties (Eastern States), latewarunionsoldiers.org.; Miller, *States at War,* 1:70, 79, 86–87, 102, 111.

47. Union Bounties (Eastern States), latewarunionsoldiers.org.; Miller, *States at War,* 1:274, 304, 306, 315. The option offered by Massachusetts provides some insight into how much longer Massachusetts veterans and new recruits thought the war would last. Opting for the $325 in advance would suggest the view that the war would be over relatively quickly. Opting for only $50 in advance and $20 per month suggests the opposite. (The crossover point was fourteen months.) Overall, just over half of reenlisting veterans took the $50 option, while only 10 percent of the new recruits did, suggesting that the veterans, while evenly split themselves, were more pessimistic than the recruits. *National Aegis and Transcript* (Worcester, MA), Mar. 5, 1864, 1.

48. Miller, *States at War,* 1:315; *Boston Congregationalist,* Aug. 26, 1864, 3; *Lowell Daily Citizen and News* (MA), July 27, 1864, 2; Union Bounties (Eastern States), latewarunionsoldiers.org. The *Daily News* itself noted that the statute did not explicitly require that the $125 ceiling be reserved for three-year volunteers but could be offered to one-year volunteers. Union Bounties (Eastern States), latewarunionsoldiers.org.

49. *Portland Daily Eastern Argus,* Dec. 11, 1863, 3 (Maine Adjutant General Order No. 25, Dec. 9, 1863); *Lewiston Evening Journal,* Dec. 17, 1863, 2; OR III:4:1, 33. For example, if a municipality paid a bounty of $50, the state bounty would be reduced to $250 and the municipality would be reimbursed $50. If the municipality paid a bounty of $350, the state bounty would be reduced to zero and the municipality would be reimbursed only $300.)

50. *Boston Daily Advertiser,* Feb. 6, 1865, 1 (Augusta correspondent); *Portland Daily Press,* Sept. 21, 1864, 2, Sept. 22, 1864, 4, Sept. 19, 1864, 2. See also Union Bounties (Eastern States), latewarunionsoldiers.org; Whitman and True, *Maine in the War for the Union,* 635–36; Miller, *States at War,* 1:208, 218; *Union Army,* 1:34.

51. Union Bounties (Eastern States), latewarunionsoldiers.org; Miller, *States at War,* 2:242–45, 276–77, 296.

52. Union Bounties (Eastern States), latewarunionsoldiers.org; Miller, *States at War,* 4:612.

53. Union Bounties (Eastern States), latewarunionsoldiers.org; Miller, *States at War,* 1:479, 486. Private subscriptions did apparently come into play, which limited the impact of the state law. *Providence Manufacturers' and Farmers' Journal,* Aug. 8, 1864, at 2; *Providence Evening Press,* Aug. 1, 1864, 4; June 16, 1864, 4; Dec. 12, 1863, 2.

54. OR III:5, 733, 735; *Boston Daily Advertiser,* Sept. 15, 1864, 1. Large numbers of men initially held to service in the draft provided substitutes. For the September 1864 draft after the July call, the burden of personal service was borne far more heavily in the Western States than in the Eastern States. OR III:5, 735.

55. OR III:3, 892.

56. OR III:5, 671–72. The need for the amount of the bounty to compete with civilian wages had been recognized at the local level in 1862. *Portland Daily Press,* July 22, 1862, 2, and Aug. 26, 1862, 3. In his postwar report, Fry concluded that "If we compare this [the federal bounty of $100/$200/$300 for one/two/three years paid in installments] with the exorbitant bounties paid in advance by local authorities . . . , its comparative insignificance will readily demonstrate how little the Government bounty effected in raising volunteers." OR III:5, 673. Still, the federal government did increase its bounty for three years from $100 to $300 and $400 for veterans.

57. Calculated from Stewart and Brown, *History of Wages,* passim; Kennedy, *Population of the United States in 1860,* passim.

58. OR III:5, 650. The study also included artillery batteries and smaller infantry units, with the same results.

59. GO No. 191, June 25, 1863, OR III:3, 414; Lerwill *Personnel Replacement System,* 109–11.

60. OR III:3, 415. The Confederate army faced an even more serious problem at the end of 1861 with the upcoming expiration of the one-year term of the volunteers from the spring of 1861. In response, the Confederate Congress offered veterans who reenlisted a $50 bounty, a sixty-day furlough, transportation home, and the opportunity to reorganize their units, including the election of officers. Noe, *Reluctant Rebels,* 104. Noe did not provide information on the Confederate reenlistment percentage.

61. OR III:3, 415.

62. GO No. 216, July 14, 1863, OR III:3, 487; OR III:5, 651.

63. OR III:5, 651; Lerwill, *Personnel Replacement System,* 109.

64. OR III:4:2, 813; Lerwill, *Personnel Replacement System,* 110–11.

65. OR III:5, 651.

66. Wiley, *Billy Yank,* 343. See also Linderman, *Embattled Courage,* 261.

67. OR IV:2, 813; Phisterer, *New York in the War of the Rebellion,* 1, 49–51 and passim.

68. In December 1863, Meade estimated that 40,586 of his infantrymen (aggregate present and absent) were eligible for reenlistment. OR 29:2, 561. Factoring in the other branches of service (see OR 36:3, 426; OR 42:1, 39–40) suggests a number in the range of 45,000 to 50,000 eligible men (aggregate present and absent). At the end of 1863, the Army of the Potomac had 146,208 men (aggregate present and absent) (OR III:3, 1198), which would suggest that roughly one-third were eligible for reenlistment. Shelby Foote states that 26,767 veterans reenlisted in the Army of the Potomac but does not provide the source. Foote, *Red River to Appomattox,* 129. Meade reported that as of January 2, 1864, 16,189 veterans had reenlisted and that he expected "many more." OR 33:347. McPherson states that that Army of the Potomac's reenlistment rate was "only 50 percent," but does not provide the source. McPherson, *Battle Cry of Freedom,* 720. (Meade estimated "more than half" in December 1863. OR 29:2, 557.) Foote's 26,767 number would be roughly 60 percent of my estimated number of eligible men.

While the veterans from 1861 and early 1862 were given the opportunity to reenlist in late 1863 and early 1864, they were not immediately discharged if they chose not to reenlist. Their original three-year term of enlistment still governed and the veterans from 1861 were generally not discharged until the last half of 1864.

69. *Yates Country Chronicle* (Penn Yan, NY), Feb. 2, 1864; *Watkins Express* (NY), Feb. 4, 1864.

70. OR III:5, 635–36.

71. *Hartford Daily Courant,* Mar. 5, 1864, 2.

72. OR III:4:1, 421.

73. *Ontario County Times* (Canandaigua, NY), July 20, 1864, 2. See also *Hartford Courant,* Aug. 11, 1864, 2.

74. OR 37:2, 384.

75. OR 37:2, 400; OR III:4:1, 515.

76. Foner, *The Fiery Trial,* 304; McPherson, *Tried by War,* 231, 238; Gallagher, *Enduring Civil War,* 117.

77. OR III:4:1, 396; OR III:5, 640.

78. OR III:4:1, 530 (Ohio); 535–36 (Minnesota); 539 (Massachusetts); 541 (Iowa); 559 (Indiana); 561 (New York); 591 (General Dix); 608 (Connecticut); 622 (Delaware). But see OR III:4: 1, 551 (twelve months); (Michigan), 552; (Rhode Island), 606; (Massachusetts), 626; (New Jersey); and 625 (Philadelphia) (three years for regiment of African American troops). Stanton apparently asked Fry about shorter terms in May. At that time, Fry recommended against one year for new organizations because they "would go out [in May 1865] at the most critical season next year if the war continues." OR III:4:1, 396. In the event, May 1865 would have cut it pretty close. Fry remained a strong believer in the superiority of the three-year term of enlistment over one year. OR III:5, 640.

79. Para. 1, Adjutant General GO No. 235 (July 26, 1864), OR III:4:1, 547. It is possible that funding of a larger than necessary force may have been a concern. Fry was opposed to reinstating large federal bounties and Congress reduced the bounties at the last minute from $200/$300/$400 to $100/$200/$300. See *Caledonian* (St. Johnsbury, VT), July 1, 1864, 2; *Burlington Daily Times,* July 1, 1864, 2.

80. OR IV:1, 421; *Pittsburg Gazette* in *American Citizen* (Butler, PA), July 13, 1864, 3. Just under fifteen thousand men had been examined. Nearly half were exempted on medical or other grounds. Two-thirds of the nonexempt men paid commutation. (Another 20 percent

provided substitutes. OR III:4:1, 421). Lincoln transmitted Stanton's recommendation to Congress with his concurrence. Basler, *Collected Works of Abraham Lincoln,* 7:380.

81. *Brooklyn Daily Eagle,* Dec. 24, 1864, 2. See also *Hartford Courant,* Aug. 11, 1864, 2; *Newburyport Morning Herald,* Aug. 1, 1864, 3.

82. Basler, *Collected Works of Abraham Lincoln,* 8:171–72; OR III:4:2, 1002–3.

83. OR III:5, 626, 636–37, 639. These numbers do not include African American volunteers and volunteers for the Regular Army, seaman, and the Marine Corps.

84. OR III:5, 729.

85. Grant, *Memoirs,* 2:500–501.

86. Grant, *Memoirs,* 2:505.

87. Grant's recommendation for a call of three hundred thousand troops in July 1864 was based in part on a strategy of taking Richmond "without attacking fortifications." OR 37:2, 384.

88. McPherson, *Battle Cry of Freedom,* 605. Where I disagree with McPherson is his conclusion that the recruits coming in under the bounty/draft system "did little to help win the war." McPherson, *Battle Cry of Freedom,* 606.

89. Escott, *Rethinking the Civil War Era,* 73, 75.

3. To Volunteer . . . or Not

1. OR III:2, 298 (Aug. 5, 1862).

2. Gallman, *Defining Duty,* 3. See also Sandow, *Contested Loyalty,* 1–3, 6, 10.

3. Gallman, *Defining Duty,* 142–43; see also 15, 16, 66.

4. Gallman, *Defining Duty,* 157; see also 15, 127, 136, 170, 186, 252–53, 255–56. The concept of loyalty was also in flux during the Civil War. Robert Sandow concludes that the essays in *Contested Loyalty* show "how a fractious and diverse Northern people ultimately failed to reach consensus on what loyalty meant or how citizens in times of war might demonstrate it." "Economic survival and opportunity were compelling forces that weakened the call of nationalists to serve and to sacrifice." Sandow, *Contested Loyalty,* 1, 7.

5. Lincoln, "Opinion on the Draft," Sept. [14?], 1863, in Basler, *Collected Works of Abraham Lincoln,* 6:445. Lincoln also opined: "I do not say that all who would avoid serving in the war are unpatriotic; but I do think every patriot should willingly take his chance under a law made with great care in order to secure entire fairness." However, his ultimate opinion was less sympathetic to a man's decision not to serve. Lincoln, "Opinion on the Draft," Sept. [14?], 1863, in Basler, *Collected Works of Abraham Lincoln,* 6:447.

6. Gallman, *Defining Duty,* 26; see also 8, 137.

7. *Rochester Daily Union and Advertiser,* July 12, 1862. See also *Ontario Repository and Messenger* (Canandaigua, NY), Aug. 20, 1862; *Penn Yan Democrat* (NY), July 25, 1862, 2; *St. Lawrence Republican and Ogdensburgh Weekly Journal* (NY), Aug. 26, 1862, 2; *Watertown New York Reformer,* July 21, 1862, 2; *Ocean Emblem* (Tom's River, NJ), July 30, 1862, 2.

8. Thirty-Seventh Congress, Sess. III, chap. LXXV, 12 Stat. 731. Section 2 also exempted men found to be "physically or mentally unfit for service." While these family exemptions might seem quite narrow from today's perspective, in an era when there was no social security and women often died in childbirth, their reach was potentially broad. Of the 250,000 men examined for the 1863 draft, nearly 165,000—roughly two-thirds—were exempted pursuant to these provisions (including physically and mentally unfit). Indeed, Fry noted that "The large proportion of exemptions defeated, in a measure, the object of the law." OR III:5, 626. He noted that many of the exemptions were subsequently repealed.

9. OR III:5, 674.

10. *Poughkeepsie Eagle,* Aug. 2, 1862, 2; Sandow, "The Limits of Northern Patriotism," 177, 186–88; *Albany Evening Journal,* July 2, 1862. There were, of course, calls for men to enlist regardless of their occupation or personal situation. *Ontario Repository and Messenger* (Canandaigua, NY), July 22, 1862; *Broome Republican* (Binghamton, NY), July 16, 1862. Murdock noted that "The principal objective of substitution, as it had been in Europe, was to permit persons in necessary occupations (agricultural or industrial) to stay on the job, since they could better promote the war effort as civilians than as soldiers," but that the concept was "corrupted" because it was not limited to specific occupations. Murdock, *One Million Men,* 178–79.

11. John Andrews War Journal, Nov. 1, 1864, John Tuttle and Arvilla Raplee Andrews Papers, Collection No. 3790, Cornell Univ., Carl A. Kroch Library, Division of Rare and Manuscript Collections.

12. Gallman, *Defining Duty,* 136; see also 26.

13. *Rochester Daily Democrat and American,* July 18, 1862 (emphasis added); *Buffalo Morning Express,* July 19, 1862, 2; *Broome Republican* (Binghamton, NY), July 23, 1862; *Hornellsville Tribune* (NY), July 24, 1862, 2; *Brockport Republican* (NY), July 31, 1862, 2; *Plattsburgh Republican* (NY), Aug. 2, 1862, 3. Other New York newspapers presented similar numbers and conclusions. *Mexico Independent,* July 24, 1862, 4); *Freeman's Journal* (Cooperstown, NY), July 25, 1862, 3; *Freeman's Journal* (Otsego, NY), July 25, 1862, 3 in Reisen, *Otsego County in the Civil War,* 22; *Poughkeepsie Eagle,* Aug. 9, 1862, 2; *Ontario Republican Times* (Canandaigua), July 23, 1862, 3; *Rochester Daily Union and Advertiser,* July 21, 1862; *Troy Weekly Times,* July 19, 1862, 2 and July 26, 1862, 2; *Frontier Patriot* (Cape Vincent, NY), July 19, 1862, 2; *Geneva Courier* (NY), July 23, 1862, 2; *Brooklyn Daily Eagle,* July 15, 1862, 2; *Yates County Chronicle* (Penn Yan, NY), July 24, 1862, 3.

The financial analysis by these newspapers is a reminder that people did not necessarily view the bounty in isolation but may have viewed the bounty as just one component of total compensation. It is important to note that the salary component of total compensation fell far behind the rate of inflation as the war progressed, despite a small pay increase in June 1864. Thus, part of the increases in the bounty over time could be viewed as compensating for the failure of the monthly salary to keep up with the rate of inflation. The monthly pay for privates increased from $11 in April 1861 to $13 in August 1861 to $16 in June 1864. See Kreidberg and Henry, *History of Military Mobilization,* 110–11. The Index of Average Wages went from 100.8 in 1861 and 102.9 in 1862 to 110.5, 125.6, and 143.1 for 1863, 1864, and 1865 respectively, so military pay increases were in line with the civilian economy, at least through 1864. Bureau of the Census, *Historical Statistics,* 66. However, the cost of living increased more than wages. From 1861 to 1864, the cost of living increased by 50 percent, with another 12 percent to 1865. Bureau of the Census, *Historical Statistics,* 235. Sherman wrote after the war that it might have been more economical to have increased a private's pay to "thirty or even fifty dollars a month" than to have paid the high bounties. Sherman, *Memoirs,* 328.

14. *Broome Republican* (Binghamton, NY), Aug. 27, 1862. As in 1861, there were many private inducements offered to sweeten the local offer. For example, the Pennsylvania Railroad contributed $50,000 for bounties (*Brooklyn Daily Eagle,* July 24, 1862, 3); the New York Produce Exchange offered an extra $10 for recruits for the Fourteenth New York (*Brooklyn Daily Eagle,* Aug. 15, 1862, 2); the Union Ferry Company of Brooklyn gave $5,000 to be used for bounties (*Troy Weekly Times,* Aug. 30, 1862, 2); the Jewish community in Syracuse, New York, raised $2,500 for a $25 bounty for an "Israelite" regiment (*Poughkeepsie Eagle,* Aug. 30, 1862, 2). And private individuals would often offer extra amounts. For example, in Buffalo, approximately ten citizens offered to pay $50 each for eight to ten volunteers (*Buffalo Morning Express,* Aug. 23, 1862, 2), and in Brooklyn, an individual offered an extra $5 per

volunteer (*Brooklyn Daily Eagle,* Aug. 23, 1862, 2). See also *Poughkeepsie Eagle,* Aug. 16, 1862, 2 (Boston merchants and American Express in Chicago).

15. *Portsmouth Journal of Literature and Politics* (NH), Aug. 16, 1862, 3.

16. For example, *Connecticut Courant,* July 19, 1862, 2; *Providence Evening Journal,* Aug. 27, 1862, 2; *Burlington Weekly Free Press,* Aug. 15, 1862, 3; *Rutland County Herald,* Aug. 28, 1862, 5; *Windham County Transcript* (CT), Aug. 25, 1864, 2; *Trenton State Gazette,* Aug. 29, 1864, 3. *Camden Democrat* (NJ), Aug. 2, 1862, in Miller, *States at War,* 4:566; *Bridgton Reporter* (ME), Aug. 29, 1862.

17. *Pennsylvania Daily Telegraph* (Harrisburg), Aug. 7, 1862, 3; Catton, *Glory Road,* 12–13.

18. *Poughkeepsie Eagle,* July 23, 1864, 2; *Ithaca Journal and Advertiser,* Aug. 31, 1864, 2; *Tri-States Union* (Port Jervis, NY), Aug. 26, 1864, 2.

19. Gallman, *Defining Duty,* 141; Shannon, *Organization and Administration,* 2:47; *Burlington Weekly Free Press,* Nov. 27, 1863, 2.

20. See Charles E. Hemphill Pension File, passim, NARA. The documents in Hemphill's pension file and CMSR are unclear as to his occupation. As to his income, a neighbor (James Bailey) stated in a January 23, 1885, affidavit that he had employed Hemphill on his farm for two or three years before he went into the army, paying him about $15 a month during the summer of 1864. (See also Mar. 23, 1885, Affidavit of S. M. Fullerton, paid about $1 a day during summer and winter of 1860 and 1861.)

21. Hemphill to Mother, Sept. 1, 1864, Pension File, NARA.

22. Hemphill to Mother, Nov. 24, 1864, Pension File, NARA. Hemphill had previously served in the military, but the circumstances are not entirely clear. Pension File, NARA; US Army Register of Enlistments, 1798–1914; US Civil War Draft Registration Records, 1863–65, Ancestry.com.

23. Charles E. Hemphill CMSR; Charles E. Hemphill to Mother, Nov. 17, 1864, Pension File, NARA; Bates, *History of Pennsylvania Volunteers,* 5:762.

24. Charles E. Hemphill CMSR, NARA.

25. Michael Kennedy to Father and Mother, Apr. 3, 5, 11, 14, 1864; April [?], 1864; July 3, 1864. Affidavit of Samuel H. Purinton, Oct. 4, 1864, Pension File; Abner Roberts to Father, June 5, 1864, Pension File, NARA. Kennedy did note after Spotsylvania that "There are a great many that would give their bounty to get back." Michael Kennedy to Father, May 20, 1864, Pension File, NARA.

26. Rutan, *179th New York Volunteer Infantry,* 45, 49; Union Bounties (Eastern States), latewarunionsoldiers.org; *Hartford Courant,* Aug. 9, 1864, 2.

27. Seymour, Annual Message to the Legislature, Jan. 1863, 18; *New London Daily Chronicle,* Aug. 26, 1862, 2; *Portland Weekly Advertiser,* July 19, 1862, 2 (emphasis in original). See also *Frontier Palladium* (Malone, NY), Aug. 28, 1862, 2. These views were expressed later in the war as well. For example, *Boston Morning Journal,* Nov. 20, 1863, 4; *Bath Daily Times* (ME), Sept. 1, 1864, 2; *Portland Daily Press,* Nov. 10, 1863, 1; *Jamestown Journal* (NY), Jan. 15, 1864, 1.

28. *Mirror and Farmer* (Manchester, NH), Aug. 16, 1862, 1; *Bridgton Reporter,* July 18, 1862, 2. I did not research the relative use of the phrases *high bounty* and *liberal bounty.* The following are examples of references to a "liberal" bounty by state and year: **Connecticut:** (1862) *Hartford Courant,* Aug. 20, 1862, 2; (1864) *Hartford Courant,* Mar. 5, 1864, 2; **Delaware:** (1862) (None located); (1864) *Delaware State Journal,* Aug. 2, 1862, 2; **Maine:** (1862) *Maine Farmer* (Augusta), July 17, 1862, 2; *Bath Daily Times,* Aug. 15, 1862, 2; *Oxford Democrat,* July 18, 1862, 3; *Portland Weekly Advertiser,* July 19, 1862, 2; Aug. 2, 1862, 2; (1864) *Bangor Daily Whig and Courier,* July 25, 1864, 2; **Massachusetts:** (1862)

(None located); (1863) *Waltham Sentinel,* Dec. 4, 1863, 2; (1864) *Springfield Daily Union,* Aug. 1, 1864, 2; (1865) *Salem Register,* Feb. 13, 1865, 2; **New Hampshire:** (1862) *Concord Independent Democrat,* Aug. 28, 1862, 3; *Exeter News-Letter and Rockingham County Advertiser,* Sept. 8, 1862, 3; *Manchester Weekly Union,* Aug. 12, 1862, 2; *Portsmouth Journal of Literature and Politics,* Aug. 16, 1862, 3; (1863); *Portsmouth Journal of Literature and Politics,* Nov. 14, 1863, 2; (1864) *New Hampshire Sentinel* (Keene), June 23, 1864, 2; **New Jersey:** (1862) *Monmouth Democrat,* July 24, 1862, 2; (1863) *Trenton State Gazette,* Aug. 25, 1863, 3; **New York:** (1862) *Brooklyn Daily Eagle,* July 15, 1862, 2; *Geneva Courier,* July 30, 1862, 2 ("generous"); *Livingston Republican* (Geneseo), Aug. 21, 1862, 2; *Ontario Repository and Messenger* (Canandaigua), Aug. 27, 1862, 2; *Rochester Democrat and Union Advertiser,* Aug. 17, 1862; *Mexico Independent,* July 24, 1862, 4; (1864) *Elmira Daily Advertiser,* July 21, 1864, 2; *Livingston Republican* (Geneseo), Aug. 18, 1864, 2; Sept. 8, 1864, 2 ("the bounty is liberal, even extravagant"); **Pennsylvania:** (1862) *Patriot* (Harrisburg), July 31, 1862, 1; (1864) *American Citizen* (Butler), Aug. 31, 1864, 3; *Pittsburgh Gazette,* July 6, 1864, 2, but see *Pittsburgh Gazette,* Aug. 7, 1862, 2 ("high"); *Daily Post* (Pittsburgh), Aug. 19, 1864, 3; *Daily Evening Express* (Lancaster), Aug. 23, 1864, 2; **Rhode Island:** (1862) *Newport Daily News,* Aug. 14, 1862, 2; (1864) *Providence Evening Press,* July 27, 1864, 4; **Vermont:** (1862) *Burlington Free Press,* Aug. 22, 1862, 2; *Vermont Journal* (Windsor), Aug. 23, 1862, 2; (1863) *Burlington Free Press,* Dec. 4, 1863, 2; *North Star* (Danville), Dec. 5, 1863, 2 ("quite liberal"); (1864) *Burlington Free Press,* Aug. 9, 1864, 2; *Green-Mountain Freeman* (Montpelier), Nov. 22, 1864, 1; *Rutland County Herald,* July 21, 1864, 8; *Rutland Weekly Herald,* Sept. 1, 1864, 4; *Vermont Phoenix* (Brattleboro), Aug. 12, 1864, 3; *Report of the Adjutant and Inspector General of the State of Vermont, from October 1, 1863 to October 1, 1864* (Montpelier: Walton's Steam Press, 1864), 15.

29. OR III: 2, 291.

30. George D. Fox to "Dear Mother," Aug. 6, 1862, Pension File, NARA. Fox did not need his parents' consent to enlist because he was nineteen. Fox chose the Ninth New Hampshire and died at Antietam. Pension File, NARA.

31. *Philadelphia Dollar Newspaper,* Aug. 13, 1862, 3; *Hornellsville Tribune* (NY), Aug. 14, 1862, 3; *Pittsburgh Daily Post,* Aug. 15, 1862, 1. See also *Union County Star and Lewisburg Chronicle* (PA), Aug. 26, 1862, 1; *Hornellsville Tribune* (NY), *July 24, 1862.* For a view of the carrot and stick in 1864, see *Providence Evening Press,* June 16, 1864, 4.

32. *Constitution* (Middletown, CT), Aug. 27, 1862, 2; *Delaware Gazette* (Delhi, NY), Aug. 13, 1862. See also *Pennsylvania Daily Telegraph* (Harrisburg), Aug. 7, 1862, 3; *Geneva Courier* (NY), July 23, 1862, 2.

33. *Syracuse Daily Courier and Union,* Sept. 5, 1864, 2.

34. Reid and White, "'A Mob of Stragglers and Cowards,'" 65; Humphreys, *Marrow of Tragedy,* 3; Gallman, *Defining Duty,* 3. Simeon Draper, the Union's first provost marshal general, observed "a population which, however imbued with military instincts, was unused to the habits of war, a people who for upward of half a century had lived in the enjoyment of profound peace (except during the brief interlude of the Mexican war)." OR III:2, 936. See also *Providence Evening Press,* June 16, 1864, 4.

35. McPherson, *Battle Cry of Freedom,* 332. Much of this section is taken from my history of the 179th New York. Rutan, *179th New York Volunteer Infantry,* 18–19.

36. Ward, *Civil War,* 58.

37. Fry wrote in his postwar report that "A knowledge of the extent of the disaster at Fredericksburg had reached and dispirited the loyal people." OR III:5, 612. See also Marvel, *Lincoln's Mercenaries,* 93, 179.

38. Faust, *This Republic of Suffering,* 11.

39. Rosenheim, *Photography and the American Civil War,* 8–9. Because these photo-graphs were not published in newspapers, it is not clear how widely they were seen. See also Adams, *Living Hell,* 16–17.

40. Faust, *This Republic of Suffering,* 11–12. The *Bradford Argus* (County, PA), July 21, 1864, reported a similar story of a photo showing a woman and a little girl, which was found on the Wilderness battlefield.

41. OR III:5, 638; Foner, *Fiery Trial,* 304; McPherson, *Tried by War,* 231, 238; Galla-gher, *Enduring Civil War,* 117.

42. US Sanitary Commission, *Narrative of Privations and Sufferings of United States Officers and Soldiers.*

43. Barton, *Glorious Recollections,* 3. See also Chamberlain, *Passing of the Armies,* 23, on later-enlisting volunteers.

44. OR 29:2, 557. Meade later acknowledged the impact of the bounties as well as the furlough. OR 33, 347. See also Nolan, *Iron Brigade,* 267–68, 270.

45. *Green-Mountain Freeman* (Montpelier, VT), Jan. 26, 1864, 1. Linderman con-cluded that the offer of a furlough was "decisive" because the veterans from 1861 were pessimistic about their chances of surviving the upcoming campaign season and the fur-lough was their opportunity to see their families one last time before dying. Linderman, *Embattled Courage,* 261–64. Cpl. George H. Uhler of the Ninety-Third Pennsylvania re-called his comrades' thinking:

> While the furloughs were only for 30 days, the government and local bounties were liberal, and as all the men had still one campaign before them, they argued that they might as well accept the offer, as if the war ended by that time they would be so much ahead; while if it did not, they would either have to enlist again or be subject to draft, and the emoluments might be much smaller. Uhler, *Camps and Campaigns of the 93rd Pennsylvania Volunteers,* 23.

46. OR III:3, 112 (GO No. 85 War Dept., AGO, Apr. 2, 1863). While three years became the standard term of enlistment early in the war, the rush of recruiting and the uncertain interplay between the federal and state government roles led to the anomaly that thirty-six two-year infantry regiments were created by New York in mid-1861. Fox, *Regimental Losses,* 477. Their terms of enlistment would expire in the late spring and early summer of 1863. In April 1863, the War Department added a thirty-day furlough to the state and local bounties available. The furlough provision was directed primarily at retention of these "two-year" New York regiments. OR III:3, 91 (GO No. 73, Mar. 24, 1863); OR III:3, 112 (GO No. 85, Apr. 2, 1863); Lerwill, *Personnel Replacement System,* 108; Miller, *States at War,* 2:244. See also OR III:3, 179 (GO No. 111, May 1, 1863).

The effort to retain these two-year infantry regiments was a failure. Of the thirty-six regiments, only one—the Seventeenth New York—was reorganized as an infantry regi-ment to serve for three more years of the war, although the Thirtieth New York was re-organized as cavalry. Reorganization of the Eighth, Ninth, Eleventh, Twentieth, Twenty-Ninth, Thirty-First, Thirty-Seventh and Thirty-Eighth New York was authorized, but either failed or was discontinued. Four companies of the Tenth New York continued in service as a battalion. Phisterer, *New York in the War of the Rebellion,* passim.

47. OR III:3, 1193; OR III:4, 4–6, 28, 154; OR III: 4:1, 30, 148, 154. Fry had "no doubt the effect of [ending the $400 bounty and going back to $100] will be to check, if it does not stop, enlistments [in general]." OR III:4, 5. Stanton noted that only the $100 bounty would be available and advised Meade to "Secure all re-enlistments of veteran volunteers possible before January 5th." Stanton to Meade, Dec. 24, 1863, Regimental Order Book, Part 2, Fifty-Third Pennsylvania Regimental Books, vol. 6, RG 94, NARA. The *Brooklyn*

Daily Eagle reported on January 6, 1864, that "Recruiting is quite dull this morning, only ten men having been enlisted, one of whom was a re-enlisted volunteer . . . This sudden lull in volunteering is accounted for by the fact, that on yesterday the Government bounty of $300 was stopped" (Jan. 6, 1864, 2).

48. *Green-Mountain Freeman* (Montpelier, VT), Jan. 26, 1864, 1. As the Sixth Vermont passed through Washington on its way home to recruit, a local observer commented that "The boys are eager to obtain the big bounty and a month's rest among home scenes and home faces. They are also very much influenced to re-enlist by the current opinion that one more campaign like that of 1863 will end the Rebellion." *Alleghanian* (Ebensburg, PA), Jan. 7, 1864, 2. See also Simeon McDuffie (Ninth New Hampshire) to "Dear Mother," Dec. 11, 1863, Pension File. McDuffie wanted to reenlist, but his mother did not want him to. McDuffie said he would give her his $402 bounty if she would let him reenlist.

49. Para. XI, GO No. 191, OR III:3, 416.

50. Letter, Dec. 23, 1863, Kingsbury, *History of the Town of Surry, Cheshire County, New Hampshire,* 118. The Vermont Adjutant and Inspector General's office also noted that "a large number" in the Army of the Potomac "arranged in advance" for the payment of local bounties. *1864 Report of the Adjutant and Inspector General,* 31.

51. OR III; 4:1, 135; *Norwich Weekly Courier* (CT), Mar. 3, 1864, 4; OR 26:1, 881; *Newport Mercury,* Dec. 19, 1863, 2. For drawing on reenlistments in the field to meet quotas, see also *Sentinel of Freedom* (Newark, NJ), Jan. 12, 1864, 3; *Newark Daily Advertiser,* Dec. 28, 1863, 2; *Vermont Watchman and State Journal* (Montpelier), Mar. 4, 1864, 2. For a discussion of motivations in the Second Corps, see Kreiser, *Defeating Lee,* 143–46. John Robertson concluded that men from Western Pennsylvania "seemed to make the decision that was more practical for them. . . . In general, soldiers from urban and higher-class backgrounds seemed to have more opportunities outside the army than those from rural and lower-class backgrounds." Robertson, "Re-enlistment Patterns of Civil War Soldiers," 35.

52. *Philadelphia Inquirer,* July 19, 1864, 4; Chamberlain, *Passing of the Armies,* 22.

53. OR III:4:2, 813. Thomas Livermore estimated that two hundred thousand veterans reenlisted. Livermore, *Numbers and Losses in the Civil War,* 1. James McPherson estimated that one hundred thousand veterans did not reenlist. McPherson, *Battle Cry of Freedom,* 720.

54. McPherson, *Battle Cry of Freedom,* 720; Chamberlain, *Passing of the Armies,* 21–22. See also Linderman, *Embattled Courage,* 263.

55. Fox, *Regimental Losses,* 479–81; OR III:3, 414. GO No. 191 was amended in September 1863 to authorize reenlistment of three-year men starting that month provided that they had less than one year left to serve. GO 305, AGO, OR III:3, 785. This meant that the three-years men from the July 1862 call would not be eligible until the late summer and fall of 1864. The reenlistment program under GO 119 was regularly extended—to December 1, 1863 (GO 324, AGO, OR III:3, 844) and to January 5, 1864 (GO 387, AGO, OR III:3, 1106). In March 1864, the program was extended without an end date, but the federal bounty was reduced to $100. (Circular No. 25, AGO, Mar. 18, 1864, OR III:4:1, 190). In July 1864, just as the one-year remaining reenlistment window for the three-year volunteers from 1862 was about to open, it was shut for them by reducing the eligibility window to less than sixty days remaining to serve. GO No. 235, AGO, OR III:4:1, 547. In September 1864, the Adjutant General's Office confirmed that reenlistment under GO No. 305 was no longer available and that GO No. 235 governed. OR III:4:2, 696 (Circular No. 72, Sept. 6, 1864). That meant that the three-year volunteers from the late summer and early fall of 1862 would not be eligible for reenlistment until the late spring and early summer of 1865. See also Fox, *Regimental Losses,* 494n. But see Marvel, *Lincoln's Mercenaries,* 204.

56. *Pittsburgh Gazette,* July 6, 1864, 2.

57. *Hornellsville Tribune* (NY), Sept. 8, 1864, 3; *Daily Evening News* (Fall River, MA), Sept. 10, 1864, 2. Two New Hampshire newspapers had made a similar point in late 1863. *Farmer's Cabinet* (Amherst), Nov. 19, 1863, 2; *Manchester Daily Mirror,* Nov. 2, 1863, 4.

58. Economic Database and Methodology—Comparison of military and civilian compensation, both latewarunionsoldiers.org.

59. Marvel, *Lincoln's Mercenaries,* xii.

60. Marvel did include anecdotal examples comparing civilian to military income but did not do so on a comprehensive basis. For example, Marvel, *Lincoln's Mercenaries,* 43, 79.

61. In rare instances, newspapers did include a quantitative comparison. *Portsmith Journal of Literature and Politics* (NH), Aug. 16, 1862, 3 ("How many men . . . are making half of it?").

"Notwithstanding the risks of war" may seem like a huge qualification. However, the risk from volunteering of death or serious injury in war can be excluded from further analysis here because the possibility of being drafted—the alternative to volunteering once the conditional draft was adopted in August 1862—presented the same risk (see chapter 2). Recent studies of hazardous occupations demonstrate that workers will accept increased risk of death or serious injury in return for financial reward, but they are of little value here because the draft removes the element of free choice. See, for example, Schnier, Horrace, and Feltoven, "The Value of Statistical Life," i, ii, 2, 10, 25.

It could be argued that the fact that large numbers of men volunteered in 1861 demonstrates that the strength of their patriotic feeling outweighed the increased risk of death or serious injury. However, that increased risk generally was not properly understood by men in 1861, in terms of both the reality and the actual duration of the war.

62. *New York Daily Herald,* Jan. 11, 1860, 7 ("Make Money. Splendid Investment. . . . Can Double Your Money Next Winter."); *Vermont Journal* (Windsor), Feb. 9, 1861, 8 ("In That Way, You Double Your Money the First Year."); *New York Observer,* Sept. 14, 1865, 5 ("Splendid Chance for Business; Double Your Money in Three Months."); *Buffalo Commercial,* June 23, 1865 ("Here Is a Chance to Double Your Money."); and *Public Ledger* (Philadelphia), Mar. 22, 1860, 3 ("BE YOUR Own Master, Conduct Your Own Business and Double Your Own Money at Every Sale.")

63. Tables 3.5 and 3.6, Tables, latewarunionsoldiers.org. See introduction, n19. Claudia Goldin and Frank Lewis concluded in 1975 that "A comparison of civilian and military wage rates indicates that this additional compensation was slight." Goldin and Lewis, "The Economic Cost of the American Civil War," 304n8g. While they apparently considered bounties, they did not state their sources for civilian wage data, nor did they state whether they considered factors such as seasonality of civilian employment or the value of military rations. Goldin and Lewis, "The Economic Cost of the American Civil War," 304n8g. See also Marvel, *Lincoln's Mercenaries,* 141.

With respect to the Western States, the one-quarter to one-half estimate probably does not hold true for three reasons. First, state and local bounties may have been lower in the Western States than the Eastern States in 1862. Second, civilian wages in the Western States (excluding California and Oregon) may have been pretty much the same as in the Eastern States. The combination of the first and second factors would likely drive the ratios for most occupations below 2.0, although for unskilled occupations, they may still have been somewhat above 2.0. Third, the percentage of farmers in the Western States was much higher. For a more thorough discussion, see "Methodology—Western States," latewarunionsoldiers.org.

I have not researched how the individual Western States met their quotas in terms of the mix among volunteers, substitutes, and draftees, but at least for the July 1864 call, it appears that the Western States relied more heavily on draftees than the Eastern States did. OR III:5, 735.

64. Tables 3.5 and 3.6, Tables, latewarunionsoldiers.org.

65. Men who enlisted in the Ninth New Hampshire, a three-year regiment recruited in August 1862, provide some anecdotal examples of the economic circumstances of the volunteers.

For the six months before he enlisted, eighteen-year-old William A. Kemp earned $15 per month. Two years before enlisting, he earned $14 to $20 per month. The summer before enlisting, he earned $13 a month working in a mill. Affidavit of Orlando J. Raymond, Apr. 18, 1876; Affidavit of Jane Wellington, Aug. 16, 1877; Affidavit of Luther King, May 5, 1878, all William A. Kemp Pension File, NARA. Even assuming full employment over the hypothetical twelve-month period, for $15 a month civilian compensation, volunteering would have represented a 3.1 ratio for Kemp.

James Hatch was an eighteen-year-old farm laborer from Conway, earning $18 a month with board. Affidavit of Thomas Towle, Mar. 12, 1886, James Hatch Pension file, NARA. Even assuming year-round employment, Hatch's ratio would have been 2.0.
Nineteen-year-old Simeon Clement earned $8 to $10 a month and board before enlisting, resulting in a ratio of 4.0. Affidavit of Herman A. Clement, Mar. 8, 1880, Simon Clement Pension File, NARA.

William Knights was an eighteen-year-old shoemaker earning fifty cents a day (about $150 per year), which results in a 2.9 ratio. Affidavit of Charles J. Cowell, Apr. 25, 1877; Francis B. Libby, Apr. 25, 1877, William S. Knights Pension File, NARA.

66. Kennedy, *Population of the United States in 1860,* passim.

67. See Sutherland, *Expansion of Everyday Life 1860–1876,* 132. The 1860 Census included information on the value of the individual's real property and personal property. However, it is not clear whether the stated values were net of indebtedness. The instructions to the census enumerators were very clear: "You are not to consider any question of lien or encumbrances; it is simply your duty to enter the value as given by the respondent." Census Office, *Eighth Census . . . Instructions,* 15, para. 12.

68. The analysis is complicated by the fact that the military used only two categories—farmer and laborer—to cover occupations that the census divided into three: farmer, farm laborer, and laborer. As explained in "Methodology—Farmers, Laborers and Farm Laborers" (latewarunionsoldiers.org), it cannot be assumed that all the men reported as "farmers" in a unit's descriptive book were farm owners or their sons. Many were actually farm laborers as reported in the 1860 Census.

69. Compiled from Muster Roll Abstract, 122nd New York Volunteers, NYSMM and 1860 Census, both Ancestry.com. One percent of the men in the 122nd New York were "Farmers" who rented their land. They were generally in their mid-to-late twenties, married (usually with several children), and had a personal estate of $100 to $350. Muster Roll Abstract, 122nd New York Volunteers, NYSMM and 1860 Census, both Ancestry.com.

70. The instructions for the census enumerators stated that the value of real property and personal property was to be provided for each person enumerated, but in practice numbers were entered only for the head of the household. Census Office, *Eighth Census, Instructions,* paras. 12 and 13, 15. Wealth data was not entered for any of the sons from the 122nd New York that I was able to identify in the 1860 Census. The economic prospects for the son of a farm owner depended on so many different circumstances that it is not practical to generalize about the economic attractiveness of volunteering.

71. Compiled from Muster Roll Abstract, 122nd New York Volunteers and 1860 Census, both Ancestry.com.

72. The Ninth New Hampshire was raised in the summer of 1862. Examples of the farms owned by the volunteers' families are the following: the father of Osborn Drown (Company D) owned a small farm worth $250 (Affidavit of Mark Pierce, Mar. 10, 1884, Osborn Drown Pension File); the parents of Frank Lovejoy (Company A) purchased a farm in 1859 for $800 (Affidavit of [?] Bickford, Oct. 9, 1888, Frank Lovejoy Pension File); the family of Sidney Spaulding (Company E) bought a farm in 1863 for $650 Affidavit, Aug. 31, 1883, Sidney Spaulding Pension File); the parents of James Hatch (Company D) purchased their farm for $600 (unstated year) (Samuel Hazelton to Mr. Dudley, Apr. 4, 1884, James Hatch Pension File); and the mother of Anthony Stevens paid $70 for five acres of land in 1863 (Affidavit of Hannah Stevens, June 26, 1880, Anthony Stevens Pension File). All Pension Files, NARA.

73. Richard Miller also added the caveat to his economic analysis that the volunteers had to be "prepared to risk their lives." For example, Miller, *States at War*, 1:49. See also note 61 above.

74. Calculated from Kennedy, *Population of the United States in 1860*, passim.

75. Economic Database, Wage Ratios (by state and period), latewarunionsoldiers.org.

76. OR III:5, 732, 734, 737, 739.

4. *The Quality of Late-War Replacements*

1. Kautz, *Customs of Service*, para. 95, 38. For today's values, go to Living the Army Values, goarmy.com.

2. Kautz, *Customs of Service*, Art. 52 (228); Art. 24 (222); Art. 2 (218).

3. *New York Evening Post*, Aug. 11, 1862, 4; *Vermont Watchman and State Journal* (Montpelier), Jan. 1, 1864, 2; *Alleghanian* (Ebensburg, PA), Sept. 8, 1864, 3; *Delaware Republican* (Delhi, NY), Aug. 25, 1862, 2; *Elmira Daily Advertiser* (NY), Sept. 14, 1864, 2; *Otsego Republican* (NY), Aug. 30, 1862; *Pittsburg Daily Commercial*, Sept. 2, 1864, 1; *Hartford Daily Courant*, Aug. 11, 1864, 2; *New York Tribune*, Aug. 5, 1862, 8. See also *Manufacturers' and Farmers' Journal* (Providence), Aug. 8, 1864, 2.

4. *New York Times* reprinted in *Rochester Daily Union Advertiser*, July 16, 1862. See also *Penn Yan Democrat* (NY), July 25, 1862.

5. *Albany Evening Journal*, July 2, 1862; *Ontario Repository & Messenger* (Canandaigua, NY), July 23, 1862; *Otsego Republican* (NY), Aug. 30, 1862, quoted in Reisen, *Otsego County in the Civil War*, 32.

6. Sherman, *Memoirs*, 328 (emphasis added); *Daily Mirror* (Manchester, NH), Dec. 11, 1863, 2; Costa and Kahn, *Heroes & Cowards*, 46.

7. *Hartford Daily Courant*, Aug. 22, 1864, 2 (emphasis in original); *Manufacturers' and Farmers' Journal* (Providence, RI), Aug. 8, 1864, 2. See also *Providence Evening Press*, July 27, 1864, 4 ("good men and true"). The $500 "order" was a note. The *Courant* believed that the bounty needed to be offered in cash.

Costa and Kahn noted the inherent dilemma in trying to raise a large army of good soldiers in *Heroes & Cowards*. After identifying the individual characteristics with the lowest probability of desertion—"being literate, being a farmer, being native-born or German born, being single, and being wealthy"—they observed that "If all soldiers had these characteristics (and they could not have, because the army would have had too few men), the desertion probability would have been 3 percent," Costa and Kahn, *Heroes & Cowards*, 111–12; see also 100–102.

8. *Coos Republican* (Lancaster, NH), Sept. 6, 1864, 2; Aug. 30, 1864, 3. The *Coos Republican* named twenty-two of the men. Based on the 1860 Census and those that can be identified with reasonable certainty, they were in fact "Lancaster" men and would have been considered to be "good" men. Six were young men living on family farms valued at $600 to $3,000; another five were small farmers; one was a blacksmith and one a station agent. Ancestry.com. The *Coos Republican* (Sept. 6, 1864, 2) also commented that recruits in other local towns "were among the most useful citizens of their several towns."

9. *Vermont Watchman and State Journal* (Montpelier), Jan. 1, 1864, 2; *Elmira Daily Advertiser* (NY), Sept. 14, 1864, 2; *Alleghanian* (Ebensburg, PA), Sept. 8, 1864, 3; Report of General Superintendent of Recruiting in Vermont Adjutant and Inspector General, *Report from Oct. 1, 1863 to Oct. 1, 1864*, 219. The Ebensburg company became part of the 209th Pennsylvania Volunteers, which distinguished itself at the Battle of Fort Stedman. See also *Pennsylvania Telegraph (Harrisburg)*, Sept. 17, 1864, 3.

10. OR III:4:2, 1251.

11. OR III:4, 710.

12. *Pittsburg Daily Commercial*, Sept. 2, 1864, 1.

13. Height is another objective criterion. Stanton reduced the minimum height for recruits from five feet three inches to five feet in November 1864. OR III:4:2, 966. I do not know how many more recruits Stanton expected would become eligible.

14. Kautz, *Customs of Service*, 11, para. 7.

15. The standard enlistment form for volunteers included a signed certification by the "Examining Surgeon" that he had "carefully examined" the recruit and that in his opinion the recruit "is free from all bodily defects and mental infirmity, which would in any way disqualify him from performing the duties of a soldier." The enlistment form also included a signed certification by the "Recruiting Officer" that he had "minutely inspected" the recruit and that to the best of his "judgment and belief," the recruit was "of lawful age" and "entirely sober." Standard enlistment form in a typical CMSR.

16. OR III:2, 236; Lerwill, *Personnel Replacement System*, 75. In December 1861, the disbursing and mustering officer in Albany, New York, wrote AG Thomas that "I am satisfied the large number of defective men in Service is owing to the want of Medical examination at the various Recruiting Rendezvous." Letter dated Dec. 26, 1861, RG 110, Entry 1764, NARA (New York City Branch). In March 1862, General Rosecrans, commanding the Mountain Department in West Virginia, complained to AG Thomas about sickness rates in his various districts in the range of only 8 percent. OR 12:3, 12.

17. OR III:4, 932. In an 1863 letter to Stanton, Fry stated more clearly that at least half of the two hundred thousand "were unfit for service when received." OR III:3, 894.

18. The enlistment form included a signed declaration by the volunteer that "I know of no impediment to my serving honestly and faithfully as a soldier." See typical CMSR. In the Fifty-Sixth Massachusetts, Pvt. Sidney Barstow was convicted of attempting to defraud the United States "by enlisting in this Regimentt, knowing himself to be physically incompetent at that time to perform the duty of a soldier." He was sentenced to being drummed out of the camp. SO No. 46, Headquarters, Fifty-Sixth Massachusetts, dated Jan. 30, 1864, Regimental Letter and Order Book, Fifty-Sixth Massachusetts Regimental Books, Vol. 3, RG 94, NARA.

19. OR III:5, 600. But see Marvel, *Lincoln's Mercenaries*, 208.

20. Grant, *Memoirs*, 2:531; Judson, *History of the Eighty-Third Regiment Pennsylvania Volunteers*, 84; Wiley, *Billy Yank*, 304.

21. OR III:5, 668–69; Costa and Kahn, *Heroes & Cowards*, 100–101. German-born soldiers actually deserted at a lower rate than native-born soldiers. Costa and Kahn, *Heroes & Cowards*, 100–101. The difference in desertion rates between native-born and

foreign-born soldiers was not as great as might be expected. For example, the probability that an Irish-born soldier would desert was about 12 percent compared to 8 percent for native-born soldiers. Costa and Kahn, *Heroes & Cowards,* 100–101.

22. Rutan, *179th New York Volunteer Infantry,* 338n110. See also Costa and Kahn, *Heroes & Cowards,* 102–3.

23. Occasionally, the actual residence of a soldier is identified as in the case of the roster of the Ninth New Hampshire, but that is the exception. Trying to match soldiers with names in the 1860 Census is somewhat speculative, not to mention quite time-consuming.

24. Grant, *Memoirs,* 2:531.

25. Kautz, *1865 Customs of Service,* 5–6; Boatner, *Civil War Dictionary,* 448–49.

26. McPherson, *For Cause and Comrades,* 11. See also Bui, "'I Feel Impelled to Write.'" Costa and Kahn, who utilized census data as well as military records, concluded that literate men were less likely to desert than illiterate men. Costa and Kahn, *Heroes & Cowards,* 101–2.

27. McPherson, *Cause and Comrades,* viii; Kautz, *Customs of Service,* 11, para. 7. Amos Judson of the Eighty-Third Pennsylvania believed that boys between the ages of sixteen and twenty made the best soldiers, and that one boy of eighteen was worth two men of thirty and three men of forty. Judson *History of the 83rd Regiment Pennsylvania Volunteers,* 85. With respect to age and the likelihood to desert, Costa and Kahn concluded that a twenty-year-old soldier had a 10 percent probability of desertion, while a forty-year-old soldier had only an 8 percent probability. Costa and Kahn, *Heroes & Cowards,* 100. The difference in desertion probability is small and it may be that the greater physical vigor of a twenty-year-old more than compensated. In a similar vein, they concluded that wealthy men were less likely to desert, but they may also have fared less well as soldiers with the hardships of service in the field.

28. McPherson, *For Cause and Comrades,* viii; Rutan, *179th New York Volunteer Infantry,* 31. Costa and Kahn noted that "Married men may be either more or less motivated to fight by the thought of loved ones," but did conclude that married men were one and a half times as likely to desert as single men. Costa and Kahn, *Heroes & Cowards,* 93–94, 100. They did note in an earlier work that studies of American soldiers in World War II found that combat performance was positively correlated with being married. Costa and Kahn, "Cowards and Heroes," 520.

29. Churchill, *Landmarks of Oswego County,* 158–70; Kennedy, *Population of the United States in 1860,* 323, 339; Snyder, "Oswego County's Response to the Civil War," 71–72, 76.

30. Churchill, *Landmarks of Oswego County,* 173–202.

31. Churchill, *Landmarks of Oswego County,* 172–74; Snyder, "Oswego County's Response to the Civil War," 73–75; Phisterer, *New York in the War of the Rebellion,* 3:2002.

32. Churchill, *Landmarks of Oswego County,* 176–77; Snyder, "Oswego County's Response to the Civil War," 76–77; Phisterer, *New York in the War of the Rebellion,* 4:2878.

33. Churchill, *Landmarks of Oswego County,* 181–82; Snyder, "Oswego County's Response to the Civil War," 84; Phisterer, *New York in the War of the Rebellion,* 4:3295; Union Bounties (Eastern States), latewarunionsoldiers.org.

34. Churchill, *Landmarks of Oswego County,* 184–85; Phisterer, *New York in the War of the Rebellion,* 5:3705; Fox, *Regimental Losses,* 237.

35. Churchill, *Landmarks of Oswego County,* 200; Phisterer, *New York in the War of the Rebellion,* 5:4052; Union Bounties (Eastern States), latewarunionsoldiers.org.

36. Phisterer, *New York in the War of the Rebellion,* 5:4104; Fox, *Regimental Losses,* 481.

37. Kennedy, *Population of the United States in 1860,* 323, 338; Clayton, *History of Onondaga County,* 135, 150; *New York Times,* Nov. 22, 1864, 5.

38. Phisterer, *New York in the War of the Rebellion,* 3:1873; 4:3174, 3439, 3731; 5:4058.

39. Phisterer, *New York in the War of the Rebellion,* 3:1873–74.

40. Phisterer, *New York in the War of the Rebellion,* 4:3174.

41. Union Bounties (Eastern States), latewarunionsoldiers.org.

42. Phisterer, *New York in the War of the Rebellion,* 5:3732; Fox, *Regimental Losses,* 238.

43. Union Bounties (Eastern States), latewarunionsoldiers.org.

44. Fox, *Regimental Losses,* 237; Biddlecom to Wife, Oct. 21, 1863; Aldridge, *No Freedom Shrieker,* 51.

45. Compiled from Descriptive Books, Regimental Books for individual regiments, RG 94, NARA. See also Methodology—Farmers, Laborers, and Farm Laborers, latewarunionsoldiers.org.

46. The Twenty-Fourth, 110th, 184th, and 193rd New York received too few replacements to justify further analysis.

47. The Twelfth, 101st, 122nd, 185th, and 193rd New York received too few replacements to warrant further analysis.

48. Compiled from Unit Roster, NYSMM website.

49. Compiled from New York Muster Roll Abstracts, Fold3.com.

50. Compiled from Unit Roster, NYSMM website.

51. The Eighty-First suffered 137 casualties at the battle of Fair Oaks and also lost many men to sickness in early 1862. The Eighty-First later suffered over two hundred casualties at Cold Harbor. Fox, *Regimental Losses,* 212, 479; Eighty-First New York Unit Roster, NYSMM website, passim.

52. Fox, *Regimental Losses,* 212, 479; Eighty-First New York Unit Roster, NYSMM website, passim. The place of enlistment was not necessarily the man's place of residence and in fact for larger commercial centers like Buffalo and Rochester, it usually was not.

53. Compiled from unit roster, NYSMM.

54. The Onondaga and Oswego County regiments appear to have had the good fortune of finding new recruits locally, or at least within New York State. That was not universally true.

55. William Marvel has found that 70 percent of the three-year volunteers came from families with below-median wealth for both the 1861 and the 1863–64 recruiting periods. Marvel, *Lincoln's Mercenaries,* 24. That suggests that there was not a meaningful difference in the socioeconomic status of the volunteers from 1861 compared to the volunteers from 1863–64. Only 62 percent of the one-year volunteers from 1864–65 came from families with below-median wealth, which suggests that the one-year volunteers from 1864–65 came from a somewhat higher socioeconomic status than the three-year volunteers from 1861. If wealth is taken as an indicator of "good" men, that suggests a slight improvement in quality over 1861. Marvel found that 67 percent of the three-year volunteers from 1862 and 57 percent of the nine-month volunteers from 1862 came from families with below-median wealth, which suggests they came from somewhat higher socioeconomic class than the three-year late-war replacements from 1863–64, but not the one-year late-war replacements from 1865. Marvel, *Lincoln's Mercenaries,* 24.

5. Desertion

1. Gen. August Kautz defined desertion as "leaving the command with the intention of not returning to it, after having been duly enlisted or mustered into service." Kautz, *Customs of Service,* 213–14. Neither the Pennsylvania nor the New Jersey desertion rates discussed here should be assumed to be representative of the Eastern States (or the Union army) as a whole. The data cited by PMG Fry in his postwar report showed a wide range

in the desertion rates among the Eastern States. OR 3:5, 668–69. Moreover, the HIBO Database does not include all Pennsylvania and New Jersey infantry regiments—only those in the Army of the Potomac on the eve of the Overland Campaign (with data going back to 1861) or thereafter. Methodology—HIBO Database, latewarunionsoldiers.org. See also the introduction, note 25.

2. Lonn, *Desertion,* 143–45; Reid and White, "'A Mob of Stragglers and Cowards,'" 65. For Confederate desertion during the Petersburg Campaign, see Freeman, *R. E. Lee,* 3:497, 516–17, 541–42; Bowery, *The Richmond-Petersburg Campaign, 1864–65,* 14–116.

3. OR III:5, 676.

4. OR III:2, 286. See also OR III:2, 247; *New York Herald* republished in *Providence Evening Press,* Aug. 4, 1862, 3; Lerwill, *Personnel Replacement System,* 75–76.

5. OR III:2, 939, 936–37; OR III:5, 676. Draper had initially been appointed as a War Department commissioner in July to address the problem of absenteeism. OR III:2, 294.

6. Lonn, *Desertion,* 145.

7. OR III:5, 612; Lonn, *Desertion,* 145.

8. Lonn, *Desertion,* 145.

9. Calculated from Lonn, *Desertion,* 233 (Table III). Lonn's numbers were based on a congressional document. The Deserters' Branch of the Provost Marshal General's Bureau reported somewhat different numbers in its final report. "In 1863 the monthly desertions averaged 4,647; in 1864 they averaged 7,333; in 1865 they averaged 4,368." OR III:5, 758.

10. Lonn, *Desertion,* 152; *American Cyclopedia* (1864), 37 ("desertions from the service during the year were not so numerous as in the early years of the war"). Four factors to consider are the following.

First, the army was somewhat larger during the high-bounty period. The aggregate number of men present and absent for the Union Army was 837,078 at the end of 1863 and 936,990 at the end of 1864, about a 10 percent difference. OR III:3, 1198; OR III:4:2, 1034.

Second, the comparison may not have been apples to apples in its treatment of draftee desertions in 1863 and 1864. The head of the Deserters Branch commented that "In 1863 the monthly desertions averaged 4,647; in 1864 they averaged 7,333; . . . [a 57.8 percent increase]. The deserters of 1864 include all drafted men who have been assigned to regiments and deserted en route to the field, and some who, being held to the draft, have deserted before reaching general rendezvous. This accounts for the increase of desertions during that year." OR III:5, 758. See Lonn, *Desertion,* 152. It seems surprising that this factor could account for the entire difference.

Third, record-keeping may have been more accurate in the later years. Lonn, *Desertion,* 152.

Fourth, volunteers from 1861 and 1862 were also among the deserters in 1864 and 1865.

Approximately 7 percent of the Pennsylvania volunteers from 1861 and from 1862 who deserted at some point during the war deserted in 1864 or 1865. See note 36.

11. Gallagher, *Enduring Civil War,* 42. See also the introduction, note 25.

12. I have not included deserters who returned to their regiment at some point, either voluntarily or involuntarily in the calculation, nor have I included deserters whose enlistment date is not available. For further discussion, see Methodology—Desertion—HIBO Database. See also the introduction, note 25.

13. OR III:4:2, 813, note a. The Adjutant General's Office explained that "This difference or loss results from desertions and discharges on account of physical disability, subsequent to muster in and prior to the men being ready to be forwarded to regiments and companies." OR III:4:2, 813, note a. I have calculated desertion percentages based on regimental records such as unit rosters and registers of deserters in descriptive books. These records are generally limited to soldiers who reported to the regiment and were officially recorded in the regimental books. These regimental records generally do not record

men who were assigned to the regiment upon enlisting but did not actually report to the regiment. The Not Taken Up Factor and the notation No Further Record in documents such as CMSRs and unit rosters are discussed further in Methodology—Desertion—Not Taken Up and No Further Record, latewarunionsoldiers.org.

14. Because the men included in the Not Taken Up group likely included substitutes and draftees as well as later-enlisting volunteers, assigning the full 10 percent to later-enlisting volunteers overstates their desertion rate somewhat.

15. New Jersey was probably at the high end of desertion among the Eastern States, but Connecticut and New Hampshire may have been higher. Fry provided overall desertion rates during the war for seven of the ten Eastern States, but these percentages likely are low because they were based on the ratio between desertions and credits, and credits included commutation and naval enlistments: Connecticut (11.7 percent); Maine (4.4 percent); Massachusetts (6.7 percent); New Hampshire (11.2 percent); New Jersey (10.7 percent); New York (8.9 percent); and Vermont (5.2 percent). Converted from OR III:5, 668. The rate for Pennsylvania was not included. OR III:5, 668. These relative relationships do not necessarily hold for later-enlisting volunteers.

16. Murdock, *One Million Men*, 342.

17. Regular administrative reporting by Union regiments identified soldiers who deserted, usually with details as to the date and place. For example, the "Descriptive Book" for each regiment included a "Register of Deserters." The CMSR for soldiers who deserted usually includes one or more "cards" with the details.

18. Murdock, *Patriotism Limited*, 81.

19. OR III:4:2, 813; Tables, latewarunionsoldiers.org. See also note 13 above.

20. The fact that the later-enlisting volunteers served in the field for a shorter time should also be considered, although desertion by later-enlisting volunteers tended to occur early in their term of service.

21. OR III:5 750, 757; Lonn, *Desertion*, 220.

22. During the course of the war, twice as many soldiers died from disease as from battle. Faust, *This Republic of Suffering*, 4.

23. While the July 1864 call was for 500,000 men, adjustments reduced the number to be raised to 234,327. The actual number raised under the July 1864 call was 272,463, only slightly lower than the 300,000 men that Grant had told Lincoln were needed on July 19, 1864. OR III: 5, 637; OR 37:2, 384. As discussed in chapter 1, Grant certainly did complain about desertion by the late-war replacements and their fighting capability, as well as possible delays in the draft, but he did not go a step further and specifically complain that he could not achieve his objectives as a result. OR III:4:2, 706; OR II:7, 614–15. Even if he had more troops, it seems unlikely that Grant would have pursued frontal assaults later in the war because of the horrendous casualties that would have resulted.

24. Lerwill, *Personnel Replacement System*, 112–16, 119–20; OR III:5, 599–600. Similarly, Sherman wrote in his memoirs that "we tried almost every system known to modern nations, all with more or less success—voluntary enlistments, the draft, and bought substitutes." Sherman, *Memoirs*, 328.

25. As Fry noted, "there can be no cause so just or so beloved that war in its behalf will not be attended by desertion among its defenders. The extent of the evil is governed by circumstances." OR III:5, 676; Lonn, *Desertion*, xiii. However, Fry and the head of the Deserters' Branch would still argue that "prompt and adequate punishment" could have significantly reduced desertion. OR III:5, 678, 755. Determining a normal or benchmark desertion rate for the Union army is problematic. For further discussion, see Methodology—Desertion Benchmark, latewarunionsoldiers.org.

26. High as the desertion rate for New Jersey substitutes seems, it may not have been

the highest among the Eastern States. The desertion rate for New Hampshire substitutes likely was around 75 percent. Livermore, *18th New Hampshire*, 10.

27. OR III:5, 668. Costa and Kahn found that foreign-born men (except for German natives) were more likely to desert than American-born men. Costa and Kahn, *Heroes & Cowards*, 101. The *Philadelphia Inquirer* (July 19, 1864, 4) noted that veterans exempt from the draft could be substitutes.

28. OR III:2, 864. The New Hampshire adjutant general wrote in a letter to local recruiters in August 1864 that "one regiment of [volunteers from New Hampshire] is more desirable than a brigade of substitutes." *Report of the Adjutant General of the State of New Hampshire for the Year Ending May 20, 1865*, 1:XXXVI. Governor Gilmore "appealed" to men considering procuring a substitute "to send no man to the front, for whose loyalty and good conduct they are not willing to be personally responsible." *Report of the Adjutant General of the State of New Hampshire for the Year Ending May 20, 1865*, 1:XXXIX. See also Boggs, *Patriotism by Proxy*, 42.

29. Livermore, *Eighteenth New Hampshire*, 27; Henry Bull to Sister Mary, Nov. 8, 1864, copy in author's collection.

30. OR III:5, 724. The Confederate experience with substitutes was far worse. As many as 90 percent of the substitutes never joined their units. Noe, *Reluctant Rebels*, 113, 120. Roughly seventy thousand substitutes were hired in the South, with advertised rates as high as $500 in 1862 and $10,000 in 1863. The Confederacy did put a limit on the number of substitutes that would be permitted—only one per company per month with the approval of the company commander required. As opposed to the Union army, a Confederate soldier already in service could hire a substitute so he could be discharged, but this apparently rarely happened. Noe, *Reluctant Rebels*, 112–20.

31. Gallagher, *Enduring Civil War*, 40.

32. OR III:5, 618.

33. OR III:4:2, 1261–62; Rutan, *179th New York Volunteer Infantry*, 50–51, 186.

34. Tables 5.11, 5.12, and 5.13, latewarunionsoldiers.org.

35. Because a late-war new regiment had only limited influence over the recruit before he reported to the regiment, I did not charge the Not Taken Up Factor against late-war new regiments. See Livermore, *Eighteenth New Hampshire*, 20. The regiment did not control transport of the recruit to the depot, but officers from the regiment often were involved in face-to-face recruiting and may have had some personal influence.

36. Table 5.14, latewarunionsoldiers.org. The experience of the men enlisting in Pennsylvania regiments in 1861 and 1862 suggests that the propensity to desert was greater earlier in their service (although the denominator for the following data was not adjusted over time to reflect casualties).

Year	Number	Deserted	%	Deserted in the Year (%)					
				1861	1862	1863	1864	1865	No date
1861	42,451	4,123	9.7	24.4	39.7	18.4	5.5	1.2	10.8
1862	28.035	3,104	11.1		51.3	31.4	6.4	1.0	9.8

Source: HIBO Database. See also Methodology–HIBO Database, latewarunionsoldiers.org.

37. A deserter in the 179th New York made the creative—but unsuccessful—argument that if he had intended to be a bounty jumper, he would have enlisted for three years and received much more money rather than enlisting for only one year as he had done. Rutan, *179th New York Volunteer Infantry*, 184–85.

38. Lonn, *Desertion*, 127–42. The fact that Lonn listed the bounty system as her eighth of nine "heads" could be erroneously interpreted to understate the intensity of her criti

cism. She elsewhere described the bounty system as "thoroughly vicious." Lonn, *Desertion,* 219–20, 226–27. Interestingly, she did not discuss conscription as a cause of Union desertion even though her statement about the South that "obviously, men conscripted for service . . . would be potential material for desertion, as their hearts were not devoted to a cause for which they had failed to volunteer" would seem to apply to the North as well. Lonn, *Desertion,* 6.

In addition to Lonn's "heads" or causes, it is also useful to recognize that desertion occurred in different contexts. These different contexts can provide additional insight into the causes of desertion because the driving motivations likely were different. In my observation, there were basically six contexts for desertion: (1) desertion on the way to the central depot, from the depot itself, or on the way to the field (collectively "desertion en route"); (2) desertion from the field; (3) desertion from hospital; (4) desertion from furlough; (5) desertion from parole camp; and (6) desertion after Lee's surrender. As an example of different motivations, a deserter from the hospital had either been wounded or was sick and may have thought that he would never be sent back to the front, so he might as well go home to recover (or, conversely, he may have recovered and did not want to return to the front).

39. Lonn, *Desertion,* 138.

40. OR III:5, 668–69, 755. See also OR III:5, 673; OR III:5, 678. Lonn, *Desertion,* 135–37; Halleck, "The Role of the Community in Civil War Desertion," 125 (citing Lonn).

41. See OR III:5, 668–69, 740–49; Kennedy, *Population of the United States in 1860,* passim; Costa and Kahn, *Heroes & Cowards,* 101–2; Tables, latewarunionsoldiers.org.

42. Costa and Kahn, *Heroes & Cowards,* 101–2; calculated from Kennedy, *Population of the United States in 1860,* passim.

43. Calculated from Kennedy, *Population of the United States in 1860,* passim. Because multiple factors were in play, in states with low percentages of foreign-born recruits, the effect of greater desertion by foreign-born recruits may be outweighed by other factors. For example, New Hampshire and Maine had identical splits of native-born (94 percent) and foreign-born (6 percent) men. While Maine had a relatively low 43.90 desertion rate, New Hampshire had a desertion ratio two and a half times higher at 112.22. OR III:5, 668.

44. Wikipedia, 1864 United States presidential election, results by state.

45. HIBO Database, latewarunionsoldiers.org.

46. HIBO Database, Thirty-Ninth and Fortieth New Jersey, Desertion, latewarunionsoldiers.org. The Thirty-Eighth New Jersey had a low desertion rate similar to that of the Thirty-Ninth New Jersey. The relatively low desertion rate in the Thirty-Eighth New Jersey is not surprising given the nature of its service. Not only was the term of enlistment only one year with the end of the war in sight, but upon arriving at the front, the Thirty-Eighth New Jersey apparently performed only garrison duty in the Army of the James. It suffered no deaths from battle and only fourteen from disease. Stryker, *New Jersey in the Civil War,* 2:1110; Fox, *Regimental Losses,* 483.

47. *Newark Daily Advertiser,* Feb. 16, 1865, 2.

48. *Newark Daily Advertiser,* Sept. 16, 1864, 2.

49. Compiled from Stryker, *New Jersey in the Civil War,* 2:1129, 1152–79; HIBO Database, Thirty-Ninth and Fortieth New Jersey, Desertion, latewarunionsoldiers.com. Once the Thirty-Ninth New Jersey reached the front, desertion all but ended. Of the fifty-two deserters from the Thirty-Ninth New Jersey's original complement, all but four deserted at Newark or en route to the front. Stryker, *New Jersey in the Civil War,* 2:1129, 1152–79.

50. *Newark Daily Advertiser,* Sept. 13, 1864, 2; *Sentinel of Freedom* (Newark), Sept. 27, 1864, 3; *Newark Daily Advertiser,* Sept. 28, 1864, 2 (dress parade every afternoon); *Newark Daily Advertiser,* Oct. 7, 1864 (patrol sent out searching for AWOL soldiers, weapon fired

at "skedadler"); *Newark Daily Advertiser,* Sept. 30, 1864, 2; *Trenton State Gazette,* June 20, 1865, 3; *Newark Daily Advertiser,* Sept. 2, 1864, 2.

51. Five companies left New Jersey on October 4, 1864, under Lt. Col. Close, another company on October 9, two more the following day, and the final two companies on October 14. Stryker, *New Jersey in the Civil War,* 2:1129. OR 46:1:2, 1057.

52. Stryker, *New Jersey in the Civil War,* 2:1152.

53. The Fortieth New Jersey lost another one hundred sixty or so to desertion between Lee's surrender and the Fortieth New Jersey's muster out date. Although deserting after hostilities have ended, but before discharge is still desertion, there is no impact on the fighting capability of the regiment. Of the roughly two hundred additional recruits who joined the Fortieth New Jersey in March as the war was ending, about 30 percent deserted, but the vast majority not until after Lee's surrender. The imminent end of the war, as well as improved security, could well have limited desertion. HIBO Database, Fortieth New Jersey, Desertion, latewarunionsoldiers.org; Stryker, *New Jersey in the Civil War,* 2:1152–79.

54. *Sentinel of Freedom* (Newark), Feb. 28, 1865, 1.

55. Another example of differences between regiments of the same state is the thirty percentage points difference between the 210th Pennsylvania and the 211th Pennsylvania, both of which were recruited in the fall of 1864. While local bounties were not uniform throughout Pennsylvania, it seems likely that factors other than the bounty would explain that difference as well. As discussed in chapter 10, the 211th Pennsylvania proved to be a high-performing unit because of a wide range of factors that would work against desertion. In contrast, the performance of the 210th Pennsylvania was mediocre.

56. There may well also have been differences among the various branches of the army. Because the focus here is on infantry regiments, I have not tested that.

The 179th New York Volunteers illustrates differences in desertion rates among companies. The first seven companies were raised in the spring and early summer of 1864. Companies A, C, and G experienced only 4 percent desertion en route, while the rate was 44 percent for Company E and 21 percent for Company F. To further illustrate the complexity, both companies E and G were primarily recruited in Buffalo. The last three companies were raised under the July 1864 call. Companies I and K experienced no desertion en route. Company H lost a fifth of its men. Rutan, *179th New York Volunteer Infantry,* 50–51, 138–39.

57. See note 36 above.

58. The lax discipline that Lonn identified could be a regiment-specific factor adversely impacting unit cohesion.

59. Costa and Kahn tested for the impact of a wide variety of factors on desertion, such as occupation and birthplace, but did so independent of bounty considerations. They did not test for the impact of bounties themselves. Costa and Kahn, *Heroes & Cowards,* 60.

6. Late-War Union Soldiers in Battle

1. McPherson, *For Cause and Comrades,* ix. A more precise inquiry would factor in, for example, the number of days in combat and the intensity of the battles. See also the limitations explained in the introduction, note 25.

2. See, for example, *Yates County Chronicle,* June 22, 1865; *Broome Republican,* June 14, 1865; *Elmira Daily Advertiser,* June 12, 1864.

3. Gordon, *A Broken Regiment,* 2.

4. Fox measured sacrifice, not combat effectiveness. He explained that "It is not claimed that these are *the* Three Hundred Fighting Regiments of the Army; but, that they are three hundred regiments which evidently did considerable fighting. There were, undoubtedly, others which did equally good or, perhaps, better fighting." Fox, *Regimental Losses,* 122 (emphasis in original).

5. Musick, "The Little Regiment."

6. C. E. Stevens wrote a sarcastic sketch in 1908 detailing why the Seventy-Seventh New York was "not a fighting regiment" despite its meritorious service. "Not a Fighting Regiment," *National Tribune,* Oct. 8, 1908, 7. See also "Surely a Fighting Regiment," *National Tribune,* Nov. 18, 1897, 2:5 (Seventy-Sixth Ohio); Smith, "Regiment [Second Delaware] to Be Proud of," *National Tribune,* Dec. 24, 1908, 7:1.

7. Wilkinson, *Fifty-Seventh Massachusetts Veteran Volunteers,* 364.

8. For example, Barram, *72nd New York,* 1; Mark, *Red, White, and Blue Badge,* 9.

9. Fox, *Regimental Losses,* 122, 136, 153, 174–76, 400–401. These regiments may have been the ones that Bruce Catton had in mind when he wrote that "several of [the high-number regiments] made excellent records." See Catton, *A Stillness at Appomattox,* 30.

10. Fox, *Regimental Losses,* 153, 175.

11. Fox, *Regimental Losses,* 122. John Horn gave the Confederate forces at Second Reams's Station an "effectiveness" rating of 34.0 and the Union forces a rating of 6.25 based on the casualties inflicted per day per hundred men. Horn, *Siege of Petersburg,* Table 4, 319. However, statistics on casualties inflicted should not be utilized without discussion of the forces' missions, which may go beyond inflicting (or avoiding) casualties.

12. Hayward, "Measurement of Combat Effectiveness," 316, 318.

13. Hayward, "Measurement of Combat Effectiveness," 316, 318; Reardon, "A Hard Road to Travel," 177; van Creveld, *Fighting Power,* 1, 173. van Creveld cautions against an exclusive focus on victory because it can obscure the "intrinsic qualities" of a unit. van Creveld, *Fighting Power,* 1, 173.

14. Coss, *All for the King's Shilling,* 3; Lynn, *Bayonets of the Republic,"* 3.

15. While the French Army generally accomplished its mission, it was not uniformly successful. For example, Lynn explains that the failure to conduct training during the winter of 1792–93 caused the reverses in the spring of 1793. Lynn, *Bayonets of the Republic,* 218–19, 10, 15.

16. Lynn, *Bayonets of the Republic,* Fig. 1, 23, 21, 39. Thirty years later, Ilya Berkovich's recent study of common soldiers in Old-Regime Europe "owes much" to Lynn's model. Berkovich, *Motivation in War,* 6, 9–10.

17. Lynn, *Bayonets of the Republic,* Fig. 1, 23.

18. For example, Linderman, *Embattled Courage,* 2; Hess, *Union Soldier in Battle,* ix; McPherson, *For Cause and Comrades,* 12. Carla Reardon did discuss several of the elements of the military system in 1998 in an article on Spotsylvania, but the discussion was not particularly focused. However, her conclusion that "in terms of military effectiveness, the Confederacy had done the better job of employing its fighting power [at Spotsylvania]" answered a question that Civil War historians should ask more frequently. Reardon, "A Hard Road to Travel," 197. Richard Sommers's reference to "combat effectiveness" is a rare example to the contrary. "Able leadership, freshness, numerical strength all contributed to [Mott's] division's impressive combat effectiveness." Sommers, *Richmond Redeemed,* 1st ed., 362. See also Hess, *Tactics,* xxi, 241.

19. Lynn, *Bayonets of the Republic,* 23–24; Coss, *All for the King's Shilling,* 14; Berkovich, *Motivation in War,* 9–10.

20. Lynn, *Bayonets of the Republic,* Fig. 1, 22, 35–36; McPherson, *For Cause and Comrades,* 12–13.

21. The state and local bounties, which were the largest component of the bounty package, were generally paid in full in advance. The $300 federal bounty was paid $60 in advance with the remainder paid in installments over three years.

22. McPherson, *For Cause and Comrades,* 174.

23. Lynn cautions that "A decline in [the] intensity . . . [of initial motivation] does not necessarily entail a major drop in sustaining or combat motivation. . . . In the camp and on the battlefield motivation derives from a set of factors different from those that first brought the soldier into the service." Lynn, *Bayonets of the Republic,* 178. But see McPherson, *For Cause and Comrades,* 12–13.

24. Lynn, *Bayonets of the Republic,* 32. Coercion would also remain as a motivating force in the second and third phases. Even if a man volunteered, once he was in the army he could not leave until his term of service expired or he was otherwise discharged and while he was in the service there were consequences for disobeying orders.

25. McPherson, *For Cause and Comrade,* 85; Lynn, *Bayonets of the Republic,* 30. See also Coss, *All for the King's Shilling,* 4. As an example, Charles Rugg of the Fifty-Seventh Massachusetts wrote his parents that his hometown friends "Billie" and "Alfred" and he "stick together like Brothers." Charles Rugg to parents, Apr. 20, 1864, Pension File, NARA. Hiram Whiting of the Fifty-Sixth Massachusetts provided an example of primary group cohesion that initially failed in a letter to his father explaining his transfer between companies: "[Company D] seems More Like home to me Now than When I was in F Company for The boys All seem to like me first rate here." Hiram Whiting to father, Apr. 18, 1864, Pension File, NARA.

26. Guilmartin, "Foreword," in Coss, *All for the King's Shilling,* xx; Reardon, "A Hard Road to Travel," 174; Coss, *All for the King's Shilling,* 3; Lynn, *Bayonets of the Republic,* 34, 168–69; Hess, *Tactics,* 241.

27. Author's conversation with Kenneth G. Miller, brigadier general, United States Air Force (Ret.) and Ben Koerselman, colonel, United States Army (Ret.), Oct. 4, 2022.

28. The guiding principle comes from Galileo: "Measure what is measurable, and make measurable what is not so." See Westphal and Guffey, "Measures of Effectiveness in Army Doctrine," https://www.benning.army.mil/armor/earmor/content/issues/2014.

29. The federal, state, and local bounties and the veteran furlough provided remunerative motivation, but they were constants. Differences in reenlistment rates are likely explained by differences in unit cohesion.

30. See Dunkelman, *Esprit de Corps,* 19–20, 30. McPherson notes that "Identification with regiment, state, country, and flag is related to but not precisely the same as . . . 'primary group cohesion.'" McPherson, *For Cause and Comrades,* 85. This study treats the former as evidencing the latter.

31. Wiley, *Billy Yank,* 50.

32. Lynn, *Bayonets of the Republic,* 166–67, 228, 235; Coss, *All for the King's Shilling,* 206–7; Mansoor, *GI Offensive in Europe,* 251, 254–55; van Creveld, *Fighting Power,* 74–75.

33. Late-war new regiments arriving in the field generally did not receive replacements, although the Seventeenth Vermont is an exception. For late-war new regiments arriving with fewer than ten companies, the remaining companies generally arrived within several months. The regiment would have to integrate these new companies into the regiment, but not new men into the original companies.

34. Dunkelman, *Esprit de Corps,* 69. McPherson, *For Cause and Comrades,* 116. McPherson cites an April 2, 1863, letter from William E. Dunn of the Eighty-Fifth New

York. McPherson, *For Cause and Comrades,* 217n36. Because the letter is dated April 1863, the "money soldiers" that Dunn was referring to were presumably recruits from 1862, not late-war replacements. Dunn had enlisted in 1861 and reenlisted on January 1, 1864. Unit Roster, Eighty-Fifth New York Volunteers, NYSMM. He presumably received a substantial bounty when he reenlisted and he might have had a different view of "money soldiers" in 1864 as a result.

35. Uhler, *Camps and Campaigns of the 93rd Regiment Penna.* vols., 23, 22, 32; Norton, *Army Letters 1861–1865,* 165. See also Bosbyshell, *48th in the War,* 142, 144–45; Judson, *History of the Eighty-Third Regiment of Pennsylvania Volunteers,* 93 ("The Eighty-third had . . . received a number of recruits during the winter, and when the spring campaign opened we started with the regiment nearly full.")

36. Simon Shuman to George H. Mowery, Nov. 1, 1863, https://sparedshared9.wordpress.com/2015/10/29/1862-simon-shuman; Macneal, *Centre County Regiment,* 95; Fox, *Regimental Losses,* 302; Bates, *History of Pennsylvania Volunteers,* 4:579. See also Dunkelman, *Esprit de Corps,* 70–71.

37. Lynn, *Bayonets of the Republic,* Fig 1, 40, 20, 285. Even in the context of an army, Lynn noted that "Some critics might accuse me of using a heavy theoretical sledgehammer to swat a rather puny methodological fly," but Lynn believed that "the results justify the effort." Lynn, *Bayonets of the Republic,* 21. Hess, *Tactics,* 229, 233.

38. van Creveld, *Fighting Power,* 1, 4, 163, 170, 174.

39. Millett, Murray, and Watman, "Effectiveness of Military Organizations," 1:2; Reardon, "A Hard Road to Travel," 171. Reardon identifies the missions of Lee's forces and Grant's forces but does not explicitly discuss the extent that Lee and Grant successfully achieved their respective missions. Defending Richmond, the Confederate capital, was Lee's primary mission. He obviously accomplished that mission, but whether he also accomplished his secondary mission of maintaining an adequate fighting force is less clear. Grant did not accomplish his mission of destroying the Army of Northern Virginia but arguably made valuable progress toward rendering it incapable of offensive operations and ultimately unable to defend itself.

40. Congressional Research Service, *Fundamentals of Military Readiness,* 1, 3.

41. I have also drawn on my army training as an intelligence analyst, Military Occupational Specialty 96B20 in 1971.

42. Lynn explained that "Morale, defined in broad terms, is one basis of motivation, and small group cohesion is another. A complex and only partially understood interaction between the two, modified by interest, results in motivation." Lynn, *Bayonets of the Republic,* 26. Reardon similarly observed that "Good morale reflects solid bonds of unit cohesion." Reardon, "A Hard Road to Travel," 172. Compartmentalizing closely related concepts incurs the problem that soldiers did not necessarily think in compartmentalized terms when they wrote their letters. Accordingly, this project treats morale and cohesion together.

Lynn followed S. L. A. Marshall's definition of morale as "the whole complex of an army's thought" and divided "the climate of opinion within an army" into five categories: "(1) basic societal and group attitudes, (2) opinions and codes from army indoctrination, (3) wartime opinions, (4) reactions to service conditions, and (5) esprit de corps." Lynn defined esprit de corps "in its fundamental form [as] identification of the individual soldier with his military unit, most commonly on the regimental to the corps level." Lynn, *Bayonets of the Republic,* 26, 25, 29–30, 172. This project uses "morale" to encompass reactions to service conditions and esprit de corps and to a lesser degree wartime opinion. Allan R. Millet, Williamson Murray, and Kenneth H. Watman have observed that "There is a growing sense based on the experience of the Vietnam war, the Falklands campaign, and the wars in the Middle East that unit cohesion may be the key to tactical effectiveness." Millett, Murray, and Watman, "Effectiveness of Military Organizations," 27. See also Guilmartin, "Foreword" in Coss, *All for the King's Shilling*, xx.

Peter Mansoor observed that the American experience in World War II counsels that "the endurance of a military force—its ability to sustain and regenerate combat power—is an integral component of combat effectiveness." Mansoor, *GI Offensive in Europe*, 266. Similarly, Martin van Creveld included "resilience" along with "morale, elan [and] unit cohesion" in his discussion of the effectiveness of the German Army during World War II. van Creveld, *Fighting Power*, 163. See also Reardon, "A Hard Road to Travel," 195. Resilience and endurance fall under motivation for this project. See also Dunkelman, *Esprit de Corps*, 5, 6–7, 8, 226.

43. van Creveld, *Fighting Power*, 127, 168; Hayward, "Measurement of Combat Effectiveness," 317; Reardon, "A Hard Road to Travel," 171; Dunkelman, *Esprit de Corps*, 205.

44. Martin van Creveld writes that "Training is undoubtedly of the highest importance for the production of fighting power." van Creveld, *Fighting Power*, 71. Training is also an important part of Lynn's analysis. Lynn, *Bayonets of the Republic*, 9, 10, 15, Fig. 1, 218–19, 239–40. Training is a central element in "build[ing] ready forces" in Department of Defense doctrine. Congressional Research Service, *The Fundamentals of Military Readiness*, 9–10. See also Griffith, "What Do the Soldiers Say?" 369. Thomas E. Hanson illustrated the importance of training in his "regimental case study" of the Twenty-Seventh Infantry Regimental Combat Team at the beginning of the Korean War. Hanson, "The Eighth Army's Combat Readiness before Korea," 167–84. For an extensive discussion of training during the Civil War, see Hess, *Civil War Infantry Tactics*, 61–80. Coss concluded that "the willingness to submit to a system of rules and regulations (both formal and informal) . . . helped turn individual soldiers into competent fighting teams." Coss, *All for the King's Shilling*, 15.

45. In Lynn's model, experience encompasses: "(1) the backlog of conception and habit carried by the men who teach and lead, i.e. the experience of the commanders; (2) the concurrent feedback from success or failure of tactics in the field; and (3) the experience that seasons troops, turning unsteady recruits into reliable veterans." Lynn, *Bayonets of the Republic*, 37. For this project, experience means the experience that seasons troops. The experience of the commanders is covered here under leadership.

46. The US Department of Defense utilizes "the ratio of unit personnel available for deployment in comparison to the total number of personnel the unit is authorized to have" as one of the principal metrics for evaluating personnel readiness. Congressional Research Service, *Fundamentals of Military Readiness*, 44. As Lynn succinctly stated, "Numbers must be considered." Because Lynn defined combat effectiveness in terms of quality, he added another step to factor in the quantitative factor of force size. "Tactical combat strength" is the "product of relative combat effectiveness multiplied by total force size." Lynn, *Bayonets of the Republic*, 38–39, 226.

47. Reardon, "A Hard Road to Travel," 181; Congressional Research Service, *Fundamentals of Readiness*, Fig. 7, 39. Lynn treats weapons as part of the tactical system and logistics as part of the administrative system. Lynn's model focuses on the technology of weapons. Lynn, *Bayonets of the Republic*, Fig. 1, 37. For a Union regiment, weapons were more a supply issue than a technology issue. Lynn notes that logistics "can have a great effect on morale, because they put food, weapons, and ammunition into the soldier's hands." Lynn, *Bayonets of the Republic*, Fig. 1, 37.

48. At the end of the eighteenth century and the beginning of the nineteenth, the composition of the national armies in Europe began following more closely the socioeconomic demographics of their countries. Lynn concluded that "the explanation of French victory in the North lies in the citizen-soldiers who made up the Armee du Nord." Lynn, *Bayonets of the Republic*, 3. Similarly, Edward Coss has demonstrated that British soldiers

were not the "scum of the earth" as described by the Duke of Wellington. They came from the working class, "mostly manual laborers but also weavers, tailors, shoemakers, tinsmiths, and men of various other trades." Coss, *All for the King's Shilling,* 3, 6. With respect to national cultures, Martin van Creveld has observed that "In Germany, beginning at the Wars of Unification, the army was highly regarded by most of the people and was considered the pride of the nation. Esteem was extended more or less automatically to any member of the army." van Creveld, *Fighting Power,* 18. Jim Webb has described the impact of "the two great defining characteristics of the Scots-Irish culture—a loyalty to strong leaders and an immediate fierceness when invaded from the outside" on the Confederate army. Webb, *Born Fighting,* 231–32. This project has not pursued the national culture dimension of effectiveness because of the inability to isolate national groups for the late-war new regiments.

49. Kreidberg and Henry, *History of Military Mobilization,* 119; Hess, *Tactics,* 61, 69; author's conversation with Kenneth G. Miller, brigadier general, United States Air Force (Ret.) and Ben Koerselman, colonel, United States Army (Ret.), Oct. 4, 2022.

7. The Overland Campaign

1. McPherson, *Battle Cry of Freedom,* 606. McPherson expressly excluded from his "three-quarters of a million new men" count the one hundred fifty thousand-plus reenlisting veterans who received bounties. McPherson, *Battle Cry of Freedom,* 606n28. While there is no way of knowing the percentage of veterans who were motivated to reenlist by the bounties, it presumably was not zero. Thus, the inducement of bounties should be given at least some credit for the number of reenlisting veterans. The conditional draft would not have had an impact because the veterans from 1861 had served more than two years in the army and therefore would not have been subject to the draft had they returned to civilian life. See OR III:4, 129, Section 6.

At the same time, a not insignificant number of the later-enlisting volunteers were returning veterans from 1861 who had been discharged from the army due to expiration of their term of service or other reason. However, these returning veterans from 1861 and 1862 do not dilute the contributions of the late-war replacements because when they returned to the army in 1864 and 1865, they were no longer "pre-bounty." See McPherson, *Battle Cry of Freedom,* 606.

2. Compiled from OR 36:1, 106–16 and Fox, *Regimental Losses,* passim.

3. Greene, *A Campaign of Giants,* 13.

4. OR 40:1, 525.

5. Extracts from April 1864 Inspection Report, Second Corps, transmitted June 11, 1864, NARA, RG 159, Entry 3, 67; OR 36:1, 320; OR 36:1, 408. See also Catton, *A Stillness at Appomattox,* 30; Bates, *History of Pennsylvania Volunteers,* 2:495 (Sixty-Third Pennsylvania). However, the Irish Brigade was subsequently sharply criticized by its division commander for its performance at Deep Bottom in August 1864. OR 42:1, 248.

6. Compiled from HIBO Database, unit rosters, latewarunionsoldiers.com.

7. In reviewing the *OR* and the works of A. Wilson Greene, Edwin C. Bearss, Gordon C. Rhea, and William F. Fox, I looked for incidents that were significant enough to draw praise—for example, taking works under heavy fire—or criticism, for example, breaking without cause. This anecdotal approach was not an effort to compile a comprehensive assessment of the unit's performance but rather to get a directional sense.

8. OR 36:1, 106–14. The Ninth Corps was not formally assigned to the Army of the Potomac until May 24, 1864. Before that it operated under Grant's direct orders. OR 36:1, 113

note*. The Sixtieth Ohio (reorganized) was not literally a high-number regiment but was formed in the spring of 1864. The original Sixtieth Ohio was organized in February 1862 and had been mustered out in November 1862. Dyer, *Compendium of the War of the Rebellion*, 3:1524–25. The 188th Pennsylvania Volunteers was not a true high-number regiment because it was organized in April 1864 "from the surplus members of the Third Pennsylvania Heavy Artillery," which had been organized in 1862. (Moreover, it was part of the Army of the James.) Fox, *Regimental Losses*, 306, 484, 488. The 182nd New York, which joined the Second Corps on May 17, 1864, also was not a true high-number regiment. The unit started out in August 1862 as the Sixty-Ninth Regiment, National Guard Artillery (also referred to as First Regiment, Corcoran Irish Legion). It was mustered into United States service on November 17, 1862. The War Department gave it the designation "182d Regiment N. Y. Volunteers" on March 21, 1864. Phisterer, *New York in the War of the Rebellion*, 5:4038.

9. OR 36:3, 135. On April 8, 1864, Fry had notified the acting assistant provost marshal generals around the North that Grant had directed that "active measures be taken to get into the field all recruits, new organizations, and all old troops that can be spared. . . . Execute this order as soon as possible." OR III: 4:1, 221. See also Miller, *States at War*, 1:504.

10. Calculated from OR 40:2, 47–48. Ten thousand men (20 percent) were late-war replacements from the rendezvous of distribution. Late-war new regiments provided just under five thousand troops (9 percent). OR 40:2, 47–48; Dyer, *Compendium of the War of the Rebellion*, 3:1017, 1018, 1235, 1259, 1348–49, 1442, 1596, 1601–2, 1610, 1620. See also Lerwill, *Personnel Replacement System*, 120.

11. OR 40:2, 47.

12. OR 40:2, 48. After the beginning of the Overland Campaign, Meade wrote to his command that "While we mourn the loss of so many gallant comrades, let us remember the enemy must have suffered equal, if not greater losses. We shall soon receive re-enforcements which he cannot expect." OR 36:1, 197. On August 23, 1864, Lee wrote the Confederate secretary of war that "Unless some measure can be devised to replace our losses, the consequences may be disastrous. Without some increase of strength, I can not see how we are to escape the natural military consequences of the enemy's numerical superiority." OR 42:2, 1199.

13. Reardon, "A Hard Road to Travel," 176n18.

14. OR 36:1, 937; Fox, *Regimental Losses*, 153; Adjutant and Inspector General of Vermont, *Report from October 1, 1863 to October 1, 1864*. 198–200; Benedict, *Vermont in the Civil War*, 2:496, 497, 499; *Union Army*, 1:122; letter, May 19, 1864, in Zeller, "The Civil War Letters of Pvt. Mark B. Slayton"; Charles Cummings to Wife, June 6, 1864, Vermont Historical Society, https://vermonthistory.org.

15. Compiled from HIBO Database, Seventeenth Vermont, latewarunionsoldiers.org.

16. Benedict, *Vermont in the Civil War*, 2:497–98; *Union Army*, 1:122. Colonel Randall could not take the field until the tenth company was mustered in in October.

17. Chap. 3, note 68; HIBO Database, Seventeenth Vermont, Occupations, latewarunionsoldiers.org.

18. The percentages were close for "laborer" (1860 Census—8.6 percent/Seventeenth Vermont—9.0 percent), "carpenter" (2.9 percent/2.1 percent), "blacksmith" (1.3 percent/1.5 percent), "shoemaker" (1.3 percent/1.5 percent) and "painter" (.6 percent/.8 percent). Calculated from Kennedy, *Population of the United States in 1860*, 499; HIBO Database, Seventeenth Vermont, Occupations, latewarunionsoldiers.org.

19. HIBO Database, Seventeenth Vermont, latewarunionsoldiers.org; Wiley, *Billy Yank*, 307. In the summer of 1864, the Seventeenth Vermont received 164 substitutes, more than 90 percent of whom were foreign-born. For the Seventeenth Vermont overall,

only two-thirds (67 percent) were native-born. HIBO Database, Seventeenth Vermont, latewarunionsoldiers.org.

20. Charles Cummings to Wife, Mar. 17, 1864, and Apr. 30, 1864, Vermont Historical Society, https://vermonthistory.org; *Vermont Adjutant and Inspector General, Report from October 1, 1863 to October 1, 1864,* 198.

21. Benedict, *Vermont in the Civil War,* 2:499, 507; Fox, *Regimental Losses,* 153; OR 36:1, 132, 148, 162, 176; *Union Army,* 1:122.

22. Anderson, *Fifty-Seventh Regiment of Massachusetts Volunteers,* 15.

23. *Union Army,* 1:202; Fox, *Regimental Losses,* 175; OR 36:1, 147, 161.

24. Wilkenson, *Mother, May You Never See the Sights I Have Seen,* xii; Fox, *Regimental Losses,* 175.

25. Provost Marshal General Circular dated June 29, 1863, *Berkshire County Eagle* (Pittsfield, MA), July 23, 1863, 3; Commonwealth of Massachusetts, Special Order No. 481, Aug. 17, 1863; *Berkshire County Eagle,* Aug. 20, 1863, 3; Circular, Oct. 28, 1863, Headquarters, Fifty-Sixth Massachusetts, Regimental Letter and Order Book, Fifty-Sixth Massachusetts Regimental Books, 3:13, RG 94, NARA.

26. OR III:3, 415; *Daily Evening News* (Fall River, MA), Dec. 31, 1863, 1; Fox, *Regimental Losses,* 174; Compiled from HIBO Database. The specific percentages of veteran recruits were: Fifty-Sixth Massachusetts (24.9 percent), Fifty-Seventh Massachusetts (21.1 percent), Fifty-Eighth Massachusetts (24.2 percent), and Fifty-Ninth Massachusetts (24.4 percent).

27. Wilkenson, *Mother, May You Never See the Sights I Have Seen,* 631, 405–623, 12; Anderson, *Fifty-Seventh Regiment of Massachusetts Volunteers,* 3.

28. Wilkenson, *Mother, May You Never See the Sights I Have Seen,* 630.

29. Compiled from HIBO Database, Fifty-Seventh Massachusetts, latewarunionsoldiers.org; Wiley, *Billy Yank,* 304; Kennedy, *Population of the United States in 1860,* 227–29. The percentage for "mariner" includes "seaman" and "sailor." The percentage for "shoemaker" includes "bootmaker."

30. Bowen, *Massachusetts in the War, 1861–1865,* 693; Weld, *War Diary and Letters,* 287–88; OR 36:1, 131; James Carlyle to Mother, May 17, 1864, Pension File, NARA; John Osborn to Father & Mother, Brother & Sister, May 18, 1864, and Declaration of Thomas Osborn, July 20, 1880, both Pension File, NA.

31. Fox, *Regimental Losses,* 175.

32. Bowen, *Massachusetts in the War,* 694; Fox, *Regimental Losses,* 174; OR 36:1, 131, 147, 161, 175.

33. Fox, *Regimental Losses,* 174; Albert Cook to Father, Mar. 14, 1864, and [Apr. 1864?], Pension File NARA; HIBO Database, latewarunionsoldiers.org.

34. Compiled from HIBO Database, Fifty-Sixth Massachusetts, Occupations, latewarunionsoldiers.org; Wiley, *Billy Yank,* 304; Kennedy, *Population of the United States in 1860.* "Mariner" includes "seaman" and "sailor."

35. Bowen, *Massachusetts in the War,* 711; OR 36:1, 131, 147, 161, 175; OR 36:2, 383.

36. Compiled from HIBO Database, Fifty-Ninth Massachusetts, Occupations, latewarunionsoldiers.org; Wiley, *Billy Yank,* 304; Kennedy, *Population of the United States in 1860,* 227–29. "Shoemaker" includes "bootmaker."

37. OR 36:2, 585; Rhea, *Battles for Spotsylvania Court House and the Road to Yellow Tavern,* 106; Birch, *The 50th Pennsylvania's Civil War Odyssey,* 272–79, 289; OR 36:1, 969.

38. *Philadelphia Daily Evening Bulletin,* Feb. 2, 1864, 4; *Philadelphia Age,* Jan. 26, 1864, 2; Fox, *Regimental Losses,* 269; HIBO Database, Fiftieth Pennsylvania, latewarunionsoldiers.org.

39. Fox, *Regimental Losses,* 292; Bates, *History of Pennsylvania Volunteers,* 3:1228–33; HIBO Database; OR 36:1, 398–99. Mulholland, *Story of the 116th Regiment, Pennsylvania Volunteers,* 176–78. The 116th Pennsylvania is noteworthy because the vast majority of its replacements came as six new companies instead of infill for existing companies. They were the equivalent of a late-war new regiment, with their own company officers.

40. Rhea, *Battle of the Wilderness,* 162–63.

41. OR 36:1, 637.

42. Fox, *Regimental Losses,* 276, 300; OR 36:1, 122, 348.

43. Rhea, *Battle of the Wilderness,* 154–55.

44. Letter from Michael Kennedy, May 14, 1864, Pension File, NARA. See also Pvt. John McGee to Mother, June 20, 1864 ("As soon as we got here we were put into a fight and we have been marching and fighting ever since."), Pension File, NARA.

45. Houston, *Thirty-Second Maine,* 78.

46. Houston, *Thirty-Second Maine,* 33–35. Thirty-some veterans of the nine-month Twenty-Seventh Maine did enlist in Thirty-Second Maine. Another twenty-some came from the Twenty-Third Maine. Compiled from "Complete Roster," Houston, *Thirty-Second Maine,* 459–534.

47. Houston, *Thirty-Second Maine,* 459–534. Houston stated in the text that 140 men out of the 1,010 men in the regiment had prior service (13.9 percent). 35–36. My methodology, which uses the "Additional Services" section of the Civil War Pension Index cards on Fold3.com results in 18.2 percent. My methodology is explained in Methodology— Prior Service, latewarunionsoldiers.org.

48. Houston, *Thirty-Second Maine,* 34–36, 43–44, 46–47, 459–534. Houston, who added a year and a half to his age to get to eighteen, suspected he was one of many who lied about their age.

49. Letters from Michael Kennedy, Apr. 3, 1864; Apr. [?], 1864; May 20, 1864; June 27, 1864; but see May 20, 1864. Henry Sproul did write that an "Albert Moadly," whom I have been unable to identify, did say "he wood not enlist again for all the money thir is in the State of Maine." Letter, July 12, 1864, Pension File, NARA; Henry Sproul to Mother, May 27, 1864, Pension File, NARA.

50. OR 33, 926, 1045; Houston, *Thirty-Second Maine,* 56, 138, 184; Whitman and True, *Maine in the War for the Union,* 583; Dyer, *Compendium of the War of the Rebellion,* 3:1228; OR 36:3, 665, 738; *Union Army,* 1:60.

51. Houston, *Thirty-Second Maine,* 39–40, 82.

52. OR 36:1, 385, 965; OR 51:1:2, 1161; Rhea, *Battles for Spotsylvania Court House and the Road to Yellow Tavern,* 80.

53. OR 36:1, 385, 386, 137, 153, 166, 370–71, 381; Bates, *History of Pennsylvania Volunteers.* 5, 128–29.

54. OR 33, 784.

55. Bates, *History of Pennsylvania Volunteers,* 5:128–29, 131.

56. Rhea, *The Battles for Spotsylvania Court House and the Road to Yellow Tavern,* 56; Judson, *History of the Eighty-Third Regiment Pennsylvania,* 96 (emphasis in original).

57. OR 36:2, 585; OR 36:1, 962, 943, 968; OR 51:1, 1161. The Sixtieth Ohio also "rendered valuable service" on June 1 (OR 36:1, 971; Rhea, *Cold Harbor,* 257) and rendered important service on June 17 in supporting Ledlie's attack (OR 40:1, 533). However, the Sixtieth Ohio's performance during the initial phase of the battle on May 9 was not as creditable as its commanders reported. The Sixtieth Ohio was positioned somewhat in advance of Christ's brigade's line and proved to be the weak point the Confederates were looking for. Rhea recounts that the Confederates "scattered [the Sixtieth Ohio] in some confusion," but did note that the Sixtieth Ohio "had been recruited less than three weeks

before and had never faced fire. This was the first day that many of its troops carried rifles." Rhea, *Spotsylvania*, 105.

58. Dyer, *Compendium of the Civil War*, 3:1525.

59. OR 36:1, 965; OR 51:1:2, 1161.

60. OR 36:1, 408–14, 428.; Rhea, *Battles for Spotsylvania Court House and the Road to Yellow Tavern*, 111, 237–38; Rhea, *To the North Ana River*, 237; MacNeal, "'Centre County Regiment,'" 118; Fox, *Regimental Losses*, 302; Bates, *History of Pennsylvania Volunteers*, 4:579.

61. Rhea, *Spotsylvania*, 163. Ruane, "An Illiterate Wife 'Wrote' Poignant Letters. . . ," https://www.washingtonpost.com/history/2018/11/09/an-illiterate-wife.

62. Fox, *Regimental Losses*, 268; Westbrook, *History of the 49th Pennsylvania Volunteers*, 4, 5, 137; HIBO Database, Forty-Ninth Pennsylvania, latewarunionsoldiers.org; Bates, *History of Pennsylvania Volunteers*, 1:1241.

63. Muster Rolls, Forty-Ninth Pennsylvania, RG 94, Boxes 4298, 4299, 4300, NARA.

64. Westbrook, *History of the 49th Pennsylvania Volunteers*, 180, 5, 67, 72, 76, 137, 178; Bates, *History of Pennsylvania Volunteers*, 1:1241. Some of the men in the Forty-Fifth Pennsylvania also played some football. William B. Glenn to Sister, Mar. 31, 1864, https://sparedandshared19.wordpress.com/2019/08/19/1864-william-b-glenn.

65. Westbrook, *History of the 49th Pennsylvania Volunteers*, 193, 76; Rhea, *Spotsylvania*, 163.

66. OR 36:1, 424–25.

67. Fox, *Regimental Losses*, 271; OR 36:1, 137, 424–25.

68. *North Branch Democrat* (Tunkhannock, PA), Jan. 13, 1864, 3; HIBO Database, Fifty-Third Pennsylvania, latewarunionsoldiers.org.

69. Fox, *Regimental Losses*, 400; OR 36:1, 154, 167; OR 36:2, 828, 911; OR 36:3, 665, 738; Dyer, *Compendium of the War of the Rebellion*, 3:1687; Aubery, *Thirty-Sixth Wisconsin Volunteer Infantry*, 61, 293.

70. OR 36:2, 828; Fox, *Regimental Losses*, 400; Aubery, *Thirty-Sixth Wisconsin Volunteer Infantry*, 293–323.; J. B. Maur to Mrs. Taylor, Apr. 9, 1864, in Alderson and Alderson, *Letters Home to Sarah*, 13–14; Aubery, *Thirty-Sixth Wisconsin Volunteer Infantry*, 30; Jacob Dubois to [?], May 8, 1864, Pension File, NARA; Guy Taylor to Wife, May 5, 1864, and May 7, 1864, in Alderson and Alderson, *Letters Home to Sarah*, 14–16. Some battalion drill had occurred. Letter from [?] to Sister, Apr. 22, 1864, Pension File, NARA. The Thirty-Sixth Wisconsin may have had only 765 men. OR 361, 434. Lt. James Aubery took a more favorable view of the officers' experience. Aubery, *Thirty-Sixth Wisconsin Volunteer Infantry*, 27.

71. OR 36:1, 483; Fox, *Regimental Losses*, 273; *North Branch Democrat* (Tunkhannock, PA), Jan. 13, 1864, 3; Bates, *History of Pennsylvania Volunteers*, 2:246, 252; Fox, *Regimental Losses*, 273; HIBO Database, Fifty-Seventh Pennsylvania, latewarunionsoldiers.org; OR 36:1, 483.

72. Bates, *History of Pennsylvania Volunteers*, 2:1257; Rhea, *To the North Ana*, 317; OR 36:1, 585; Judson, *History of the 83rd Pennsylvania Volunteers*, 100.

73. Fox, *Regimental Losses*, 176; OR 36:1, 175; Bowen, *Massachusetts in the War*, 707–8.

74. HIBO Database, Fifty-Eighth Massachusetts, Occupations, latewarunionsoldiers. org; Kennedy, *Population of the United States in 1860*, 227–29. "Mariner" includes "seaman" and "sailor." "Shoemaker" includes "bootmaker."

75. McPherson, *For Cause and Comrades*, viii. The average age for the Union army was 25.8, compared to 26.3 for the Fifty-Eighth Massachusetts.

76. Bowen, *Massachusetts in the War*, 708; Regimental Books, Fifty-Eighth Massachusetts, NARA; *Union Army*, 1:203.

77. Fox, *Regimental Losses*, 176; OR 36:1, 131; OR 36:2, 324, 364; F. E. C., *History of the 58th Regt. Massachusetts*, 4–6.

78. Fox, *Regimental Losses,* 136; *Union Army,* 1:59. General Griffin said after Bethesda Church that "It also gives me great pleasure to add my evidence to the well-known fact that the Thirty-first Maine has made for itself a most brilliant record and won for its officers and men imperishable renown." Whitman and True, *Maine in the War for the Union,* 578–79.

79. Fox, *Regimental Losses,* 136; Dyer, *Compendium of the War of the Rebellion,* 3:1228; OR 36:1, 132, 176, 148.

80. Compiled from Whitman and True, *Maine in the War for the Union,* 577–78; Ancestry.com; Fold3.com.

81. Bates, *History of Pennsylvania Volunteers,* 5:151; OR 36:3, 665–66; OR 36:1, 167 (110 casualties at Cold Harbor).

82. Bates, *History of Pennsylvania Volunteers,* 5:151.

83. Rhea, *Cold Harbor,* 370–71.

84. Fox, *Regimental Losses,* 270.

85. Fox, *Regimental Losses,* 270; Bates, *History of Pennsylvania Volunteers,* 2:10; HIBO Database, Fifty-First Pennsylvania, latewarunionsoldiers.org.

86. Rhea, *Cold Harbor,* 236.

87. Bates, *Pennsylvania Volunteers,* 2:1207; HIBO Database, Eighty-Second Pennsylvania, latewarunionsoldiers.org; OR 36:3, 520.

88. Rhea, *Cold Harbor,* 149; Hess, *Trench Warfare under Grant & Lee,* 191–92; OR 36:3, 685–86; Bosbyshell, *48th in the War,* 155–56.

89. *Philadelphia Inquirer,* Jan. 20, 1864, 8; Fox, *Regimental Losses,* 267.

90. OR 36:1, 124, 142, 157, 171; Rhea, *Battle of the Wilderness* (no reference); Rhea, *Battles for Spotsylvania Court House and the Road to Yellow Tavern,* 288; Rhea, *To the North Ana,* 71; Rhea, *Cold Harbor* (no reference); Bearss, *Eastern Front Battles,* 15; letter from "Veteran," June 8, 1864, *Agitator* (Wellsborough, PA), June 29, 1864, 1; letters from Samuel Haynes, June 5, 1864, and June 6, 1864, in Albert, *History of the Forty-Fifth Regiment Pennsylvania,* 259. The performance of the Eleventh Pennsylvania, which incurred three hundred casualties; the Ninety-Third Pennsylvania; the Ninety-Fifth Pennsylvania, which suffered 175 casualties; and the One Hundredth Pennsylvania, which incurred over two hundred fifty casualties also did not stand out.

91. For the Union army overall, Lerwill minimized the impact of the late-war replacements prior to August 1864. Lerwill, *Personnel Replacement System,* 105. Gordon Rhea observed a "prevailing pattern" that "new regiments lost heavily while veteran regiments, knowledgeable of risks entailed in attacking entrenched positions, generally took only light casualties." Rhea, *Cold Harbor,* 361. By "new" regiments, he was not necessarily referring to the late-war new regiments, which usually had 10–20 percent veterans in their enlisted ranks led by experienced officers. Rhea seemed to focus primarily on the heavy artillery regiments converted to infantry, which had been organized in 1861 and 1862. He did give the Fifth New Hampshire as an example of an old regiment with a large number of late-war replacements that incurred heavy casualties.

8. *The Petersburg Campaign during 1864*

1. Rutan, *179th New York Volunteer Infantry,* 57–58.

2. Michael Kennedy to Father, June 27, 1864, Pension File, NARA.

3. Howe, *Petersburg Campaign.*

4. OR 40:1, 220, 359; Myers, *We Might as Well Die Here,* 207–12; Bearss, *Eastern Front Battles,* 86–88.

5. OR 40:1, 404, 222.

6. OR 40:1, 222, 404. The Sixty-Third Pennsylvania was mustered out on September 9, 1864, upon the expiration of its three-year term, and the remaining reenlisted men and replacements—only sixty-seven men—were transferred to the Ninety-Ninth Pennsylvania. Fox, *Regimental Losses*, 276; Bearss, *Western Front Battles*, 497.

7. OR 40:1, 220.

8. OR 40:1, 363.

9. Bates, *History of Pennsylvania Volunteers*, 5:151.

10. Bearss, *Eastern Front Battles*, 92; OR 40:1, 530.

11. OR 40:1, 569; Charles Cummings to Wife, June 18, 1864, Vermont Historical Society, https://vermonthistory.org.

12. Fox, *Regimental Losses*, 176; OR 40:1, 530–31; Greene, *Campaign of Giants*, 150.

13. Eden, *Sword and the Gun*, 19–20, 28; Fox, *Regimental Losses*, 401.

14. Fox, *Regimental Losses*, 401; Dyer, *Compendium of the War of the Rebellion*, 3:1687; OR 36:3, 724, 739, 666; Eden, *Sword and the Gun*, 8, 16–17. The other two companies apparently arrived in the field sometime during July. Compare OR 40:2, 550 (Thirty-Seventh commanded by a captain) with OR 40:3, 734 (commanded by a colonel).

15. Eden, *Sword and the Gun*, passim; Ancestry.com, Civil War Collection. Colonel Harriman, Lieutenant Colonel Doolittle, and Major Kershaw all had previously served, but two of them only as captains and the third as a first lieutenant. Only one of the company commanders had previously served as a captain. At least two had not previously served at all. Most of the lieutenants had previously served, but only one as an officer.

16. OR 40:1, 573; Birch, *50th Pennsylvania's Civil War Odyssey*, 302.

17. OR 40:1, 582; Bates, *History of Pennsylvania Volunteers*, 1:12.

18. OR 40:1, 230; Sixtieth Ohio Volunteer Infantry, Rootsweb, C. C. Caruthers, Co. G.

19. Fox, *Regimental Losses*, 175; William Larzelare Diary, June 17, 1864 (copy in author's collection); Franklin B. Doty to Helen Finch, June 18, 1864, https://sparedshared18.wordpress.com/2018/12/14/1864-franklin-benjamin; Wilkenson, *Mother, May You Never See the Sights I Have Seen*, 185.

20. Greene, *Campaign of Giants*, 164–65; OR 40:1, 533.

21. Rutan, *179th New York Volunteer Infantry*, 49–50, 92, 132–33; OR 36:3, 666, 724, 739.

22. Phisterer, *New York in the War of the Rebellion*, 3:1994, 5:4032–38; Rutan, *179th New York Volunteer Infantry*, 28.

23. Rutan, *179th New York Volunteer Infantry*, 12–13. The Twenty-Third New York and the Thirty-First New York were two-year regiments from 1861 that had been mustered out in mid-1863. Phisterer, *New York in the War of the Rebellion*, 3:1994, 2089.

24. Rutan, *179th New York Volunteer Infantry*, 62–65.

25. OR 40:1, 533.

26. Dyer, *Compendium of the War of the Rebellion*, 3:1688; OR 36:3, 509, 733, 739; Quiner, *Military History of Wisconsin*, 845–46.

27. Quiner, *Military History of Wisconsin*, passim; Ancestry.com, Civil War Collection. Colonel Bintliff had previously served as a captain, but he could not join the Thirty-Eighth Wisconsin in the field until October, when organization of the tenth company was completed. Lieutenant Colonel Pier had served only as a private in the First Wisconsin. Major Larkin had previously served as a lieutenant.

28. OR 40:1, 523.

29. Fox, *Regimental Losses*, 176; Lieutenant Colonel Whiton to Brigadier General Schouler, Dec. 16, 1864, Fifty-Eighth Massachusetts, Regimental Books, NARA; OR 40:1, 229.

30. Greene, *Campaign of Giants*, 192, 195–96. OR 40:1, 223.

31. Bates, *History of Pennsylvania Volunteers,* 5:222–23; OR 40:1, 458, 223, 254, 457; Greene, *Campaign of Giants,* 192, 196; Dyer, *Compendium of the War of the Rebellion,* 3:1623; OR 36:3, 602, 652.

32. Dyer, *Compendium of the War of the Rebellion,* 3:622–23; OR 36:2, 802; OR 36:3, 666 (nine hundred ninety men), 739 (eight hundred men); Bates, *History of Pennsylvania Volunteers,* 5:222.

33. Bates, *History of Pennsylvania Volunteers,* 5:223; Dyer, *Compendium of the War of the Rebellion,* 3:1622–23; OR 36:2, 802.

34. OR 40:1, 309, 311, 324–25, 331–32, 339, 345, 346; OR 40:3, 696; OR 42:1, 265–66. In its report, the Twenty-Eighth Massachusetts claimed credit for the flanking movement. OR 40:1, 336.

35. OR 42:1, 302, 130; Bates, *History of Pennsylvania Volunteers,* 5:151–52.

36. Bosbyshell, *48th in the War,* 172; Rutan, *179th New York Volunteer Infantry,* 82; OR 40:1, 558, 549, 91.

37. Fox, *Regimental Losses,* 174; OR 40:1, 246; Bearss, *Eastern Front Battles,* 221.

38. Rutan, *179th New York Volunteer Infantry,* 98; Greene, *Campaign of Giants,* 441.

39. OR 40:1, 246, 538.

40. OR 40:1, 579, 582; Bates, *History of Pennsylvania Volunteers,* 2:12.

41. OR 40:1, 547–48, 553; Homer Shunk Thompson to Lydia, Aug. 4, 1864, https:/spared shared23.com/2022/08/18/1864-homer-shunk-thompson; letter from Samuel Haynes, Aug. 4, 1864, in Albert, *History of the Forty-Fifth Regiment Pennsylvania,* 260.

42. OR 40:1, 567, 247.

43. Letter, June 26, 1864, Pension File, NARA.

44. Greene, *Campaign of Giants,* 442; Whitman and True, *Maine in the War for the Union,* 586.

45. Sixtieth Ohio Memoirs, Charles C. Caruthers Autobiography, freepages.roots-web.com.

46. Thirty-First Maine, Regimental Order Book, Regimental Books, 4:51, Aug. 23, 1864, RG94, NARA.

47. OR 42:1, 551; *Union Army,* 1:203.

48. OR 42:1, 551.

49. Houston, *Thirty-Second Maine,* 377, 380.

50. Rutan, *179th New York Volunteer Infantry,* 119.

51. OR 42:1, 551, 557; Bates, *History of Pennsylvania Volunteers,* 3:563.

52. OR 42:1, 127; Bates, *History of Pennsylvania Volunteers,* 2:12.

53. OR 40:1, 530; OR 42:1, 127; Birch, *50th Pennsylvania's Civil War Odyssey,* 312–13.

54. Houston, *Thirty-Second Maine,* 396.

55. Whitman and True, *Maine in the War for the Union,* 580.

56. Rutan, *179th New York Volunteer Infantry,* 143, 119.

57. Rutan, *179th New York Volunteer Infantry,* 145–46; Phisterer, *New York in the War of the Rebellion,* 5:4029.

58. Rutan, *179th New York Volunteer Infantry,* 132–33, 148.

59. Lieutenant Colonel Whiton to Brig. Gen. William Schouler, Dec. 16, 1864, Regimental Books, NARA; Bearss, *Western Front Battles,* 36.

60. Bearss, *Western Front Battles,* 36; Bates, *History of Pennsylvania Volunteers,* 1:1070; Albert, *History of the Forty-Fifth Regiment Pennsylvania,* 164, 167. The Forty-Fifth Pennsylvania's regimental history stated: "We got decidedly the worst of it . . . , but the result was no reflection on the bravery and good conduct of the men. Bad management or carelessness by superior officers was the cause . . . Our brigade was pushed forward too

far without proper support, and the enemy . . . got in our flanks and rear." Albert, *History of the Forty-Fifth Regiment Pennsylvania,* 166. Postwar recollections of soldiers are often suspect, but this one sounds correct.

61. OR 42:3, 479–80, 544.

62. OR 42:1, 553.

63. OR 42:1, 558.

64. OR 42:1, 567.

65. OR 42:1, 378.

66. Birch, *50th Pennsylvania's Civil War Odyssey,* 248, 316–17, 327, 330. Just before the Battle of Poplar Spring Church, the terms of the veterans from 1861 who had not reenlisted expired, leaving the Fiftieth Pennsylvania with forty-six men and three officers. (The forty-six enlisted men left may not be correct. Compare Birch *50th Pennsylvania's Civil War Odyssey,* 248 with 316–17.) On October 12, the Fiftieth Pennsylvania received 147 replacements, mostly substitutes and draftees. Because of the shortage of officers, the Seventeenth Michigan loaned two lieutenants to assist with drilling the replacements.

67. Benedict, *Vermont in the Civil War,* 2:520, 524–25; *Union Army,* 1:122–23.

68. HIBO Database, Seventeenth Vermont, Desertion, latewarunionsoldiers.org.

69. Fox, *Regimental Losses,* 176; F. E. C., *History of the 58th Regt. Massachusetts Vols.,* 18–20.

70. Lieutenant Colonel Whiton to Brigadier General Schouler, July 7, 1864, Fifty-Eighth Massachusetts, Regimental Books, RG 94, NARA.

71. *Union Army,* 1:59.

72. Whitman and True, *Maine in the War for the Union,* 581; Dyer, *Compendium of the War of the Rebellion,* 3:1228; *Union Army,* 1:60; OR 46:2, 974.

73. *Cincinnati Daily Enquirer,* Aug. 15, 1864, 2; *Cleveland Leader,* Oct. 12, 1864, 2; Dyer, *Compendium of the War of the Rebellion,* 3:1525; HIBO Database, Sixtieth Ohio, latewarunionsoldiers.org; OR 42:1, 578.

74. Quiner, *Military History of Wisconsin,* 846, 849, 853; OR 42:1, 558.

75. Bates, *History of Pennsylvania Volunteers,* 5:152.

76. OR 42:3, 1042, 1116.

77. Bates, *History of Pennsylvania Volunteers,* 5:129–30. Number of transfers compiled from Bates, *History of Pennsylvania Volunteers,* 131–50. The Seventy-Second Pennsylvania was mustered out in Philadelphia on August 24, 1864. Dyer, *Compendium of the War of the Rebellion,* 3:1597. The Seventy-Second Pennsylvania was one of Fox's Three Hundred. Fox, *Regimental Losses,* 279.

78. Compiled from HIBO Database, latewarunionsoldiers.org; Lerwill, *Personnel Replacement System,* 105.

79. *Cincinnati Daily Inquirer,* Aug. 15, 1864, 2; OR 42:3, 565, 578 (Lincoln 93/McClellan 41).

80. White, *Emancipation, the Union Army, and the Reelection of Abraham Lincoln,* 6, 5. White contends that the soldiers' vote for Lincoln was more a vote against the Democratic Party "as a party that routinely appeared anti-patriotic and anti-soldier." White, *Emancipation, the Union Army, and the Reelection of Abraham Lincoln,* 4, 5. White also argues that the high percentage of soldiers' votes for Lincoln also reflects the possibility that Democratic soldiers "disproportionately exited the army by not re-enlisting or deserting." White, *Emancipation, the Union Army, and the Reelection of Abraham Lincoln,* 4. If so, that may have advanced unit cohesion by limiting a source of friction.

81. White, *Emancipation, the Union Army, and the Reelection of Abraham Lincoln,* 6; "Presidential Election of 1864: A Resource Guide," *Library of Congress,* https://www.loc. gov/rr/program/bib/elections/election1864.html.

82. Because voter support for a particular candidate can vary significantly in different parts of a state, it would be better to compare a regiment's voting percentage to the locality where it was raised rather than to the whole state. Unfortunately, regiments were generally raised among the men of multiple counties. For example, the 210th and 211th Pennsylvania were each raised in eight different counties (Bates, *History of Pennsylvania Volunteers,* vol. 5), which makes a comparison to individual county numbers impractical. At the same time, because Pennsylvania had over sixty counties, a comparison to the statewide number is still imperfect. The 185th New York was raised primarily in one county. The 185th New York voted 89 percent for Lincoln compared to 56 percent in Onondaga County.

83. White, *Emancipation, the Union Army, and the Reelection of Abraham Lincoln,* 6.

84. Powell, *Fifth Army Corps,* 748, 751; Humphreys, *Virginia Campaign of '64 and '65,* 310; Rutan, *179th New York Volunteer Infantry,* 200–201; Shackleton to Mother, Dec. 29, 1864, Pension File, NARA.

85. Rutan, *179th New York Volunteer Infantry,* 201. The Thirty-Sixth Wisconsin's Lt. James Aubery wrote of the importance of noncombat experience. "Battle is one trial of a soldier's quality; the March is another scarcely less severe. It tries endurance." Aubery, *Thirty-Sixth Wisconsin,* 31.

9. Second Reams's Station

1. Foner, *Fiery Trial,* 304; McPherson, *Tried by War,* 231, 238; Gallagher, *Enduring Civil War,* 117; Basler, *Collected Works of Abraham Lincoln,* 7:514.

2. OR 42:1, 226; Sommers, *Richmond Redeemed,* 234, rev. ed. 2014, 230.

3. OR 42:1, 222; Hess, *In the Trenches at Petersburg,* 135; Humphreys, *Virginia Campaign of '64 and '65,* 278–79.

4. OR 42:1, 244.

5. OR 42:1, 222; Humphreys, *Virginia Campaign of '64 and '65,* 278–79.

6. OR 42:1, 227, 262, 290. Hess does note that Grant "probably wanted to lure the Confederates into another attack." Hess, *In the Trenches at Petersburg,* 135.

7. OR 42:1, 253, 226.

8. OR 40:3, 729; SO No. 164, June 26, 1864 (Second Corps), vol. 4, Regimental Books, Fifty-Second New York, RG 94, NARA. See also OR 36:1, 199; OR 40:2, 543; OR 40:3, 729.

9. Horn, *Siege of Petersburg,* 256.

10. OR 42:1, 245 (Second Corps memorandum); Gibbon, *Personal Recollections of the Civil War,* 258; OR 42:1, 421 (Twelfth New York Battery); OR 42:1, 423 (First Rhode Island Light Artillery). General Heth reported that "This charge and its results has proved to me that nothing is impossible to men determined to win. The coolness and determination as evinced by all and expressed by many officers and men as I passed down the line, a few minutes before the attack . . . , carried with it a conviction of success." OR Supplement, vol. 7 (Addendum), vol. 42 (Serial No. 87), 475; Hess, *In the Trenches at Petersburg,* 138, 140; Kreiser, *Defeating Lee,* 208. Hess did also consider the fact that "the [Second Corps'] ranks were filled by a lot of newly inducted men with little experience and less will to fight" to be a key factor in the Union defeat. Hess, *In the Trenches at Petersburg,* 140. See also *Army and Navy Journal,* Sept. 3, 1864, 18:2.

11. OR 42:1, 288–89.

12. OR 42:1, 245.

13. OR 42:1, 252.

14. OR 42:1, 288, 245.

15. Horn, *Siege of Petersburg,* 252–53, 256. The "Third" Brigade occupied the left side of the Consolidated Brigade's position, with its left resting on Depot Road. The "Second" Brigade occupied the right, with its right resting on the railroad. Horn, *Siege of Petersburg,* 234. While I do not know their specific positions in relation to each other, the Seventh New York, Thirty-Ninth New York, and Fifty-Second New York constituted the "Third" Brigade's left, while the 111th New York, 125th New York, and 126th New York constituted its right. Horn, *Siege of Petersburg,* 256; OR 42:1, 288. John M. Pellicano states that the regiments were located left to right from Depot Road: Seventh New York, Thirty-Ninth New York, Fifty-Second New York, Fifty-Seventh New York, 111th New York, 125th New York, and 126th New York, but does not provide any citation. Pellicano, *Conquer or Die,* 154.

16. OR 42:1, 289, 47–48, 117, 288; OR Supplement, vol. 7 (Addendum) vol. 42 (Serial No. 87), 475; Walker, *History of the Second Corps in the Army of the Potomac,* 582; Hess, *In the Trenches at Petersburg,* 136; Bearss, *Eastern Front Battles,* 342. As to the lack of abatis for McRae, Cooke "had to advance over an almost impenetrable entanglement" and Heth thought that the portion of the Union breastworks "protected by obstructions formed by felling timber for 150 yards in front, render[ed] the works seemingly unapproachable from the front." OR Supplement, vol. 7 (Addendum) vol. 42 (Serial No. 87), 474–75. How the numbers present for duty at Second Reams's Station for the individual regiments were calculated is explained in Methodology—Second Reams's Station Present for Duty, latewarunionsoldiers.org.

West Point Prof. Dennis Hart Mahan, who taught virtually all of the cadets who later served on either side during the Civil War, wrote in his treatise on field fortifications that "The troops may be drawn up for the defense either in one, two, or three ranks . . . Each man will occupy one yard, linear measure, along the linear crest . . . A more vigorous defense will require, at least, two ranks." Mahan, *A Complete Treatise on Field Fortifications,* 25–26, 154.

The 148th Pennsylvania was held in reserve but was "not posted in the pits." OR 42:1, 289. Miles viewed the center of the line as "strong." OR 42:1, 251.

17. Horn, *Siege of Petersburg,* 255–56.

18. OR 40:1, 346; Phisterer, *New York in the War of the Rebellion,* 2:1805; Horn, *Siege of Petersburg,* 256. The Seventh New York had arrived in the field from garrison duty with a diverse array of 168 old guns for 250 men. A Second Corps inspector had declared all of the weapons unserviceable. Regimental Books, vol. 1, Orders, 4–5, RG 94, NARA. Company E, which was mustered in New York on August 9, apparently did not reach the Second Corps in full force until two days after Second Reams's Station (OR 42:1, 44), but some men from Company E apparently had arrived earlier. The unit roster shows one man from Company E as having been captured at Second Reams's Station and another as having deserted, as well as one man having deserted at Deep Bottom. NYSMM website. The Seventh New York was posted in the reserve in the battle occurring on July 30 but suffered twenty-seven casualties at Strawberry Plains on August 14. OR 40:1, 346; Phisterer, *New York in the War of the Rebellion,* 2:1806. That would have provided some live-fire training for at least some of the men.

The Seventh New York was not "entirely new." When the two-year volunteers were discharged in 1863, the three-year recruits were assigned to the Fifty-Second New York and then reassigned to the Seventh New York in July 1864. Phisterer, *New York in the War of the Rebellion,* 2:1788.

19. The brigades of Miles's Division were deployed in numerical order from right to left, which suggests there was no particular consideration given to which brigade could best defend which position.

20. Inspector general's report for April 1864, transmitted to General Halleck June 11, 1864, NARA, RG 159, Entry 3, 1:67.

Two days after the battle of Second Reams's Station, the Second Corps directed its regiments to report the number of officers and enlisted men "present with the Command on May 4, 1864 and at the battle of Reams Station." See Report, Headquarters, Fourth Brigade, First Div., 2AC, Aug. 29, 1864. The request would appear intended to set up the argument that the defeat at Second Reams's Station was the fault of the late-war replacements. The August 1864 inspector general's report for the Second Corps included the following opinion: "A great part of the 1st Div. . . . deserves censure, especially the 7th, 52nd, 39th, 125th and 126th N. Y. . . . It should be stated that the Corps was greatly fatigued, had suffered very heavily in loss of officers, and is largely made up of Recruits. It has been ascertained that but about 2500 men, who started on the Campaign in May, were present at Reams. The Regiments particularised by name have lately been filled up with Recruits, mostly Foreigners." NARA, RG 159, Entry 3, 1:276. The report included the notation "Report of this subject reserved until further examination."

At the same time the Second Corps also requested a report on the number of men "who returned to camp without arms" and the number who would be charged for the cost of their lost equipment. See Report, Headquarters, Fourth Brigade, First Division., Second Corps, Aug. 29, 1864.

21. Hancock's full quotation was: "the Irish Brigade . . . attacked the enemy vigorously on his right and drove his line for some distance. The Irish Brigade was heavily engaged, and although four-fifths of its numbers were recruits, it behaved with great steadiness and gallantry, losing largely in killed and wounded." OR 36:1, 320.

22. Fox, *Regimental Losses*, 118, 169, 202, 204, 217, 292.

23. OR 40:3, 729. The 116th Pennsylvania was in the Fourth Brigade of Miles's Division. OR 40:3, 730.

24. OR 40:1, 324–25.

25. Phisterer, *New York in the War of the Rebellion*, 3:2415.

26. OR 29:1, 266; Fifty-Second New York, "Historical Sketch," NYSMM Unit History website; *Fourth Annual Report of the Bureau of Military Statistics of the State of New York*, 169. The relative proportions of substitutes and conscripts among the recruits is not clear. Frank's praise may not have been universally justified. A dozen or so of the new recruits were captured at Bristoe Station and its aftermath. Unit Roster, NYSMM. Lt. Col. C. G. Freudenberg of the Fifty-Second New York also favorably commented on the presence of six hundred "conscripts": "They bore the fatigue of the severe marches admirably, and acted under fire better than could have been expected of recruits." OR 29:1, 267. Maj. Henry Abbott of the Twentieth Massachusetts also commented on the substitutes in his regiment at Bristoe Station: "the coolness and obedience of the men of this command . . . of course to be expected from the veteran soldiers, was to many unexpected on the part of the substitutes who had but recently joined, and who formed one-half the regiment." OR 29:1, 286.

27. *Fourth Annual Report of the Bureau of Military Statistics of the State of New York*, 169–70. The reference to panic subsiding may have been to the Third Brigade in general, not just the Fifty-Second New York. The Bureau did not mention Second Reams's Station in its history of the Fifty-Second New York. *Fourth Annual Report of the Bureau of Military Statistics of the State of New York*, 169–70.

28. Phisterer, *New York in the War of the Rebellion*, 3:2416; Compiled from Unit Roster, Fifty-Second New York Volunteers, NYSMM.

29. Regimental Order No. 130, Aug. 30, 1864, Fifty-Second New York, Regimental Books, 4:158, NARA, Record Group 94. Three of the sergeants had enlisted in 1861 and

the fourth in January 1862. Three other sergeants were also demoted, although only one of them appears to have been demoted based on poor performance.

30. Compiled from Unit Roster, Fifty-Second New York, NYSMM website. See also Regimental Books, vol. 4, Oct. 9 and Oct. 10, 1864.

31. For a discussion of the performance of short-timers in the Second Corps in general, see Kreiser, *Defeating Lee*, 162–63, 172.

32. Phisterer, *New York in the War of the Rebellion*, 3:2188–89. The original complement was quite diverse: three companies of Germans, three of Hungarians, one Swiss, one Italian, one French, and one Spanish and Portuguese.

33. Bacarella, *Lincoln's Foreign Legion*, 174–75; OR 40:2, 622–23; Compiled from Unit Roster, NYSMM.

34. Phisterer, *New York in the War of the Rebellion*, 4:3477–78, 3497–98.

35. Seventy-three of the late-war replacements in the 125th New York and sixteen in the 126th New York could have been at Second Reams's Station, but not necessarily were. Compiled from Unit Rosters, NYSMM website. As of August 8, 1864, the 125th New York had only about 140 men in the field. OR 40:1, 352.

The 125th New York's chaplain, who wrote the regimental history, acknowledged that "we failed" at Second Reams's Station. "There is no excuse to offer that they were not held." Simons, *The One Hundred and Twenty-Fifth New York State Volunteers*, 242–43.

36. Kreiser, *Defeating Lee*, 210; OR 42:1, 129–30; Fox, *Regimental Losses*, 475. In his brief comments on Second Reams's Station, Joshua Chamberlain did not refer to the late-war replacements. Instead, he commented that "After every purpose and prospect of success, these *veterans* were quickly driven from their entrenchments, even abandoning their guns." Chamberlain, *Passing of the Armies*, 20–21 (emphasis added).

The Seventh New York lost twenty-seven killed or wounded and thirty-three missing; the Thirty-Ninth New York lost six killed or wounded and twenty-one missing, and the Fifty-Second New York lost four men killed or wounded and twenty-six missing. Phisterer, *New York in the War of the Rebellion*, 3:1806, 2189, 2416.

37. OR 42:1, 253; Bearss, *Eastern Front Battles*, 383.

38. OR 42:3, 544. See also OR 42:3, 1071–72. A small Confederate force was threatening the rear of the Second Corps' Second Division. The division commander, Brig. Gen. Thomas W. Egan, reported that the Thirty-Sixth Wisconsin "charged at their head, capturing nearly the whole, with their officers and colors. I consider this brilliantly done, and that the Thirty-sixth, during the whole movement behaved most nobly." OR 42:1, 297, 299. See also OR 42:1, 303, 316. Hancock noted in his report that the Thirty-Sixth Wisconsin had "captured more prisoners than the regiment had men." OR 42:1, 234.

39. OR 42:1, 253; 226. The Sixty-First New York was Miles's old regiment, which could raise doubt about his objectivity, but his praise was justified by the facts.

40. Compilation based on the Sixty-First New York Volunteers' Roster, NYSMM website and Sixty-First New York's Carded Medical Records, NARA. The Sixty-First New York suffered thirty-nine casualties at Second Reams's Station—three killed, eleven wounded, and twenty-five missing in action. Fox, *Regimental Losses*, 201. Two of the three killed had been mustered into the army only three weeks before. At least three of the eleven wounded were replacements. Almost all of the twenty-five missing in action were replacements from the end of July and the beginning of August.

41. Kreiser, *Defeating Lee*, 132.

42. RG 159, Entry 3, 1:276, NARA. Captain Weaver, who commanded the 148th at Second Reams's Station, reported that "The men in many instances knocked their assailants down with the butts of their guns, and many retired when the right and left flanks were

completely overpowered and the enemy not only had possession of the works but occupied the railroad. The command fell back beyond the church and reformed." OR 42:1, 287.

43. Fox, *Regimental Losses,* 302; Bates, *History of Pennsylvania Volunteers,* 4:579. It does appear that a disproportionately small number of the replacements were killed or wounded at Second Reams's Station. See Bates, *History of Pennsylvania Volunteers,* 4:583. The performance of the 148th Pennsylvania was criticized by the subsequent commander of the Consolidated Brigade in his after-action report. OR 42:1, 288, 289. There is no indication of exceptional performance by the 148th Pennsylvania in Horn's recounting of the battle. See Horn, *Siege of Petersburg,* 234, 237–38, 248, 253. However, in September, General Hancock did honor the 148th Pennsylvania as the regiment in the first division to receive Spencer repeating rifles. Fox, *Regimental Losses,* 302; OR 42:1, 48, 254; OR 43:3, 412, 1000.

44. OR 42:1, 226. See also OR 42:1, 245, 253.

45. OR 42:1, 227, 226. Gibbon agreed with the criticism. OR 42:1, 293–94.

46. OR 42:1, 226. In the opinion of the inspecting officer, "the whole of the 2nd Div. . . . deserve censure for its conduct in this action, especially the 152nd N. Y. which is reported to have run away under disgraceful circumstances." Inspector general's report for Apr. 1864, transmitted to General Halleck June 11, 1864, NARA, RG 159, Entry 3, 1:67. Miles had specifically positioned the 152nd New York for a flank counterattack should the Confederates attack the Consolidated Brigade. Miles was understandably upset by the 152nd New York's failure to perform its mission. OR 42:1, 253, 313–14; Horn, *Siege of Petersburg,* 248–49.

47. Phisterer, *New York in the War of the Rebellion,* 5:3767.

48. Estimated based on Unit Roster, NYSMM website.

49. OR 42:1, 227, 222, 250–51, 287–88. Moreover, to get to the start point for the move on Reams's Station, the Second Corps had endured what Hancock described as "one of the most fatiguing and difficult [marches] performed by the troops during the campaign, owing to the wretched condition of the roads" after leaving Deep Bottom the night of August 20. OR 42:1, 222. They were on the march again on August 21. On August 22, they worked on repairing roads and at noon the First Division was ordered to the Weldon Railroad to cover the work parties and assist in destroying the railroad track.

50. OR 36:1, 434.

51. NARA, RG 159, Entry 3, 1:247.

52. OR 40:3, 729. Gibbon emphasized this factor in his memoirs. "Some of the brigades were commanded by Lieutenant Colonels the regiments by Captains and companies by sergeants. [F]or renown in the future it could not hope, except through a thorough reorganization. The other divisions were little if any better off." Gibbon, *Personal Recollections,* 259–60.

53. OR 42:1, 288, 251, 291; Unit Roster, Eighty-Eighth New York Volunteers, 17, NYSMM; Walker, *History of the Second Army Corps in the Army of the Potomac,* 592. But see Horn, *Siege of Petersburg,* 222.

54. OR 42:1, 288.

55. OR 42:1, 289 (Consolidated Brigade); OR 42:1, 421 (Twelfth New York Battery); Horn, *Siege of Petersburg,* 253.

56. OR 40:3, 729. The failure to withdraw the picket line is not chargeable to the late-war replacements, regardless of whether a field-grade officer would not normally have accompanied the picket line (or a field-grade officer ordered Penfield to keep the picket line in place).

57. Hess, *In the Trenches at Petersburg,* 140.

58. OR 42:1, 224, 252; Hess, *In the Trenches at Petersburg,* 135. See also Second Corps memoranda: "very defectively located and constructed." OR 42:1, 245; Walker, *History of the Second Corps in the Army of the Potomac,* 582–83, 604. In Earl Hess's view, "the field defenses at Reams's Station failed to serve Hancock's needs" and were one of three major factors causing the Union defeat. Hess, *In the Trenches at Petersburg,* 140. Hancock did order some minor improvements. See Bearss, *Eastern Front Battles,* 363. Gibbon extended the entrenchments to protect his flank. OR 42:1, 293.

59. OR 42:1, 293 (Gibbon); Mulholland, *116th Regiment,* 299.

60. See map, "Battle of Reams's Station," page 150.

61. OR 42:1, 289.

62. See Hess, *In the Trenches at Petersburg,* 136. Among other things, movement of troops and supplies between the railroad embankment and the line to the west was difficult. Hess, *In the Trenches at Petersburg,* 136; Horn, *Siege of Petersburg,* 220–21; Bearss, *Eastern Front Battles,* 342. For example, the Tenth Battery, Massachusetts Light Artillery had to reserve fire during the last Confederate attack because it had run low on ammunition. Horn, *Siege at Petersburg,* 255.

63. OR 42:1, 294.

64. Gibbon, *Personal Recollections,* 259–60.

65. Gibbon, *Personal Recollections,* 259. See also Walker, *History of the Second Corps in the Army of the Potomac,* 604–5. The Army of the Potomac arguably had been in "semicontinuous" combat since the beginning of the Overland Campaign on May 4, 1864, roughly 110 days by the time of Second Reams's Station. Studies of World War II combat soldiers found that their performance deteriorated precipitously over time. Keegan, *Face of Battle,* 328–29. See also Lynn, *Bayonets of the Republic,* 29.

66. Walker, *History of the Second Corps in the Army of the Potomac,* 606.

67. Only two months after Second Reams's Station, Hancock commended the performance of his troops at Boydton Plank Road on October 27, 1864, "particularly . . . the regiments whose conduct was open to censure on a previous occasion." OR 42:1, 240.

68. Bearss, *Eastern Front Battles,* 407; Horn, *Siege of Petersburg,* 223; Humphreys, *Virginia Campaign of '64 and '65,* 278–79.

10. Fort Stedman

1. Conrad Slusie from the 200th Pennsylvania wrote home in October 1864 that "the war will soon be over now. The rebs are giving up fast. . . . They say their it is no use for fighting any longer. They had nothing hardly to eat anymore . . . All their are waiting for is the presidential Election." Conrad Slusie to [?], Oct. [?], 1864, Pension File, NARA.

2. Rhea, "Foreword" in Young, *Lee's Army during the Overland Campaign,* ix. For an analysis of the numbers behind the "breaking point," see Hess, *In the Trenches at Petersburg,* 254.

3. Hess, *In the Trenches at Petersburg,* 246; Greene, *Final Battles of the Petersburg Campaign,* 108, 112; Humphreys, *Virginia Campaign of '64 and '65,* 316–18.

4. Greene, *Final Battles of the Petersburg Campaign,* 112; Hess, *In the Trenches at Petersburg,* 246, 250.

5. Charles E. Hemphill to Father, Mar. 6, 1865, Pension File, NARA.

6. Hartranft, "Recapture of Fort Stedman," 584–89.

7. How important was the contribution of Hartranft's Division to the victory at Fort Stedman? The decisive Union response was composed of four elements: (1) stubborn

resistance at Fort Haskell, which prevented the Confederate forces from expanding the breakthrough to the south; (2) stubborn resistance at Battery No. IX and Fort McGilvery, which prevented the Confederates from expanding the breakthrough to the north; (3) withering artillery fire from an arc of positions to the east, which made it difficult for the Confederates to advance east, north, and south; and (4) timely containment of the Confederate advance east from Fort Stedman toward Meade Station. Hartranft's Division provided the bulk of the force for the fourth factor. (The Fifty-Seventh Massachusetts, another late-war new regiment, played an important role in slowing down the advance of the Confederates until Hartranft's Division arrived.)

How important, in turn, was the Union victory at Fort Stedman? I agree with A. Wilson Greene that the Confederate assault "could have succeeded only had the Federals demonstrated rank incompetence and demoralization." Greene, *Final Battles of the Petersburg Campaign,* 140. However, Hartranft's Division did act quickly and effectively. Because of the low chance of Confederate success, Greene spent little time on Fort Stedman and only briefly refers to Hartranft's "untested regiments." Greene, *Final Battles of the Petersburg Campaign,* 114, 116.

8. Dyer, *Compendium of the War of the Rebellion,* 3:1624–25. These six regiments were not only high-number, they were comprised of high-bounty men. At the time these regiments were raised, the federal bounty was $100 for a one-year term of enlistment. Pennsylvania did not offer a state bounty, but many local governments did offer bounties. In the areas where the six regiments of Hartranft's division were raised, local governments offered bounties ranging from $200 to $530, but not all localities offered a bounty. Johnstown: "handsome sum" of $400, *Alleghanian,* Sept. 1, 1864, 3; Bedford Borough, Bloody Run Borough, Broadtop Township: $530, *Bedford Inquirer* (PA), Sept. 30, 1864, 3; Union, Armagh, and Brown: "offering liberal bounties," *Lewistown Gazette* (PA), Aug. 10, 1864; Lewistown: $200, *Lewistown Gazette,* Aug. 10, 1864, 3; Catawissa, Montour, Scott Centre, Mifflin, and Bloom filled quotas with bounties from $350 to $500, *Star of the North* (Coudersport, PA), Sept. 7, 1864, 2; Greenwood: $500, *Star of the North,* Sept. 7, 1864; Scott Township "and other townships in Columbia County": $400, *Star of the North,* Aug. 31, 1864, 3; Alleghany, Hebron, Sharon, Clara, and Oswego offering $200, *Potter Journal* (Coudersport, PA), Aug. 17, 1864, 3; Coudersport: $200, *Potter Journal,* July 27, 1864, 3.

Ebensburg, home to Company C of the 209th Pennsylvania Volunteers, offered a $310 town bounty. The local newspaper, the *Alleghanian,* asked rhetorically, "Looking at the matter solely in a pecuniary point of view, what undertaking will *pay* so well as volunteering just now?" and detailed the components, Aug. 25, 1864 (emphasis in original). The Ebensburg town bounty had been increased from $200 on Aug. 22. *Alleghanian* (Ebensburg, PA).

9. Letter from J. M., Mar. 26, 1865, excerpted in the *Potter Journal,* Apr. 5, 1865, 3. In November 1864 while at Bermuda Hundred, Gamma of the 209th Pennsylvania had written: "what we may prove in time of battle yet remains to be seen." Letter to the Editor, Nov. 8, 1864, *Alleghanian* (Ebensburg, PA), Nov. 17, 1864, 3.

10. GO No. 12, Headquarters, Third Division, Ninth Army Corps, Mar. 25, 1865, Regimental Books, 205th Pennsylvania Infantry, Regimental Letter & Order Book, NARA, RG 94. Hartranft also similarly stated: "The officers and men of my division, composed entirely of new troops, deserve great credit for their promptness in moving forward to the point of attack, to which great measure is owing the success of the day, and for their gallant conduct throughout the action." OR 46:1, 348. He especially praised the 200th Pennsylvania.

11. OR 46:1, 318. See also 316. Catton grudgingly acknowledged that the six regiments "seem to have contained good men—not all of the recruits were worthless bounty jumpers and substitutes." Catton, *A Stillness at Appomattox,* 337.

12. OR 46:3, 174 (General Orders No. 13) The *Philadelphia Press*'s "special correspondent" wrote that "As their numbers indicate, these are all new organizations, yet their conspicuous gallantry doubtless saved the day." Mar. 28, 1865, 2.

13. OR 46:1, 345; Hartranft, "Recapture of Fort Stedman," 584; OR 46:1, 317; OR 46:1, 354; Hodgkins, *Battle of Fort Stedman,* 15, 29; Barton, *Glorious Recollections,* 49–50; Bates, *Pennsylvania in the Civil War,* 5:520, 636, 672, 692, 710–11, 752; Trudeau, *Last Citadel,* 346–47. The regiments probably were not placed near the military railroad with the thought that the railroad could be used to move them to battle. Peebles Farm was the only battle during the Petersburg Campaign when the military railroad was used to move troops into battle, and even then it was not a large number. More likely, the regiments were stationed near the military railroad in order to protect it in the event of a Confederate breakthrough and to facilitate their own supply. James H. Blankenship Jr., email to author, Jan. 3, 2017.

14. OR 46:1, 330.

15. Hartranft, "Recapture of Fort Stedman," 585. Trudeau says 4:20 A.M. Trudeau, *Last Citadel,* 346; OR 46:1, 345.

16. OR 46:1, 345; Hartranft, "Recapture of Fort Stedman," 585. The 200th Pennsylvania and the 209th Pennsylvania may already have been on the move in response to orders by General Willcox—contingency plans provided that in the event of an attack in Willcox's sector they would respond as reserves to his orders because they were closer to his headquarters. Hartranft, "Recapture of Fort Stedman," 585; OR 46:1, 346.

17. OR 46:1, 346; Hartranft, "Recapture of Fort Stedman," 585; Trudeau, *Last Citadel,* 351.

18. OR 46:1, 346.

19. OR 46:1, 323, 351, 353. Sending the 200th Pennsylvania north rather than west toward Fort Stedman seems like a mistake, but Willcox probably was relying on the initial report that he may have received from the front that the Confederates were moving north toward the Appomattox River after their breakthrough.

20. OR 46:1, 351.

21. OR 46:1, 346; Hodgkins, *Battle of Fort Stedman,* 31; Wilkenson, *Mother, May You Never See the Sights I Have Seen,* 332. In both his after-action report and his article for *Battles & Leaders* written twenty years later, Hartranft stated that Willcox ordered the 209th from Meade Station to Friend House and the 200th from its camp to the nearby Dunn House Battery. OR 46:1, 346; Hartranft, "Recapture of Fort Stedman," 585. Capt. William Hodgkins one of Hartranft's staff officers, wrote the same in 1889. Hodgkins, *Battle of Fort Stedman,* 30. This is the reverse of Willcox's report after the battle that he had ordered the 200th to move to Friend House and the 209th to the front of the Dunn House Battery. The after-action reports by the regimental commanders of the 200th and the 209th Pennsylvania make it clear that Willcox's version is the correct one. OR 46:1, 351; OR 46:1, 353. But see Trudeau, *Last Citadel,* 350–51. This illustrates the difficulty of reconstructing the movements of small units in the heat of battle.

22. OR 46:1, 339; OR 46:1, 333; OR 46:1, 346; Hartranft, "Recapture of Fort Stedman," 584; Trudeau, *Last Citadel,* 348n2. Both the division and brigade commanders of the Fifty-Seventh Massachusetts praised their actions. Lt. Col. Julius Tucker of the Fifty-Seventh described their actions in more detail. OR 46:1, 339.

23. OR 46:1, 339, 346.

24. OR 46:1, 346; OR 46:1, 351.

25. OR 46:1, 346, 339.

26. OR 46:1, 346, 351.

27. OR 46:1, 346, 351, 354.

28. Wyrick in Bearss with Suderow, *Western Front Battles,* 276.

29. Wyrick in Bearss with Suderow, *Western Front Battles,* 276.

30. Hodgkins, *Battle of Fort Stedman,* 42.

31. OR 46:1, 348.

32. Charles Dellinger to "Dear Friend," Mar. 2, [1865], Pension File, NARA.

33. Barton, *Glorious Recollections,* 160.

34. OR 46:1, 353 (209th Pennsylvania Report); Barton, *Glorious Recollections,* 69.

35. Hodgkins, *Battle of Fort Stedman,* 31; Barton, *Glorious Recollections,* 230–32.

36. Barton, *Glorious Recollections,* 160.

37. Barton, *Glorious Recollections,* 69, 160, 194–95.

38. OR 46:1, 343; Barton, *Glorious Recollections,* 72, 231.

39. OR 46:1, 343, 353; Hodgkins, *Battle of Fort Stedman,* 31–32.

40. OR 46:1, 353–54 (209th Pennsylvania Report, Mar. 28, 1865); Barton, *Glorious Recollections,* 160.

41. OR 46:1, 346.

42. Hartranft, "Recapture of Fort Stedman," 584; Bearss, *Western Front Battles,* 271.

43. OR 46:1, 352.

44. OR 46:1, 352.

45. OR 46:1, 341; OR 46:1, 333; Barton, *Glorious Recollections,* 79.

46. OR 46:1, 347, 333; OR 46:1, 350; Barton, *Glorious Recollections,* 195; Hodgkins, *Battle of Fort Stedman,* 38.

47. Bates, *History of Pennsylvania Volunteers,* 5:692.

48. 208th Pennsylvania, Morning Reports, Regimental Books, RG 94, NARA.

49. Hartranft, "Recapture of Fort Stedman," 585.

50. OR 46:1, 347; Bates, *History of Pennsylvania Volunteers,* 5:672.

51. OR 46: 1, 347, 354; Hodgkins, *Battle of Fort Stedman,* 40–41; Letter from J. M., Mar. 26, 1865, excerpted in *Potter Journal* (Coudersport, PA), Apr. 5, 1865, 3. Hardee defined "double-quick time" as 160 regulation steps (thirty-three inches) per minute. Hess, *Civil War Infantry Tactics,* 245. In theory, troops could cover five miles in one hour at the "double-quick," but even one mile at "double-quick" was hard on the soldiers. Hess, *Civil War Infantry Tactics,* 245, 92.

52. Hodgkins, *Battle of Fort Stedman,* 40–41.

53. OR 46:1, 354; Bates, *History of Pennsylvania Volunteers,* 5:636–37, 672.

54. OR 46:1, 347.

55. OR 46:1, 347.

56. Bates, *History of Pennsylvania Volunteers,* 5:752.

57. Barton, *Glorious Recollections,* 195; Bates, *History of Pennsylvania Volunteers,* 5:752.

58. Bates, *History of Pennsylvania Volunteers,* 5:752. On March 24, the 211th reported 643 men and 27 officers present for duty. Regimental Books, vol. 1, RG 94, NARA. In his postbattle report, Hartranft wrote that the 211th numbered "about 600 muskets." OR 46:1, 348. See also Barton, *Glorious Recollections,* 208.

59. Trudeau, *Last Citadel,* 354.

60. OR 46:1, 347–48; Barton, *Glorious Recollections,* 196; Trudeau, *Last Citadel,* 352; Hartranft, "Recapture of Fort Stedman," 588–89. Hartranft stated that he was ready to attack with nearly four thousand men, but that was for five regiments, which excluded the 211th Pennsylvania, which joined the attack at the last moment. OR 46:1, 347; Barton, *Glorious Recollections,* 75.

61. OR 46:1, 347–48.

62. Bates, *History of Pennsylvania Volunteers,* 5:521.

63. Nelson Statler to Wife, Mar. 26, 1865, https://statler850624931.wordpress.com/letter-by-nelson-statler.

64. OR 46:1, 321; Barton, *Glorious Recollections,* 196.

65. OR 46:1, 348, 321.

66. Barton, *Glorious Recollections,* 76; John K. Satterfield to Editor, Mar. 25, 1865, *Bedford Inquirer* (PA), Apr. 7, 1865, 2.

67. OR 46:1, 350.

68. Munden and Beers, *Union: A Guide to Federal Archives Relating to the Civil War,* 353.

69. Regimental Books, 203rd Pennsylvania, RG94, Box 4607, NARA.

70. See, for example, Muster Roll of Lt. John T. Andrews, Company D of the One Hundred and Seventy-Ninth Regiment of New York Vols. Infantry, United States Army, Col. William M. Gregg, from the Thirty First day of October 1864, when last mustered, to the Thirty First day of December 1864, Collection No. 3790, Cornell Univ. The muster roll form does not provide a definition of the criteria, stating only that "It is made the special duty of the Inspector and Mustering Officer to add the appropriate remarks touching 'Discipline,' 'Instruction,' &c., according to the facts exhibited in the course of his inspection, with such other remarks as may be necessary or useful for the information of the War Department." "Discipline" was defined in the *1865 Customs of Service for Officers of the Army* as follows: "The preservation of order, the prevention of all kinds of offences, and the faithful performance of every kind of duty, without delay or interruption, is what is meant by discipline." Kautz, *1865 Customs of Service for Officers of the Army,* 286, para. 562. I have not found definitions of the other criteria. Similar assessments apparently were not performed at the regimental level. See, for example, the standard form for a regiment's Monthly Return.

71. War Department, Inspector General's Office, monthly reports, 374, reports for Sept. 1864 transmitted Nov. 28, 1864. See also 385. RG159, Entry 3, vol. 1. The 205th Pennsylvania was assigned to the Engineering Brigade at City Point at this time. Bates, *History of Pennsylvania Volunteers,* 5:521, 636. See OR 42:3 520; 42:3, 10. It is not clear whether the 211th Pennsylvania was included in the inspection report.

72. War Department, Inspector General's Office, monthly reports, 380, Army of the James Provisional Brigade, Oct. 1864 reports transmitted Nov. 20, 1864.

73. War Department, Inspector General's Office, 455; Dec. 1864 reports transmitted Jan. 20, 1865.

74. War Department, Inspector General's Office, 489–90, Jan. 1865 reports transmitted Feb. 22, 1865; Feb. 1865 reports transmitted Mar. 22, 1865 (523–25). The first brigade was cited for "Corps Div and Brig commanders visit and inspect their commands seldom" and overdrawn clothing in January 1865. The Third Division as a whole was cited for seldom reading the Articles of War in December 1864, January 1865, and February 1865 and "no recitations in army regulations and tactics" in January 1865.

75. Extracts from Monthly Inspection Report, Third Division, Ninth Army Corps for Feb. 1865, 205th Pennsylvania Regimental Letter & Order Book, RG 94, NARA.

76. Third Brigade SO #16, Feb. 27, 1865, 205th Pennsylvania Regimental Letter & Order Book, Regimental Books, RG 94, NARA.

77. Regimental Order No. 5, Oct. 3, 1864, Regimental Letter and Order Book, RG 94, NARA. At the end of December 1864, as brigade commander Mathews stated that "it is a matter of regret that so little interest is manifested on the part of the officers in the discharge of their plain duties. . . . [I]t will be the commanding officer's duty to send all incompetents before a commission with a view to their dismissal from the service." SO No. 9, Second Brigade, Dec. 30, 1864, 205th Pennsylvania, Regimental Letter and Order Book. This order apparently related to all three regiments in the Second Brigade, not just the 205th.

78. Letter from Richard Bohn, Mar. 4, 1865, p. 050, Univ. of Virginia.

79. Lynn, *Bayonets of the Republic*, 29. In his framework, "Morale" is one component of the "Motivational System," along with "Primary Group Cohesion" and "Motivation." He also considers the impact of "Interest" on the Motivational System. Lynn, *Bayonets of the Republic*, Fig. 1, 22.

80. Letters from the front come with the caveat that soldiers may depict things as better than they in fact are so that family and friends will not worry as much.

81. Rutan, *179th New York Volunteer Infantry*, 208; Bui, "'I Feel Impelled to Write': Male Intimacy, Epistolary Privacy, and the Culture of Letter Writing during the American Civil War," unpublished doctoral dissertation, Univ. of Illinois at Urbana-Champaign, 2016, 3–4.

82. Letter, Jan. 3, 1865, *Alleghanian* (Ebensburg, PA), Jan. 12, 1865.

83. Undated letter p. 060, Richard F. Bohn Civil War Letters 1862–1865 Collection, Univ. of Virginia, Special Collections Department, Accession Number 11418.

84. John Shell to Father, Jan. 6, 1865, Pension File, NARA; letter dated Nov. 8, 1864, *Alleghanian* (Ebensburg, PA), Nov. 17, 1864.

85. Letter dated Nov. 8, 1864, *Alleghanian* (Ebensburg, PA), Nov. 17, 1864. Sept. 15, 1864, 3. See also *Bedford Inquirer*, Oct. 21, 1864.

86. *Philadelphia Press*, Sept. 27, 1864, 1.

87. Henry H. Otto to Father, Dec. 30, 1864, sparedeshared13.wordpress.com, posted by Griff, Sept. 9, 2016.

88. J. V. L. to [?], undated letter, *Agitator* (Tioga County), Jan. 4, 1865, 4.

89. *Columbia Democrat and Bloomsburg General Advertiser* (PA), Jan. 14, 1865, 1.

90. Letter, Jan. 18, 1865, *Alleghanian* (Ebensburg, PA), Jan. 26, 1865 (emphasis in original). Lemmon attributed that in part to the religious faith of "quite a number of the men." See also letters from Gamma, Dec. 5 and 15, 1864, *Alleghanian;* Jan. 3 and 12, 1865, *Alleghanian;* Jan. 16 and 26, 1865, *Alleghanian.* For a discussion of the role of religious faith in a soldier's life, see Rutan, *179th New York Volunteer Infantry*, 162–68.

91. Henry C. Staily to Editor, Jan. 15, 1865, *Bedford Inquirer*, Jan. 27, 1865, 2.

92. Samuel Maynard to Father, Feb. 9, 1865, Pension File, NARA.

93. Dellinger to "Dear Friend," Mar. 2 [1865], Pension File, NARA.

94. Nelson Statler to Wife, Mar. 17 and 24, 1865, https://statler850624931.wordpress.com/letters-by-nelson-statler.

95. Letter, Jan. 18, 1865, *Alleghanian* (Ebensburg, PA), Jan. 26, 1865, 2. Cpl. Nelson Statler in the 211th Pennsylvania had noted in December that there is "good water and plenty of it." Nelson Statler to Wife, Dec. 22, 1864, https://statler850624931. Gamma had complained about water being "exceedingly scarce" at a previous camp. Letter, Sept. 21, 1864, *Alleghanian,* Oct. 6, 1864, 2. Col. McCalmont of the 208th Pennsylvania praised the men's quarters in November and again in January. McCalmont, *Extracts from Letters,* Nov. 19, 1864, 100, and Jan. 20, 1865, 113–14.

96. Undated letter, p. 057, Richard F. Bohn Civil War Letters 1862–1865 Collection, Univ. of Virginia, Special Collections Department, Accession Number 11418.

97. Nelson Statler to Wife, Dec. 24, 1864. See also letters, Jan. 1, 1865, and Feb. 3, 1865, https://statler850624931.wordpress.com/letters-by-nelson-statler.

98. Oct. 30, 1864, letter (pp. 053–54); Mar. 4, 1865 letter (p. 050); [late 1864] undated letter (p. 038), Richard F. Bohn Civil War Letters 1862–1865 Collection, Univ. of Virginia, Special Collections Department, Accession Number 11418; *Columbia Democrat and Bloomsburg General Advertiser* (PA), Jan. 14, 1865, 2. James Parmlee of the 211th Pennsylvania wrote his mother to explain that his morale was not as bad as his brother apparently had told her: "Of course I am somewhat dissatisfied with some operations I see here, but I don't think I am homesick or anything else the matter with me . . . True, I should like

to see Warren [hometown] & Warren friends once more, but I am content to wait till the time comes that I can do so honorably." Letter, Nov. 7, 1864, https://sparedshared16.word-press.com/2018/10/11/1864-james-oliver-parmlee.

99. White, *Emancipation,* 11.

100. John E. Satterfield, Company K. 208th Pennsylvania, wrote on September 23, 1864: "All are looking forward to the election of old Abe with much anxiety; of course they don't look for the election of anybody else. The Johnnies say if McClellan is elected, their independence will be established and the war shall go on, but if Lincoln is elected they will give up, for they are fully acquainted with *Lincoln's* policy" (emphasis in original). *Bedford Inquirer,* Oct. 21, 1864, 1. See also letters from Gamma, Oct. 31, 1864, *Alleghanian* (Ebensburg, PA), Nov. 10, 1864, 3, and Nov. 14, 1864; *Alleghanian,* Nov. 24, 1864, 3.

101. *Pittston Gazette* (PA), Nov. 17, 1864 at 2 (roughly forty regiments from Pennsylvania in the Army of the Potomac cast 5,170 votes for Lincoln and 2,455 for McClellan.

102. The *Huntington Monitor* reported an incident in which the 205th Pennsylvania reputedly snubbed Lincoln. Reported in *Lewistown Gazette,* Sept. 28, 1864, 2. However, Milton from Company F of the 205th vehemently denied that the incident occurred. *Lewistown Gazette,* Oct. 19, 1864, 1. The 205th Pennsylvania's vote was not reported. OR 42:3, 569.

103. Muster Rolls, 200th Pennsylvania, RG 94, 8W3/6/15, NARA; Muster Rolls, 205th Pennsylvania, Box 4608, NARA.

104. OR 46:1, 344–45.

105. *Wellsboro Gazette* (PA), Nov. 2, 1864, 1.

106. A. B. Cloos to [?], undated letter, *Agitator* (Tioga County, PA), Jan. 4, 1865, 4.

107. George Aumiller to Sister and Mother, Feb. 11, 1865, https://sparedshared22.word-press.com/2020/08/03/1865-george-aumiller.

108. Hess, *Civil War Infantry Tactics,* 43, 44–45.

109. Sommers, *Richmond Redeemed,* 229. See also Catton, *A Stillness at Appomattox,* 337. Sommers provides a detailed analysis of the senior Union leadership in the Army of the Potomac on the eve of the Battle of Poplar Spring Church. Sommers, *Richmond Redeemed,* 225–30. He describes the Union high command as "not brilliant but, on the whole, sound, competent, and above-average, with however, some weak spots." Sommers, *Richmond Redeemed,* 230.

110. Boatner, *Civil War Dictionary,* 382; Wikipedia.

111. Peter Mansoor has emphasized the importance of staff leadership: "What made outstanding divisions so good? First and foremost, they had good senior leadership and capable staff officers at the division level." Mansoor, *The GI Offensive in Europe,* 265. *Carbon Advocate* (Leighton, PA), Apr. 23, 1881, 3.

112. OR 46:1, 346–49; Hodgkins, *Battle of Fort Stedman,* 38n1; Fox, *Regimental Losses,* 270, 388.

113. Estimates compiled from the regimental descriptive books and the Civil War pension file index cards. See chap. 7, note 47. Professor Barton's team concluded that fourteen of the ninety-four men of Company F of the 209th Pennsylvania (15 percent) had prior service. Barton, *Glorious Recollection,* 250. My calculation based on the Civil War Pension File Index is 21.5 percent. Barton's team did not state how they calculated their number.

114. OR 42:3, 520.

115. OR 46:1, 348–49; compiled from descriptive books and pension file index as described above; Fox, *Regimental Losses,* passim. All eight officers were commended by Hartranft in his after-action report.

116. Reardon, "A Hard Road to Travel," 187; Maj. Isaac B. Brown, "Historical Sketch of the Third Division," in Barton, *Glorious Recollections,* 202–3.

117. G. M. B. to [?], undated letter, *Agitator* (Tioga County, PA), Jan. 4, 1865, 5. Hiram Roblyer in Company C of the 207th Pennsylvania wrote his parents that "we have a good old Cornel. He is a fine man. When we went on the [march?] some of the boys got tired. He would get off from his horse and let the boys ride, but the mager wouldn't." Hiram Roblyer to parents, Jan. 1, 1865, Pension File, NARA.

118. Letter from J. R. O'Neal, Nov. 9, 1864, *Bedford Inquirer,* Nov. 25, 1864, 3. See *Bedford Inquirer,* Oct. 21, 1864, 1; letter from 1Lt. William G. Eicholz, Nov. 15, 1864, *Bedford Gazette,* Dec. 2, 1864, 2. The connection of the men with Major Bobb was not stated, but it seems that he was a prominent citizen.

119. Letter from Gamma, Nov. 21, 1864, *Alleghanian,* Dec. 1, 1864, 3; Barton, *Glorious Recollections,* 181.

120. George Aughenbaugh to Wife, Oct. 19, 1864, https://sparedshared18.wordpress.com/2018/10/141864-george-washington-aughenbaugh.

121. George Aughenbaugh to Wife, Oct. 19, 1864, https://sparedshared18.wordpress.com/2018/10/141864-george-washington-aughenbaugh; Hiram Robyler to [?], Jan. 1, 1865, Pension File, NARA.

122. Henry C. Staily to Editor, Jan. 15, 1865, *Bedford Inquirer,* Jan. 27, 1865, 2. Colonel McCalmont described the company officers of the 208th Pennsylvania as "very competent and faithful." McCalmont, *Extracts from Letters,* Nov. 19, 1864, 103, and Jan. 20, 1865, 112. Lynn treats noncommissioned officers as a "crucial level of command, especially because of the importance of the small groups they lead." Lynn, *Bayonets of the Republic,* 38.

123. Bohn letters, Oct. 26, 1864 (p. 033) and undated, p. 056, Univ. of Virginia.

124. Compiled from Pension File Index, fold3.com. As to the 158th, 165th, and 166th Pennsylvania, see Fox, *Regimental Losses,* 487, and Bates, *History of Pennsylvania Volunteers,* 4:834, 1084, and 1100. Of the five enlisted men whom Hartranft singled out for distinguished service in his after-action report, all five had prior service. OR 46:1, 349; Pension File Index, Fold3.com; Civil War Soldiers, Ancestry.com. Of the three reported as having captured Confederate colors, two had prior service while one did not. OR 46:1, 349; Pension File Index, Fold3.com; Civil War Soldiers, Ancestry.com.

125. Muster Rolls for Oct. 31, 1864; Dec. 31, 1864; and Feb. 28, 1865, RG 94, NARA. Companies were evaluated individually, but most companies received the same rating.

126. "Training readiness does not lend itself to quantifiable evaluation as easily as [other factors]; it relies more heavily on the commander's professional military judgment." Congressional Research Service, "The Fundamentals of Military Readiness," 45. Colonel McCalmont of the 208th Pennsylvania described his men as "very obedient and well behaved." McCalmont, *Extracts from Letters,* Jan. 10, 1865, 112. See also Nov. 19, 1864, 103.

127. Maj. Isaac B. Brown, "Historical Sketch of the Third Division," in Barton, *Glorious Recollections,* 202. The 209th arrived at Bermuda Hundred only three days after its regimental organization had been completed and without a single drill. Barton, *Glorious Recollections,* 19.

128. Veritas to Friend Cobb, Sept. 23, 1864, *Agitator* (Tioga County, PA), Oct. 5, 1864, 2.

129. Barton, *Glorious Recollections,* 27. See also Bates, *History of Pennsylvania Volunteers,* 5:710–11. Capt. John B. Landis from Company A of the 209th Pennsylvania recalled that "A large proportion of the command was . . . kept on constant and exhausting picket and garrison duty; yet company and battalion drill were actively prosecuted, and by great diligence on the part of its officers and men, the regiment attained a large degree of efficiency and discipline." Maj. Isaac Brown recalled that "These few months of service had disciplined, and in a measure, veteranized us." Barton, *Glorious Recollections,* 227, 205.

130. Letter, Nov. 14, 1864, *Alleghanian* (Ebensburg, PA), Nov. 24, 1864, 3.

131. Bates, *History of Pennsylvania Volunteers,* 5:636.

132. Dec. 16, 1864, letter, Univ. of Virginia.

133. OR 51:1,1191–92; OR 42:1, 71.

134. Communication to Colonel Mathews from Headquarters, Third Division, Ninth Corps, Jan. 4, 1865, Regimental Letter & Order Book, 205th Pennsylvania Infantry, RG 94, NARA. See also Regimental Letter & Order Book, 207th Pennsylvania.

135. Jan. and Feb. 1865 Morning Reports, Company I, Regimental Books, 200th Pennsylvania Volunteers, RG 94, NARA. Samuel Bates noted that "During the winter the [200th] regiment was thoroughly drilled." Bates, *History of Pennsylvania Volunteers,* 5:519. Colonel McCalmont wrote that the 208th Pennsylvania had reviews and brigade drills every day or two. McCalmont, *Extracts from Letters,* Jan. 20, 1865, 114.

Bell Wiley described the "typical routine" for a unit in service for two or three months: "an hour or so of squad drill early in the morning" followed by "an equal stint of company drill" and "about an hour and a half of battalion drill in the late afternoon." As training advanced, "an hour or two of company drill in the forenoon and of battalion drill after lunch" replaced squad drill. After a few weeks of this schedule, "company drill might be dispensed with or held only on alternate days, and brigade drill introduced in the afternoon." Wiley, *Billy Yank,* 50. At the beginning of December 1864, the schedule for what was then the Ninth Corps' Provisional Brigade was similar. SO #3, Provisional Brigade, 205th Pennsylvania Regimental Letter and Order Book, RG 94, NARA.

136. Barton, *Glorious Recollections,* 56. On January 23, 1865, Peter Simpson from Company B of the 209th wrote home that "our men have not been doing much yet here but drill." H. Simpson to Rev. Murray, Jan. 23, 1865, Barton, *Glorious Recollections,* 134, 138.

137. Bates, *History of Pennsylvania Volunteers,* 5:752. But see John Shell, Company H, 207th Pennsylvania: "we needen stant picket yet and dond get much drilled." Letter, Feb. 28, 1865 to [?], Pension File, NARA. The 211th Pennsylvania's Cpl. Nelson Statler wrote that "we did not drill any for three or four weeks [in February]." Cpl. Nelson Statler to Wife, Mar. 7, 1865. See also letter, Mar. 5, 1865. In January, he had complained to his wife that "I can hardly get as much time as to write a letter anymore as we have so much duty to perform—drilling, fatigue and police duty." Cpl. Nelson Statler to Wife, Jan. 20, 1865, https://statler850624931.wordpress.com/letters-by-nelson-statler.

138. Wiley, *Billy Yank,* 26–27, 50. For the importance of live-fire training, see Lynn, *Bayonets of the Republic,* 230–31; Hanson, "The Eighth Army's Combat Readiness Before Korea," 170–71.

139. Morning Reports, Regimental Books, 200th, 207th, and 208th Pennsylvania Infantry, RG 94, NARA; George Aughenbaugh (Co. H, 200th Pennsylvania) to Wife, Oct. 19, 1864, https://sparedshared18.wordpress.com/2018/10/14/1864-george-washington-aughenbaugh.

140. Letter from J. M., Mar. 26, 1865, excerpted in *Potter Journal* (Coudersport, PA), Apr. 5, 1865, 3; Bates, *History of Pennsylvania Volunteers,* 5:692; Barton, *Glorious Recollections,* 72.

141. Veritas to Friend Cobb, Sept. 23, 1864, *Agitator* (Tioga County, PA), Oct. 5, 1864, 2.

142. Bates, *History of Pennsylvania Volunteers,* 5:710.

143. When the six regiments first went on picket duty after being assigned to the Army of the James in October 1864, they served in a sector where there was an informal understanding by the men on both sides that they would not shoot at each other while on picket. Barton, *Glorious Recollections,* 35; Bates, *History of Pennsylvania Volunteers,* 5:751. That understanding was broken on November 17, 1864, when the Confederates attacked the picket lines, capturing twenty-two men from the 205th Pennsylvania, including its commanding officer, Colonel Tobias, and killing or wounding another six. Barton, *Glorious Recollections,* 36.

144. Lynn, *Bayonets of the Republic*, 35. See also Costa and Kahn, *Heroes & Cowards*, 3, 9–10 ("long marches" as tests of adversity).

145. Company B of the 205th Pennsylvania (40 percent); Company G of the 209th Pennsylvania (37 percent); and Company I of the 211th Pennsylvania (38 percent). The lowest percentage was 13 percent (Company H of the 200th Pennsylvania). Compiled from Pension File Index Cards, Fold3.com.

146. Rutan, *179th New York Volunteer Infantry*, 200–201.

147. Letter from A Soldier to Editor, Jan. 1865, *Star of the North* (Bloomsburg, PA), Feb. 8, 1865, 2. Nelson Statler of the 211th Pennsylvania wrote his wife that "The weather was very bad—raining and snowing and cold." Nelson Statler to Wife, Dec. 14, 1864, https://statler850624931.wordpress.com/letters-by-nelson-statler; Colonel McCalmont of the 208th Pennsylvania, who had previously served in the 142nd Pennsylvania, wrote his brother that "I never experienced so rough a march." McCalmont, *Extracts from Letters*, Dec. 14, 1864, 107. As grueling as the experience was, "none regretted the trip for the rich supply [of turkies, chickens and pigs from foraging] fully repaid us." See also Lt. A. B. Cloos to [?], undated letter, *Agitator* (Tioga County, PA), Jan. 4, 1865, 4; G. M. B. to [?], undated letter, *Agitator* (Tioga County, PA), Jan. 4, 1865, 4; Brown in Barton, *Glorious Recollections*, 207; Landis in Barton, *Glorious Recollections*, 229. But see McCalmont, *Extracts from Letters*, Dec. 14, 1864, 108.

148. A. B. Cloos to [?], undated letter, *Agitator* (Wellsborough, PA), Jan. 4, 1865, 4.

149. OR 46:1, 344; George Aumiller to Sister and Mother, Feb. 11, 1865, https://spared-shared22.wordpress.com/2020/08/03/1865-george-aumiller.

150. Quoted in Keegan, *Face of Battle*, 329. See also Lynn, *Bayonets of the Republic*, 29 ("men can only bear the burden of fear for a given amount of time before they collapse under its weight").

151. Reardon, "A Hard Road to Travel," 170.

152. Rutan, *179th New York Volunteer Infantry*, 105.

153. See, for example, McPherson, *Battle Cry of Freedom*, 735.

154. Boatner, *Civil War Dictionary*, 612. While the actual size of a unit is purely a quantitative factor (Lynn, *Bayonets of the Republic*, 39), a unit well below authorized strength could have morale problems.

155. HIBO Database; Regimental Books, NARA. The 209th Pennsylvania left Camp Curtin with 988 men. Barton, *Glorious Recollections*, 227.

156. Present for Duty (that is, not including the following categories of "present": special duty, extra and daily duty, and sick).

	Officers	Men	Total
200th Pennsylvania	14	719	733
205th Pennsylvania	23	748	771
207th Pennsylvania	24	630	654
208th Pennsylvania	22	679	701
209th Pennsylvania	20	662	682
211th Pennsylvania	27	643	670

200th Pennsylvania Regimental Books, vol. 3, Morning Reports; 205th Pennsylvania Regimental Books, vol. 1, Regimental Descriptive List and Consolidated Morning Reports; 207th Pennsylvania Regimental Books, vol. 1, Consolidated Morning Reports; 208th Pennsylvania Regimental Books, vol. 4, Morning Reports; 209th Pennsylvania Regimental Books, vol. 1, Regimental Descriptive List and Morning Reports; 211th Pennsylvania Regimental Books, vol. 1, Regimental Descriptive List and Consolidated Morning Reports; all NARA, RG 94. Earl Hess states that an average Union regiment had three hundred men by 1863. Hess, *Civil War Infantry Tactics,* 176.

157. Calculated based on the "Organization of the Army of the Potomac" (number of regiments) and Inspection Reports (number of men in corps). As of March 31, 1865, of the nearly seventy regiments in the Second Corps, only four had a "present" strength in excess of six hundred—the Second, Fourth, and Eighth New York Artillery and the Seventh New Jersey. Four regiments were below one hundred—the Sixty-Sixth and 126th New York, the First Minnesota and the 106th Pennsylvania. OR 46:1, 692–94. (Using the "Average strength present during March, 1865" numbers in the March 31, 1865, report of the medical inspector on the Second Corps yields an average per regiment of 327. OR 46:1, 692–94)

158. Tables, latewarunionsoldiers.org.

159. 200th Pennsylvania: 114 deserters (11 percent), all but one in Pennsylvania in Aug. and Sept. 1864; 205th Pennsylvania: seventy-one deserters (7 percent), all but one in Pennsylvania in Aug. and Sept. 1864; 207th Pennsylvania: fifty or fifty-three deserters (5 percent), all but one in Pennsylvania in Aug. and Sept. 1864; 208th Pennsylvania: seventy-six deserters (8 percent), all in Pennsylvania from Aug. through Oct. 1864; 209th Pennsylvania: 115 deserters (12 percent), all but one in Pennsylvania in Aug. and Sept. 1864; and 211th Pennsylvania: ten deserters (1 percent), all but one in Pennsylvania in Aug. and Sept. 1864. "Numerator" taken from the Provost Marshal General's "Descriptive List of Deserters from Pennsylvania Military Units during the Civil War (1866), (Penn State Univ. Libraries, "The People's Contest: A Civil War Era Digital Archiving Project," https://peoplescontest.psu.edu/descriptive-list-deserters-pennsylvania-military-units-during-civil-war). "Denominator" compiled from Descriptive Books, Regimental Books, Record Group 94, NARA. See also HIBO Database.

160. OR III:3, 386–87; OR 45:2, 344–45.

161. Barton, *Glorious Recollections,* 28. But see letter from Gamma, Nov. 8, 1864, *Alleghanian* (Ebensburg, PA), Nov. 17, 1864, 3. See also George Aughenbaugh to Wife, Oct. 19, 1864, https://sparedshared18.wordpress.com/2018/10/14/1864-george-washington-aughenbaugh. ("There are quite anumber sick in our regiment at present.") Augenbaugh also noted that "There are quite a number of them that I think are too lazy to do anything. Some are afraid to go into a fight and are trying to make themselves sick."

162. Letter from Gamma, Oct. 26, 1864, *Alleghanian* (Ebensburg, PA), Nov. 10, 1864, 3. See also *Alleghanian,* Oct. 20, 1864, 3 (Company C, 209th Pennsylvania); *Bedford Inquirer* (PA), Oct. 21, 1864 , 1 (Company K, 208th Pennsylvania); *Alleghanian,* Oct. 27, 1864, 3 (Company C, 208th Pennsylvania); *Bedford Inquirer,* Nov. 18, 1864, 3 (208th Pennsylvania); *Alleghanian,* No. 24, 1864, 3 (Company C, 209th Pennsylvania); *Alleghanian,* Dec. 8, 1864 (Company C, 209th Pennsylvania); *Alleghanian,* Dec. 15, 1864, 3 (Company C, 209th Pennsylvania); *Alleghanian,* Jan. 12, 1865, 3 (Company C, 209th Pennsylvania); *Alleghanian,* Jan. 26, 1865, 3 (Company C, 209th Pennsylvania); *Bedford Inquirer,* Jan. 27, 1865, 2 (Company K, 208th Pennsylvania); *Star of the North* (Bloomsburg, PA), Feb. 8, 1865, 2 (209th Pennsylvania).

163. Consolidated Morning Reports, Regimental Books, NARA: 200th Pennsylvania (not calculated); 205th Pennsylvania (forty-four); 207th Pennsylvania (forty-nine); 208th Pennsylvania (not available); 209th Pennsylvania (forty-five); 211th Pennsylvania (seventy-six).

164. Muster Rolls, 200th, 205th, 207th, 208th, 209th, and 211th Pennsylvania Volunteers, Boxes 4608, 4611, 4611, 4612, 4613, 4615, RG 94, NARA. The spaces on the muster rolls for the 209th Pennsylvania were not filled in.

165. Muster Rolls, 200th, 205th, 207th, 208th, 209th, and 211th Pennsylvania Volunteers, Boxes 4608, 4611, 4612, 4613, 4615, RG 94, NARA. The spaces on the muster rolls for the 209th Pennsylvania were not filled in.

166. Nelson Statler to Wife, Jan. 7, 1865, https://statler850624931.wordpress.com/letters-by-nelson-statler. Statler did question the quality of the food; George Aughenbaugh to Wife, Oct. 19, 1864, https://sparedshared18.wordpress.com/2018/10/14/1864-george. George Aumiller to Sister and Mother, Feb. 11, 1865, https://sparedshared22.wordpress.com/2020/08/03/1865-george-aumiller.

167. For example, Morgan Hofius to Henry Hofius, Dec. 2, 1864 (211th Pennsylvania), https://sparedshared4.wordpress.com/letters/1864-morgan-b-hofius.

168. McPherson, *For Cause and Comrades,* viii. Because these numbers include the late-war replacements, they are not a perfect basis for comparison.

169. Descriptive Books, Regimental Books, RG 94, NARA. Several companies had higher percentages of foreign-born men: Company E, 205th Pennsylvania (17 percent German-born, 4 percent Irish-born); Company G, 200th Pennsylvania (24 percent Irish-born); and Company H, 200th Pennsylvania (17 percent German-born).

170. Wiley, *Billy Yank,* 307.

171. Wiley, *Billy Yank,* 304. See Halleck, "The Role of the Community in Civil War Desertion," 127.

172. Compiled from Descriptive Books, Regimental Books, RG 94, NARA. There are variations in individual companies.

11. The Five Forks Offensive

1. Hess, *In the Trenches at Petersburg,* xx.

2. Hess, *In the Trenches at Petersburg,* xx; Bearss, *Western Front Battles,* 310–11.

3. OR 46:1:1, 568–69.

4. OR 46:1:1, 570. The 190th and 191st Pennsylvania in Gwyn's Brigade of Ayres's Division were "high-number" regiments in numerical order only. When the regiments in the Pennsylvania Reserve Corps were mustered out at the end of May 1864, "a large number of veterans and recruits, whose terms had not expired, still remained." These men were organized into the 190th and 191st Pennsylvania. Bates, *History of Pennsylvania Volunteers,* 5:279; Dyer, *Compendium of the War of the Rebellion,* 3:1623. There were late-war replacements in both regiments, but veterans from 1861 and 1862 predominated. See Unit Rosters, Bates, *History of Pennsylvania Volunteers,* 288–330.

5. OR 46:1:2, 796, 1101; Chamberlain, *Passing of the Armies,* 39; Bearss, *Western Front Battles,* 329.

6. OR 46:1:2, 845, 847; Chamberlain, *Passing of the Armies,* 42; Wood, *Under Chamberlain's Flag,* 184–85.

7. OR 46:1:2, 847; Chamberlain, *Passing of the Armies,* 42–43.

8. OR 46:1:2, 1286; OR 46:1, 845–46; OR 46:3:1, 730–31; Chamberlain, *Passing of the Armies,* 53.

9. OR 46:1:2, 847; Chamberlain, *Passing of the Armies,* 43. A good bit ahead of the rest of Chamberlain's Brigade, Glenn's Battalion may have advanced to the woods beyond the Lewis Farm and been forced back to the Lewis Farm buildings before the rest of Chamberlain's Brigade arrived. Wood, *Under Chamberlain's Flag,* 189–90.

10. OR 46:1:2, 847–48; Chamberlain, *Passing of the Armies,* 43–45.

11. OR 46:1:2, 848. Chamberlain quoted Griffin as saying: "If you can hold on there ten minutes, I will give you a battery." Chamberlain, *Passing of the Armies,* 50.

12. OR 46:1:2, 848, 1287; Chamberlain, *Passing of the Armies,* 50–52.

13. OR 46:1, 848:2; Chamberlain, *Passing of the Armies,* 52–53; *Harper's Weekly,* Apr. 22, 1865, 244.

14. OR 46:1:2, 853.

15. OR 46:1:2, 848.

16. OR 46:1:2, 847; Wood, *Under Chamberlain's Flag,* 206.

17. OR 46:1:2, 847–48, 850; Wood, *Under Chamberlain's Flag,* 199.

18. OR 46:1:2, 802.

19. OR 46:3:1, 266, 1102; Bearss, *Western Front Battles,* 348.

20. OR 46:1:2, 810, 846.

21. OR 46:1:2, 812, 813, 814.

22. OR 46:1:2, 814, 868; Chamberlain, *Passing of the Armies,* 70.

23. OR 46:1:2, 878, 879; Bearss, *Western Front Battles,* 418.

24. OR 46:1:2, 814, 846.

25. OR 46:1:2, 814–15.

26. OR 46:1:2, 754–56, 745, 750–51. The 148th Pennsylvania averaged 340 men present during March 1865. OR 46:1:1, 693.

27. OR 46:1:2, 745. The 116th Pennsylvania averaged 298 men present during the month of March 1865. OR 46:1:1, 693.

28. OR 46:1:2, 815.

29. OR 46:1:2, 846, 849; Chamberlain, *Passing of the Armies,* 73.

30. OR 46:1:2, 816, 846, 849; Chamberlain, *Passing of the Armies,* 75.

31. Chamberlain, *Passing of the Armies,* 77; Bearss, *Western Front Battles,* 433–34; OR 46:1:2, 849, 853, 858.

32. OR 46:1:2, 846, 849; Bearss, *Western Front Battles,* 435.

33. OR 46:3, 266; OR 46:1:2, 1103; Chamberlain, *Passing of the Armies,* 109–10.

34. Bearss, *Western Front Battles,* 463–64.

35. Chamberlain, *Passing of the Armies,* 109–10.

36. OR 46:1:2, 1100, 1104.

37. OR 46:1:2, 1100.

38. OR 46:3, 367; OR 46:1, 817, 822, 849; Bearss, *Western Front Battles,* 462, 476–78.

39. OR 46:1:2, 830, 880; see also OR 46:1:2, 1104.

40. Bearss, *Western Front Battles,* 486; Chamberlain, *Passing of the Armies,* 127; Humphreys, *Virginia Campaign of '64 and '65,* 347.

41. OR 46:1:2, 832, 833, 850, 869, 880.

42. Ayres described the Confederate positions around the return. "The left flank of the enemy . . . was thrown back at right angles with his main line and covered by a strong breast-work, screened behind a dense undergrowth of pines and about 100 yards in length." OR 46:1:2, 869–70. Warren described the return as "a very short line." OR 46:1:2, 832.

43. Bearss, *Western Front Battles,* 483, 487, 495; OR 46:1:2, 850.

44. Bearss, *Western Front Battles,* 496, 505; Humphreys, *Virginia Campaign of '64 and '65,* 349; OR 46:1:2, 879.

45. Bearss, *Western Front Battles,* 496; OR 46:1:2, 861, 865, 868. I do not know the relative positions of the First Michigan and the Twentieth Maine.

46. OR 46:1:2, 854; see also OR 46:1:2, 858.

47. Making sure that the right was not exposed, Lieut. Col. Daniel Myers of the 187th Pennsylvania "hop[ed] that we might arrive in time to get into action, but when we arrived we found the firing had ceased and the day was won." OR 46:1:2, 856.

48. Bearss, *Western Front Battles,* 496–97; OR 46:1:2, 838.

49. Bearss, *Western Front Battles,* 499, 505; OR 46:1:2, 838, 870, 881.

50. Bearss, *Western Front Battles,* 509; OR 46:1:2, 1105.

51. OR 46:1:2, 890; Bearss, *Western Front Battles,* 510.

52. Lynn, *Bayonets of the Republic,* 27–28; McPherson, *For Cause and Comrades,* 131; Coss, *All for the King's Shilling,* 236–37.

53. "Battle Flag for the New Onondaga Regiment," *Syracuse Daily Courier and Union,* Sept. 23, 1864, 2; unidentified newspaper, Nov. 12, 1864; E. W. F. to the *Syracuse Standard,* Oct. 3, 1864; W. G. to *Syracuse Journal,* Nov. 1, 1864; Lew to the *Syracuse Standard,* Oct. 3, 1864, all 185th New York newspaper clippings, NYSMM except the first.

54. Letter from E. W. F., Oct. 24, 1864; Letter from H. W. to the *Syracuse Journal,* Oct. 14, 1864; Letter from Lew to *Syracuse Standard,* Oct. 3, 1864; letter from W. G. to *Syracuse Journal,* Oct. 30, 1864; letter from A. H. S. to *Syracuse Standard,* Nov. 7, 1864; letter from [?] to *Syracuse Journal,* Nov. 7, 1864; Letter from W. G. to the *Syracuse Journal,* Dec. 12, 1864, all NYSMM Unit History Project website. E. W. F. may have been Cpl. Edwin W. Fryer; H. W. may have been Pvt. Henry Weber or Pvt. Hiram Ward; Lew may have been Pvt. Ladroit E. Washburn; A. H. S. may have been Capt. Abram H. Spear; and W. G. may have QM William Gilbert or Pvt. Warren Gilbert. See Unit Roster, 185th New York Volunteers, NYSMM.

55. Wood, *Under Chamberlain's Flag,* 102. See also H. W. to *Syracuse Journal,* Oct. 14, 1864; E. W. F. to *Syracuse Standard,* Oct. 24, 1864, both NYSMM, Unit History Project website.

56. *New York Daily Reformer* (Watertown), Nov. 5, 1864, 2; *Syracuse Standard,* undated, 185th New York newspaper clippings, NYSMM; Alburtus Peckham to Mr. and Mrs. Eggleston, Oct. 15, 1864, https://sparedshared23.com/2022/05/17/1864-alburtus-h-peckham.

57. 185th New York Muster Rolls, RG 94, Box 3415, NARA.

58. Undated letter from T. S. M. to *Syracuse Journal;* E. W. F. to unidentified newspaper, Oct. 24, 1864; Lew to *Syracuse Standard,* Oct. 3, 1864; undated letter to the Editor, unidentified newspaper, all NYSMM Unit History website; HIBO Database, Table 5.7. While soliciting volunteers, T. S. M. cautioned: "But don't send us any substitutes for the sake of our reputation," undated letter, *Syracuse Journal,* undated newspaper clippings, 185th New York Volunteers, NYSMM.

59. Author's conversation with Kenneth G. Miller, brigadier general, United States Air Force (Ret.) and Ben Koerselman, colonel, United States Army (Ret.), Oct. 4, 2022.

60. WG to *Syracuse Journal,* Oct. 2, 1864, Unit History Project website, Civil War newspaper clippings, 185th New York Volunteers, NYSMM.

61. *Syracuse Standard,* Oct. 3, 1864; *Syracuse Journal,* Dec. 19, 1864; undated letter in unidentified newspaper; *Syracuse Journal,* Dec. 12, 1864; *Syracuse Standard,* Oct. 24, 1864, all 185th New York newspaper clippings, NYSMM.

62. Unsigned letter to the Editor, unidentified newspaper, ca. Sept. 29, 1864, NYSMM, Unit History Project website, Civil War newspaper clippings, 185th New York Volunteers.

63. Compiled from Phisterer, *New York in the War of the Rebellion,* 5:4059–66.

64. LEW to *Syracuse Standard,* Oct. 3, 1864, NYSMM, Unit History Project website, Civil War newspaper clippings, 185th New York Volunteers.

65. LEW to the *Syracuse Standard,* Feb. 9, 1865, NYSMM; OR 46:1:1, 267.

66. W. L. Winslow to J. W. Yale, Oct. 15, 1864; T. S M. to the *Syracuse Journal,* Dec. 19, 1864, and Feb. 9, 1865; DRAUGHTGILSIVAD to *Syracuse Journal,* Oct. 21, 1864, and undated letter; LEW to the *Syracuse Standard,* Dec. 3 and 13, 1864; letter from [?] to [?], Apr. 25, 1865, all NYSMM Unit History website.

67. DRAUGHTGILSIVAD to *Syracuse Journal,* Oct. 21, 1864, NYSMM, Unit History Project website, Civil War newspaper clippings, 185th New York Volunteers.

68. *Syracuse Journal,* Dec. 19, 1864, 185th New York, newspaper clippings, NYSMM.

69. DRAUGHTGILSIVAD to *Syracuse Journal,* Oct. 21, 1864, NYSMM, Unit History Project website, Civil War newspaper clippings, 185th New York Volunteers. See also *Syracuse Daily Journal,* Oct. 19, 1864, in Wood, *Under Chamberlain's Flag,* 102n261.

70. Lew to the *Syracuse Standard,* Dec. 3, 1864, NYSMM, Unit History Project website, Civil War newspaper clippings, 185th New York Volunteers.

71. DRAUGHTGILSIVAD to *Syracuse Journal,* Oct. 21, 1864, NYSMM, Unit History Project website, Civil War newspaper clippings, 185th New York Volunteers.

72. Muster Rolls, 185th New York, RG 94, Box 3415, NARA.

73. Unsigned letter to the Editor, unidentified newspaper, ca. Sept. 29, 1864, NYSMM, Unit History Project website, Civil War newspaper clippings, 185th New York Volunteers.

74. Lynn, *Bayonets of the Republic,* 222, 232. "Petite guerre" as practiced by the French involved small, independent actions such as "patrols, raids and ambushes." Lynn, *Bayonets of the Republic,* 222, 232.

75. OR 42:3, 22; Phisterer, *New York in the War of the Rebellion,* 5:4059; Wood, *Under Chamberlain's Flag,* 173.

76. LEW to *Syracuse Standard,* Dec. 13, 1864; letter to "Dear Brother," Dec. 13, 1864, unidentified newspaper. See also T. S. M. to *Syracuse Journal,* Dec. 19, 1864, both NYSMM, Unit History Project website, Civil War newspaper clippings, 185th New York Volunteers. The Fifth Corps' medical director reported that during Hatcher's Run in February 1865, "The cold was the most intense encountered in any movement during the winter." OR 46:1:1, 263.

77. *Syracuse Daily Courier and Union,* Sept. 23, 1864, 2.

78. LEW to *Syracuse Standard,* Oct. 3, 1864, NYSMM, Unit History Project website, Civil War newspaper clippings, 185th New York Volunteers.

79. *Syracuse Standard,* Oct. 3 and 21, 1864, 185th New York, newspaper clippings, NYSMM. Gilbert and Mowry were later criticized in the press, but TSM came to their defense. Undated and unidentified newspaper, 185th New York newspaper clippings, NYSMM.

80. Muster Rolls, 185th New York, RG 94, Box 3415, NARA.

81. See chap. 4, p. 73. Compiled from Descriptive Books for Companies A–K, Mar. 28, 1865, 185th New York Regimental Books, RG 94, NARA.

82. *Syracuse Standard,* Feb. 9, 1865, 185th New York, newspaper clippings, NYSMM.

83. *Philadelphia Inquirer,* Sept. 19, 1864, 8.

84. Muster Rolls, 198th Pennsylvania, RG 94, Box 4599, NARA.

85. OR 42:3, 577; *Union County Star and Lewisburg Chronicle* (PA), Nov. 11, 1864, 2; Jacob O. Wilson to Brother, [October 1864?] and Wilson to Uncle Samuel, Oct. 29, 1864, both https://sparedsheet18.wordpress.com/2018/11/12/1864-jacob-o-wilson; "Pennsylvania Presidential Election Returns 1864," https://staffweb.wilkes.edu/harold.cox/pres/PaPress.

86. Letter, Feb. 28, 1865, James Daily Pension File, Fold3.com and NARA; letter, Mar. 9, 1864, Morgan Shaffer Pension File, NARA. See also Henry Dibel to Mother and Father, Mar. 19, 1865, Pension File, NARA.

87. HIBO Database; Wood, *Under Chamberlain's Flag,* 31.

88. Letter, Feb. 19, 1865, Henry Dieble Pension File, NARA. I do not know what a "Solger's Memorial" was. From Dieble's description, it may have been a preprinted decorative form that a soldier could fill in with the appropriate details.

89. Boatner, *Civil War Dictionary,* 760; OR 42:2, 964, 990, 1000; OR 42:1, 58.

90. Compiled from Ancestry.com, US Civil War Soldiers, 1861–65; Wood, *Under Chamberlain's Flag,* 30, 32.

91. Diary of Joseph Shuman, passim, USAHEC; GO No. 7, Oct. 18, 1864, Headquarters, 198th Pennsylvania, Order Book, Company C, Regimental Books, 198th Pennsylvania, RG94, NARA.

92. Muster Rolls, 198th Pennsylvania, RG 94, Box 4599, NARA.

93. Compiled from Bates, *History of Pennsylvania Volunteers,* 5:468–93, Ancestry.com, and Fold3.com.

94. Wood, *Under Chamberlain's Flag,* 102; OR 42:1, 462; OR 42:1, 139, 155.

95. OR 46:1:1, 266.

96. OR 46:1:1, 267; OR 46:1, 65; Jordan Lear to Isaac Lear, Feb. 12, 1865, https://spared-shared9.wordpres.com/2015/12/20/1865-jordan-h-lear; Josiah Shuman, Civil War Diary, Feb. 5, 1865, USAHEC.

97. Hess, *Civil War Infantry Tactics,* 43, 44–45. The Adjutant General's Office authorized a battalion of four additional companies because "a surplus of men for the 198th have already been enlisted with the understanding that they would serve with the 198th." Thomas Vincent to Governor of Pennsylvania, Sept. 21, 1864, RG 94, Box 4599, NARA. One hundred men who had enlisted in Reading were sent to Philadelphia for muster into the 198th Pennsylvania. Letter, Sept. 6, 1864, RG 94, Box 4599, NARA.

98. Muster Rolls, 198th Pennsylvania, RG 94, Box 4599, NARA.

99. Circular, Nov. 22, 1864, Headquarters, 198th Pennsylvania, Order Book, Company C, Regimental Books, RG 94, NARA.

100. Phisterer, *New York in the War of the Rebellion,* 5:4074; Union Bounties (Eastern States), latewarunionsoldiers.org; HIBO Database. Cattaraugus had a county bounty, but I have been unable to determine the specific amount. Local bounties ranged from $40 to $760. Chautauqua had no county bounty with local bounties ranging from $300 to $800. Erie County had a bounty of $600. Most towns offered no local bounty, but Buffalo offered $400 to $500. Niagara County had a county bounty, but I have been unable to determine the specific amount. Local bounties ranged from $100 to $500. Union Bounties (Eastern States), latewarunionsoldiers.org.

101. Compiled from Unit Roster (NYSMM, Unit History website and Muster Roll Abstract (Fold3.com), 187th New York Volunteers.

102. Phisterer, *New York in the War of the Rebellion,* 5:4074, 4078; OR 42:1, 459; OR 42:3, 309.

103. Undated, unsourced clipping in NYSMM, Unit History website misfiled with 186th New York.

104. Phisterer, *New York in the War of the Rebellion,* 5:4075–80.

105. Phisterer, *New York in the War of the Rebellion,* 4:2747, 1:667–68, 5:4075–76.

106. Compiled from Pension Index, 187th New York Volunteers, fold3.com. Joshua Chamberlain recalled that the 187th, 188th, and 189th New York were "new" regiments, "but mostly old soldiers." Chamberlain, *Passing of the Armies,* 39.

107. Dunham, *Alleghany to Appomattox,* 93.

108. DKN to *Courier,* Oct. 29, 1864, NYSMM, Unit History website (misfiled with 186th New York); Phisterer, *New York in the War of the Rebellion,* 5:4074 (seventy-seven casualties).

109. DKN to *Courier,* Oct. 29, 1864, NYSMM, Unit History website (misfiled with 186th New York)

110. *Albany Evening Journal,* Oct. 31, 1864, 1 (Lincoln 219/McClellan 9); *New York Daily Reformer* (Watertown), Nov. 5, 1864, 2 (212/9); *Syracuse Courier,* NYSM. Clippings, letter dated Oct. 29, 1864, from D. K. N.

111. Phisterer, *New York in the War of the Rebellion,* 5:4080; Union Bounties (Eastern States), latewarunionsoldiers.org; OR 42:3, 264, 271, 292, 302, 325, 327.

112. Compiled from Phisterer, *New York in the War of the Rebellion,* 5:4080–88.

113. OR 46:1:2, 859; Phisterer, *New York in the War of the Rebellion,* 3:1897; 4:3068, 3238; 5:4081–88.

114. *Jamestown Journal* (NY), Jan. 27, 1865, 3; Phisterer, *New York in the War of the Rebellion,* 5:4080.

115. Dunham, *Allegany to Appomattox,* 86–87.

116. *New York Daily Reformer* (Watertown), Nov. 5, 1864, 2 (Lincoln 508/McClellan 87).

117. Phisterer, *New York in the War of the Rebellion,* 5:4088; Union Bounties (Eastern States); HIBO Database, latewarunionsoldiers.org.

118. OR 42:3, 378, 410, 487; Phisterer, *New York in the War of the Rebellion,* 5:4088. To facilitate initial organization of the regiment, four companies originally recruited for the 175th New York were assigned to the 189th New York. An unassigned New York company joined the 189th in the field, bringing it to ten companies. Phisterer, *New York in the War of the Rebellion,* 5:4088; OR 42:3, 519, 892, 999.

119. Compiled from Phisterer, *New York in the War of the Rebellion,* 5:4089–95.

120. Henry Bull to Father, Nov. 17, 1864; Henry Bull to Sister Mary, Nov. 8, 1864. Two weeks earlier, Bull had not been as enthusiastic about going to the front. "I heard that they was a going for to keep us here [City Point] for to build breast-works and call us the Engineers corps. I am in hopes that they will do it." Henry Bull to Father, Oct. 28, 1864. Copies of letters in author's possession.

121. *Albany Evening Journal,* Oct. 31, 1864 (Lincoln 481/McClellan 77); *New York Daily Reformer* (Watertown), Nov. 5, 1864, 2 (same); HIBO Database.

122. OR 42:2, 1136; HIBO Database.

123. Bates, *History of Pennsylvania Volunteers,* 5:729.

124. OR 46:1:2, 876; OR 46:1:1, 156; Bates, *History of Pennsylvania Volunteers,* 5:729.

125. Bates, *History of Pennsylvania Volunteers,* 5:729; OR 46:1:1, 66. Gwyn did not single out the 210th Pennsylvania for praise in his after-action report other than noting that the 210th Pennsylvania had led the initial march. OR 46:1:1, 283.

126. OR 42:3, 577.

127. OR 42:3, 264; OR 42:1, 213; OR 42:3, 264, 272; OR 42:3, 343.

128. Dyer, *Compendium of the War of the Rebellion,* 3:1018; OR 42:3, 293, 519, 1114.

129. OR 46:1:1, 570; OR 46:3:2, 926.

Conclusion

1. Gallagher, *Enduring Civil War,* 28.

2. Gallman, *Defining Duty in the Civil War,* 26.

3. OR III:5, 673.

4. See Murdock, *One Million Men,* 334–37. Murdock concluded that the "major mistakes" in raising the Union army were "failure to equalize local bounties, lenient treatment toward bounty jumpers and deserters, failure to regulate brokers until the war was almost over, and the repeal of commutation without abolishing substitution" (337). While Murdock properly recognized that an unrestricted draft would not have been politically acceptable, he did not give appropriate weight in my view to the political challenge from local communities that equalizing local bounties and/or eliminating substitution would have incurred. I do agree that strict disciplinary measures (short of execution) should have been taken against deserters in general and bounty jumpers in particular and that bounty brokers should have been regulated sooner.

5. McPherson, *War That Forged a Nation,* 5. See also Gallagher, *Enduring Civil War,* 130–31.

6. "Armed Forces of the United States—Statistics & Facts," www.statista.com; www.goarmy.com; myarmybenefits.usarmy.mil. The army does not pay the bonuses upon enlistment the way state and local governments typically did during the Civil War, but the

army does typically pay them upon completion of training, rather than spreading them over the term of service. It is also worth noting that the US Army relied very heavily on civilian contractors in Afghanistan and Iraq to perform what traditionally would have been viewed as military work.

7. Sherman, *Memoirs,* 328. See also OR III:3, 1051. I agree with Sherman that a significant increase in monthly pay would have been preferable to increased bounties. By leaving monthly pay at $16, the federal government pushed the compensation burden to the state and local governments through bounties (or state increases in monthly pay). Increased monthly pay would not have provided an advance payment feature, which Fry and others recognized was attractive to potential volunteers.

8. James McPherson has commented that "The half-billion dollars paid in bounties by the North represented something of a transfer of wealth from rich to poor—an ironic counterpoint to the theme of a rich man's war/poor man's fight." McPherson, *Battle Cry of Freedom,* 605. See also Wilkenson, *Mother, May You Never See the Sights I Have Seen,* 6.

9. The *Elmira Daily Advertiser* (NY) wrote that the money spent on high bounties had "reverted back to the benefit of our loyal citizens generally" because the money was being used to support families and pay off debts, including mortgages. The *Daily Advertiser* (Sept. 14, 1864, 2) concluded that "the good accomplished by the use and circulation of so large sums of currency will redound to the growth and prosperity of the business interests of our city and town."

10. The question is less clear for substitutes. While the typical Pennsylvania substitute may not have been a deserter by a narrow margin, it does appear that the typical New Hampshire substitute was a deserter. Livermore, *Eighteenth New Hampshire,* 9.

11. Lonn, *Desertion,* 230; Gallagher, *Enduring Civil War,* 40; Weitz, "Desertion, Cowardice and Punishment," www.essentialcivilwarcurriculum.com; Frawley, "Voting with Their Feet," 298.

12. Houston, *Thirty-Second Maine Regiment,* 431. See also Reid and White, "'A Mob of Stragglers and Cowards,'" 73 ("The constant breaking up of units invariably provoked a wave of desertions."); Bearman, "Desertion as Localism," 321–42 ("[North Carolina] men deserted because their identity as Southerners was eroded by an emergent localism, sustained and organized within the Confederate army. Desertion rates were highest in companies that evidenced a high degree of local homogeneity—company solidarity thus bred rather than reduced desertion rates.") (321). A similar issue could have arisen in the Sixty-Third Pennsylvania. See Hays, *Under the Red Patch,* 276–77. Another example of intraregiment tension is the Thirty-Seventh New York, which brought together Irish-born men from New York City and rural men from Cattaraugus County. See Rutan, *179th New York Volunteer Infantry,* 31, 338, n. 110.

13. Lonn, *Desertion,* 230.

14. In his introduction to the 1998 reprint of Lonn's *Desertion during the Civil War,* William Blair noted that Lonn had relied primarily on the OR and had not pursued the broad range of other records at NARA, nor had she drawn on soldiers' letters. He observed that "the work involved in this kind of research would be tedious and exhausting, which perhaps explains why no one has done it yet." Lonn, *Desertion,* x. See also Gallagher, *Enduring Civil War,* 150–51; Frawley, "Voting with Their Feet," 298, 4–5, 79.

15. OR III:5, 669; Rutan, *179th New York Volunteer Infantry,* 187. Lonn did note that "Natural solicitude for their families entered into the restiveness and discontent of the soldiers," but did so in the context of irregular pay. Lonn, *Desertion,* 134.

16. Reid and White, "'A Mob of Stragglers and Cowards,'" 69; White, *Emancipation,* 78. But see Manning, *What This Cruel War Was Over,* 5. John A. Miller of the 148th Penn-

sylvania was the rare soldier who openly discussed the possibility of deserting in letters to his wife. In October 1862, two months after he had enlisted, he wrote her that "When I left home, I went to fight for the Constitution and to put down the Rebellion. But it appears now that the object of the war is to make the n[—]s free and for that I [don't] want to fight if I can help it." Macneal, "'The Centre County Regiment,'" 36. Similarly, Daniel B. Lee of the 179th New York wrote his wife in May 1864 that "it is just for slavery that does keep this thing [illegible]. If it wasn't for that we would all be to home about our domestic business in peas." Lee did not specifically speak of desertion in his letters to his wife, but he was reported as a deserter in July 1864 (although the better evidence is that he was captured while going for water for his company in no man's land). Rutan, *179th New York Volunteer Infantry*, 46, 78, 363n47.

17. The "Early Indicators" database is an extremely important resource—nearly 40,000 Union soldiers in 331 companies—and Costa and Kahn's *Heroes & Cowards* illustrates its value in analyzing desertion. Hess, "The Early Indicators Project," 380, 385–86. However, my research for "*If I Have Got to Go and Fight, I Am Willing*," as well as my preliminary research for this book, suggested to me that there were important insights to be gained from the regimental approach I have pursued here. While the company was the relevant unit for analyzing the relationships studied by Costa and Kahn, units were deployed in battle as regiments rather than companies.

18. Costa and Kahn, *Heroes & Cowards*, 101.

19. Costa and Kahn, 178–79. See also Reardon, "A Hard Road to Travel," 174 (impact on unit cohesion of "shotgun marriages" of the Army of the Potomac's Corps).

20. Costa and Kahn, *Heroes & Cowards*, xix, 60. Costa and Kahn did not explain in *Heroes & Cowards* how they controlled for bounties. They certainly could have controlled for the fact of receiving a bounty, but only to a limited degree for the amount. The service records utilized to populate the "Early Indicators" database do include information about receipt of a federal bounty and the amount of the federal bounty, but they rarely contain information about receipt or the amount of any state or local bounty and the state and local bounties generally exceeded the federal bounty by a fair amount during the high-bounty period.

21. Reardon, "A Hard Road to Travel," 170, 189; Reid and White, "'A Mob of Stragglers and Cowards,'" 75; Cleaves, *Meade of Gettysburg*, 277.

22. Livermore, *Eighteenth New Hampshire*, 13.

23. Brokaw, *Greatest Generation*. Most of the individuals featured by Brokaw volunteered early in the war, but he did feature at least one who was drafted in 1943. Brokaw, *Greatest Generation*, 47.

24. Grant, *Memoirs*, 2:531. See also Perret, *There's a War to Be Won*, 543. ("When [World War II] ended the [American] Army had several million battle-hardened combat troops, tactical nuclear weapons, TOT artillery fire, 100 percent mobility, medical evacuation helicopters, the best battlefield communications anywhere and much else besides. It was at least a decade ahead of any other army in the world.")

Bibliography

Archives

Cornell Univ., Carl A. Kroch Library, Division of Rare and Manuscript Collections, Ithaca, NY, John Tuttle and Arvilla Rapleee Andrews Papers, Collection 3790.
Minnesota Historical Society, St. Paul, MN, William Bird Jr. Papers, A/m.B618.
National Archives and Records Administration, Washington, DC.
    Carded Medical Records, selected Union regiments (Record Group 94)
    Compiled Military Service Records, selected Union regiments (Record Group 94)
    Inspector General Records (Record Group 159)
    Muster Rolls, selected Union regiments (Record Group 94)
    Pension Files, selected Union veterans (Record Group 15)
    Provost Marshal General Bureau (Record Group 110) (New York City Branch)
    Regimental Book Records, selected Union regiments (Record Group 94)
    Reports of Operations (Record Group 393)
Univ. of Virginia, Special Collections Department, Charlottesville, VA, Richard F. Bohn Civil War Letters 1862–65 Collection, Accession no. 11418.
US Army Heritage and Education Center, Carlisle, PA. Various collections of soldiers' letters and diaries.

References

Adjutant General of the State of Connecticut. *Annual Report, April 1, 1865.* 1865. Reprint, Ithaca, NY: Cornell Univ., 2020.
Adjutant General of the State of Maine. *Annual Report for the Year Ending December 31, 1863.* Augusta: Stevens & Sayward, Printers to the State, 1863.
———. *Report for the Years 1864 and 1865.* Augusta: Stevens & Sayward, Printers to the State, 1866.
Adjutant General of the State of Massachusetts. *Annual Report for the Year Ending December 31, 1863.* Boston: Wright & Potter, State Printers, 1864.

Adjutant General of the State of New Hampshire. *Report for the Year Ending May 20, 1865.* Vol. 1. Concord: Amos Hadley, State Printer, 1865.

Adjutant General of the State of New Hampshire. *Report for the Year Ending June 1, 1866.* Vol. 2. Concord: George E. Jenks, State Printer, 1866.

Adjutant General of Pennsylvania. *Annual Report for the Year 1862.* Harrisburg: Singerly & Myers, State Printers, 1863.

Adjutant and Inspector General for the State of Vermont. *Report from October 1, 1863, to October 1, 1864.* Montpelier: Walton's Steam Press, 1864.

Aldrich, Nelson Wilmarth. *Wholesale Prices, Wages and Transportation. Part 1.* Washington, DC: Government Printing Office, 1893.

American Annual Cyclopedia and Register of Important Events of the Year 1864. New York: D. Appleton & Co., 1864.

Basler, Roy P., ed. *The Collected Works of Abraham Lincoln.* 3 vols. New Brunswick: Rutgers Univ. Press, 1955.

Bates, Samuel Pennman. *History of Pennsylvania Volunteers 1861–1865.* 5 vols. Harrisburg: B. Singerly State Printer, 1869–1871. Reprint, Delhi, India: Facsimile Publications, n.d.

Benedict, G. G. *Vermont in the Civil War: A History of the Part Taken by the Vermont Soldiers and Sailors in the War for the Union, 1861–5.* 2 vols. 1888. Reprint, Breinigsville, PA/ La Vergne, TN: Hard Press Classics Series and Scholar Select, 2020.

Boatner, Mark M., III. *The Civil War Dictionary.* Rev. ed. New York: Vintage Books, 1981.

Bowen, James L. *Massachusetts in the War, 1861–1865.* Springfield, MA: Clarke W. Bryan & Co., 1889.

Bureau of the Census, US Department of Commerce. *Historical Statistics of the United States 1789–1945.* Washington, DC: Government Printing Office, 1949.

Census Office, US Department of the Interior. *Eighth Census, United States—1860: Instructions to U.S. Marshals.* Washington, DC: Geo. W. Bowman, Public Printer, 1860.

———. [Ninth Census] *The Statistics of the Population of the United States.* Vol. 1. Washington, DC: Government Printing Office, 1872.

Collins, Darrell L. *The Army of the Potomac: Order of Battle, 1861–1865, with Commanders, Strengths, Losses and More.* Jefferson, NC: McFarland & Company, Inc., 2013.

Dyer, Frederick H. *A Compendium of the War of the Rebellion.* 3 vols. New York: Thomas Yoseloff, Publisher, 1959.

Eaton, J. H. *The Army Paymaster's Manual, or Collection of Official Rules, or the Information and Guidance of Officers of the Pay Department of the United States Army.* Washington, DC: Government Printing Office, 1864. Reprint, London: Forgotten Books, 2016.

Fox, William F. *Regimental Losses in the American Civil War 1861–1865.* Albany, NY: Albany Publishing Company, 1889.

Kautz, August Valentine. *Customs of Service for Non-Commissioned Officers and Soldiers as Derived from Law and Regulations and Practised in the Army of the United States.* 1864. Reprint, Nabu Public Domain Reprints, 2013.

———. *1865 Customs of Service for Officers of the Army.* 1866. Reprint, Mechanicsburg, PA: Stackpole Books, 2002.

Kennedy, Joseph C. G. *Population of the United States in 1860.* Washington, DC: Government Printing Office, 1864.

Lebergott, Stanley. *Manpower in Economic Growth: The United States Record Since 1860.* New York: McGraw-Hill Book Company, 1964.

Livermore, Thomas L. *Numbers and Losses in the Civil War in America: 1861–65.* 1900. Reprint, Lavergne, TN: Kessinger Publishing, 2011.

Long, Clarence D. *Wages and Earnings in the United States 1860–1890.* Princeton: Princeton Univ. Press, 1960.

Miller, Richard F. *States at War: A Reference Guide for Connecticut, Maine, Massachusetts, New Hampshire, Rhode Island and Vermont in the Civil War.* 4 vols. Hanover, NH: Univ. Press of New England, 2013.

Munden, Kenneth W., and Henry Putney Beers. *The Union: A Guide to Federal Archives Relating to the Civil War.* 1962. Reprint, NARA, 2004.

Murdock, Eugene C. *The Civil War in the North: A Selective Annotated Bibliography.* New York: Garland Publishing, Inc., 1987.

New York Bureau of Military Statistics. *Third Annual Report.* Albany: G. Wendell, Printers, 1866.

———. *Fourth Annual Report.* Albany: Week Parsons & Co., 1867.

———. *Fifth Annual Report.* Albany: C. Van Benthuysen & Sons' Steam Printing House, 1868.

Parsons, Stanley B., William W. Beach, and Michael J. Dubin. *United States Congressional Districts and Data, 1843–1883.* New York: Greenwood Press, 1986.

Phisterer, Frederick. *New York in the War of the Rebellion 1861–1865.* 3rd. ed. 5 vols. Albany: J. B. Lyon Company, State Printers, 1912.

Plante, Trevor K. *Military Service Records at the National Archives, Reference Information Paper 109.* Washington, DC: National Archives and Records Administration, 2007.

Quiner, E. B. *Military History of Wisconsin: A Record of the Civil and Military Patriotism of the State, in the War for the Union.* Chicago: Clarke & Co., Publishers, 1866.

Rhode Island. *Public Laws Passed at the Sessions of the General Assembly from January 1857 to January 1867.* Providence: Providence Press Co., Printers to the State, 1867.

Sauers, Richard A. *The National Tribune Civil War Index.* Vol. 1, *1877–1903.* El Dorado, CA: Savas Beatie, LLC, 2019.

Scheiber, Harry N., Harold G. Valter, and Harold Underwood Faulkner. *American Economic History.* 9th ed. New York: Harper & Row, Publishers, 1976.

Secretary of the Interior. *Statistics of the United States (Including Mortality, Property, & c.) in 1860.* Washington, DC: Government Printing Office, 1866.

Stewart, Estelle May, and Jesse Chester Brown. *History of Wages in the United States from Colonial Times to 1928.* Bulletin of the Bureau of Labor Statistics, Issue 604. Washington, DC: Government Printing Office, 1934.

Stryker, William S. *Record of Officers and Men of New Jersey in the Civil War, 1861–1865.* 2 vols. Trenton, NJ: John L. Murray, Steam Book and Job Printer, 1876.

The Union Army: A History of Military Affairs in the Loyal States 1861–65. 8 vols. Madison, WI: Federal Publishing Company, 1908.

US Sanitary Commission. *Narrative of Privations and Sufferings of United States Officers and Soldiers While Prisoners of War in the Hands of the Rebel Authorities.* Philadelphia: King & Baird, Prs, 1864.

War Department: Office of the Chief of Staff. *Bibliography of State Participation in the Civil War 1861–1866.* War Department Library Subject Catalogue no. 6, 1913. Reprint, Charlottesville, VA: Allen Publishing Co., Inc., 1961.

The War of the Rebellion: A Compilation of the Official Records of the Union and Confederate Armies. 128 vols. Washington, DC: Government Printing Office, 1890s.

Weeks, Joseph D. (Census Office, Department of the Interior). *Report on the Statistics of Wages in the Manufacturing Industries.* Washington, DC: Government Printing Office, 1886.

Whitman, William E. S., and Charles H. True. *Maine in the War for the Union: A History of the Part Borne by Maine Troops in the Suppression of the American Rebellion.* Lewiston: Nelson Dingley Jr. & Co., Publishers, 1865.

Wright, John D. *The Language of the Civil War.* Westport, CT: Oryx Press, 2001.

Online Resources

American Civil War Research Database: http://www.civilwardata.com

American Presidency Project: "Voter Turnout in Presidential Elections 1828–2016," https://www.presidency.ucsb.edu/

Ancestry.com: Federal Census Collection and US, Civil War Soldiers, 1861–65 Collection

Chronicling America: Historic American Newspapers, https://chroniclingamerica.loc.gov

Congressional Research Service: *The Fundamentals of Military Readiness* (R46559), Oct. 2, 2020. https://crsreports.congress.gov

DifferenceBetween.net: "Difference Between VEP and VAP," http://www.differencebetween.net/miscellaneous/politics/difference-between

Fold3.com: Civil War Veterans Pension Index; New York Muster Roll Abstracts; "Widow's" Pensions and Massachusetts and Vermont Compiled Military Service Records

Genealogybank.com: newspapers.

Hickox, Will. "The Civil War's 11th Hour Soldiers." Opinionator, *New York Times,* Apr. 6, 2015. archive.nytimes.com

latewarunionsoldiers.org: Economic Database, HIBO Database, Methodology, Tables, Union Bounties (Eastern States)

Library of Congress: "Presidential Election of 1864: A Resource Guide," https://guides.loc.gov/presidential-election-1864

Maine Newspaper Project: https://digitalmaine.com/newspapers

New Jersey Digital Newspaper Project: https://collections.libraries.rutgers.edu/new-jersey-digital-newspaper-project

New York Historic Newspapers: https://nyshistoricnewspapers.org

New York State Military Museum and Veterans Research Center: Unit History Project (Muster Rolls, Rosters, and Newspaper clippings by regiment), https://museum.dmna.ny.gov/unit-history/conflict/us-civil-war-1861–1865

Newspapers.com

Pennsylvania Civil War Deserters Database: https://desertersroster.psu.edu/site/searchtips

Pennsylvania Newspaper Archive: https://panewsarchive.psu.edu

Pennsylvania Volunteers of the Civil War: http://www.pacivilwar.com

Seymour, Horatio. Annual Message to the Legislature, Jan. 7, 1863, Senate Doc. No. 2, New York State Library Digital Collections, https://www.nysl.nysed.gov>nysgovmessage

US Elections Project: "National Turnout Rates 1789-Present," https://www.electproject.org/national-1789-present

Westphal, CPT Tom W., and Guffey, CPT Jason. "Measures of Effectiveness in Army Doctrine," eArmor, https://www.benning.army.mil/armor/earmor/content/issues/2014

Wikipedia: Various subjects

Books, Articles, and Unpublished Manuscripts

Achorn, Edward. *Every Drop of Blood: The Momentous Second Inauguration of Abraham Lincoln.* New York: Grove Press, 2020.

Adams, Michael C. C. *Living Hell: The Dark Side of the Civil War.* Baltimore: Johns Hopkins Univ. Press, 2014.

Albert, Allen D. *History of the Forty-Fifth Regiment Pennsylvania Veteran Volunteer Infantry 1861–1865.* Williamsport, PA: Grit Publishing Company, 1912.

Alderson, Kevin, and Patsy Alderson, eds. *Letters Home to Sarah: The Civil War Letters of Guy C. Taylor, 36th Wisconsin Volunteers.* Madison: Univ. of Wisconsin Press, 2012.

Aldridge, Katherine M. *No Freedom Shrieker: The Civil War Letters of Union Soldier Charles Biddlecom*. Ithaca, NY: Paramount Market Publishing, Inc., 2012, 2015.

Alexander, Edward S. "Mapping the Attack on Fort Mahone, April 2, 1865." *Emerging Civil War*. emergingcivilwar.com/2017/10/13/.

Ambrose, Stephen E. *Band of Brothers: E Company, 506th Regiment, 101st Airborne from Normandy to Hitler's Eagle's Nest*. New York: Simon & Schuster, 1992, 2001.

Anderson, John. *The Fifty-Seventh Regiment of Massachusetts Volunteers in the War of the Rebellion*. Boston: E. B. Stillings & Co., Printers, 1896.

Aubery, James M. *The Thirty-Sixth Wisconsin Volunteer Infantry*.1900. Reprint, Monee, IL: Old South Books, 2022.

Bacarella, Michael. *Lincoln's Foreign Legion: The 39th New York Infantry, The Garibaldi Guard*. Shippensburg, PA: White Maine Publishing, Inc., 1996.

Baier, Bret. *Three Days in January: Dwight Eisenhower's Final Mission*. New York: William Morrow, an imprint of Harper Collins Publishers, 2017.

Baquet, Camille. *History of the First Brigade, New Jersey Volunteers from 1861 to 1865*. Trenton, NJ: MacCrellish & Quigley, State Printers, 1910.

Barram, Rick. *The 72nd New York Infantry in the Civil War: A History and Roster*. Jefferson, NC: McFarland & Company, 2014.

Barton, Michael, ed. *Glorious Recollections, J. Howard Wert's Lost History of the 209th Regiment Pennsylvania Volunteer Infantry, 1864–1865*. Bloomington, IN: Xlibris, 2016.

Bearman, Peter S. "Desertion as Localism: Army Unit Solidarity and Group Norms in the U.S. Civil War." *Social Forces* 70, no. 2 (Dec. 1991): 321–42.

Bearss, Edwin C., with Bryce A. Suderow. *The Petersburg Campaign*. Vol. 1, *The Eastern Front Battles June–August 1864*. El Dorado Hills, CA: Savas Beatie LLC, 2012.

———. *The Petersburg Campaign*. Vol. 2, *The Western Front Battles September 1864 to April 1865*. El Dorado Hills, CA: Savas Beatie LLC, 2014.

Berkovich, Ilya. *Motivation in War: The Experience of Common Soldiers in Old-Regime Europe*. Cambridge: Cambridge Univ. Press, 2017.

Bicknell, Thomas Williams. *A History of Barrington, Rhode Island*. Providence, RI: Snow & Farnham, Printers, 1898.

Bilby, Joseph G. *Three Rousing Cheers: A History of the Fifteenth New Jersey from Flemington to Appomattox*. Rev. ed. Hightstown, NJ: Longstreet House, 2001.

Birch, Harold B. *The 50th Pennsylvania's Civil War Odyssey*. Bloomington, IN: Harold B. Birch, 2003.

Boggs, Colleen Glenney. *Patriotism by Proxy: The Civil War Draft and the Cultural Formation of Citizen Soldiers, 1863–1865*. Oxford: Oxford Univ. Press, 2020.

Bosbyshell, Oliver Christian. *The 48th in the War Being a Narrative of the Campaigns of the 48th Regiment, Infantry, Pennsylvania Veteran Volunteers during the War of the Rebellion*. Philadelphia: Avil Printing Co., 1895.

Bowery, Charles R., Jr. *The Richmond-Petersburg Campaign, 1864–65*. Santa Barbara, CA: Praeger, 2014.

Brokaw, Tom. *The Greatest Generation*. New York: Random House, 1998.

Bui, L. Bao. "'I Feel Impelled to Write'": Male Intimacy, Epistolary Privacy, and the Culture of Letter Writing during the American Civil War." PhD diss., Univ. of Illinois at Urbana-Champaign, 2016.

Catton, Bruce. *The Army of the Potomac: Glory Road*. Garden City, NY: Doubleday & Company, 1952.

———. *The Army of the Potomac: A Stillness at Appomattox*. Garden City, NY: Doubleday & Company, 1953.

———. *Grant Takes Command.* Boston: Little, Brown and Company, 1968.

Chamberlain, Joshua Lawrence. *The Passing of the Armies: An Account of the Final Campaign of the Army of the Potomac, Based upon Personal Reminiscences of the Fifth Army Corps.* 1915. N.p.: Alpha Editions, 2020.

Chernow, Ron. *Grant.* New York: Penguin Press, 2017.

Churchill, John Charles. *Landmarks of Oswego County, New York.* Syracuse: D. Mason & Company, Publishers, 1895.

Clayton, W. W. *History of Onondaga County, New York.* Syracuse: D. Mason & Co., 1878.

Cleaves, Freeman. *Meade of Gettysburg.* Norman: Univ. of Oklahoma Press, 1960.

Cogswell, Leander W. *A History of the Eleventh New Hampshire Regiment Volunteer Infantry in the Rebellion War 1861–1865.* Concord: Republican Press Association, 1891.

Coss, Edward J. *All for the King's Shilling: The British Soldier under Wellington, 1808–1814.* Norman: Univ. of Oklahoma Press, 2010.

Costa, Dora L., and Matthew E. Kahn. "Cowards and Heroes: Group Loyalty in the American Civil War." *The Quarterly Journal of Economics* (May 2003): 519–48.

———. "Deserters, Social Norms, and Migration." *Journal of Law & Economics* 50, no. 2 (May 2007): 323–53.

———. *Heroes & Cowards: The Social Face of War.* Princeton: Princeton Univ. Press, 2008.

de Tocqueville, Alexis. *Democracy in America.* 1835. Reprint, London: Penguin Books, 2003.

Dunham, Valgene. *Alleghany to Appomattox: The Life and Letters of Private William Whitlock of the 188th New York Volunteers.* Syracuse: Syracuse Univ. Press, 2013.

Dunkelman, Mark H. *Brothers One and All: Esprit de Corps in a Civil War Regiment.* Baton Rouge: Louisiana State Univ. Press, 2004.

Eden, R. C. *The Sword and the Gun, A History of the 37th Wis. Volunteer Infantry from Its Organization to Its Final Muster Out.* Madison: Atwood & Ruble, Printers, 1865.

Escott, Paul D. *Rethinking the Civil War Era: Directions for Research.* Lexington: Univ. Press of Kentucky, 2018.

Etcheson, Nicole. "Making War on the Draft." In *The New York Times: Disunion: A History of the Civil War,* edited by Ted Widmer. New York: Oxford Univ. Press, 2016.

Faust, Drew Gilpin. *This Republic of Suffering: Death and the American Civil War.* New York: Alfred A. Knopf, 2008.

F. E. C. *History of the 58th Regt. Massachusetts Vols. From the 15th day of September, 1863, to the Close of the Rebellion.* Washington, DC: Gibson Brothers, Printers, 1865.

Foner, Eric. *The Fiery Trial: Abraham Lincoln and American Slavery.* New York: W. W. Norton & Company, 2010.

Foote, Shelby. *The Civil War a Narrative: Red River to Appomattox.* 1974. Reprint, New York: Vintage Books, 1986.

Ford, Owen. "A History of the Bounty System Used during the Civil War." MA thesis, Univ. of the Pacific, 1933. https://scholarlycommons.pacific.edu/uop_etds/943.

Frawley, Jason Mann. "Voting with Their Feet: Union Desertion in the Army of the Potomac, 1861–1865." Legacy ETDs. Master's thesis, Georgia Southern Univ., 2003. https//digitalcommons.georgiasouthern.edu/etd_legacy/298.

Freeman, Douglas Southall. *R. E. Lee a Biography.* Vol. 3. New York: Charles Scribner's Sons, 1935.

Gallagher, Gary W. *The Enduring Civil War: Reflections on the Great American Crisis.* Baton Rouge: Louisiana State Univ. Press, 2020.

———. *The Union War.* Cambridge, MA: Harvard Univ. Press, 2011.

Gallman, J. Matthew. *Defining Duty in the Civil War: Personal Choice, Popular Culture and the Union Home Front.* Chapel Hill: Univ. of North Carolina Press, 2015.

Gallman, Matt. Review of *Patriotism by Proxy: The Civil War Draft and the Cultural Formation of Citizen-Soldiers, 1863–1865* by Colleen Glenney Boggs. *Civil War History* 68, no. 3 (Sept. 2022): 331.

Gates, Paul W. *Agriculture and the Civil War.* New York: Alfred A. Knopf, 1965.

———. *The Farmer's Age: Agriculture 1815–1860.* Armonk, NY: M. E. Sharpe, Inc., 1960.

Geary, James W. *We Need Men: The Union Draft in the Civil War.* DeKalb: Northern Illinois Univ. Press, 1991.

Gibbon, John. *Personal Recollections of the Civil War.* 1928. Reprint, Dayton, OH: Morningside Bookshop, 1988.

Glasson, William Henry. *Federal Military Pensions in the United States.* 1918. Reprint, San Bernadino, CA: Filiquarian Publishing, 2014.

Goldin, Claudia, and Frank Lewis. "The Economic Cost of the American Civil War: Estimates and Implications." *The Journal of Economic History* 35, no. 2 (1975): 299–326.

Goodwin, Doris Kearns. *Team of Rivals: The Political Genius of Abraham Lincoln.* New York: Simon & Schuster, 2005.

Gordon, Lesley J. *A Broken Regiment: The 16th Connecticut's Civil War.* Baton Rouge: Louisiana State Univ. Press, 2014.

Grant, Ulysses S. *Personal Memoirs of U. S. Grant.* Vols. 1 and 2. New York: Charles L. Webster & Company, 1886.

Greene, A. Wilson. *A Campaign of Giants: The Battle for Petersburg.* Vol. 1, *From the Crossing of the James to the Crater.* Chapel Hill: Univ. of North Carolina Press, 2018.

———. *The Final Battles of the Petersburg Campaign: Breaking the Backbone of the Rebellion.* 2nd ed. Knoxville: Univ. of Tennessee Press, 2008.

Griffith, James. "What Do the Soldiers Say? Needed Ingredients for Determining Unit Readiness." *Armed Forces & Society* 32, no. 3 (Apr. 2006): 367–88.

Guilmartin, John F. "Foreword." In *All for the King's Shilling: The British Soldier under Wellington, 1808–1814,* by Edward J. Coss. Norman: Univ. of Oklahoma Press, 2010.

Haines, Alanson A. *History of the Fifteenth Regiment New Jersey Volunteers.* New York: Jenkins & Thomas, Printers, 1883.

Halleck, Judith Lee. "The Role of the Community in Civil War Desertion." *Civil War History* 29, no. 2 (June 1983): 123–34.

Hanson, Thomas E. "The Eighth Army's Combat Readiness before Korea: A New Appraisal." *Armed Forces & Society* 29, no. 2 (Winter 2003): 167–84.

Hartranft, John F. "The Recapture of Fort Stedman." In *Battles and Leaders of the Civil War.* Vol. 4. 1887. Reprint, Secaucus, NJ: Castle, a division of Book Sales, Inc., n.d.

Hays, Gilbert Adams. *Under the Red Patch: Story of the Sixty Third Regiment Pennsylvania Volunteers 1861–1864.* 1908. Reprint, Breinigsville, PA: Alpha Editions, 2019.

Hayward, Philip. "The Measurement of Combat Effectiveness." *Operations Research* 16, no. 2 (Mar.–Apr. 1968): 314–23.

Hess, Earl J. *Civil War Infantry Tactics: Training, Combat, and Small-Unit Effectiveness.* Baton Rouge: Louisiana State Univ. Press, 2015.

———. "The Early Indicators Project: Using Massive Data and Statistical Analysis to Understand the Life Cycle of Civil War Soldiers." *Civil War History* 63, no. 4 (Dec. 2017): 377–99.

———. *In the Trenches at Petersburg: Field Fortifications & Confederate Defeat.* Chapel Hill: Univ. of North Carolina Press, 2009.

———. *Into the Crater: The Mine Attack at Petersburg.* Columbia: Univ. of South Carolina Press, 2010.

———. *Trench Warfare under Grant & Lee: Field Fortifications in the Overland Campaign.* Chapel Hill: Univ. of North Carolina Press, 2007.

———. *The Union Soldier in Battle*. Lawrence: Univ. Press of Kansas, 1997.

Hodgkins, William Henry. *The Battle of Fort Stedman (Petersburg, Virginia) March 25, 1865*. Boston: Privately printed, 1889.

Holberton, William B. *Homeward Bound: The Demobilization of the Union and Confederate Armies, 1865–1866*. Mechanicsburg, PA: Stackpole Books, 2001.

Hopkins, William Palmer. *The Seventh Regiment Rhode Island Volunteers in the Civil War, 1862–1865*. 1903. Reprint, n.p. and n.d. Nabu Public Domain Reprint.

Horn, John. *The Siege of Petersburg: The Battles for the Weldon Railroad, August 1864*. Rev. ed. El Dorado Hills, CA: Savas Beatie LLC, 2015. Originally published as *The Petersburg Campaign: The Destruction of the Weldon Railroad—Deep Bottom, Globe Tavern and Reams Station*. Lynchburg, VA: H. E. Howard, Inc., 1991.

Houston, Henry C. *The Thirty-Second Maine Regiment of Infantry Volunteers: An Historical Sketch*. Portland: Press of Southworth Brothers, 1903.

Howe, Thomas J. *The Petersburg Campaign; Wasted Valor, June 15–18, 1864*. 2nd ed. Lynchburg, VA: H. E. Howard, Inc., 1988.

Humphreys, Andrew A. *The Virginia Campaign of '64 and '65*. 1883. Reprint, Edison, NJ: Castle Books, 2002.

Humphreys, Margaret. *The Marrow of Tragedy: The Health Crisis of the American Civil War*. Baltimore: Johns Hopkins Univ. Press, 2013.

Hyde, Thomas W. *Following the Greek Cross Or, Memoirs of the Sixth Army Corps*. Boston: Houghton Mifflin and Company, 1894.

Jordan, Brian Matthew. *Marching Home: Union Veterans and Their Unending Civil War*. Philadelphia: Liveright Publishing Corporation, 2014.

Judson, Amos, M. *History of the Eighty-Third Regiment Pennsylvania Volunteers*. 1865. Reprint, n.p.: Scholar Select, (Andesite Press), 2017.

Keegan, John. *The American Civil War: A Military History*. New York: Alfred A. Knopf, 2009.

———. *The Face of Battle*. New York: Viking Press, 1976.

Kingsbury, Frank Burnside. *History of the Town of Surry, Cheshire County, New Hampshire*. Concord: Concord Press, 1925.

Kreidberg, Marvin, and Merton G. Henry. *History of Military Mobilization in the United States Army 1775–1945*. Pamphlet no. 20–212. Washington, DC: Department of the Army, 1955.

Kreiser, Lawrence A., Jr. *Defeating Lee: A History of the Second Corps Army of the Potomac*. Bloomington: Indiana Univ. Press, 2011.

Krick, Robert E. L. "Repairing an Army: A Look at the New Troops in the Army of Northern Virginia in May and June 1864." In *Cold Harbor to the Crater: The End of the Overland Campaign*, edited by Gary W. Gallagher and Caroline E. Janney, 33–72. Chapel Hill: Univ. of North Carolina Press, 2015.

LaRocca, Charles J. *The 124th New York State Volunteers in the Civil War*. Jefferson, NC: McFarland & Company, Inc., 2012.

Lerwill, Leonard L, *The Personnel Replacement System in the United States Army*. Department of the Army Pamphlet no. 20–211, Aug. 1954.

Linderman, Gerald F. *Embattled Courage: The Experience of Combat in the American Civil War*. New York: Free Press, 1987.

Livermore, Thomas L. *History of the Eighteenth New Hampshire Volunteers*. Boston: Fort Hill Press, 1904.

Lonn, Ella. *Desertion during the Civil War*. Lincoln: Univ. of Nebraska Press, 1998.

Lord, Edward O., ed. *History of the Ninth Regiment, New Hampshire Volunteers in the War of the Rebellion*. Concord, NH: Republican Press Association, 1895.

Luskey, Brian P. *On the Make: Clerks and the Quest for Capital in Nineteenth-Century America.* New York: New York Univ. Press, 2010.

Lynn, John A. *The Bayonets of the Republic: Motivation and Tactics in the Army of Revolutionary France, 1791–94.* 1984. Reprint, Boulder, CO: Westview Press, 1996.

Macneal, Douglas. "'The Centre County Regiment': Story of the 148th Regiment, Pennsylvania Volunteers." *Centre County Heritage* 36, no. 1 (2000): 1–160.

Mahan, Dennis Hart. *A Complete Treatise on Field Fortifications.* 1836. Reprint, New York: Greenwood Press, 1968.

Manning, Chandra. *What This Cruel War Was Over: Soldiers, Slavery and the Civil War.* New York: Vintage Books, 2007.

Mansoor, Peter R. *The GI Offensive in Europe: The Triumph of American Infantry Divisions, 1941–1945.* Lawrence: Univ. Press of Kansas, 1999.

Mark, Penrose G. *Red, White, and Blue Badge, Pennsylvania Veteran Volunteers. A History of the 93rd Regiment, Known as the "Lebanon Infantry" and "One of the 300 Fighting Regiments" from September 12th, 1861, to June 27th, 1865.* N.p.: Alpha Editions, 2019.

Marten, James. *Sing Not War: The Lives of Union & Confederate Veterans in Gilded Age America,* Chapel Hill: Univ. of North Carolina Press, 2011.

Marvel, William. *Lincoln's Mercenaries: Economic Motivation among Union Soldiers during the Civil War.* Baton Rouge: Louisiana State Univ. Press, 2018.

———. *Race of the Soil: The Ninth New Hampshire Regiment in the Civil War.* Wilmington, NC: Broadfoot Publishing Company, 1988.

Matthews, Richard E. *The 149th Pennsylvania Volunteer Infantry Unit in the Civil War.* Jefferson, NC: McFarland & Company, 1994.

McCalmont, Alfred B. *Extracts from Letters Written by Alfred B. McCalmont 1862–1865.* N.p.: Privately printed by Robert McCalmont, 1908.

McPherson, James M. *Battle Cry of Freedom: The Civil War Era.* 1988. Reprint, New York: Oxford Univ. Press, 2003.

———. *For Cause and Comrades: Why Men Fought in the Civil War.* New York: Oxford Univ. Press, 1997.

———. *Tried by War: Abraham Lincoln as Commander in Chief.* New York: Penguin Press, 2008.

———. *The War That Forged a Nation: Why the Civil War Still Matters.* New York: Oxford Univ. Press, 2015.

Miller, Richard F. *Harvard's Civil War: A History of the Twentieth Massachusetts Volunteer Infantry.* Lebanon, NH: Univ. Press of New England, 2005.

Millet, Allan R., Williamson Murray, and Kenneth Watman. "The Effectiveness of Military Organizations." In *Military Effectiveness,* new ed., vol. 1, *The First World War,* edited by Allan R. Millet and Williamson Murray, 1–30. Cambridge: Cambridge Univ. Press, 2010.

Mitchell, Wesley C. "The Value of the 'Greenbacks' during the Civil War." *Journal of Political Economy* 6, no. 2 (Mar. 1898): 144.

Mowris, J. A. *A History of the 117th Regiment, N. Y. Volunteers (Fourth Oneida).* 1866. Reprint, Hamilton, NY: Edmonston Publishing, Inc., 1996.

Mulholland, St. Clair A. *The Story of the 116th Regiment, Pennsylvania Volunteers in the War of the Rebellion.* 1899. Reprint, New York: Fordham Univ. Press, 1996.

Murdock, Eugene C. *One Million Men: The Civil War Draft in the North 1862–1865: The Civil War Draft and the Bounty System.* Madison: State Historical Society of Wisconsin, 1971.

———. *Patriotism Limited,* Kent, OH: Kent State Univ. Press, 1967.

Musick, Michael P. "The Little Regiment: Civil War Units and Commands." *Prologue* 27, no. 2 (Summer 1995): 151–71.

Myers, Irvin G. *We Might as Well Die Here: The 53rd Pennsylvania Veteran Volunteer Infantry.* Shippensburg, PA: White Maine Books, 2004.

Nevins, Allan. *The War for the Union: The Organized War to Victory 1864–1865.* New York: Charles Scribner's Sons, 1971.

Newsome, Hampton. *Richmond Must Fall: The Richmond Petersburg Campaign, October 1864.* Kent, OH: Kent State Univ. Press, 2013.

Noe, Kenneth W. *Reluctant Rebels: The Confederates Who Joined the Army after 1861.* Chapel Hill: Univ. of North Carolina Press, 2010.

Nolan, Alan T. *The Iron Brigade: A Military History.* Bloomington: Indiana Univ. Press, 1994.

Norton, Oliver Wilcox. *Army Letters 1861–1865.* 1903. Reprint, Monee, IL: Big Byte Books, 2016.

Parsons, George W. *Put the Vermonters Ahead: The First Vermont Brigade in the Civil War.* Shippensburg, PA: White Maine Publishing Company, Inc., 1996.

Pellicano, John M. *Conquer or Die: The 39th New York Infantry: Garibaldi Guard.* Flushing, NY: John M. Pellicano, 1996.

Perret, Geoffrey. *There's a War to Be Won: The United States Army in World War II.* New York: Random House, 1991.

Powell, William H. *The Fifth Army Corps (Army of the Potomac): A Record of Operations during the Civil War in the United States of America, 1861–1865.* 1896. Reprint, N.p.: Scholar Select (Wentworth Press), 2016.

Pride, Mike, and Mark Travis. *My Brave Boys: To War with Col. Cross and the Fighting Fifth.* Hanover, NH: Univ. Press of New England, 2001.

Proceedings Reunion of the Third Division, Ninth Corps, Army of the Potomac, Held at York, PA., March 25, 1891. Harrisburg, PA: Harrisburg Publishing Company, 1892.

Ramold, Steven J. *Across the Divide: Union Soldiers View the Northern Home Front.* New York: New York Univ. Press, 2013.

Reardon, Carol. "A Hard Road to Travel: The Impact of Continuous Operations on the Army of the Potomac and the Army of Northern Virginia in May 1864." In *The Spotsylvania Campaign,* edited by Gary W. Gallagher, 170–202. Chapel Hill: Univ. of North Carolina Press, 1998.

Reid, Brian Holden, and John White. "'A Mob of Stragglers and Cowards': Desertion from the Union and Confederate Armies, 1861–65." *Journal of Strategic Studies* 5, no. 1 (1985): 64–67.

Reisen, Dominick J., ed. *Otsego County in the Civil War.* 2nd ed. Voorheesville, NY: Square Circle Press, 2011.

Rhea, Gordon C. *The Battle of the Wilderness May 5–6, 1864.* Baton Rouge: Louisiana State Univ. Press, 1994.

———. *The Battles for Spotsylvania Court House and the Road to Yellow Tavern May 7–12, 1864.* Baton Rouge: Louisiana State Univ. Press, 1997.

———. *Cold Harbor: Grant and Lee May 26–June 3, 1864.* Baton Rouge: Louisiana State Univ. Press, 2002.

———. "Foreword." In *Lee's Army during the Overland Campaign: A Numerical Study,* by Alfred C. Young III. Baton Rouge: Louisiana State Univ. Press, 2013.

———. *To the North Ana River: Grant and Lee May 13–25, 1864.* Baton Rouge: Louisiana State Univ. Press, 2000.

———. *On to Petersburg: Grant and Lee June 4–15, 1864.* Baton Rouge: Louisiana State Univ. Press, 2017.

Rhodes, James Ford. *History of the Civil War, 1861–1865.* New York: MacMillan Company, 1917.

———. *History of the United States from the Compromise of 1850.* New York: MacMillan Company, 1902.

Robertson, John. "Re-enlistment Patterns of Civil War Soldiers." *Journal of Interdisciplinary History* 32, no. 1 (Summer 2001): 15–35.

Rogers, William H. *History of the One Hundred and Eighty-Ninth Regiment of New-York Volunteers.* 1865. Reprint, Lexington, KY: BiblioLife, 2016.

Rosenheim, Jeff. *Photography and the American Civil War.* New York: Metropolitan Museum of Art, 2013.

Rutan, Edwin P., II. *"If I Have Got to Go and Fight, I Am Willing": A Union Regiment Forged in the Petersburg Campaign, the 179th New York Volunteer Infantry 1864–1865.* Park City, UT: RTD Publications, LLC, 2015.

Sandow, Robert M., ed. *Contested Loyalty: Debates over Patriotism in the Civil War North.* New York: Fordham Univ. Press, 2018.

———. "The Limits of Northern Patriotism: Early Civil War Mobilization in Pennsylvania." *Pennsylvania History: A Journal of Mid-Atlantic Studies* 70, no. 2 (Spring 2003): 175–203.

Schnier, Kurt E., William C. Horrace, and Ronald G. Felthoven. "The Value of Statistical Life: Pursuing the Deadliest Catch." (2009). Center for Policy Research, Syracuse Univ. Maxwell School. https://surface.syr.edu/cpr/49.

Shannon, Fred Albert. *The Organization and Administration of the Union Army, 1861–1865.* 2 vols. 1928. Reprint, Gloucester, MA: American Council of Learned Societies, 1965.

Shea, Robert F. "Aspects of the History of Westerly [Rhode Island] during the Civil War." Master's thesis, Univ. of Rhode Island, 1957. Open Access Masters Theses. Paper 720. https://digitalcommons.url.edu/theses/720.

Sherman, William Tecumseh. *Memoirs of Gen. William T. Sherman.* 1875. Reprint, Las Vegas, NV: Pantianos Classics, n.d.

Simons, Ezra D. *A Regimental History: The One Hundred and Twenty-Fifth New York State Volunteers.* New York: Ezra D. Simons, 1888.

Snyder, Charles M. "Oswego County's Response to the Civil War." *New York History* 42, no. 1 (Jan. 1961): 71–92.

Sommers, Richard J. *Richmond Redeemed: The Siege at Petersburg.* Garden City, NY: Doubleday & Company, 1981.

———. *Richmond Redeemed: The Siege at Petersburg.* Rcv. ed. El Dorado, CA: Savas Beatie, 2014.

Stevens, George T. *The Sixth Corps, The Army of the Potomac, Union Army, during the American Civil War.* 1866. Reprint, N.p.: Leonaur Ltd., 2007.

Sutherland, Daniel E. *The Expansion of Everyday Life 1860–1876.* Fayetteville: Univ. of Arkansas Press, 1989, 2000.

Trudeau, Noah Andre. *The Last Citadel: Petersburg June 1864–April 1865.* Rev ed. El Dorado Hills, CA: Savas Beastie LLC, 2014.

Uhler, George H. *Camps and Campaigns of the 93rd Regiment Penna. Vols.* Harrisburg, PA: State Library of Pennsylvania, 1898.

Upton, Emory. *The Military Policy of the United States.* Washington, DC: Government Printing Office, 1917.

van Creveld, Martin. *Fighting Power: German and U.S. Army Performance, 1939–1945.* Westport, CT: Greenwood Press, 1982.

Ventner, Bruce M. "Hancock the (Not So) Superb: The Second Battle of Reams' Station, August 25, 1864." *Blue & Gray* 23, no. 5 (2007): 42.

Walker, Francis A. *History of the Second Corps in the Army of the Potomac.* New York: Charles Scribner's Sons, 1886.

Ward, Geoffrey C., with Ric Burns and Ken Burns. *The Civil War: An Illustrated History.* New York: Alfred A. Knopf, 1991.

Webb, Jim. *Born Fighting: How the Scots-Irish Shaped America*. New York: Broadway Books, 2004.

Weld, Stephen Minot. *War Diary and Letters of Stephen Minot Weld, 1861–1865*. 1912. Reprint, N.p.: Nabu Public Domain Publishing, n.d.

Westbrook, Robert S. *History of the 49th Pennsylvania Volunteers*. Altoona, PA: Altoona Times Print, 1898.

Weygant, Charles H. *History of the One Hundred and Twenty-Fourth Regiment N.Y.S.V.* 1877. Reprint, Gaithersburg, MD: Butternut Press, 1986.

White, Jonathan W. *Emancipation, The Union Army and the Reelection of Abraham Lincoln*. Baton Rouge: Louisiana State Univ. Press, 2014.

Wiley, Bell Irwin. *The Life of Billy Yank: The Common Soldier of the Union*. Baton Rouge: Louisiana State Univ. Press, 1952, 1971.

Wilkenson, Warren. *Mother, May You Never See the Sights I Have Seen: The Fifty-Seventh Massachusetts Veteran Volunteers in the Last Years of the Civil War*. New York: Harper & Row, 1990.

Wilson, Sven Eric. "Prejudice & Policy: Racial Discrimination in the Union Army Disability Pension System, 1865–1906." *American Journal of Public Health* 100, no. S1 (Apr. 2010): S56–S65.

Wood, Jeffrey L. *Under Chamberlain's Flag: The Stories of the 198th Pennsylvania and the 185th New York Volunteers*. Victoria, BC: Trafford Publishing, 2008.

Wyrick, William C. "Bursting of the Storm: Action at Petersburg March 25, 1865." *Blue & Gray* 28, no. 5 (2012): 7.

———. "Lee's Last Offensive: The Attack on Fort Stedman March 25, 1865." *Blue & Gray* 25, no. 1 (2008), 6.

Young, Alfred C., III. *Lee's Army during the Overland Campaign: A Numerical Study*. Baton Rouge: Louisiana State Univ. Press, 2013.

Zeller, Paul G. "In Their Words: 'My Soldier Boy Mark': The Civil War Letters of Pvt. Mark B. Slayton." *Vermont History* 82, no. 1 (Winter/Spring 2014): 45–62.

Index

Adjutant General's Office, 79–81

advertising, 59

African Americans: recruitment of, 9, 83; in the Union army, 24, 173, 209

age, of soldiers, 69, 71

Albany Atlas & Argus, 37

Albany Bounty Jumper, 20. *See also* bounty jumpers

Albany Evening Journal, 65

Alexandria, VA, 54

Allegany County, NY, 200

Alleghenian, 66

American Annual Cyclopedia, 20

American Legion, 31

American Revolution, 34

Ames, Adelbert, 117

Anderson, Richard H., 178–79, 181

Andersonville, 52

Andrews, John, 49–50, 134

anecdotes, in history, 19–20

Annapolis, MD, 113

Antietam, Battle of, 37, 54, 117, 123, 167, 169

Appomattox Court House, VA, 151

Appomattox River, 155

Ap Rees, Henry, 139

Arlington Heights, 129

Army of Northern Virginia, 32, 139, 152; defeat of, 2. *See also* Confederate army

Army of the James, 125, 162, 170, 195

Army of the Potomac: casualties in, 97–99, 110; combat effectiveness of, 211; demographics of, 197; desertion rates of, 78–81, 88, 90, 93, 95–96, 207; at Five Forks, 188; Grand Review of, 30, 211; historiography of, 6, 15, 31–32; inspections in, 162–63; late-war new regiments in, 109–11, 123, 128, 130, 170, 195, 201; late-war Union soldiers in, 3, 8, 13, 107–8; officers of, 27; performance of late-war new regiments in, 11, 98–99, 111, 139, 209; at Petersburg, 46, 125–26, 139; recruitment for, 2, 35–37, 44, 46; reenlistment in, 55; regiments in, 115, 173–74, 176; supplies of, 152, 174–75; training of, 110, 209; voting in, 166. *See also* Union army

Army of the Tennessee, 24, 30

Arnold, John, 119

artillery, 180–81

Atlanta, 137, 152

Aubery, James, 121

Aughenbaugh, George, 169

Augusta, ME, 41

Aumiller, George, 166, 172–73, 175

Ayres, Romeyn B., 178

Ayres's Division, 178, 181–83, 185–87, 201

Bacon, Theodore C., 31
Barber, Albern, 192
Bartlett, William Francis, 114, 187
Bartlett's Brigade, 116, 118, 178, 185, 187
Barton, George, 128
Barton, John, 128
Bates, Samuel, 123, 161, 171, 174, 201
Bath, NY, 200
Battle Cry of Freedom (McPherson), 1, 14
Baxter, Henry, 190
Bayonets of the Republic, The (Lynn),
    100–101, 163–64
Bearss, Edwin, 126, 184
Beauregard, P. G. T., 125
Beaver, James A., 119
Bell, Charles H., 25
Belle Plain, 123
Benham, Henry Washington, 168
Berkshire County Eagle, 38
Bermuda Hundred, VA, 164, 170
Bertolette, John D., 159, 167–68
Bethesda Church, Battle of, 121
Biddlecom, Charles, 74
Bintliff, James, 136
Bismarck Weekly Tribune (SD), 29
Blair County, PA, 16
Blanchard, Peter, 166
Boal, James, 51
Bobb, Alexander, 169
Bohn, Richard, 164–65, 169–70
Boker, James, 128
Boston, 17, 115
bounty jumpers, 19–20, 22, 66, 80–82, 84,
    89–90; historiography of, 15–16, 78, 80
bounty system, 3; advance payment, 41, 43,
    61, 205; carrot and stick, 3, 37, 53, 204;
    desertion and, 14, 78–81, 84, 86, 92–94,
    96, 208–9; draft and, 42–43, 83–84;
    economics of, 51, 58, 61–63; federal, 43,
    45; geography and, 68–69; historiog-
    raphy of, 4, 14–15, 48, 64, 67, 92, 101;
    history of, 20, 37–38, 204–5; liberal
    versus high bounty, 52–53, 63, 203–4;
    local governments and, 5, 37–43, 63,
    205; military views of, 22–23, 26–27, 29;
    motivation and, 189, 193, 197; newspa-
    pers on, 29, 52–53, 66; patriotism and,
    52, 56–57, 59, 203–4; politics of, 77;
    reenlistment and, 56; regiments and,

114; reputation of, 5, 203–4; role of, 33,
    47; soldiers' use of bounties, 206–7;
    states and, 39–42, 199–200; taxes and,
    16, 40–42; unit cohesion and, 102–3;
    veterans' views of, 4, 13, 29, 203
Brady, Matthew, 54–55
Bragg, Edward Stuyvesant, 116
Bridgton Reporter, 52–53
Bristoe Station, 118; Battle of, 144
Bristol, NH, 52
Broady, Oscar, 148–49
Brooke, John, 108, 119–20
Brooklyn, 37
Brooklyn Daily Eagle, 5, 38, 46
Broome Republican, 50
Brown, Isaac, 169
Brown, John Marshall, 117
Brown, T. Fred, 142
Buffalo, NY, 76, 197
Bull, Henry, 26, 200
Bull Run, First Battle of, 34–35, 133, 167
Burgess's Mill, Battle of, 135, 145, 192–93,
    196, 198–99
Burlington Weekly Sentinel, 40
Burns, Ken, 20
Burnside, Ambrose, 108, 115, 119, 127, 129–31
Byron, John, 147

Camp Schuyler, 65
Canadian-born men in the Union army,
    114, 175, 198
Canandaigua, NY, 31, 65
Cape Cod, 122
Carlyle, James, 114
Carpenter, George, 23
Caruthers, Charles, 132
Cattaraugus County, NY, 68
Catton, Bruce, 1, 9, 15
cavalry, 177–78, 184–86
Cedar Run, 119
Census of Veterans, 80
Chamberlain, Joshua, 57, 129, 177–81, 183,
    188, 197, 202
Chamberlain's Brigade: at Five Forks, 178,
    180, 183–84, 187, 201–2; late-war new
    regiments in, 10, 101, 105, 201–2; at Pe-
    tersburg, 129
Chancellorsville, Battle of, 103, 144
chaplains, 190

Charleston, SC, 157

citizen-soldiers, 48

City Point, 189–90, 199, 201

Civil War: advertising and, 59; in American history, 1; bounties during, 203–4; combat effectiveness in, 10; combat experience in, 173; contributions to, 211; culture and, 48, 54; desertion during, 91; documents from, 207; economy and, 33–34, 47; end of, 152; historiography of, 14–15, 20, 101, 207–8, 210; politics of, 137–38; qualifications for soldiers, 64–65; recruitment in, 14, 16, 33–37; regiments in, 166–67; soldiers' experiences in, 209; views of late-war soldiers during, 4

Civil War, The (documentary series), 20

class: recruitment and, 65, 67–68; reputation of soldiers and, 7, 176

Clearfield County, PA, 51

Cleveland, Grover, 29

Cloos, A. B., 166, 172

Coburn, Abner, 41

Cold Harbor, Battle of, 112–13, 115, 118, 121–23, 125, 127–29; tactics at, 142

Columbia Spy, 37

combat: late-war new regiments in, 98–101, 124, 139, 196, 199, 201–2; late-war replacements in, 97, 124, 139, 147; shirking, 1, 9, 17, 29–30, 57, 97, 135, 144, 146, 207

combat effectiveness, 10, 99–105, 176, 209–11; experience and, 173

commutation, 2, 46–47, 63, 205

companies, 169–70

Concord, Battle of, 34

Concord, NH, 40

Confederate army, 11–12; age of soldiers, 69; at Cold Harbor, 123; combat effectiveness of, 173; at the Crater, 131–32; desertion from, 79, 82, 189, 193, 207; at Five Forks, 177–82, 184–85, 187–88; at Fort Stedman, 152–53, 156–61, 172; at Ny River, 115; at Petersburg, 2, 17–19, 126–28; at Poplar Spring Church, 28, 133–34; at Second Reams's Station, 130, 140–43, 148–49; supplies of, 138, 140, 151

Confederate States, 137–38; defeat of, 152; manpower of, 82; mistreatment of

prisoners, 55; recruitment in, 36; war effort of, 47

Congress (US), 56, 104–5, 206; draft and, 38, 46, 49, 83; recruitment and, 35

Congressional Medal of Honor, 18

Connecticut, 40–42; military pay in, 58–61; recruitment in, 57

conscription. *See* draft

conscripts. *See* draftees

Consolidated Brigade (Union army), 141–44, 147–49, 151

Constantia, NY, 200

Constitution (Middletown), 53

Cony, Samuel, 56

Cook, Albert, 115

Coos Republican, 66

Costa, Dora L., 89, 93, 95, 208

Coulter, William A., 159, 168

Cox, Robert C., 160, 168–69

Crandall, Levin, 147

Crater, Battle of the, 128, 130–32, 168, 173

Crawford's Division, 186–87

Cross, Edward J., 99

Cross, George, 208

Cumberland Heights, 128

Cummings, Charles, 112, 127

Curtin, Andrew Gregg, 39

Curtin's Brigade, 134

Customs of Service (Kautz), 69

Dabney's Mill, Battle of, 201

Daily, James, 193

Daily Mirror (Manchester, NH), 65

Dalien, Prosper, 154, 158, 168

Davis, Jefferson, 12

Deep Bottom, Battle of, 130

Deering, Arthur, 117

Defense Department (US), 10, 104

Delaware, 42, 62, 93

Delaware Gazette (NY), 53

Delaware regiments, 8th Delaware, 178, 201

Delhi, NY, 53

Dellinger, Charles, 157, 164

Democratic Party, 137

demographics, 7, 67, 68, 105, 175, 192–93, 197

desertion: absent without leave, 79, 82; birthplace and, 92, 93; bounties and, 14, 78–81, 84, 86, 92–94, 96, 208–9; communities and, 68; from Confederate army, 79, 82, 189, 193, 207; draft and, 8, 83–84, 86–87; at Fort Stedman, 153; historiography of, 17, 78, 207; in late-war new regiments, 88–90, 93–94, 136, 174, 189, 193, 197, 199–201; late-war replacements and, 7–9, 20, 22, 96–97, 207; location of, 210; rates of, 78–84, 86–90, 165, 205, 207; reasons for, 91–92, 95–96, 208

Dieble, Henry, 195

Dinwiddie Courthouse, VA, 177–78, 184–85

disabilities: Pension Act and, 28–29; soldiers with, 8–9, 67, 83

discipline. *See* training

Diven, C. W., 168–69

Dollar Newspaper (Philadelphia), 53

Doolittle, Isaac, 199

Doty, Franklin B., 24, 128, 132–33

draft, 2–3, 21–23, 34, 36–38, 50, 53, 65; bounties and, 42–43, 83–84; debates about, 4, 66–67; desertion and, 8, 82–84, 86–87; exemptions from, 49; federal policy and, 44–46; history of, 205–6; Lincoln on, 48–49, 53; morale and, 166; Murdock on, 14; opposition to, 47; politics of, 5, 77, 83, 92, 204–5; state policy and, 93

draftees, 20–21, 28, 30, 46, 82; in combat, 97; desertion rates and, 84, 86–87; historiography of, 107; late-war new regiments and, 74; morale of, 166; in the Overland Campaign, 108; performance of, 64; reputation of, 207; veterans and, 103, 145

Draper, Simeon, 79

Dunn House Hill, 154, 159

Eastern States, 3, 203; bounty system in, 5, 40–42; desertion rates in, 92; military pay in, 6, 15, 51–53, 59, 62

Ebensburg, PA, 66

economics, enlistment and, 58–60

economy, of the Union, 33–34, 47

Eden, R. C., 30–31, 127

elections, 137–38, 140, 165–66, 189, 193, 198–201

Ellsworth, Ephraim, 54

Ellsworth American (ME), 26

Elmira Daily Advertiser, 66

emancipation, 137

English-born men in the Union army, 175

English language, 7, 27, 68

enlistment term, one year versus three years, 45–46, 57–58, 90, 94

Enrollment Act, 14, 43, 49–50

Erie County, PA, 51

Escott, Paul, 47

Essex County, NJ, 94

Europe, 68–69

Fair Oaks, Battle of, 144

family, 208; volunteering and, 49, 69, 204

farmers, 93, 112, 115, 176, 197–98, 206; drafting of, 49; income of, 60–61; recruitment of, 68, 74–76

farm laborers, 61–62, 74, 112; draft and, 65

Fay, Augustus, 17

Ferrero, Edward, 173

Fesq, Frank, 18

Fifth Corps (Union army), 140, 170, 172, 192; at Five Forks, 177–78, 181, 183, 185; late-war new regiments in, 10, 177–78, 196, 199–201; at Petersburg, 125–26, 129; at Poplar Spring Church, 28

Five Forks, Battle of, 184–88, 201

Five Forks Campaign, 10, 105, 125, 177–78, 184–88, 193, 196–97, 201–2

flags, 134

food, in Union army, 175

football, 120

Foote, Shelby, 20–21

Fort Haskell, 153, 155, 158–59

fortifications, 149, 165–66, 170, 172

Fort Mahone, 95

Fort Prescott, 154, 159

Fortress Monroe, 190

Fort Stedman, Battle of, 51, 152–62, 165, 177; late-war new regiments in, 10, 25, 30, 105, 125, 167, 171–75, 202

Fox, George D., 53

Fox, William F., 9; on late-war new regiments, 99, 113, 116; list of 300 regiments, 16, 98–99, 107, 121, 123, 143, 146, 168, 210; on Petersburg, 127–28

France: Army of Revolutionary France, 10, 100, 104, 191; World War II, 173

Frank, Paul, 144

Frederick, George W., 168

Fredericksburg, Battle of, 37, 54, 116–17, 144, 167
Fry, James, 26, 37, 43–46, 49, 55–56, 66–67; on bounties, 13–14, 21–23, 206; on desertion, 8, 83, 87, 92, 95, 208; on health of soldiers, 84
furloughs, 55–56, 79, 102–3, 121, 165

Gallagher, Gary, 79, 203
Gallman, J. Matthew, 2, 48, 50, 203
generals, views of late-war Union soldiers, 4–5, 26–27
German Army, 104
German-born men in the Union army, 175, 198
Getty, George, 30
Gettysburg, Battle of, 27, 107, 117, 169; casualties of, 55, 103, 116, 144–45
Gibbon, John, 10, 140, 142, 147, 150–51
GI Bill, 206
Gilkyson, Stephen, 19
Gilmore, Joseph Albree, 26, 40, 57
Glatthaar, Joseph T., 165
Glenn, Edwin A., 178–79, 181, 183, 196–97
gold, 41
Gordon, John, 152
Gordon, Lesley, 98
Grand Army of the Republic, 29, 31
Grand Review, of the Army of the Potomac, 30, 211
Grant, Ulysses S.: correspondence of, 110; on the draft, 66; Meade and, 195; memoirs of, 33–34, 47, 68, 211; at Petersburg, 125; portrayal of, 1; on recruits, 69; strategies of, 9, 12, 139–40, 151–52, 181, 184; views of class, 68; views of recruitment, 21–22, 45; views of regiments, 24; views of troop numbers, 82; views of Union army, 211
Gravelly Run (Lewis Farm), 178, 181, 183, 188, 201
Greene, A. Wilson, 17, 29, 95, 107–8, 129
Gregg, William, 24, 128, 134, 139
Gregory, Edgar, 178, 180, 187
Gregory's Brigade, 178, 180, 184–85, 202
Griffin, Charles, 177, 180, 183, 202
Griffin, Simon, 111, 122, 133
Griffin's Brigade, 131–33
Griffin's Division, 10, 125, 177–78, 181–83, 185–87, 199

Griswold, Charles E., 115
Guilmartin, John, 102

Haight, Thomas, 122
Halleck, Henry W., 110
Hancock, Winfield Scott, 108, 113, 125, 130; at Second Reams's Station, 10, 27, 140–44, 146–47, 149–50
Harper, James, 16–17
Harpers Ferry, WV, 145
Harper's Weekly, 180
Harriman, Samuel, 135
Harrisburg, PA, 66, 130
Harrisburg Pennsylvania Daily Telegraph, 51
Harrison's Creek, 158
Hartford Daily Courant, 38, 44–45, 52
Hartranft, John, 30, 123, 131, 135, 154–59, 170–71; at Fort Stedman, 154–59, 161, 166–68; at Poplar Spring Church, 28
Hartranft's Brigade, 28, 132
Hartranft's Division: demographics of, 175; at Fort Stedman, 10, 105, 125, 153–54, 161; late-war new regiments in, 10–11, 101, 105, 125, 161, 165–66, 169–73, 176, 202; officers of, 25
Haskell, Frank A., 121
Hatcher's Run, Battle of, 166, 168, 171–73, 176–77, 192, 196, 201
Haynes, Samuel, 131
health: of recruits, 7; of soldiers, 67, 84, 174
Heintzelman, George M. T., 168
Hemphill, Charles E., 51–52, 153, 155
Henry, Merton G. 105
Hess, Earl J., 27, 31–32, 142, 166–67
Heth's Division, 108, 119
HIBO Database, 8, 11
Hicksford, VA, 139
Hicksford Raid, 138–39, 166, 172, 190, 192–93, 196
high-bounty men. *See* later-enlisting volunteers
high-number regiments. *See* late-war new regiments
Hill, A. P., 132
historians: on bounties, 204; on effectiveness of units, 99–100; views of desertion, 17, 78, 207; views of late-war Union soldiers, 6–7, 13–15, 17, 19–20, 48, 64, 67, 97
Hodgkins, William Henry, 157, 159, 168

Holbrook, Frederick, 112
Hood, John Bell, 12
Hooker, Joseph, 79
Horn, John, 142
Hornellsville Tribune (NY), 26, 53
horses, 169
Houston, Henry Clarence, 117
Howe, Thomas J., 126
Hudson, John, 133
Humiston, Amos, 55
Humphreys, Andrew A., 27, 172
Hunton, Eppa, 183–84
Hyde, Thomas W., 29–30

immigrants, 68, 76–77, 86, 92–93, 95, 175, 198, 208
Internet, 208
Irish-born men in the Union army, 65, 68, 114, 175, 198
Irish Brigade (Union army), 108, 116, 143
Italy, 168, 173

James River, 144
Jamestown Journal, 199
Jenney, Edwin, 190–91, 196
Johnson, Bushrod, 178–79
Johnston, Joseph E., 152
Judson, Amos, 68, 118, 121–22

Kahn, Matthew E., 89, 93, 95, 208
Kansas, 208
Kaufman, Tobias B., 169
Kautz, August V., 69
Kennedy, Michael, 51–52, 116–17, 125
Kreidberg, Marvin A., 105
Kreiser, Lawrence, 145

labor, 39, 43
laborers, 63–65, 68, 93, 115, 176, 197–98; recruitment of, 68
Lake Ontario, 70
Lamont, William, 134
Lancaster, NH, 66
language, 68
Larzalere, William, 128
later-enlisting volunteers, 46; casualty rates of, 97; criticism of, 140–41, 146; definition of, 3; desertion rates of, 7–8, 78–82, 84, 86–87; at Fort Stedman, 162; health of, 84; historiography of, 1–4, 15–16, 20,

101; late-war new regiments and, 209; from Pennsylvania, 108; performance of, 9–10, 12; recruitment of, 124; reputation of, 29–30, 63, 207; role of, 107; at Second Reams's Station, 146; at Spotsylvania Court House, 119; veterans and, 103
late-war new regiments, 2–3; casualties in, 135; at Cold Harbor, 123; creating versus refilling old regiments, 3, 21, 23–26, 209–10; in combat, 98–101, 124, 139, 196, 199, 201–2; combat effectiveness of, 105; at the Crater, 130–31; criticism of, 145, 162–63; definition of, 3; demographics of, 175–76, 192, 197–98, 200; desertion and, 88–90, 93–94, 136, 174, 189, 193, 197, 199–201; at Five Forks, 177–78, 181, 187–88, 201–2; at Fort Stedman, 154, 161–62; in the Hicksford Raid, 138–39; historiography of, 7, 17, 30–31; later-enlisting volunteers and, 209; leadership of, 166–70; morale of, 165–66; officers of, 24–25, 110, 190, 198–201; officers' views of, 4–5, 21, 23–24; in the Overland campaign, 109–10; pensions for, 28–29; performance of, 10–12, 176, 197, 199, 201–2, 210; at Petersburg, 125–26; at Poplar Spring Church, 28; readiness of, 162–66, 172–73, 176, 188–202; recruitment for, 26, 44, 74, 209; reputation of, 30; role of, 139; strength of, 173–75, 192, 196–98, 200–201; training of, 170–71, 190–91, 195–96, 198–99, 202; unit cohesion of, 102, 163–64, 166, 176, 188–90, 193, 195; veterans in, 170–72, 176, 191, 199; voting in, 137
late-war replacements: birthplaces of, 76; in combat, 97, 124, 139, 147; combat effectiveness of, 100; contributions of, 32; demographics of, 70–77; desertion and, 7–9, 20, 22, 96–97, 207; in existing regiments, 74–75; health of, 67; historiography of, 1, 31, 48, 64, 97, 100, 107, 203; in the Overland Campaign, 108–12; performance of, 176, 209; at Petersburg, 126–29; politics of, 137; quality of, 70–77, 97, 99; recruitment of, 44, 70; reputation of, 21, 143–44; role of, 139; at Second Reams's Station, 143–47, 151; unit cohesion and, 102; veterans and, 25–26, 117, 120

late-war Union soldiers: accounts of, 51–52; definition of, 3; historiography of, 6–7, 13–15, 17, 19–20, 48, 64, 67, 97; in the Overland Campaign, 107–12, 143–44, 146; patriotism of, 189; payment of, 58–59; performance of, 10–11; reputation of, 13, 15–17, 207

Laurel Hill, engagement at, 118

leadership, of regiments, 105, 166–70, 190, 195

Lear, Jordan, 196

Ledlie, James, 128–32

Lee, Robert E., 9–10, 12, 129, 151, 170, 198; at Five Forks, 177, 184; in the Overland Campaign, 110; at Petersburg, 82; strategies of, 152

Lemmon, J. S., 164–65

Lewis Farm, Battle of, 177–81, 188, 199, 202

Lewiston Evening Journal, 41

Lewistown Gazette, 38–39

Lexington, Battle of, 34

Lincoln, Abraham, 21, 23–24; on bounties, 56; correspondence of, 67; on the draft, 48–49, 53; political support of, 93; portrayal of, 1; recruitment policy, 34–36, 38, 43–46, 57, 70, 82–83; reelection of, 137–38, 152, 165–66, 189, 193, 198–201; soldiers' views of, 165–66; strategies of, 33, 47; views of reelection, 140

Lincoln's Mercenaries (Marvel), 6, 58

literacy, 69

Livermore, Thomas, 24–27, 210

Loeb, Daniel, 198

Lonn, Ella, 14, 91–92, 95, 207

Lowell Daily Citizen and News, 41

Lynch, J. C., 130

Lynn, John A., 10, 99–101, 103–4, 163–64, 172, 188, 191

Maceuen, C. Z., 181

Mackenzie's Division, 185–86

MacRae, William, 142

Mahone, William, 132

Maine, 37, 93; bounties in, 41; draft in, 43; military pay in, 61; recruitment in, 66, 117

Maine regiments: 14th Maine, 56; 20th Maine, 117; 31st Maine, 99, 122–23, 127, 131–33, 136, 207; 32nd Maine, 51, 116–18, 125, 132–33, 136, 207

Manchester, NH, 65

Manufacturers' and Farmers' Journal (Providence), 65–66

Marks, John, 199

Martin, Edward, 199

Marvel, William, 1, 5–6, 58

Massachusetts: bounties in, 37, 41; desertion rates in, 93; draft in, 42; economy of, 61; recruitment in, 114–15; soldiers from, 17

Massachusetts regiments, 24; 56th Massachusetts, 99, 114–15, 122, 131–32; 57th Massachusetts, 98–99, 113–14, 128, 132, 156; 58th Massachusetts, 99, 122, 127, 129, 134, 136; 59th Massachusetts, 115

Mathews, J. A., 163, 165, 169

Maynard, Samuel, 164

McCall, W. H. H., 168

McClellan, George, 23, 36, 137, 152, 165–66, 193, 209

McLaughlen, Napoleon B., 158

McPherson, James, 5, 20, 54, 97, 101, 205; on bounties, 14–15; on late-war replacements, 1, 31, 107; on literacy, 69; on reenlistments, 57

Meade, George, 55, 127, 139, 151, 154, 195; at Five Forks, 182, 185; views of regiments, 24, 134

Meade Station, VA, 153, 156–57, 159

Mellin, Gideon, 111

Memoirs (Grant), 33–34, 47, 68, 211

mercenaries: definition of, 13; use of word, 203–4

merchants, 68

Merritt, Wesley, 185

Mexican War, 54

Meyer, Abram, 139

Michigan regiments, 17th Michigan, 158

Middletown, CT, 53

Miles, Nelson A., 140, 142, 145–46, 183

military compensation package, 6, 59, 205–6

military effectiveness model, 104

Militia Act, 34–35

Miller, John, 119

Millet, Allan R., 104

Monroe County, NY, 199

morale, 165–66, 188–90, 193, 195, 198–200

Morgan, Edwin D., 23, 41

Morrow, B. M., 168

motivation: to fight, 2, 3, 10–11, 13–14, 100–102, 105–6, 163–66, 188–90, 193, 195; to volunteer, 2, 3, 5–6, 13–16, 23, 31, 35, 37, 44, 48–63, 90, 203–4, 206
Mule Shoe Salient, 27, 119
Munford, Thomas T., 186
Murdock, Eugene, 5–6, 14, 16, 80, 204–5
Murray, Williamson, 104
Musick, Michael, 98
Myers, Daniel, 198

National Tribune, 29, 98
Neeper, William B., 126
Newark, NJ, 94
New England, 39
New Hampshire, 17; bounties in, 40; draft in, 42; military pay in, 61; recruitment in, 66; soldiers from, 53
New Hampshire Patriot and State Gazette, 40
New Hampshire regiments, 20; 6th New Hampshire, 56; 9th New Hampshire, 17; 18th New Hampshire, 24–25, 27, 210
New Jersey: bounties in, 42; draft in, 93; politics of, 93; soldiers from, 8
New Jersey regiments, 78–82, 84, 87–88, 93–95; 6th New Jersey, 19; 7th New Jersey, 25; 10th New Jersey, 19; 15th New Jersey, 19; 39th New Jersey, 93–95; 40th New Jersey, 17–19, 93–95
New London Daily Chronicle, 52
Newsome, Hampton, 31
newspapers, advertising in, 59
New York: bounties in, 37, 41–42, 56, 66, 72–73, 199–200; draft in, 42; farmers in, 60–61; military pay in, 60–61; recruitment in, 44, 57, 197; soldiers from, 17, 198–200
New York City, 17, 37–38, 189; draft in, 87; soldiers from, 68
New York Evening Post, 29, 37
New York Harbor, 143
New York regiments, 7, 23–24, 27, 70–77; 23rd New York, 24; 37th New York, 68; 39th New York, 142, 144–45, 147–49; 52nd New York, 142, 144, 147–49; 61st New York, 146–47; 70th New York, 143; 81st New York, 70, 74–75; 110th New York, 70–71; 121st New York, 65; 122nd New York, 60–61, 72–73; 147th

New York, 70–71, 74; 148th New York, 16; 149th New York, 72, 74; 152nd New York, 146–47; 179th New York, 2, 24–25, 52, 128, 131–34, 139, 208, 210; 184th New York, 7, 70–71; 185th New York, 7, 10–11, 70, 72–73, 177–81, 183, 188–93, 196, 201–2; 187th New York, 177, 184, 187, 197–99, 202; 188th New York, 178, 184, 187, 198–99, 202; 189th New York, 178, 184, 187, 198, 200, 202; 193rd New York, 70–71, 76
New York Sanitary Commission, 7, 48, 67
New York Times, 30, 37, 54–55; on recruits, 65
Ninth Corps (Union army), 28, 107–10, 119, 125; casualties in, 132; at the Crater, 130–31; at Fort Stedman, 152–54; late-war new regiments in, 95, 109, 113, 118–19, 126–27, 129, 135, 170–71; regiments in, 174
Noe, Kenneth, 3
North Ana River, Battle of, 113–15, 118, 121–22
North Carolina, 114, 152
Norton, Oliver, 103
Nottoway River, 139, 176
Ny River, Battle of the, 115, 119

occupation, of recruits, 67–68, 71, 73–77, 112, 176, 198
officers: as casualties, 147; experience of, 24–25; of late-war new regiments, 24–25, 110, 190, 198–201; soldiers' views of, 168–69; views of late-war new regiments, 4–5, 21, 23–24; views of late-war replacements, 27
Ohio regiments, 60th Ohio, 99, 119, 127, 132, 136
Oneida County, NY, 200
One Million Men (Murdock), 80
Onondaga County, NY, 7, 60, 70, 72–74, 76–77, 192
Ontario County Times, 45
Ontario Repository and Messenger, 38, 65
Osborn, John, 114, 200
Oswego, NY, 70
Oswego County, NY, 7, 70–72, 74–77
Otsego Republican, 65
Otto, Henry H., 164

Overland Campaign, 8, 10–11, 78–79; casualties of, 27, 32, 45, 115; impact of, 25, 31–32, 82, 151–52, 209; late-war new regiments in, 99, 105, 109–12, 117, 119–20, 124–26, 135; late-war Union soldiers in, 107–12, 143–44, 146
Oxford Democrat, 36

Paris, Maine, 36
Parke, John, 28, 154–56, 159, 161
Paterson Daily Press, 12
patriotism, 5–7, 15–16, 31; bounties and, 52, 56–57, 59, 203–4; enlistment and, 59, 65; late-war replacements and, 64, 137; of late-war Union soldiers, 189; recruitment and, 47–49, 53, 84
Patriotism Limited (Murdock), 14
Patton, John, 51
Peck, James, 112
Peckham, Albertus, 189
Peebles Farm, Battle of, 192
Pegram, John, 149
Peninsula Campaign, 36
Pennsylvania, 38; casualties from, 97; Civil War in, 130, 170; draft in, 42–43, 93; economy of, 62; elections in, 93, 137, 166; military pay in, 58, 60; recruitment in, 39, 66; soldiers from, 8–9, 16–17, 108, 175, 207; volunteers from, 209
Pennsylvania regiments, 23–24, 87–91, 93, 154, 161, 164–75; 48th Pennsylvania, 123–24, 131, 168; 49th Pennsylvania, 119–20; 50th Pennsylvania, 115–16, 132–33, 135; 51st Pennsylvania, 123; 53rd Pennsylvania, 120, 126, 183; 57th Pennsylvania, 121; 61st Pennsylvania, 29–30; 76th Pennsylvania, 16; 82nd Pennsylvania, 123; 83rd Pennsylvania, 68, 118, 121–22; 93rd Pennsylvania, 103, 111; 100th Pennsylvania, 132; 116th Pennsylvania, 108, 116, 126, 183; 139th Pennsylvania, 16–17; 148th Pennsylvania, 103, 119, 126, 146–47, 183; 183rd Pennsylvania, 109, 118, 130, 136–37, 183; 184th Pennsylvania, 99, 109, 123, 126, 130, 136; 187th Pennsylvania, 129–30; 198th Pennsylvania, 10–11, 139, 177–81, 183–84, 188, 193, 195–97, 201–2; 200th Pennsylvania, 154–59, 161–64, 166, 168–69, 171, 175–76; 205th Pennsylvania, 154, 158–59, 161, 163–66, 168–70, 176; 207th Pennsylvania, 154, 158–66, 169–71, 174, 176; 208th Pennsylvania, 154–55, 158, 161–63, 166, 168–71, 175–76; 209th Pennsylvania, 55, 154–59, 161–65, 168–71, 174, 176; 210th Pennsylvania, 178, 182–83, 187, 200–202; 211th Pennsylvania, 51, 154, 158–59, 161, 163–66, 170–71, 174–76
Pennsylvania regiments, late-war replacements in, 11, 78–82, 84, 96, 102–3, 105, 108, 111, 124
Penrose, William Henry, 17–19
Penrose's Brigade, 17
Pension Act, 28–29
pensions, for the Union army, 4, 28–29
Petersburg, VA, 157, 189
Petersburg Campaign, 45–47, 110, 123, 125–29, 165, 184, 209; historiography of, 29; impact of, 25, 82, 149, 152; late-war new regiments in, 11, 17–19, 105, 131, 135, 139; late-war Union soldiers in, 2, 108, 126–29, 143–44, 146; supply lines for, 140
Philadelphia, 17, 53, 129–30, 193, 197
Philadelphia Inquirer, 56
Philadelphia Press, 164
Philips, Cyrus A., 189
photography, 54–55
Pickett's Charge, 27
Pittsburgh Daily Commercial, 66
Pittsburgh Daily Post, 53
Pittsburgh Gazette, 57
Poplar Spring Church, Battle of, 5, 27–28, 128, 133–36, 168
Po River, engagement at, 119
Portland Daily Press, 41
Portland Weekly Advertiser, 52
Portsmouth Journal of Literature and Politics, 50
Portugal, Wellington's Campaign, 99
Potter, Robert, 28, 112, 123, 129, 134, 139
Poughkeepsie Eagle, 38, 49, 51
Prentiss, John, 128
prisoners of war, 55
Provost Marshal General's Bureau, 8, 20, 43, 82, 84, 86; purpose of, 79
Pulitzer Prize, 14

Ramold, Steven J., 16

Randall, Francis, 112

Rapidan River, 109–10, 134

Rawlins, John, 110

readiness, 104–5; of late-war new regiments, 162–66, 172–73, 176, 188–202

Reams's Station, Second Battle of, 5, 9–10, 26–27, 97, 130, 133, 139–51

Reams's Station, VA, 139, 141, 149, 151

Reardon, Carol, 104, 173, 209

recruitment, 2, 33–39, 66, 74–77, 112–15, 117, 197, 204; class and, 65, 67–68; for late-war new regiments, 26, 44, 74, 209; morale and, 166; patriotism and, 47–49, 53, 84; policies for, 21–23, 34–36, 38, 43–46, 57, 70, 82–83; veterans and, 103

Red River to Appomattox (Foote), 21

reenlistment, 55–57, 102–3, 123, 207

regimental effectiveness, 105

regiments: cohesion of, 95, 102–3; combat effectiveness of, 103–5, 176; generals' views of, 24, 134; inspection of, 162–63; leadership of, 168–69; performance of, 11, 210; reputation of, 98–99; strength of, 192, 196. *See also* late-war new regiments

Reilly, James, 199

Reynolds, William, 112–13

Rhea, Gordon, 118–19, 123

Rhode Island, 37, 42, 60, 62

Rhodes, James Ford, 14, 20

Richards, John, 201

Richmond, VA, 45, 118

Richmond Redeemed (Sommers), 27, 140

Robyler, Hiram, 169

Rochester, NY, 76, 199

Rochester Daily Democrat and American, 50

Rochester Daily Union and Advertiser, 49

Rogers, Niles, 60

Rowanty Creek, 140, 178

Savannah, Georgia, 157

Schriver, Edmund, 162

Second Corps (Union army), 125–26, 172, 177, 181, 183; late-war replacements in, 143–44; reputation of, 27, 140, 151; at Second Reams's Station, 10, 27, 97, 140–41, 145, 149–51

Sentinel of Freedom (Newark, NJ), 26

Sergeant, William, 201

Seward, William H., 21–22, 36

Seymour, Horatio, 38, 41–42, 52

Shackleton, William, 139

Shaffer, Morgan, 193

Shannon, Fred Albert, 5, 14–15, 20

Shell, John, 164

Sheridan, Philip, 177–78, 184–85, 187–88, 201

Sherman, William Tecumseh, 23–24, 30, 65, 152, 206; views of recruitment, 34

Shiloh, Battle of, 54

Shorkey, George, 168

Shuman, Joshua, 196

Shuman, Simon, 103

Sickel, Horatio, 181, 188, 193, 195–97, 201

Sixth Corps (Union army), 126, 141, 149, 161

slavery, 34, 47, 208; end of, 1

Slayton, Mark, 111–12

Sloan, J. Barnette, 128

Smith, William, 125

Sniper, Gustavus, 180, 190–91, 202

soldiers: criteria for recruitment, 70; demographics of, 70–77; effects of combat on, 173; geography of, 68–69; health of, 174; letters of, 164, 207–8; motivation of, 101–5; occupations of, 176; politics of, 137–38, 189, 193, 198–201; qualifications for, 64–65; use of bounties, 206–7; views of officers, 168–69; writing to home, 164. *See also* late-war replacements; late-war Union soldiers

Sommers, Richard, 10, 27, 140, 167

South Side Railroad, 177, 184

Spain, Wellington's Campaign, 99

Spotsylvania Court House, Battle of, 51, 113–17, 119–22, 144–45, 167, 169; historiography of, 104, 173, 209

Sproul, Henry, 117–18, 132

Staily, Henry C., 164

Stanton, Edwin, 24, 36, 44–46, 56, 86; draft and, 21–22, 66–67, 82, 87; furlough policy of, 79

Stanton, John, 181, 183

Statler, Nelson, 161, 164–65, 175

St. Cyr (French military academy), 168

Steuart, George, 119

Steuben County, NY, 26, 200

Stevens, Charles, 60

Stillness at Appomattox, A (Catton), 15

Stone, Roy, 116
substitutes, in Union Army, 3, 16, 19, 28, 46, 136, 205; birthplaces of, 76; in combat, 97; desertion rates and, 84, 86–87, 92; historiography of, 20–21, 101, 107; late-war new regiments and, 74; motivations of, 86, 90–91; reputation of, 66, 207
supply, 105, 174, 192, 197
Surry, NH, 56
Sutton, John F., 183
Sweeney, Patrick, 199
Syracuse, NY, 72, 188–89
Syracuse Daily Courier and Union, 53
Syracuse Standard, 189, 192–93

Talbot, Stephen, 122
taxes. *See under* bounty system
Tennessee, 108
Thomas, Emory, 113
Thomas, George, 24
Thomas, Henry, 173, 209–10
Thomas, Lorenzo, 86
Thompson, Homer, 131
"Three Hundred Fighting Regiments" (Fox), 16, 98–99, 107, 121, 123, 143, 146, 168, 210
Tocqueville, Alexis de, 34
Totopotomy Creek, engagement at, 123
training, 94, 105, 108, 110, 113, 121, 127, 209; of late-war new regiments, 170–71, 190–91, 195–96, 198–99, 202
Troy Weekly Times (NY), 36

Uhler, George, 103
Union (US Civil War): citizens of, 203; preservation of, 1; society of, 5; victory of, 30, 152; views of war in, 54–55, 208; war effort of, 47, 82
Union army: age of soldiers, 69, 71; casualty rates of, 98; causes of desertion from, 91–92, 95–96; combat effectiveness of, 101–5, 173; at the Crater, 131–32; demographics of, 68, 112, 114, 175–76, 198; desertion rates of, 78–81, 84, 87–90, 207; economics and, 6; at Five Forks, 177–78, 181, 184–85; at Fort Stedman, 153–56, 158–61; historiography of, 31–32, 203; later-enlisting volunteers

in, 9, 11–12; late-war new regiments in, 199, 202; late-war replacements in, 26; late-war Union soldiers in, 13–14, 107–8; morale of, 164–66; numbers of, 82–83; officers in, 24, 147; pay of, 23, 50–51, 205–6; politics of, 137–38; portrayal of, 1; prisoners of war from, 55; recruiting standards of, 67; recruitment of, 21–23, 33–37, 43–46, 64–67, 76–77, 204; regiments in, 176, 192, 196; reputation of, 210–11; at Second Reams's Station, 140–43, 149; strategies of, 47; training of, 105, 108, 110, 113, 121, 127, 170–71; unit cohesion in, 102–3; victory of, 30, 152; volunteers for, 2–4; war preparedness of, 48. *See also* Army of the James; Army of the Potomac
Union of Union Veterans, 31
unit cohesion, 101–3, 105, 207–8; desertion and, 95, 207; of late-war new regiments, 102, 163–64, 166, 176, 188–90, 193, 195
United States: draft in, 49; military history of, 34, 204, 206; soldiers born in, 175; in World War II, 210. *See also* Union (US Civil War)
United States Sanitary Commission, 55
Upton, Emory, 142
Upton's charge, 119–20
US Army, 104, 173
US Census, 6, 112

Van Benschoten, Moses, 128
Vermont, 39–40, 42, 61; recruitment in, 66, 112; soldiers from, 55–56, 112
Vermont regiments, 17th Vermont, 99, 111–13, 117, 127, 132, 135–36
veterans: government programs for, 206; pensions for, 4, 28–29
veterans, in the Union army; bounties and, 4, 13, 29, 103, 203; combat and, 97; contributions of, 210–11; furloughs for, 102–3, 121; historiography of, 107–8; in late-war new regiments, 170–72, 176, 191, 199; morale of, 108, 210; reenlistment of, 55–57, 102–3, 123, 207; retention of, 43–44, 46; role in Union victory, 11–12; at Second Reams's Station, 140–41, 144–45, 151; views of late-war Union

soldiers, 3–4, 13, 15–17, 25, 117, 120, 203, 209; as volunteers, 43–44, 55, 113

Veterans of Foreign Wars, 31

Veterans Reserve Corps, 9, 83

veteran volunteers, 43–44, 55, 113

Vicksburg, Battle of, 107

Vietnam War, 14, 206

Virginia, 95, 113, 164, 170–71, 174, 191

Virginia Campaign of 1864 and 1865, The (Humphreys), 27

volunteering, 21–23, 48–50; in the modern military, 206; motives for, 53–54, 204

volunteers, 2–4, 46; birthplaces of, 76; desertion rates of, 79, 81–82, 84, 86, 209; economics and, 58–59; morale of, 166; reputation of, 66–67; states and, 57–58

voting rights, 68

wages, recruitment and, 59–62, 65

Wagner, Philip, 198

Walker, Francis, 151

Ward, Geoffrey, 20

War Department, 43, 55, 79, 105, 130

Warner, Clement, 121

Warren, Gouverneur K., 139, 172, 182, 185–86, 192

Washington, DC, 30, 34, 208

Watkins Express, 44

Watman, Kenneth H., 104

Watts, Richard, 161, 168

Wayne Township, Erie County, PA, 51

Webb, Alexander, 113

Weekly Chronicle (New London), 37

Weld, Stephen, 114–15

Weldon Railroad, 140, 149–50, 172, 193, 201

Weldon Railroad, Battle of, 132–33, 138–39

Wellington, Duke of, 99, 157

Wentworth, Mark, 117

Wert, J. Howard, 55, 170–71, 174

Westbrook, Robert, 120

Westbrook, Steven, 101

Western States: desertion rates in, 92; military pay in, 6; pensions and, 29

Wheaton, Frank, 17–19

Wheaton's brigade, 120

White, Jonathan W., 137, 208

White, Julius, 132

White Oak Road, Battle of, 10, 177, 181–84, 188, 201

Whitlock, William, 199

Whitman, Edward, 201

Whiton, John Chadwick, 129, 134, 136

Wilderness, Battle of the, 111–16, 122, 145, 147, 167, 169; historiography of, 173, 209; late-war Union soldiers in, 108, 120, 143

Wiley, Bell, 15–16, 31, 102, 207–8

Wilkenson, George, 60–61

Willcox, Orlando Bolivar, 115, 119, 127, 153, 156, 158

Willcox's Division, 28, 129, 135, 152–53, 155, 157–58

Williston, VT, 66

Wilson, William, 143

Winslow, W. L., 189

Wisconsin, 129

Wisconsin regiments: 36th Wisconsin, 99, 121, 145; 37th Wisconsin, 30–31, 99, 109, 127, 135; 38th Wisconsin, 129, 135–36

World War II, 104, 173, 206, 209–10

Wyrick, William, 157

Yates County Chronicle (NY), 44

Zentz, Carl, 198